BUTTERWORTHS ANNOTATED LEGISLATION SERVICE

STATUTES SUPPLEMENT No. 223

HOUSING ACT 1974

By

JOHN MACEY, C.B.E., F.R.I.C.S., F.I.H.M.,
formerly Director of Housing, Greater London Council

LONDON
BUTTERWORTHS
1975

ENGLAND:	BUTTERWORTH & CO. (PUBLISHERS) LTD. LONDON: 88 Kingsway, WC2B 6AB
AUSTRALIA:	BUTTERWORTHS PTY LTD. SYDNEY: 586 Pacific Highway, Chatswood, NSW 2067 MELBOURNE: 343 Little Collins Street, 3000 BRISBANE: 240 Queen Street, 4000
CANADA:	BUTTERWORTH & CO. (CANADA) LTD. TORONTO: 2265 Midland Avenue, Scarborough M1P 4S1
NEW ZEALAND:	BUTTERWORTH OF NEW ZEALAND LTD. WELLINGTON: 26/28 Waring Taylor Street, 1
SOUTH AFRICA:	BUTTERWORTH & CO. (SOUTH AFRICA) (PTY.) LTD. DURBAN: 152/154 Gale Street

ISBN 0 406 54736 x

Printed in Great Britain by
Butler and Tanner, Ltd, Frome and London

PREFACE

A life-time's interest in housing is not brought to an end by retirement from front line service. The war against bad housing conditions continues to be a major pre-occupation of central and local government, and of those engaged in the housing association movement, and I am glad still to be able to play some part therein.

The Housing Act 1974 will be welcomed as representing the views of a wide cross-section of moderate people of all political parties. It will, I trust, prove a valuable weapon in the hands of all those engaged in housing administration. The housing association movement will be provided with better resources and the few weaker members subject to a fitness test. A better armoury is provided for the battle against bad housing conditions in housing action areas, which call for aggressive action. Of course, this will not succeed without a great increase in housing production, but that is outside the scope of the Act and this book.

I should like to feel that this book will prove a useful guide and reference book to everyone engaged as an elected representative, or a professional adviser, in the promotion of better housing, whether through central and local government, or in the voluntary housing movement, or as landlords and tenants with a limited but no less serious concern with the improvement of a particular street or group of houses.

November 1974 JOHN MACEY

CONTENTS

TABLE OF STATUTES

References in this Table to "*Statutes*" are to Halsbury's Statutes of England (Third Edition) showing the volume and page at which the annotated text of the Act will be found. Paragraph numbers printed in bold type indicate where the Housing Act 1974 is set out.

TABLE OF CASES

In the following Table references are given to the English and Empire Digest showing where a digest of the case will be found

PARA.

O

INTRODUCTION

[1] The decision of the Conservative Government to go to the country in February 1974 led to the demise of the Housing and Planning Bill, whose terms enjoyed a wide measure of support from the major political parties. The Housing Bill, introduced by the Labour Government in April 1974 is substantially a rebirth of the earlier Bill, except that it omits the controversial clauses dealing with "Unoccupied Office Premises" and contains slightly stronger conditions as to the future occupation of houses improved with the aid of grants. It also introduces a new concept—"Priority Neighbourhoods"; amends the law on leasehold enfranchisement; and makes a number of miscellaneous changes, particularly in the law of landlord and tenant.

[2] In the early post-war years the whole emphasis was on the provision of additional houses by new building; the amount of demolition for slum clearance was severely restricted; and very little resources in the way of manpower or money could be spared for house improvement. The provisions of the Housing Acts of 1949 and 1959 for stimulating improvements formed only a very minor part of housing strategy and the concept of improvement over complete areas did not appear until the Housing Act 1964, in which measures for compulsory improvement were first introduced. Unfortunately this Part of the 1964 Act strangled itself with its own red tape and no advance was made.

[3] The Housing Act 1969 contained the first effective measures for stimulating improvements by individual owners on a large scale, stimulated by the incentive of increased rents, and also soundly based measures for area improvements. In addition to grants in respect of the improvement of the houses themselves grants were also available for the improvement of amenities generally in the neighbourhood.

[4] The Housing Finance Act 1972 aided the progress of improvement work by simplifying the process of conversion to regulated tenancies of houses provided with all the standard amenities (Part III), and the provisions in Part IV for the wholesale conversion of rent control to rent regulation also no doubt had a beneficial effect. Unfortunately progress has been impeded by the rent-freeze imposed in March 1974.

[5] Behind these legislative reforms there lies a series of changes in housing policy. At first improvement work was regarded as a very minor part of housing strategy, but later there was a growing realisation that in some areas houses were falling into the state of unfitness faster than the elimination of other unfit properties under the slum clearance programme. This led to measures to plug the leak, not very successful because of rent limitations, and still not appreciably diminishing the importance attached to demolition and large-scale redevelopment.

[6] More recently the preservation and improvement of existing housing has come to be regarded as an alternative to massive redevelopment. The latter destroys not only the old houses and streets but also part of the neighbourhood's

social structure. During the interval, often amounting to two years or so, between the departure of the last family to be rehoused and the arrival of the first occupants of the new blocks, churches have lost their congregations, scout troops and girl guides have been wound up, pubs and shops have lost their customers, and these are grievous losses accompanied by the disappearance of what was in many cases a not unattractive street scene. Moreover it is by no means easy to create a new sense of community and neighbourliness among the tenants of the new development, particularly if this is at high density and includes a number of tall blocks.

[**7**] Not so openly admitted are the financial advantages of preservation and improvement in this era of phenomenal rises in building costs. Nevertheless the incentive is there and it may cloud the judgment of housing authorities and lead in some cases to the preservation of groups of old and worn-out housing which are suitable only for demolition. Great skill and wide experience are necessary in deciding upon the right choice between preservation and redevelopment for any particular neighbourhood.

[**8**] The Conservative Bill was based upon two White Papers—"Widening the Choice: The Next Steps in Housing" (Cmnd. 5280) and "Better Homes—The Next Priorities" (Cmnd. 5339), and many sections in the new Act are couched in terms identical with those in the Housing and Planning Bill—a welcome indication of the wide support the new legislation commands.

[**9**] The second White Paper contains a wealth of statistics to support the policy. It was estimated that by the end of 1973 the number of slum houses would have declined from 1·8 million in 1967 to less than a million. But the number of houses lacking the basic amenities of a hot-water supply, a bath or an indoor W.C., which amounted to 4 million in 1967, still stood at about 2·5 million at the end of 1973. That is to say that almost one family in every six lives in a dwelling which is deficient in at least one of these basic amenities. The rate of progress can be measured by the fact that about 70,000 unfit houses are dealt with in clearance areas each year, and about 300,000 grants for improvements are approved each year.

[**10**] A great sense of urgency is required. Hence the provisions for high pressure attacks on "Housing Action Areas", and the stimulus from the fact that improvements and conversions in such areas will attract grant at the rate of 75 per cent, compared with 60 per cent, for premises in a general improvement area, and 50 per cent for dwellings outside such areas. At the same time there is a return to the idea of attaching conditions to such grants, in an effort to ensure that large profits are not made from the subsequent sale of properties improved with the aid of substantial grants from public funds.

All these points are more fully discussed in Chapters IV to IX which deal with those parts of the Act which affect the widest cross-section of the population.

[**11**] However, there are also provisions in Parts I, II and III for the enlargement of the powers of the Housing Corporation; and registration of Housing Associations; and for greater financial assistance to Housing Associations. These are of less widespread interest but of considerable importance so far as overall housing strategy is concerned. The proportion of houses in owner-occupation is now over 50 per cent. So far as rented accommodation is concerned the private

sector is steadily shrinking and now stands at 21 per cent while the proportion of publicly-owned rented housing has risen to 29 per cent. If the publicly-owned houses were managed by one or more *ad hoc* bodies the political implications might be less serious but there are obviously political dangers where, in any particular district, the division is, say, 60 per cent Council tenants, 35 per cent owner occupiers, and 5 per cent privately rented.

[**12**] The development of an alternative to local authority ownership is therefore widely regarded, and not only by Conservatives, as a matter of considerable importance to the general wellbeing of the Country. The objects of these three Parts of the Act are to expand the work of housing associations, and at the same time to deal with the criticism that the mushroom growth of small associations over the past five or six years results in senseless competition for available properties and the waste of skilled management manpower. There are also some suggestions that not all housing associations are actuated by purely altruistic motives.

[**13**] The means by which these objects are to be achieved are, firstly, the extension and strengthening of the powers of the Housing Corporation. Secondly, the requirement that all housing associations desiring to work with Government financial aid shall become registered, and thus largely controlled by the Housing Corporation. Thirdly, financial aid to registered associations will be on a more certain and generous basis than hitherto. Indeed, the aid amounts to the shouldering by the Government, through the Corporation, of the whole of the approved net deficit on each new housing scheme, plus some cushioning against an overall revenue deficit on an association's accounts.

[**14**] Hitherto the Corporation, which was created in 1964, have played only a minor role in housing. They made advances to co-ownership housing societies, and to societies providing houses on a "cost-rent" basis, for people who did not wish, or were not in a position to rent or buy in the open market, and who yet had little or no expectation of being housed by local authorities. Essentially the Corporation operated in the field of non-subsidised housing using Exchequer money to make advances. However, their powers were slightly extended by the Housing Finance Act 1972, as described in Chapter One.

[**15**] Now the Corporation become the channel through which grants and subsidies to housing associations will be disbursed, and they will have wide powers to acquire land, to develop and manage housing, to dispose of land, to borrow money not only from the Exchequer but also from other sources; and powers to exercise a degree of control over housing associations through the machinery for their registration and the system of approvals of housing schemes proposed by registered housing associations. These functions are in addition to those they possessed prior to 1972. The changes are more fully discussed in Chapters I, II and III below.

[**16**] The financial effects of the Act arise from the following:

(*a*) contributions to local authorities towards the cost of improvement, intermediate, repair, and special grants, made by them to private owners;

(*b*) contributions to local authorities towards the cost of improvements and conversions carried out by them;

(*c*) contributions to local authorities towards approved expenditure in "housing action" and "general improvement" areas;

(*d*) grants to housing associations in respect of estimated net deficits on the approved cost of schemes for the acquisition, construction, improvement, or conversion of dwellings and hostels etc., management grants and revenue deficit grants;

(*e*) any increase in rate support grant or rising costs subsidy resulting from expenditure by local authorities under the Act.

[17] It has been estimated that in four or five years' time the Act will increase public expenditure annually by about £100 million in England and Wales and by £2 million in Scotland.

[18] The explanatory memorandum issued with the Bill said that the effect on Public Service Manpower was expected to be only slight. Some modest increase in the staff of Government Departments might occur. So far as local authorities were concerned the effect would also be slight, much of the work being covered by a re-ordering of priorities. Local authorities are likely to receive this suggestion with scepticism. There would, however, be an increase in the staff of the Housing Corporation to cover its enlarged responsibilities.

CHAPTER 1

THE HOUSING CORPORATION: EXTENDED FUNCTIONS

[**19**] *Background.* The Housing Act 1964 set up a new central body, sponsored by the Government, known as the Housing Corporation. It was created as a means of helping people who did not wish, or were unable, to purchase or rent a house on the open market, and who, at the same time, were unlikely to qualify for the offer of a Council house at a subsidised rent.

[**20**] The Corporation's original task was to encourage and assist housing societies to build new homes for letting at cost-rents (*i.e.* without subsidy) or on the basis of co-ownership. They were given power to make loans to housing societies, buy lands for them, and to give architectural and other advice. They were given power to acquire land compulsorily for these purposes if the local authority were unwilling to do so on behalf of a housing society.

In addition the Corporation could give directions for the transfer of the interests of a society which ran into difficulties to another society, or to the Corporation themselves.

[**21**] Exchequer money (£150 million rising to £300 million) was made available to the Corporation which had power to join with building societies and similar bodies in providing finance for housing societies.

[**22**] The broad division of responsibility was therefore that local authorities continued to provide loans, grants, annual rate-fund subsidies, and other assistance to housing associations providing dwellings to let at less than cost-rents, and also provided a channel for Government subsidies payable to such associations; while the Corporation carried out the functions described above in relation to other housing associations and societies.

[**23**] A housing association is defined in the Housing Act 1957 (s. 189) as meaning "A society, body of trustees or company established for the purpose of, or amongst whose objects or powers are included those of, constructing, improving or managing or facilitating or encouraging the construction or improvement of houses, being a society, body of trustees or company who do not trade for profit or whose constitution or rules prohibit the issue of any capital with interest or dividend exceeding the rate for the time being prescribed by the Treasury etc."

[**24**] The same section of the Housing Act 1957 defines a "Housing Trust" as a body "which by the terms of its constituent instrument is required to devote the whole of its funds, including any surplus . . . to the provision of houses for persons the majority of whom are in fact members of the working classes, and to other purposes incidental thereto."

[**25**] Thus the term "housing association" is, in law, a generic one, which

can cover bodies whose title includes the word "society". However, for convenience, many people use the term "association" to describe one which deals wholly or mainly with subsidised housing, and the term "society" when referring to one which deals with the provision of "cost-rent," or "co-ownership" schemes.

[**26**] The term "housing society" does not appear to have been statutorily defined before 1964, when, for the purpose of the Housing Act 1964 it was defined (s. 1 (7) and (8)) as a society which was registered under the Industrial and Provident Societies Act 1893; which does not trade for profit; and whose objects and powers include the provision of houses to be kept available for letting or co-ownership.

As with "housing associations" it is the constitution, aims and objects, which determine the classification, not the words included in the title.

[**27**] *Extension of powers in 1972.* The Housing Finance Act 1972 extended the powers of the Corporation by enabling them to lend money to any type of housing association, not merely to those which are "housing societies" as defined in the Housing Act 1964. At the same time local authorities ceased to be the channel through which all Exchequer subsidies were paid to housing associations. Existing subsidies were abolished, and transitional subsidies, and new ones, were paid direct by the Exchequer to the associations. From 1972 onwards any association which needed only a loan, and not a local authority grant as well, could ask the Corporation for a loan. Many associations disliked asking local authorities for grants and loans because they regarded the local authorities' conditions as too onerous; and they welcomed this alternative source of loans.

[**28**] *Extended functions in 1974.* The new Act provides for the continuation of the Corporation's functions as described above, and for their very considerable extension.

[**29**] *Section 1* states that the functions of the Corporation include promoting and assisting registered housing associations and unregistered self-build societies. This introduces the new rule that only those associations which become registered under the Act are eligible for help from the Corporation. For the past ten or twelve years there has been a proliferation of associations and societies, many with practically no financial resources or management and technical potential, and often in competition with each other for houses to be purchased for conversion and sites for redevelopment. Self-build societies are rather a different matter since the members are putting a great deal of their own time and effort into the provision of homes for their own occupation. They are therefore eligible for help even though they are not registered. The Corporation will be responsible for the proper exercise of the functions of registered housing associations and unregistered self-build societies.

The Corporation are to establish a register, which will enable them to exercise supervision and control of such associations, and they will normally be the agent of the Secretary of State for the making of grants to registered associations. Section 1 also states that the Corporation have power themselves to provide and manage dwellings for sale or letting, and hostels. This they can do by construction, acquisition, conversion, improvement or otherwise. This is much wider than the Corporation's former power under s. 5 of the Housing Act 1964.

The number of members of the Corporation is increased from nine to fifteen—see Sch. 1, p. 174, *post*.

[30] *Section 2* gives the Corporation power to control the disposal of any land held by a registered housing association and of any grant-aided land held by an unregistered association. In this connection "grant-aided" is defined in Sch. 2 as meaning any land in respect of which grants or subsidies are payable in respect of any period after 24 January 1974 under the enactments listed in paragraph 2 (*a*)–(*f*); or land in respect of which any repayments of capital or interest fall to be made after that date—see para. 3. There are two exceptions which do not require the consent of the Corporation. The first covers a disposal by a registered charity, where the disposal requires the sanction of an order of the Charity Commissioners; the second covers disposal of land which is not "grant-aided" (as defined in Sch. 2) and which also does not require the sanction of an order under s. 29 of the Charities Act 1960 because it is excluded under sub-s. (3) of s. 29 of the 1960 Act. Sub-s. 3 of s. 2 provides that the Charity Commissioner's shall consult the Corporation before making any order under s. 29 of the Charities Act 1960.

[31] Control of disposals under s. 2 of the new Act does not apply to a lease for a term of less than 7 years and 3 months unless there is an option for renewal or the lease is granted in consideration of a fine.

See Notes on s. 2 and on Sch. 2.

[32] *Section 3* states that the Corporation may acquire land by way of purchase, lease, exchange or gift, for the purpose of selling it to a registered housing association or an unregistered self-build society; or for the purpose of their general functions.

The Secretary of State may authorise the Corporation to acquire land for such purposes by compulsory purchase.

[33] These powers may be exercised even though the land is not required immediately for use in connection with the exercise of the Corporation's functions. Section 3 also deals with acquisitions in Scotland, and amends the law relating to acquisitions by agreement, or compulsorily.

[34] *Section 4* gives the Corporation power to provide or improve dwellings or hostels on any land belonging to them. The powers are enumerated in detail and include site clearance, construction of roads, and sewers, and the provision of open spaces, and gas, water and electricity supplies. They may also carry out ancillary development to provide land or buildings for commercial, recreational or non-domestic use, in connection with the provision of dwellings or hostels.

[35] *Section 5* states that the Corporation may not dispose of any land except in accordance with this section. Where they have not used their powers to improve or develop, disposals may be made to a registered housing association or an unregistered self-build society; to a subsidiary of the Corporation; or any other body in which the Corporation hold an interest.

[36] Where the corporation have used their powers under s. 4 (1) to develop or improve the land, they have greater freedom and may dispose of it to a registered housing association, or to the council of a county district or London borough, the Greater London Council, or the Common Council of the City of London; the Commission for the New Towns or a development corporation;

or a subsidiary of the Corporation. In Scotland they may sell to a housing authority as defined in s. 78 (1) of the Housing (Financial Provisions) (Scotland) Act 1972.

[37] Furthermore, the Corporation may sell or lease individual dwellings to persons for their own occupation, *i.e.*, they are not restricted to providing houses for rent.

[38] The Corporation may dispose of any ancillary buildings or land but "not for less than the best consideration", except with the consent of the Secretary of State.

If they so desire the Corporation may dispose of land not required for the purposes for which it was acquired, but if the land was acquired compulsorily either by the Corporation or on their behalf, or it is to be disposed of for less than the "best consideration", the consent of the Secretary of State will be necessary. Where land is to be disposed of for less than the best consideration for use as, or in connection with, a highway or street such consent is not necessary.

[39] *Section 6* gives the corporation power to acquire securities of a body corporate and to promote such a body. Some anxieties about this power and the power to build houses for sale were expressed at Committee stage but an assurance was given that the Corporation could use this, and their other powers under Part I only in the legitimate exercise of their functions under the Act. Presumably the Corporation could acquire control of a brickworks or gravel extraction plant, but only if these were required in connection with their development and other operations. In short, they must not act *ultra vires*.

[40] *Section 7* sets out the Corporation's borrowing powers. These include powers to borrow from the Secretary of State, or by way of overdraft. There is also a power to borrow in currency other than sterling.

In all cases the consent of the Secretary of State is necessary, and he will not act without the approval of the Treasury.

[41] The aggregate indebtedness of the Corporation may not exceed £400 million, or such greater sum not exceeding £750 million as the Secretary of State may by order specify. A draft of any such order must be laid before and approved by the House of Commons before it is made.

[42] *Section 8* deals with Treasury guarantees and is self-explanatory.

[43] *Section 9* describes the lending powers of the Corporation. They may lend to any bodies of the type listed in sub-s. (1), and may also lend to an individual who wishes to acquire from one of such bodies, or from the Corporation themselves, a dwelling for his own occupation.

[44] The Treasury is involved in that its consent is necessary to any directions given to the Corporation as to the terms of such loans. Subject to such directions the Corporation is free to determine the terms on which such loans are granted. However, there is one not insignificant qualification. The terms of any loan to any of the bodies listed in sub-s. 1 may include terms preventing repayment of the loan before a specified date without the consent of the Corporation. No such stipulation may be included in the terms of a loan to an individual. It will be apparent that this could bear hardly on an association which was able, and willing, to repay a loan at a high rate of interest, and thus reduce its outgoings.

This section also deals with loans to self-build societies.

[45] *Section 10* contains miscellaneous financial provisions, such as guarantees by the Corporation (limited in aggregate to £100 million); or power for the Corporation to "turn their resources to account" when not required for its functions; and provision for the Secretary of State to direct the Corporation to pay to him all or part of any sums standing to their credit and not required for the exercise of their functions.

[46] *Section 11* deals with the exclusion of certain disposals from the tax on capital gains.

[47] *Section 12* covers interpretations relating to Part I.

CHAPTER 2

REGISTRATION OF HOUSING ASSOCIATIONS

[**48**] Reference has already been made in Chapter 1 to one of the Corporation's new functions, *i.e.*, to establish and maintain a register of housing associations and to exercise supervision and control over such associations. This part of the Act lays down the procedure to be followed for setting up and maintaining such a register, the effect of registration on the powers and duties of housing associations, and allied matters.

[**49**] From the late 1960s onwards there has been phenomenal growth both in the number of housing associations and in the scope of their work. Churches and philanthropic bodies became more aware of the practical help they could give to the homeless and ill-housed by forming a housing association which would augment the efforts of the hard-pressed local authorities. Associations could obtain from the more helpful local authorities loans covering 90 or even 100 per cent of their capital costs; plus in some cases, annual rate fund contributions to help them hold their rents down to a reasonable level, if the Government subsidies, administered through local authorities, were insufficient for this purpose. Local authorities also provide technical advice on acquisition and conversion.

[**50**] Local authorities find themselves in a difficult position because they cannot house an overcrowded family who have only just arrived in the area except at the expense of a family whose living conditions may be nearly as bad, and who have been on the waiting list for years. In these, and other problem cases, certain housing associations have rendered immense service to housing because they need not be subject to procedures and priorities in the same way as local authorities. Many also adopt a tolerant attitude and grant tenancies to tenants with, for instance, a poor rent record.

[**51**] As an extension of this help to families at the lower end of the eligibility scale, some associations collaborate with local authorities in dealing with "short-life" properties which a local authority feels unable, for good reasons, to re-let, but which can be let by an association on a temporary basis to families it can re-accommodate elsewhere when the time comes for the short-life property to be demolished. Such arrangements have proved very useful in dealing with squatters, some of whom attempt to jump the local authority housing queue.

[**52**] Sheer enthusiasm led many groups of people to form their own associations without stopping to consider whether it might have been wiser to offer their energies to an existing association. This led to the proliferation of housing associations, and the uneconomic use of scarce resources both in cash and trained manpower. In addition, it often happened that two, or even three

associations, would be in the market for the same house, marked down as suitable for conversion.

[**53**] There is considerable scope for unification of housing associations, for schemes of joint management, or agency management by larger associations on behalf of smaller ones; and for staff training schemes. The competition for available vacant houses can be overcome by "zoning", *i.e.* the local authority delineates certain areas within which acquisitions and conversions by nominated associations are the only ones they will recognise for grants and loans. Such arrangements need to be elastic in order to provide openings for new associations and avoid the creation of too tight a monopoly interest for the nominated associations.

[**54**] So far I have described briefly the scope for rationalisation among genuinely altruistic and enthusiastic housing associations. There have also been pleas for more control on the grounds that associations have been formed by professional people with the ulterior motive of providing them with an income from fees plus possible future benefits from the fact that they acquire a share in the equity and may benefit from the growth in the value of the associations assets, due to inflation. However, in recent years the tendency has been to require that associations applying for grants should be incorporated under the Industrial and Provident Societies Act 1965, or should be registered charities. There are various ways of ensuring that grants are given only to genuine non-profit making bodies and of limiting fees. Further information on housing associations and societies is given in "Housing Management" by Macey and Baker (*Estates Gazette*). It is against this general background that the following provisions of Part II should be considered.

[**55**] *Section 13* states that a register shall be established and maintained by the Corporation, in which they may register any housing association which—

(*a*) is a registered charity and not an exempt charity or

(*b*) is a society registered under the Industrial and Provident Societies Act 1965 and fulfils the conditions in sub-s. (2) of the 1974 Act.

[**56**] The definition covers cost-rent and co-ownership societies. Reference is also made to an association's "additional purposes or objects"—sub-s. 3.

In deciding whether to register an association the Corporation shall have regard to the advice of the Advisory Committee (see below) and to whether the association satisfies such criteria as the Corporation may from time to time establish following consultation with this Advisory Committee. The Act makes no provision for an association to appeal against a refusal by the Corporation to register it.

[**57**] *Section 14* states that there shall be a committee called "The Housing Associations Registration Advisory Committee". Its functions are to advise the Corporation generally on the exercise of their power with regard to registration and to advise on the question whether any particular association whose application is referred to the Committee by the Corporation should be registered. They also have the function of advising on the establishment and variation of criteria for the registration of associations.

[**58**] The chairman and the members are to be appointed by the Secretary of State, who may pay them salaries or other remuneration as laid down in

sub-s. 4. The Corporation may pay them travelling and other expenses, and make similar payments to persons attending meetings at the request of the Committee.

[**59**] *Section 15* deals with the removal of bodies from the register. The Corporation may remove associations from the register only in accordance with the terms of this section. There is no provision for the association itself to resign or withdraw from the register. This is what one would expect in view of the benefits which registration brings in the way of loans and subsidies, and also in view of the intention to exercise control over associations which have had, or are receiving, aid from public funds.

[**60**] This section contains an express provision for appeals against the decision of the Corporation. An association aggrieved by a decision of the Corporation to remove it from the register may appeal to the High Court or, in Scotland, to the Court of Session.

[**61**] No payments shall be paid in respect of a housing association grant or a hostel deficit grant to a body which has been removed from the register. The Corporation will still have powers of control over disposals of land, just as it had before the association was removed from the register (s. 2).

[**62**] *Section 16* provides that the corporation must give notice of registration, or of de-registration, as soon as may be to the Charity Commissioners in the case of a registered charity which is not an exempt charity or to the appropriate registrar if the association is registered under the Industrial and Provident Societies Act 1965.

[**63**] There is also provision for these bodies to be notified of any appeal by an association which is being removed from the Corporation's register.

[**64**] *Section 17* states that, on and after 1 April 1975, no loan shall be made under any of the enactments listed in paragraphs 3 (*b*) or 3 (*c*) of Sch. 2 unless the association is a registered one. Nor can any local authority, including a county council, use its powers under s. 119 of the Housing Act 1957, or under paragraphs (*a*) and (*c*) of sub-s. (2) of s. 152 of the Housing (Scotland) Act 1966 to make future grants or loans to, and to guarantee payments in respect of money borrowed, unless at that time the association is registered.

[**65**] There is a similar restriction in sub-s. (3) on the power of the Secretary of State to make grants for affording tax relief.

[**66**] These provisions do not apply where the association has applied for registration and the application has not been disposed of by the Corporation.

[**67**] They do not apply to special associations of the kind covered by s. 80 of the Housing Finance Act 1972, *e.g.*, the North Eastern Housing Association.

[**68**] There are transitional provisions in sub-s. (4), as to the making of loans (but not grants) in respect of schemes approved before the operative date.

[**69**] *Section 18* has important effects so far as tenancies are concerned. The special position of housing association tenants referred to in sub-s. (5) of s. 5 of the Rent Act 1968 (or sub-s. (4) of s. 5 of the Rent (Scotland) Act 1971) will be preserved so far as registered associations are concerned but tenancies of unregistered associations will not be covered and such tenancies will become ordinary regulated tenancies unless—

(*a*) The association is of the special type covered by s. 80 of the Housing Finance Act 1972, *e.g.* the North Eastern Housing Association; or

(*b*) the association is a society registered under the 1965 Act (cost-rent or co-ownership schemes); or

(*c*) the association has made application for registration before the operative date and the corporation has not yet dealt with the application.

[70] It should, however, be remembered that tenancies of a housing trust which is a charity within the meaning of the Charities Act 1960 cannot be protected or statutory tenancies because of s. 5, sub-s. (1), (2) and (3) of the Rent Act 1968, and this position is unaffected by changes made by the Housing Act 1974, whether the trust is a registered housing association or not.

[71] Associations whose tenancies become protected tenancies by virtue of this section must give notice to their tenants that they are no longer excluded from protection, and there are penalties for failure to do so.

[72] *Section 19* deals with "registered 1965 Act associations" and gives the Corporation power to conduct an enquiry into the affairs of any such association. The person appointed to conduct the enquiry need not be a member of the Corporation's staff. There are penalties for failure to comply with a notice served by the person appointed, requiring the association to produce books, accounts, and other documents, or to supply information. The Corporation may require an audit, and, if so, they will bear the cost. The definition of "registered 1965 Act associations" is given in s. 28.

[73] *Section 20* gives the Corporation power, where an enquiry or audit under s. 19 satisfies them that there has been misconduct or mismanagement, to—

(*a*) remove any member of the committee of the association, or any officer, agent or servant;

(*b*) order any bank or person holding money or securities on behalf of the association not to part with them without the Corporations approval;

(*c*) restrict the transactions of the association.

The section contains a number of other provisions for dealing with misconduct or mismanagement.

[74] *Section 21* should be read with ss. 19 and 20. It gives the Corporation power in the case of misconduct or mismanagement, to transfer land belonging to the association concerned. This is subject to the approval of the Secretary of State. It is clear that this may result in the dissolution of the association. See also s. 23.

[75] *Section 22* gives the Corporation power to petition for the winding up of certain registered housing associations, on the grounds that an association is failing properly to carry out its purposes or objects.

[76] *Section 23* deals with the transfer of the net assets on the dissolution of any registered 1965 Act association. The property of such an association shall be transferred on dissolution to the Corporation, or to a registered association specified in a direction by the Corporation, after the liabilities of the dissolved association have been met. The Corporation cannot dispose of such property in any other way. Where the dissolved 1965 Act association is a charity the

Corporation may not dispose of the property except to another registered association which is a charity, and whose objects appear to the Corporation to be, as nearly as practicable, akin to those of the dissolved association. This section may be compared with s. 5 of the Housing Act 1964.

[**77**] *Section 24* places restrictions on the exercise of certain powers by registered 1965 Act associations. For example, such an association cannot exercise a power to amalgamate with other societies, or to transfer its engagements with the Corporation's consent. A copy of the consent must be sent to the appropriate registrar under the 1965 Act. There is a similar restriction on any registered 1965 Act association which wishes, by special resolution, to be voluntarily wound up. The consent of the Corporation to any of the moves set out in section 24 is to be given by order under the seal of the Corporation.

[**78**] *Section 25* deals with changes in the objects of registered charities which are registered housing associations. If such a charity is neither a company incorporated under the Companies Act 1948 nor an exempt charity, no power to vary or add to its objects may be exercised without the consent of the Charity Commissioners and before giving consent the Commissioners must consult the Corporation.

[**79**] *Section 26* bans gifts and payments by way of dividends or bonus by a registered housing association (*a*) to its members, (*b*) to any person who is a member of the family of a member, and (*c*) to any company of which a person as described in (*a*) or (*b*) is a director. Nor can payments be made to any Scottish firm of which the association member, or one of his family, is a member. This section applies to gifts or payments by way of dividend (or bonus) but not to sums paid in accordance with the rules by way of interest on capital or shares. For the exceptions see sub-s. 2 (*b*).

[**80**] This section also enables the Corporation to specify the maximum amounts which may be paid by a registered housing association, other than a registered charity which is not an exempt one, by way of fees, remuneration or expenses, to a member of the association.

[**81**] The corporation may also lay down conditions governing the circumstances in which a member of a registered 1965 Act association may enter into a contract with the association.

[**82**] *Section 27* lays down rules as to disclosure of their interests, if any, by members of the committee of a registered 1965 Act association.

[**83**] *Section 28* covers the interpretation of Part II.

CHAPTER 3

FINANCIAL ASSISTANCE FOR HOUSING ASSOCIATIONS

[84] The new arrangements for financial assistance are of vital importance to housing associations. The withdrawal by the Housing Finance Act 1972 of all pre-existing subsidies, and their replacement by (*a*) the basic residual subsidy, (*b*) the special residual subsidy, and (*c*) the new building subsidy had not worked as satisfactorily as was hoped by the Government in 1971. Additional income from other houses under the "fair rents" policy had at first come in only slowly and was then the subject of a "rent freeze" in March 1974; building costs and interest rates had risen much faster than in previous years; and the expectation that each new project would show deficits diminishing year by year had not been realised.

The Government has decided to ease matters by checking the rate of diminution of the basic residual subsidy and the special residual subsidy—see paragraphs 30 to 32 of Sch. 13.

[85] Against this background the Act introduces new types of financial assistance which will apply to all housing projects approved after the appointed day, and which may be applied to certain existing schemes under the transitional arrangements embodied in s. 35 of the Act. This financial help, known as "housing association grants" will be on a "project" or "scheme" basis, and, broadly speaking, will result in the Government meeting the net cost of the project to the registered association. Housing association grants may be payable in respect of projects for (*a*) providing housing or residential accommodation, (*b*) improving it, (*c*) repairing it, and (*d*) providing land or buildings which, in the opinion of the Secretary of State, will be for the benefit of persons for whom the housing is, or is to be, provided.

[86] In addition there are management grants payable to associations which, before 1973, provided dwellings without grant aid—see comments below on s. 31, revenue deficit grants (s. 32) and hostel deficit grants (s. 33).

[87] *Section 29.* The Secretary of State may pay housing association grants to registered housing associations, other than those falling within 18 (1) (*b*) of the Act, *i.e.* 1965 Act associations, whose rules restrict membership to tenants, or prospective tenants of the association. Such grants may be made for housing projects approved by him for any of the various types of activity listed in this section, including hostels, or part of a hostel.

[88] If the registered association is seeking a loan from the local authority under s. 119 of the Housing Act 1957, in connection with a project in England and Wales, it must make application for the housing association grant to that local authority. Otherwise it must submit its application to the Corporation.

In Scotland application for the grant may be made to a local authority, the Corporation or the Secretary of State. The recipients of any such application, other than the Secretary of State, are to forward it to the Secretary of State, with their own assessment of the project.

[89] The grant will be equal to the net cost of the project to the association, but this is qualified by the fact that it is the Secretary of State's opinion as to what is the "reasonable and appropriate" expenditure, and also his opinion as to what is the estimated income from rents and grants or subsidies under any enactment which will determine the net cost, and therefore the amount of grant. The Secretary of State also has power to determine maximum levels of cost, or of grant, applicable to projects generally, or to a particular project or description of project, and this may limit the amount which an association receives (sub-s. (5)). Indeed, the Secretary of State is given power to determine the net cost of a project in any manner he considers appropriate (sub-s. (7)).

[90] During the committee stage of the Bill much concern was expressed about associations which were in danger of becoming insolvent owing to rising interest rates and the rent freeze, which were having serious effects on schemes in course of erection or recently completed. One case was quoted of a scheme for which the borrowing rate had risen from $7\frac{7}{8}$ to $12\frac{7}{8}$ per cent. between 1969 and 1973. The Government promised to consider amending its proposals to provide for a revenue deficit subsidy in addition to the project subsidies and this promise is fulfilled in s. 32.

[91] *Section 30* enables the Secretary of State to pay housing association grant as a single sum on completion of a project, or by way of annual instalments over such number of years as he may determine, but in either case he may make payments on account before the project is completed.

[92] The Secretary of State may specify conditions, and reduce or suspend, or discontinue payments if these conditions have not been complied with.

[93] He may pay all or part of the grant to another registered housing association to which any dwelling, hostel, or part thereof is transferred, by lease or vesting. Leasing means leased for a term exceeding 7 years, or for less than 7 years with an option to the lessee for renewal carrying the total term beyond 7 years.

[94] The Secretary of State has powers to recover all or part of the grant if it appears to him that any building is no longer available for use for the purpose for which approval was originally given.

Application for grant may be made before the operative date but no payment may be made before that date.

[95] The Secretary of State may appoint the Corporation, the Greater London Council, a district council, or other local housing authority to act as his agent in respect of payments of housing association grants (sub-s. 8).

[96] *Section 31* introduces another new type of grant known as a "management grant". Such grants are payable only to a housing association which before 1 January 1973 provided any dwellings without any grant, contribution, etc., from the Secretary of State or a local authority, other than grants under s. 93 of the Finance Act 1965 (grants affording tax relief). The dwellings must, for the whole or part of the association's accounting year, have been subject to tenancies to which Part VIII of the Housing Finance Act 1972 or ss. 60 to 66 of the Housing (Financial Provisions) (Scotland) Act 1972, applied. Application must be made within certain time limits, and must be approved by the Corporation. The association must be a registered one.

[**97**] *Section 32* introduces a new grant known as the revenue deficit grant. It is not restricted in the same way as management deficit grants, to bodies which provided housing without subsidies or grants before 1 January 1973. The Secretary of State may pay this grant to a registered housing association, other than a society registered under the 1965 Act whose membership is restricted to its tenants or prospective tenants, or to a special association such as the North Eastern Housing Association. It is payable only in respect of an accounting year ending after 1 January 1974. Application may be made forthwith and must be made within 15 months of the end of the relevant accounting year, but no payments will be made until after the "operative date". However sub-s. (6) empowers the Secretary of State to make advance payments on account. The formula for calculating the grant is laid down in the section.

[**98**] The grant may be payable where the expenditure for any given year exceeds the income for that year. There is no suggestion that any credit balance brought forward from the previous year should be taken into reckoning, but the Secretary has armed himself with ample powers to regulate the method of computation.

[**99**] *Section 33* relates to hostel deficit grants. These may be paid in respect of any accounting year of an association ending after the operative date of the Act, in which a deficit is incurred in relation to the hostel. Where an association has more than one hostel the Secretary of State may treat all the associations' hostels, or two or more of them, as a single hostel for the purpose of deciding whether a deficit was incurred.

Here, too, the grant may be paid in a single sum, or in instalments.

[**100**] Amendments were made in committee to this section, and s. 35, to provide better transitional arrangements, and are dealt with under s. 35 below. Where contributions or hostel subsidies are payable under s. 92 of the Housing Finance Act 1972 or s. 21 of the Housing (Financial Provisions) Scotland Act 1968 they will continue for both registered and unregistered associations unless application is made for an alteration under s. 35 (5) of this Act.

[**101**] *Section 34* provides for the transfer to the Corporation of the rights and obligations of the Secretary of State under agreements in force immediately before the appointed day in relation to certain advances made to co-ownership or cost-rent societies under s. 7 of the Housing Act 1961 or s. 23 of the Housing (Financial Provisions) (Scotland) Act 1968. Some £25 million had been lent by the Secretary of State directly to housing associations providing cost-rent or co-ownership schemes in England and Wales. The corresponding figure for Scotland is about £3 million.

[**102**] *Section 35* covers transitional arrangements for grants and subsidies. After the operative date no further approvals may be given involving new building subsidy under. s. 75 or hostel subsidy under s. 92 of the Housing Act 1972, or the equivalent Acts for Scotland. Schemes which have been submitted but not approved will be treated as if they were applications for housing association grant under the new Act. There is the possibility of changing over to grant under the new Act even where approval has already been given under earlier

Acts, and some payments have been made, but the arrangements differ according to whether the project is a new building scheme, a hostel scheme, or an improvement scheme. For full details see Appendix 1, s. 35 of the Act, and the Notes thereon.

[**103**] Transitional arrangements for improvement grants are set out in sub-ss. (6) and (7). These make it possible to break a large scheme down into small blocks, with contributions payable as each is completed, so that some may be subject to grants or subsidies under earlier Acts and some will attract grant under this Act.

CHAPTER 4

HOUSING ACTION AREAS

[**104**] The provisions of Part IV of the Act are largely based upon an earlier Government's studies of the best ways of dealing with areas of older housing; as set out in a White Paper "Better Homes—The Next Priorities" (Cmnd. 5339) issued in June 1973. Slum clearance remains a serious problem for some local authorities. When the first "National House Condition Survey" was made in 1967, it was concluded that there were 1·8 million slum houses in England and Wales. According to the 1973 White Paper the number of unfit houses would have been reduced to 1 million by the end of 1973, and the rate of reduction was about 70,000 a year. It was forecast that all existing slums would have been dealt with by 1982. This clearance programme and the urgent need to provide for the homeless clearly requires a high and sustained rate of new housebuilding, but the outlook in mid-1974 is far from encouraging. The Act does not deal with new productions.

[**105**] The acute overall shortage accentuates the need to preserve and improve the national stock of older housing. The White Paper states that in 1967 nearly 4 million dwellings lacked such basic amenities as running hot water, a bath, and decent indoor sanitation. It was estimated that by the end of 1973 the figure of 4 million would be reduced to $2\frac{1}{2}$ million. In 1972 approvals for house improvement grants for 319,000 houses were given. To solve this part of the housing problem policy should be, as all parties seem to agree, to continue making improvement grants generally, but to concentrate as much of the effort, public and private, as possible, on areas which were not suitable for slum clearance, but where overcrowding and housing stress were most acute. The concept of housing action areas is very similar to that of the "general improvement area" under the Housing Act 1969, but the intention is that the action should be faster and more concentrated.

[**106**] With this object in view greater powers are given to local authorities, and greater incentives to owners, in the shape of higher rates of grant for properties in housing action areas.

[**107**] The criteria, or some of them, by which a housing action area may be selected cover both social and housing factors, such as—

Households living at a density exceeding 1·5 persons per room.
Furnished tenancies.
Shared accommodation.
Elderly people and large families.
Houses lacking basic amenities.

[**108**] Before deciding to declare an area to be a housing action area the local authority will have to be satisfied that the broad criteria are met and that the

action is consistent with general planning proposals. They will also need to consider priorities as between one area and another, in any district where the problem is of more than minimal. Since the essence of the idea is to make a blitz attack on bad conditions it is not sensible to try to tackle too many areas simultaneously, or to make the areas too large. Each district council must therefore consider the whole housing problem in its area, the demands of slum clearance, and other high priority work, against its probable resources over the next few years, in the shape of money, manpower, new housing production, and availability of relets.

[**109**] These factors vary so much as between one district and another, between London and the large industrial cities, and small provincial authorities, that to lay down any average size for a housing action area would be unrealistic. An area containing 50 houses might represent as serious a problem for a small authority as one of 300 would for a larger authority. The White Paper states: "Typically an area might include four or five hundred dwellings". However, experience indicates that this represents a very heavy commitment, even for a large London borough, and especially if much rehousing is involved, against the basic policy that the intention is to complete the uplift of the area within five years, or, at the most, seven.

[**110**] There is an added complication in that action in one area to reduce multiple-occupation and overcrowding may well lead to dispersal into adjoining areas where conditions would then deteriorate. Hence the provisions of Part VI with regard to Priority Neighbourhoods.

[**111**] *Section 36* describes how the declaration of an action area may be initiated. The starting point is a report "by a person or persons appearing to the authority to be suitably qualified". Such "persons" need not necessarily include an officer of the authority, and thus an "action group" of local residents may take the initiative, but it does not follow that they will secure the declaration of the area. It is for the local authority to decide whether the criteria are satisfied and, presumably, whether they have the necessary resources. They are required also, by sub-s. (3), to act in accordance "with such guidance as may from time to time be given by the Secretary of State".

[**112**] The local authority must be satisfied that the requirements of sub-s. (2) are satisfied, *i.e.* that the living conditions are unsatisfactory and can most effectively be dealt with within a period of 5 years so as to secure—

(*a*) the improvement of the housing accommodation in the area as a whole, and
(*b*) the well-being of the persons residing in the area, and
(*c*) the proper and effective management and use of that accommodation.

[**113**] Having made the declaration the authority must take the steps laid down in sub-s. (4) as to publicity; must send the stipulated information to the Secretary of State, and also send him a statement of their proposals for the participation of registered housing associations in dealing with the area.

[**114**] The word "accommodation" covers dwellings, houses in multiple occupation, and hostels.

[**115**] *Section 37* describes the functions of the Secretary of State. He may within a period of 28 days send a notification to the effect that the area is no

longer a housing action area; or may exclude certain land from the area; or state that he requires more time to consider the matter.

Any decision of the Secretary of State is to be publicised locally.

[116] *Section 38* provides that a general improvement area, a priority neighbourhood, or parts thereof, may be included in a housing action area; subject to the approval of the Secretary of State. From the date of the local authority's resolution the "relevant land" will be excluded from the general improvement area or priority neighbourhood.

[117] *Section 39* states that an area declared under s. 36 shall be an action area for a period of 5 years from the date of the resolution declaring it to be an area, but provision is made for this period to be extended, subject to the approval of the Secretary of State, by 2 years, if the local authority so resolve not less than 3 months before the 5 years' period expires.

[118] On the other hand the local authority is given power to resolve that an area shall cease to be a housing action area.

[119] The various steps which may be taken under this section, such as a resolution to extend the 5 years, a resolution that the area shall cease to be an action area, or a notification by the Secretary of State varying the date of expiry, must all be publicised locally.

[120] *Section 40* enables a local authority, by resolution, to exclude land from a housing action area, and such a resolution must be publicised.

[121] *Section 41* imposes upon the local authority a duty to bring to the attention of residents and owners of property in housing action area details of the action they propose to take and also information as to the assistance available for the improvement of housing accommodation in the area, *e.g.* details of loans and grants. They must do this from time to time and this publicity will augment that required under ss. 36, 37, 38 and 39.

[122] *Section 42* makes it a duty of the local authority to furnish the Secretary of State with information as specified in any direction issued by him.

[123] *Section 43* states that the Secretary of State may authorise a local authority to acquire compulsorily any land in the area on which are situated premises which include living accommodation. It also makes clear that they have power to acquire such land by agreement. If the area ceases to be an action area this section continues to apply—see sub-ss. (3) and (4). This section also deals with the restriction on recovery of possession after the making of a compulsory purchase order and amends s. 131 of the Local Government Act 1972.

[124] *Section 44* sets out the powers of a local authority in relation to land acquired under s. 43 (1) after the housing area was declared, either compulsorily or by agreement. Subject to the Secretary of State's approval under s. 105 the local authority may provide housing accommodation by constructing, converting or improving buildings, and may carry out works for the improvement or repair of housing accommodation, including works to the exterior, or on land within the curtilage of the housing accommodation.

[125] They may manage housing accommodation on the land, and may provide furniture, fittings or services. Similar powers are already available to local authorities under ss. 92, 94, 96 and 111 of the principal Act, the Housing Act 1957.

[**126**] *Section 45* gives the local authority power to give assistance in order to improve living conditions in a housing action area. This applies to the carrying out of environmental works to the exterior, or on land within the curtilage, of buildings containing housing accommodation, or on other land, for the purpose of improving the amenities of the area. Works in respect of which grant has been approved under Part VII of the Act are excluded from such assistance, in order to avoid duplication. The various forms of assistance are set out in sub-s. (2). Grants may be payable by instalments. The arrangements under s. 45 and s. 46 are more generous than those in the original version of the Bill.

[**127**] *Section 46* gives the Secretary of State powers to pay contributions to local authorities towards expenditure incurred by them in giving assistance under s. 45. His contributions are limited to 50 per cent. of the expenditure incurred or to be incurred by the local authority in giving such assistance, and, moreover, the aggregate amount of expenditure for which the Secretary of State may make contributions under this section is £50 multiplied by the aggregate of the numbers of dwellings, houses in multiple occupation, and hostels, in the area at the time it was declared.

[**128**] The Secretary of State has power under s. 44 (6) to vary the sum of £50 by order, and may apply different variations to particular authorities, or descriptions of authority, and to different types of housing action area.

[**129**] *Section 47* requires a landlord of housing accommodation in a housing action area who issues a notice to quit to notify the local authority within 7 days. He is not required to state his reason for serving the notice to quit but may do so if he considers it appropriate—see Sch. 4.

[**130**] Where a tenancy is due to expire by the effluxion of time the landlord is required to serve a similar notice upon the authority but in this case he must notify the authority at least 4 weeks before the tenancy expires.

[**131**] The section also requires persons disposing of land to give notice to the local authority not less than 4 weeks nor more than 6 months before the disposal is carried out.

[**132**] The local authority must, as soon as practicable, acknowledge receipt of the notification and within 4 weeks inform the landlord of the action they propose to take. Certain exceptions are laid down in sub-s. (6).

There are substantial penalties for offences under this section.

[**133**] The object is to enable the local authority to secure that the best use, from the point of view of attaining the objects of the housing action procedure, is made of the resultant vacancy. They may acquire the property or find other ways of using the property to advantage.

[**134**] *Section 48* covers the application of certain provisions of the Housing Act 1957 to this Part of this Act. They relate to powers of entry for inspection, penalties for obstruction, service of notices, and power to require information. Section 70 (review of housing conditions by local authorities) of the Housing Act 1969 is extended to apply to this Part of this Act.

[**135**] *Section 49* specifies which are the authorities for this Part of the Act. They are the councils of districts and London boroughs and the Common Council of the City of London.

[**136**] The Greater London Council may exercise the powers of a local authority under Part IV but only with the agreement of the London borough

council concerned. Where this is obtained, and the Greater London Council deals with a housing action area, it will have within that area certain powers it does not normally possess and to the exclusion of the London borough council concerned.

CHAPTER 5

GENERAL IMPROVEMENT AREAS

[**137**] *Section 50.* In the light of experience and having regard to the new powers to deal with housing action areas, it has been decided to make some curtailment in the powers of a local authority under the Housing Act 1969 to declare improvement areas. The amendments are contained in Sch. 5, Parts I and II. The authority will first have to pass a "preliminary resolution", and then submit a copy thereof, with plans and other documents as listed, within 6 months, to the Secretary of State. The latter may then send a notification to the authority within "the appropriate period" say, stating that—

(*a*) they may not pass a confirmatory resolution, or

(*b*) he requires more time to consider the matter.

[**138**] The "appropriate period" is normally 28 days, but may be longer. See Sch. 5, new s. 28 (7), and, as to publicity, new s. 28A of the Housing Act 1969.

[**139**] There are interim provisions in s. 50 (2) which operate where a local authority has declared a general improvement area on or after 12 June 1973 and before this section comes into operation. These enable the Secretary of State to terminate the status of the area. These interim provisions also deal with the case where, or on after the same date, a local authority has by resolution included land in an existing improvement area.

[**140**] *Section 51* and Part II of Sch. 5 make amendments to Part II of the Housing Act 1969. These—

(*a*) provide that a general improvement area shall not include, but may surround, a housing action area;

(*b*) deal with the situation where works have begun before an area ceases to be an improvement area;

(*c*) remove the power of a local authority to include adjoining land in a general improvement area;

(*d*) amend the powers of a local authority to make grants under s. 32 of the Housing Act 1969;

(*e*) enable the Secretary of State to increase the amount of £100 used to determine the maximum of the aggregate expenditure of local authorities on environmental improvements which shall be eligible for a contribution from him.

CHAPTER 6

PRIORITY NEIGHBOURHOODS

[**141**] It has been realised for many years that an attempt to control any particular housing evil, such as excessive multiple-occupation, in one area is apt to lead to an increase in its incidence in nearby areas. This spread of the disease may not be confined to areas which are actually contiguous, but also to others beyond.

[**142**] This Part of the Act is an attempt to safeguard areas which adjoin a housing action area or general improvement area from a worsening of housing conditions due, in whole or in part, to the campaign of improvement in the housing action area or general improvement area.

[**143**] The risk is greater where the proposed priority neighbourhood is an area which might itself have been declared a housing action area if the local authority's resources had been sufficient. Work in priority neighbourhoods does not qualify for higher percentage grants under s. 59.

The provisions of this Part of the Act are, broadly speaking, very similar to those of Part IV.

[**144**] *Section 52* closely resembles s. 36 as regards the procedure for initiating a priority neighbourhood as the result of a report followed by a resolution. This section lays down what kind of area is "appropriate" to be a priority neighbourhood. The living conditions will be unsatisfactory; it must surround or have a common boundary with a housing action, or general improvement area; but the circumstances must be such that it is not, at the date of the resolution, practicable to declare the area to be a housing action area, or a general improvement area.

[**145**] The local authority must be satisfied that it is necessary to secure "all or any of the objectives in paragraphs (*a*) to (*c*) of s. 36 (2) and that that need can best be met by declaring the area to be a priority neighbourhood. Obviously it is unlikely that all those objectives can be secured as in such a case the area could have been a housing action area.

[**146**] As with housing action areas the Secretary of State may give guidance to local authorities. The process of submitting a scheme for his approval is to be the same as that laid down in s. 37.

[**147**] *Section 53* deals with the incorporation into priority neighbourhoods of housing action areas, or general improvement areas, or parts thereof. This is apparently a downgrading of status in terms of urgency.

[**148**] *Section 54* applies many of the provisions of Part IV (housing action areas) to priority neighbourhoods, including s. 47 (notification of notice to quit or land disposal). The local authority will be able to provide, improve and repair housing accommodation as under s. 44.

[**149**] Whereas a housing action area has a duration of 5 years, which can be

extended by 2 years, the extension for a priority neighbourhood may be a further 5 years, making 10 years in all.

[150] *Section 55* specifies the local authorities for the purposes of Part VI. The Greater London Council will, as with Parts IV and V, have a power to act under Part VI, but only with the agreement of the London borough council concerned.

CHAPTER 7

FINANCIAL ASSISTANCE TOWARDS WORKS OF IMPROVEMENT, REPAIR AND CONVERSION

[**151**] The broad pattern of grants remains much as it was under the Housing Acts 1969 and 1971; and the general basis will continue to be that the grant is a percentage of the eligible expense. Some confusion may arise from the fact that the old standard grants for standard amenities are now to be known as "intermediate grants", but these will continue to be mandatory, whereas all the other grants referred to in Part VI of the Act are discretionary. There is a new 'repairs grant" applicable where the works are not associated with other works for the provision or improvement of a dwelling.

[**152**] Table 1 below summarises the grants now available under Part VII. Part 1 of the Housing Act 1969 is repealed.

[**153**] An interesting feature is the re-introduction of conditions as to the future occupation of the dwelling for owner-occupation or letting. Another feature is the prohibition of grants for owner-occupied dwellings above certain limits of rateable value.

[**154**] Encouragement is given to the carrying out of improvement works in housing action areas and general improvement areas by fixing higher "appropriate percentages" for such areas than those which apply elsewhere.

[**155**] This Part of the Act should be read with Part VIII, which deals with compulsory improvements.

The types of grant, the "ceiling" of eligible expense, and the "appropriate percentages" are summarised in Table 1 below.

[**156**] As to whether the grants are discretionary or mandatory it was stated in the Commons during the Committee stage that "local authorities have discretion whether or not to approve applications for improvement grants, special grants, or repairs grants, but where intermediate grants are concerned, provided certain requirements are met, the local authority must approve the application". The sections are worded accordingly.

[**157**] *Section 56* describes the types of grant and the purposes for which local authorities may make them. These are enumerated in Table 1 below. Normally local authorities may not entertain an application, for a grant for the conversion, improvement or repair of a dwelling erected after 2 October 1961, but some elasticity is provided in sub-s. 4. Improvement grants and intermediate grants have been enlarged to take account of the needs of disabled persons.

[**158**] *Section 57* lays down general provisions relating to applications for grants under this Part of the Act. The applicant must satisfy the local authority that he holds an estate in fee simple absolute in possession, or a lease for a

Table 1

SUMMARY OF GRANTS AND GRANT CONDITIONS IN HOUSING ACTION AREAS, GENERAL IMPROVEMENT AREAS, AND ELSEWHERE

Type of grant	*Purpose*	*Amount of eligible expense*	*Appropriate percentage*		
			HAA	*GIA*	*Elsewhere*
"Improvement"	Provision of dwellings by conversion or the improvement of dwellings beyond the provision of standard amenities	£2,000, or £2,400 for a dwelling provided by the conversion of a house or building of three or more storeys, ss. 63 and 64	75 max. or 90 where proviso in s. 59 (2) applies	60 max.	50 max. See Note 2
"Intermediate"	Provision of standard amenities where the dwelling lacks all or any of them	Up to £800 for repairs and replacements plus the cost of amenities as laid down in s. 68 and schedule 6	75 or 90 where s. 59 (2) applies See Note 1	60 max. See Note 1	50 max. See Note 1
"Special"	Provision of standard amenities in houses in multiple occupation	Maximum sums per amenity as laid down in s. 70 and schedule 6	75 max. or 90 where s. 59 (2) applies	60 max.	50
"Repairs"	Carrying out of works of repair or replacement to a dwelling, but only if it is in housing action area or a general improvement area, not being works linked with other works for conversion or improvement	Up to £800, ss. 71 and 72	75 max. or 90 where s. 59 (2) applies	60 max.	Nil. Grant is not available except in Housing Action, and General Improvement Areas

Note 1. The local authority may fix a grant at a figure below the appropriate percentage for improvement grants, special grants, and repair grants but must give reasons—see s. 80. They have no such discretion in relation to intermediate grants.

Note 2. At the time of going to press we learn that the Minister for Housing and Construction is about to make an order increasing the limits of eligible expense for improvement grants to £3,200 or to £3,700 if the building is of three or more storeys.

term of years absolute of which not less than 5 years remain unexpired at the date of application. He must supply particulars of the works and an estimate of their cost. The local authority must not approve a grant for works already begun unless they are satisfied that there were very good reasons for beginning the works before approval was given. There is provision for revising the estimated expense if it transpires that the original estimate is not sufficient (sub-s. (7)).

[159] *Section 58*, taken with Sch. 6, Part 1, defines "standard amenities". The Secretary of State may vary the provisions of Section 6 by order.

[160] *Section 59* defines the "appropriate percentages" to be used in determining the amount, or maximum amount of any grant. These percentages are shown in Table 1 above. There is a special power in sub-s. 2 to deal with cases of hardship, for which local authorities may increase the appropriate percentage up to 90 per cent of the cost of the works, but only in respect of houses in a housing action area.

The Secretary of State has power to vary these appropriate percentages by order, the draft of which must be approved by the House of Commons.

[161] *Section 60* deals with certificates of future occupation. A local authority shall not entertain an application for grant (other than a special grant) unless it is accompanied by a certificate as to future occupation. This will be either a certificate of owner-occupation or a certificate of availability for letting. See also ss. 73–77.

IMPROVEMENT GRANTS

[162] *Section 61* sets out the circumstances in which a local authority shall pay or approve an improvement grant. They must pay the grant if the application has been approved by them and the conditions for the payment of grant are fulfilled. However, they may approve an application for grant in such circumstances as they think fit, and therefore the critical point is the approval stage. They may fix the amount of an improvement grant at a figure below "the appropriate percentage"—see ss. 64 and 80.

The authority must not approve an application unless they are satisfied that when the works are completed the dwelling will attain the required standard. To attain this it must:

(*a*) be provided with all the standard amenities, for the exclusive use of its occupants;
(*b*) be in good repair (disregarding internal decorative repair) having regard to its age character and locality;
(*c*) be in conformity with such standards of construction etc. as may be laid down from time to time by the Secretary of State; and
(*d*) be likely to provide satisfactory housing accommodation for a period of 30 years.

[163] However the local authority may temper conditions if it appears to them that it is not practicable at reasonable expense to provide the dwelling with all the standard amenities and to comply with conditions (*b*) and (*c*). They also have power to reduce the period of 30 years if they consider it reasonable to do so, but the minimum period is 10 years.

[164] *Section 62* limits grants in respect of owner-occupied dwellings to those which have at the date of application a rateable value at or below a certain limit.

[165] *Section 63* empowers the local authority to determine the amount of expenses proper to be incurred in relation to an improvement grant. This is known as "the estimated expense". Not more than 50 per cent. of the total can be allowed for repair and replacement. The figure for "estimated expense" may be increased by the local authority if the applicant satisfies them that this is justifiable.

[166] *Section 64* lays down that the "amount of improvement grant" is to be fixed by the local authority when it approves the application but it must not exceed the appropriate percentage of the eligible expense. The appropriate percentage is laid down in s. 59 and is set out in Table 1 above. There is discretion to fix an amount which represents a lower percentage. The "eligible expense" for an improvement grant shall be so much of the "estimated expense" as does not exceed the "relevant limit". The relevant limit of eligible expense is £2,000 per dwelling or such amount as the Secretary of State may by order specify, but for a dwelling provided by the conversion of a house or building consisting of three or more storeys the relevant limit is £2,400 or such amount as the Secretary of State may by order specify.

If the local authority are satisfied that there are good reasons for increasing the amount they may seek the approval of the Secretary of State to a higher relevant limit in respect of a particular case, or description of case.

[**167**] The "relevant limit" in relation to an improvement grant shall be reduced if an intermediate grant, a repairs grant, or a standard grant, as defined in the Housing Act 1969, has been made within the previous 10 years, or the period laid down in sub-s. (7). The amount of the reduction is shown in this sub-section.

INTERMEDIATE GRANTS

[**168**] *Section 65* states that a local authority shall pay an intermediate grant if they have approved an application and the conditions of grant are fulfilled. This section must be read with s. 67 and together they are less permissive than s. 61. The section specifies the amenities to be provided and makes it clear that grant will not be approved except for amenities which the dwelling lacks, and has lacked, for the 12 months prior to the date of application. This is qualified by sub-s. (3).

[**169**] *Section 66* sets out the standards which the dwelling must attain. The local authority must not approve an application for intermediate grant unless they are satisfied that, on completion of the works, the dwelling will comply with the following conditions, *i.e.*:

(*a*) be provided with all the standard amenities for the exclusive use of its occupants; and
(*b*) be in good repair, having regard to its age, character and locality, and
(*c*) conform with specified standards of thermal insulation and
(*d*) be in all respects fit for human habitation, and
(*e*) have a life of 15 years.

These conditions may be modified and the period of 15 years may be reduced, as set out in sub-ss. (3) to (6).

[**170**] *Section 67* deals generally with applications for intermediate grant and makes approval (and therefore payment) mandatory providing the requirements of the sections set out in sub-s. (1) are satisfied. This section also makes some relaxations in conditions so far as applications for grant in respect of compulsory improvements are concerned. These are applications which are the result of an improvement notice, or an undertaking accepted, under Part VIII of the Act. The section also covers the case where the works specified in an application for

intermediate grant go beyond the works of repair or replacement which the local authority consider necessary.

[171] *Section 68* describes how the local authority shall determine "the estimated expense" and the "amount" of an intermediate grant. They must determine those amounts which are in respect of repair and replacement separately from those which are proper solely for the provision of the standard amenities. This is necessary because the "eligible expense" itself is calculated in two parts: The "eligible expense" is the aggregate of:

(*a*) the estimated expense of repair and replacement, but this may not exceed £800, and

(*b*) so much of "the estimated expense of actually providing each of the standard amenities as does not exceed the limits laid down in Part 1 of Schedule 6".

[172] The amount of the intermediate grant will be "the appropriate percentage" (as defined in s. 52) of the "eligible expense".

There is provision for varying "estimated expense" and "the eligible expense" if the work proves more costly than was expected. The inclusion of a "repairs element" in intermediate grants should do much to encourage the flow of applications.

SPECIAL GRANTS

[173] *Sections 69 and 70* describe the powers and duties of local authorities in approving applications for "special grant", that is grants towards the provision of standard amenities in houses which are in multiple occupation. The pattern is very similar to that for "intermediate grants" adjusted to take account of the fact that the house may need to be provided with more than one of any particular standard amenity, and an amenity will often not be for the exclusive use of one household, whereas with an intermediate grant no payment can be made towards the provision of a second amenity of any given kind, and the amenities must be for the exclusive use of the occupants of the dwelling—s. 66. The local authority has discretion to pay less than the "appropriate percentage".

REPAIRS GRANTS

[174] *Section 71* provides that a local authority shall pay a repair's grant if the application is approved by them and the conditions for payment are fulfilled, but it should be noted that they may approve the application in such circumstances as they see fit. In other words, they have a wide discretion. They may take the applicants' means into account—sub-s. 2.

Repairs grants are payable only in respect of dwellings in a housing action area or a general improvement area—s. 56.

[175] The local authority shall not approve an application unless they are satisfied that the dwelling will attain the relevant standard when the works are completed, *i.e.*, it must then be in good repair having regard to its age, character and locality, see s. 56 (2) (*d*). As with improvement grants and special grants, the local authority has discretion to fix a repairs grant at a figure below the "appropriate percentage" but must give reasons—s. 80.

[176] *Section 72* describes the local authority's power to determine the estimated expense. There is a maximum "eligible expense" of £800 or such other amount as may be prescribed. The maximum grant will be the appropriate percentage of the eligible expense. As with other grants there is power to revise the estimated expense—sub-s. (5).

GRANT CONDITIONS

[177] *Section 73* deals with the standard conditions as to future occupation, already referred to under s. 60 above. Additional conditions may be imposed under s. 74.

[178] Where the application for grant was accompanied by a certificate of owner-occupation it shall be a condition that, if at any time during the second or subsequent years of "the initial period" (5 years) the owner is not occupying it as his only or main residence, the dwelling shall be let, or available for letting as a residence, and not for a holiday, to persons other than members of the owner's family. This is modified by sub-s. (3).

[179] Where the application was accompanied by a "certificate of availability for letting" it shall be a condition throughout the 5-year period that the dwelling will be let or available for letting as a residence, and not for a holiday, to persons other than members of the owner's family.

There is also a condition as to the supply of information by the owner to the local authority in respect of occupancy.

[180] *Section 74* enables a local authority to impose, as additional conditions of any grant except a special grant:

(*a*) that the dwelling will be let or available for letting on a regulated tenancy or Part VI contract;

(*b*) that if the local authority serve notice on the owner he will, within 21 days, furnish a certificate that the condition set out at (*a*) is being fulfilled.

(*c*) as to tenants supplying the owner with information to enable him to comply with (*b*), and

(*d*) that if, on the certified date (s. 75), there is no registered rent for the dwelling, application will be made to the rent officer or the rent tribunal for the registration of a rent under either Part IV or Part VI of the Rent Act 1968, as amended by the Rent Act 1974,

(*e*) that such application will be diligently pursued, and

(*f*) that no premium will be required.

The imposition of these conditions is mandatory if the grant is in respect of a dwelling in a housing action area, a general improvement area, or a priority neighbourhood.

[181] Sub-s. (3) exempts certain housing associations from the imposition of any condition under this section. See also sub-s. 3 (*b*) and 3 (*c*).

It will be noted that this section carries matters beyond s. 60 and s. 73 by making it possible for the local authority not only to ensure that the dwelling is let, but that is let at a registered rent, or a "reasonable rent" fixed by a Rent Tribunal. See Notes on s. 74 in Appendix 1.

[182] *Section 75* deals with the enforceability of conditions imposed under s. 74. They run for 5 years from the "certified date", and for 7 years if the dwelling is in a housing action area.

[183] *Section 76* enables the local authority to enforce repayment of grant in the event of a breach of a condition of grant, at a time when the condition is binding on the owner by virtue of s. 75 (2). When an owner has satisfied the liability to make a payment under this section, the condition shall cease to be in force in respect of the dwelling.

[184] It is interesting to note that a local authority is free not to demand any amount to which they are entitled under this section. They can waive all or part of it.

[185] *Section 77* enables an owner or mortgagee to discharge any potential liability under s. 76 by making a voluntary payment to the local authority.

CONTRIBUTIONS

[186] *Section 78* deals with contributions by the Secretary of State towards the expense incurred by a local authority in making grants under Part VII. The contribution shall be a sum payable annually for 20 years equal to the "relevant percentage" of the annual loan charges on the local authority's expenditure on grants. The "relevant percentage" is 90 per cent for dwellings in general improvement or housing action areas, and 75 per cent for dwellings elsewhere.

The Secretary of State has power, subject to approval by the House of Commons, to make an order varying either or both of these percentages.

[187] Where the Secretary of State decides that an area is no longer to be a housing action area, or that certain land is to be excluded from an area, he may reduce the percentage grant to 75 per cent, but he has discretion to leave it at 90 per cent.

[188] *Section 79* provides that the Secretary of State may make "improvement contributions" towards the expenses incurred by a local authority in providing dwellings by conversion, or improving its own dwellings. Here again the contribution will be a sum payable annually for a period of 20 years, in respect of schemes approved by him.

[189] The Secretary of State will determine the estimated expense for each scheme, and the "eligible expense" for the purpose of "improvement contribution" is limited to a maximum of £2,000 per dwelling provided by conversion, or improved. The contribution will be 37·5 per cent of the annual loan charges on the eligible expenses. Presumably a substantial amount of the other 62·5 per cent will be recoverable as increased rent income, resulting from the improvements, providing there is no rent "freeze".

SUPPLEMENTARY

[190] *Section 80.* It is an important provision of this Act that where a local authority does not approve an application for grant, or fixes the amount of an improvement grant at less than the appropriate percentage of the eligible expense, they shall inform the applicant in writing their reasons for doing so.

[191] *Section 81* provides that grants are restricted to an applicant or his personal representatives.

[192] *Section 82* sets out a number of miscellaneous provisions as to payment of grants such as time limits for the completion of works; a power to extend such time; and payments by instalments.

[193] *Section 83* contains special provisions as to parsonages. It is also of importance to charity trustees.

[194] *Section 84* deals with the interpretation of Part VII.

CHAPTER 8

COMPULSORY IMPROVEMENT OF DWELLINGS

[195] The policy behind legislation dealing with general improvement areas under the Housing Act 1969, and housing action areas under this Act, is to secure a general uplift in the housing conditions and the environment throughout a complete area. If the operation were to rely wholly upon the voluntary co-operation of owners and owner-occupiers, many difficulties and delays would arise and some such schemes might fail to achieve their goal. Odd groups of unimproved houses not only affect the tenants directly concerned but have a detrimental effect on the living conditions of occupants of adjoining houses. They may even bring the area improvement scheme as a whole into jeopardy. The policy in the Housing Act 1969, in this respect, was "first persuasion, and co-operation, with compulsion to be used only in the last resort". The somewhat cumbersome machinery for making compulsory improvements, instituted by the Housing Act 1964, was abandoned within a year or two. The attitude from 1969 to 1973 was to rely on persuasion and example, but in the last resort only, local authorities could acquire dwellings in improvement areas compulsorily. They could then carry out the improvements themselves. The new Act reverses the policy in the 1969 Act. Part VIII of this 1974 Act revives the power to secure, by compulsion if necessary, the improvement by the provision of standard amenities, in houses in general improvement areas, in the new housing action areas, and in individual dwellings outside such areas. So far as the latter are concerned the initiative lies with the occupying tenant. However, as with s. 19 of the Housing Act 1964, the local authority has discretion whether to proceed or to take no action.

[196] This return to compulsory improvements reflects the fact that the sense of urgency has been lost in the pursuit of persuasion.

[197] It remains to be seen whether the concept of housing action areas, where owners, local authorities, tenants, and others concerned, will be faced with the need to complete the operation within five years, will really achieve speedier progress. Certainly provision for compulsion was necessary but with proper safeguards, which seem to have been provided.

[198] The first portion of Part VIII of the Act describes the compulsory methods to be used where necessary, in general improvement areas, and housing action areas. The second portion deals with the compulsory improvement, at the tenants' request, of individual houses outside general improvement and housing action areas.

DWELLINGS IN GENERAL IMPROVEMENT AREAS AND HOUSING ACTION AREAS

[**199**] *Section 85* describes how the local authority may bring into action the machinery for compulsory improvements. This they may do by serving a "provisional notice" on the person having control of any dwelling where it appears to them that one of the standard amenities is lacking; that the dwelling could be improved to the full standard, or the reduced standard; and that it was provided by erection or conversion before 3 October 1961. They may not take this step in respect of an owner-occupied dwelling unless it appears to them that any dwelling (not owner-occupied) in the same block cannot be improved without effecting the improvement of the owner-occupied dwelling.

[**200**] The provisional notice will specify the works which the local authority consider necessary; state a date at least 21 days after service of the notice when the proposals, and any alternative proposals, any housing arrangements, and the views of the tenant, may be discussed. The section requires the service of a copy of the notice on various other classes of person who may have an interest, such as an owner, lessee, or mortgagee.

There is thus an interval between the service of a "provisional notice" and an "improvement notice" during which representations from the interested parties may be discussed and the possibility of undertakings (s. 87) may be explored.

[**201**] *Section 86* deals with "housing arrangements" which may be made, temporarily or permanently, in connection with the improvement works. This covers the rehousing of an occupying tenant during the works, and/or after they have been completed.

[**202**] *Section 87* gives the local authority power, prior to the service of an improvement notice, to accept an undertaking from the person having control of the dwelling, or any person having an estate or interest in the dwelling, to improve the dwelling to the required standard, *i.e.* "full" or "reduced", as defined in s. 66. Before accepting an undertaking the local authority must satisfy themselves that the tenant's interests are protected, and that the undertaking incorporates his written and signed consent. They must also be satisfied that the person giving the undertaking has the right to carry out such works.

[**203**] Once the local authority have accepted such an undertaking they may not serve an improvement notice unless the works have not been carried out within the stipulated period, or they consider that, owing to a change of circumstances, the undertaking is not likely to be fulfilled. Copies of the various notices must be served upon the parties concerned.

[**204**] *Section 88* sets out the various conditions which must be satisfied before a local authority can serve an improvement notice, as distinct from a provisional notice, in respect of a dwelling in a general improvement area or housing action area. The limiting periods in sub-s. (3) should be particularly noted.

DWELLINGS OUTSIDE GENERAL IMPROVEMENT AREAS AND HOUSING ACTION AREAS

[**205**] *Section 89* gives an occupying tenant of such a dwelling the right to make representations in writing to the local authority with a view to their exercising their powers to bring about the improvement of the dwelling. The

local authority must notify the person having control of the dwelling of any representations they receive.

[**206**] If they are satisfied on the various points set out in sub-s. (3) the local authority may either serve a provisional notice on the person having control or send the occupying tenant a written statement setting out their reasons for deciding not to serve a provisional notice.

An improvement notice may be served in due course.

GENERAL PROVISIONS AS TO IMPROVEMENT NOTICES

[**207**] *Section 90* lays down the content of an improvement notice and provides for it to be registered by the local authority in the register of local land changes.

[**208**] *Section 91* covers appeals to the county court against improvement notices by the person having control of the dwelling, the occupying tenant, or any other person having an estate or interest in it. The county court may confirm, or quash, or vary the improvement notice, but the power to vary is limited by sub-s. (5).

[**209**] *Section 92* states that, if no appeal is brought within 6 weeks from the date of service of an improvement notice on the person having control, the notice becomes operative at the end of the 6 weeks' period. The local authority is given a power to withdraw an improvement notice at any time.

[**210**] *Section 93* deals with the enforcement of improvement notices. If the works have not been carried out within the time allowed the local authority may themselves complete the works. See ss. 94 and 95 as to recovery of costs.

[**211**] If the person having control of the dwelling notifies the local authority that he does not intend, or is unable, to do the works, the authority may do the works without waiting for the expiry of the period laid down in the original notice.

[**212**] There is also a power for the local authority to press the person having control for evidence of his intentions with regard to the work, before the expiry of the time limit, but not earlier than 6 months after the improvement notice became operative.

[**213**] *Section 94* provides for the recovery of expenses incurred by a local authority in cases of default. The section includes a provision that the amount of the local authority's demand shall become a charge on the premises. This section also covers appeals to the county court against a demand for such expenses.

[**214**] *Section 95* deals with charging orders in favour of the owner, or person having control, who is executing the works.

SUPPLEMENTARY

[**215**] *Section 96* contains provisions on such matters as rights of entry to survey the premises, and rights as against the occupying tenant and other persons to take steps to comply with an improvement notice. Section 97 states that s. 159 of the Housing Act 1957 (powers of entry of local authorities) shall apply, and gives the local authority other minor powers.

[**216**] *Section 98.* Consequential modifications of the Agricultural Holdings Act 1948 are dealt with in this section.

[**217**] *Section 99* lists the various types of owner excluded, or partly excluded, from this part of the Act. No provisional notice or improvement notice may be served in respect of a dwelling in which there is a Crown or Duchy interest except with the consent of the appropriate authority. Where such consent is given this Part of the Act applies in the normal way.

No provisional notice, or improvement notice, may be served if "the person having control" is a local authority or any of the other bodies named in sub-s. 2.

Sub-s. (6) widens considerably the list of bodies covered by the term "local authority", but only so far as this section is concerned.

[**218**] *Section 100* imposes upon local authorities the duty of offering loans to meet all or part of the expenses of compulsory improvement. This will be subject to the deduction of the amount of any improvement grant or intermediate grant. The local authority shall not make an offer of a loan unless they are satisfied as to the nature and value of the applicant's interest.

[**219**] *Section 101* gives the person having control who has been served with an improvement notice the right to serve a purchase notice upon the local authority.

[**220**] *Section 102* deals with the situation where an area ceases to be a general improvement area or housing action area after an improvement notice has been served, or an undertaking has been accepted. It also covers the position where the land is later excluded from either type of area. The provisions of this Part of the Act shall continue to apply as if no change had occurred.

[**221**] *Section 103* sets out certain requirements as to the service of notices.

[**222**] *Section 104* contains definitions and interpretations applicable to Part VIII.

CHAPTER 9
MISCELLANEOUS

[**223**] *Section 105* states that a housing authority may not incur any expenses in providing dwellings by conversion, or improving dwellings, except in accordance with proposals approved by the Secretary of State. The necessity for this degree of control was challenged during the committee stage. It appears from the Minister's reply that the object of the section is not to introduce detailed interference with local expenditure but to establish strategic control. Resources are not limitless and the needs of stress areas must take priority over other work. Most older council estates had already been improved but there is a great deal of urgent work involved in buying up, converting and improving older houses. Full consultation with local authorities was promised.

[**224**] *Section 106.* For many years income and expenditure in connection with hostels provided by local authorities and new town corporations in England and Wales has been excluded from their statutory Housing Revenue Accounts.

The reforms carried out under the Housing Finance Act 1972 left this rule undisturbed so far as hostels were concerned, and extended it to include lodging houses as well—now they are both to be included in the Housing Revenue Account for the year 1975–76 and subsequent years. Until then the present practice is to be continued. This section makes the necessary amendments to earlier Acts and brings subsidies under earlier Acts to an end for 1975–76 and later years.

[**225**] *Section 107* deals with hostels provided by housing authorities in Scotland. To enable the Secretary of State to make grants under ss. 29 (1) to (7), 30 (1) to (7), 33 and 35 of this Act in respect of their expenditure on hostels, such an authority shall be treated as a registered housing association.

[**226**] *Section 108* was introduced during the committee stage in the House of Commons. Its effect is to abolish the clearance order procedure under Part III of the Housing Act 1957. Having declared an area to be a clearance area under Part III the local authority had then to secure the demolition of all the buildings in the area either by themselves purchasing the land and demolishing the buildings, or by making one or more clearance orders. This alternative procedure is now repealed, though the transitional situation is covered by sub-s. (1) (*b*). In the 1950s owners frequently asked for clearance orders, and accepted the cost of demolition, because they wished to retain ownership of the site, *e.g.* for an extension of an adjoining factory. By the 1970s the proportion of houses dealt with by clearance orders had shrunk to only about 4 per cent. of the total number of houses to be cleared under Part III powers. In any event, where only a few houses are involved, and the authority does not need the site, the authority can use its powers under Part II of the 1957 Act to secure demolition without acquisition.

[**227**] This section also deals with payments in respect of "well-maintained houses" in clearance areas. The necessary amendments to existing legislation are made by Sch. 9 and 13. This section came into operation on 31 August 1974.

[**228**] *Section 109* should be read with ss. 110–116 which relate to "listed buildings" in clearance areas; the temporary rehabilitation of unfit houses; and adjustments to the compensation code arising from these sections. S. 109 links the legislation applicable in Scotland with the legislation applicable in England and Wales.

[**229**] *Section 110* applies where a compulsory purchase order has been made under Part III of the Housing Act 1957 (clearance areas) and subsequently any building comprised in the order is included in a list of buildings of special architectural interest. The local authority may apply to the Secretary of State for his consent to the demolition of the building. There is a time limit for such applications. If no application is made within the time limit, or consent is refused, and the building has not vested in the authority, or been the subject of a notice to treat, the building will no longer be on the clearance area, and the compulsory purchase order will cease to apply to it. In that event, if the building is unfit for human habitation, the local authority shall proceed to deal with it under Part II of the 1957 and so secure its repair or closure.

[**230**] Where the property has vested in, or will become vested in, the local authority, the acquisition will be treated as if it had been made under Part V instead of Part III of the 1957, or Part VI of the Act of 1971, and compensation will be adjusted accordingly. See also ss. 115 and 116.

[**231**] *Section 111* runs parallel to s. 110 except that it deals with buildings acquired by agreement, and not by compulsory purchase, under Part III of the Housing Act 1957, and which, at any time, become "listed buildings". The local authority may seek the consent of the Secretary of State to demolition. If the application is refused, or made too late, the local authority shall cease to be under a duty to demolish it, and the property shall be treated as appropriated under Part V of the Housing Act 1957, if it is a house, or if it is not, as appropriated under Part VI of the Town and Country Planning Act 1971. This affects the compensation. See ss. 115, 116 and Sch. 10.

[**232**] *Section 112* is roughly in parallel with ss. 110 and 111, except that it relates to buildings which have been included in clearance areas under Part III of the Housing Act 1957 and then made subject to clearance orders. Where any such building becomes a "listed building" after confirmation of the order the local authority may apply for consent to its demolition. If the local authority apply to the Secretary of State for his consent to demolition and consent is refused, or the application is too late, the building will cease to be in a clearance area and cease to be subject to the clearance order. If it is unfit for habitation the local authority shall deal with it under Part II of the 1957 Act and secure its repair or closure. The building will not be subject to acquisition. Sub-ss. (6) and (7) deal with the possible repayment to the local authority of payments made under certain enactments, *e.g.* well-maintained houses and payments of full value instead of Site value to certain owner-occupiers.

[**233**] *Section 113* applies ss. 110, 111, and 112, with modifications, to buildings in conservation areas under the Town and Country Planning (Amendment) Act 1972. See also ss. 115 and 116.

[**234**] *Section 114* enables a local authority to submit a "rehabilitation order" to the Secretary of State for his approval, in respect of an unfit building included in a clearance area. The building must have been purchased by agreement prior to the date on which this section comes into operation, or be included in a compulsory purchase order made before that date and confirmed within 3 months thereafter. The local authority must be satisfied that it can be improved to the full standard under s. 66 of this Act or s. 16 (3) of the Housing (Scotland) Act 1974. The full procedure for making rehabilitation orders, and for dealing with objections to them, is set out in Sch. 10, which, incidentally, widens the scope of s. 114 to embrace properties other than those defined in sub-s. (1). The local authority can make arrangements with owners for the improvement of the property, instead of its demolition.

[**235**] If the rehabilitation order is approved the local authority is under a duty to improve the house to the full standard, or to secure that some other person does so.

The order may involve the assessment of compensation under Part V instead of Part III of the 1957 Act—see Sch. 10 and s. 116.

[**236**] *Section 115* deals with the assessment of compensation where, under ss. 110 and 111, it has to be assessed as if the acquisition or appropriation was made under Part V, instead of Part III, of the 1957 Act. It also refers to payments in respect of well-maintained houses, and other payments—see sub-s. 10.

[**237**] *Section 116* amends s. 4 of the Compulsory Purchase Act 1965 and the Lands Clauses Consolidation (Scotland) Act 1845 to resolve difficulties which might otherwise arise under ss. 110, 113 or 114 of this Act.

[**238**] *Section 117* removes the time limit for the completion of works eligible for higher grants or contributions. These higher rates for improvements in development areas and intermediate areas were conditional upon the works being completed within 3 years from 23 June 1971. This condition, contained in the Housing Act 1971, shall no longer have effect where the application was approved on or before 30 September 1973, and the local authority have, before 23 June 1974, fixed the amount of grant at the higher rate of 75 per cent. (instead of 50 per cent.) applicable to these special areas.

Sub-s. (3) extends the concession in sub-s. (1) to certain housing association schemes carried out under s. 21 of the Housing Act 1969.

See also sub-s. (4) as to housing association schemes in Scotland.

[**239**] *Section 118* raises the rateable value limits for enfranchisement or extension of leases under the Leasehold Reform Act 1967 and makes certain other changes in that Act.

[**240**] *Section 119*, and Sch. 11 amend Part II of the Housing Subsidies Act 1967, so far as option mortgages are concerned.

[**241**] *Section 120* deals with tax exemptions for self-build societies, and amends the Income and Corporation Taxes Act 1970.

[**242**] *Section 121* lays down penalties for failure without reasonable excuse to supply a written statement of the landlord's name and address in response to a written request from the tenant. This is amplified by sub-s. (2) in relation to cases where the landlord is a body corporate.

This section came into operation on 31 August 1974.

[**243**] *Section 122* makes it the duty of a new landlord to notify his tenant in

writing of the change of ownership, and of the name and address of the new landlord. This section came into operation on 31 August 1974.

[244] *Section 123* tightens the law with regard to the form and content of notices to quit, which must be in writing and contain information to be prescribed by the Secretary of State.

[245] *Section 124* deals with service charges and gives tenants' rights, additional to those in s. 90 of the Housing Finance Act 1972. Either the landlord or the tenant may apply to the High Court or the county court for a declaration that any works are, or are not, to a reasonable standard and that the amount payable for them is, or is not, reasonable. Recognition is given to tenants' associations which represent not less than 60 per cent of the potential membership. This section came into force on 31 August 1974.

[246] *Section 125* makes important changes in the law with regard to specific performance of a landlords' repairing covenants. It came into operation on 31 July 1974.

[247] *Section 126* covers the enforceability of certain covenants in agreements relating to the development of land. If a "principal council" (defined in the section) and a person having an interest in land in their area become parties to an instrument executed for the purpose of carrying out works on, or developing, the land etc, and the instrument contains a covenant on the part of any person having an interest in land . . . the covenant shall be enforceable against any person deriving title from the original covenantor. Also the principal council may, without prejudice to any other method of enforcement, enter on the land and carry out the works which the covenantor has failed to do, and they may recover their expenses from him. There are various other provisions as to giving prior notice, penalties for obstruction and so on.

[248] *Section 127* gives authority for defraying out of money provided by Parliament any sums required by the Secretary of State for the payment of grants, subsidies, and contributions.

[249] *Section 128* lays down, *inter alia*, that any power of the Secretary of State to make Orders shall be exercisable by statutory instrument, and provides that the order may be varied or revoked by a subsequent order.

[250] *Section 129* deals with interpretation of this Act, with separate sets of definitions for (*a*) England and Wales and (*b*) Scotland.

[251] *Section 130* is formal and covers the changes and repeals made by Sch. 13, 14, and 15 of the Act.

[252] *Section 131* gives the short title, citation, commencement and extent.

[253] *Section 131* (*3*) states that, except in so far as the Act otherwise provides this Act shall come into force on such day as the Secretary of State may by order appoint.

The commencement dates so far decided are set out below.

	Title	*Date*	*Authority*
Part I			
Section			
1	Extension of powers of corporation	18 Sep. 74	S.I. 1974 No. 1562
2	Control by corporation of land disposals by associations	20 Aug. 74	S.I. 1974 No. 1406
3	Acquisition of land by corporation		
	sub-s. (1), (2) and (6)	18 Sep. 74	S.I. 1974 No. 1562
	remainder		

Section	*Title*	*Date*	*Authority*
4 to 8	Provision of dwellings, land disposal; Acquisition of securities, borrowings etc.	18 Sep. 74	S.I. 1974 No.1562
9	Lending powers except sub-ss. (1) (*a*) and (*b*) and sub-ss. (5) and (6)	18 Sep. 74	,,
10, 11, 12	Miscellaneous	18 Sep. 74	,,
Part II			
13	Registration of housing associations	20 Aug. 74	S.I. 1974 No. 1406
14	Registration Advisory Committee	20 Aug. 74	,,
15, 16, 17	Control of register, etc.	2 Dec. 74	S.I. 1974 No. 1791
18	Tenancies of housing associations	2 Dec. 74 (except as already in operation)	,,
19 to 28	Various matters affecting registration	2 Dec. 74	,,
Part III			
29 to 33 and 35	Financial assistance to housing associations	18 Sep. 74	S.I. 1974 No. 1562
Part IV			
36 to 49	Housing Action Areas	2 Dec. 74	S.I. 1974 No. 1791
Part V			
50 and 51	General Improvement Areas	2 Dec. 74	S.I. 1974 No. 1791
Part VI			
52 to 55	Priority Neighbourhoods	2 Dec. 74	S.I. 1974 No. 1791
Part VII			
56 to 84	Financial assistance towards works of improvement, repairs and conversion	2 Dec. 74	S.I. 1974 No. 1791
Part VIII			
85 to 104	Compulsory Improvements	2 Dec. 74	S.I. 1974 No. 1791
Part IX			
105	Powers of Secretary of State		not stated
106	Lodging houses and hostels	2 Dec. 74	S.I. 1974 No. 1791
107	Hostels provided in Scotland	18 Sep. 74	S.I. 1974 No. 1562
108	Abolition of Clearing Orders	31 Aug. 74	The Act
109	Interpretation for Scotland	2 Dec. 74	S.I. 1974 No. 1791
110 to 113	Listed buildings	2 Dec. 74	,,
114	Temporary rehabilitation provisions	2 Dec. 74	,,
115 and 116	Compensation	2 Dec. 74	,,
117	Time limit for certain grants	20 Aug. 74	S.I. 1974 No. 1406
118	Leasehold enfranchisement	31 Jul. 74	The Act
119 (parts)	Option mortgages For details see the Order in Appendix III	2 Dec. 74	S.I. 1974 No. 1791
120	Tax exemption for self-build societies	2 Dec. 74	,,
121	Disclosure of landlord's identity	31 Aug. 74	The Act
122	Assignment of landlord's interest	31 Aug. 74	The Act
123	Form of notice to quit	2 Dec. 74	S.I. 1974 No. 1791
124	Service charges	31 Aug. 74	The Act
125	Specific performance of repairing covenants	31 Jul. 74	The Act
126	Enforceability of agreements relating to land development	2 Dec. 74	S.I. 1974 No. 1791
127 to 129	General	20 Aug. 74	S.I. 1974 No. 1406
130	For details of amendments, savings and repeals, and their operative dates see Appendix III—Statutory Instruments 1974, Nos. 1406, 1562 and 1791		
Schedules			
1	Housing corporation	18 Sep. 74	S.I. 1974 No. 1562
2	Grant-aided land	20 Aug. 74	S.I. 1974 No. 1406
3	Housing Association tenancies	2 Dec. 74 (except in so far as already in operation)	S.I. 1974 No. 1791
4	Notification procedure	2 Dec. 74	S.I. 1974 No. 1791
5	General Improvement Areas	2 Dec. 74	,,
6	Standard amenities	2 Dec. 74	,,
7	Lodging houses etc.—accounting	2 Dec. 74	,,
8	Leasehold enfranchisement	See s. 118	—
9	Well-maintained houses etc.	See s. 108	—
10	Rehabilitation orders	2 Dec. 74	S.I. 1974 No. 1791
11	Option mortgages (in part)	2 Dec. 74	,,
12	Service charges	31 Aug. 74	The Act
13 to 15	See S.I. 1974, Nos. 1406, 1562, and 1791 in Appendix III		

APPENDIX I

HOUSING ACT 1974

(1974 c. 44)

ARRANGEMENT OF SECTIONS

PART I

THE HOUSING CORPORATION: EXTENDED FUNCTIONS

PART II

REGISTRATION OF HOUSING ASSOCIATIONS

PART III

FINANCIAL ASSISTANCE FOR HOUSING ASSOCIATIONS

An Act to extend the functions of the Housing Corporation and provide for the registration of, and the giving of financial assistance to, certain housing associations; to make further provision in relation to clearance areas and other areas in which living conditions are unsatisfactory or otherwise in need of improvement; to provide for the making of grants towards the improvement, repair and provision of housing accommodation and for the compulsory improvement of such accommodation; to amend the law relating to assistance for house purchase and improvement and expenditure in connection with the provision and improvement of housing accommodation and of hostels; to raise the rateable value limits under the Leasehold Reform Act 1967; to amend the Housing Finance Act 1972; to amend the law relating to the rights and obligations of landlords and tenants and the enforceability of certain covenants relating to the development of land; and for purposes connected therewith. [31st July 1974]

PART I

THE HOUSING CORPORATION: EXTENDED FUNCTIONS

1. Continuation of Housing Corporation with extended functions

(1) There shall continue to be an authority called the Housing Corporation and the provisions of Schedule 1 to the 1964 Act (constitution, proceedings and other matters relating to the Corporation) as amended by Schedule 1 to this Act shall continue to apply in relation to the Corporation.

(2) Without prejudice to any specific function conferred on the Corporation by or under the following provisions of this Act or any other enactment, the Corporation shall have the following general functions, namely,—

(*a*) to promote and assist the development of registered housing associations and of unregistered self-build societies;

(*b*) to facilitate the proper exercise and performance of the functions, and to publicise the aims and principles, of registered housing associations and unregistered self-build societies;

(*c*) to establish and maintain a register of housing associations, to exercise supervision and control over registered housing associations and, to such extent as the Secretary of State may require, to act as his agent with respect to the consideration of applications for and the payment of grants to registered housing associations; and

(*d*) to undertake, to such extent as the Corporation consider necessary, the provision (by construction, acquisition, conversion, improvement or otherwise) of dwellings for letting or for sale and of hostels and the management of dwellings or hostels provided by the Corporation.

(3) The Corporation shall exercise their general functions subject to and in accordance with the provisions of this Part of this Act and Parts II and III thereof. **[254]**

GENERAL

From its modest role when created in 1964 the Housing Corporation is now to become an important national body with heavy responsibilities as the Government agency responsible not only for giving advice to, and making loans to, housing societies providing housing without subsidy, but also for encouraging, supervising and, to some extent, controlling, the activities of the large number of existing housing associations and trusts who have provided, and are providing subsidised, or grant-aided housing. See Chapter 1 for a general description of the functions of the Corporation under the Housing Act 1964. Schedule 1 of this Act enlarges the number of members of the Corporation from a maximum of nine to a maximum of fifteen, and also deals with disclosure of members' interests and allied matters. Schedules 13 and 15 amend or repeal a number of relevant sections in the Housing Act 1964.

One of the main duties of the Corporation will be to establish a register of housing associations—see Part II. In future, no association will be eligible to receive grant aid, as distinct from loans, unless it is registered. Self-build societies do not seek grant aid and their activities are confined to providing homes for the members themselves. There is, therefore, not the same need for control. It will be noted that the Corporation's first general function is to promote and assist the development of both registered housing associations and unregistered self-build societies.

The Corporation also has power under section 1 (2) (*d*) to make direct provision by construction, acquisition, etc. of dwellings for letting or sale, and of hostels.

See Circular 133/74 in Appendix II, and s. 17 below.

DEFINITIONS
"Dwelling"—see s. 129 (1) and (2)
"Hostel"—see s. 129 (1) and (2)
"Housing association"—see s. 129 (1) and (2)
"Registered association" means registered in the register of housing associations under s. 13 of the Act. See also s. 129 (1) and (2)
"self-build society"—see s. 12

2. Control by Corporation of dispositions of land by housing associations

(1) Subject to the following provisions of this section,—

(*a*) a registered housing association may not sell, lease, mortgage, charge or otherwise dispose of any land, and

(*b*) an unregistered housing association may not sell, lease, mortgage, charge or otherwise dispose of any grant-aided land, as defined in Schedule 2 to this Act,

except with the consent of the Corporation.

(2) Subsection (1) above shall not apply to a disposition by a housing association which is a registered charity if—

(*a*) the disposition is one which, by virtue of subsection (1) or subsection (2) of section 29 of the Charities Act 1960 (certain disposals not to take place without an order of the court or of the Charity Commissioners), cannot be made without such an order as is mentioned in that section; or

(*b*) the disposition is of land which is not grant-aided land, as defined in Schedule 2 to this Act, and is one for which the sanction of an order under the said section 29 is not required by virtue of subsection (3) thereof (certain dispositions excluded from the requirements of that section).

(3) The Charity Commissioners shall consult the Corporation before making any order under section 29 of the Charities Act 1960 permitting a disposition which, apart from subsection (2) above, would be a disposition requiring the consent of the Corporation.

(4) Subsection (1) above shall not apply to the grant of a lease for a term ending within the period of 7 years and 3 months beginning on the date of the grant unless—

(*a*) there is conferred on the lessee (whether by the lease or otherwise) an option for renewal for a term which, together with the original term, would expire outside that period; or

(*b*) the lease is granted wholly or partly in consideration of a fine.

(5) Without prejudice to the generality of the expression "dispose" in subsection (1) above, in subsection (4) above the expression "lease" includes an

agreement for a lease and a licence to occupy and the expressions "grant" and "term" shall be construed accordingly.

(6) Any reference in this section to the consent of the Corporation is a reference to an order under the seal of the Corporation giving their consent. **[255]**

GENERAL

A higher degree of control is applicable to a registered housing association than to an unregistered one, in that a registered association needs the consent of the Corporation to the disposal of any land, whereas an unregistered association needs consent only for the disposal of grant-aided land. This is one of the sections which is designed to give closer control over the many associations, not all wholly altruistic or well-managed, which have sprung up in the last 5 or 6 years.

If a registered charity is a registered housing association the consent of the corporation to a disposition (whether of grant-aided or non-grant aided land) will be necessary under s. 2 (1), but not if the disposition is one which requires an order under s. 29 of the Charities Act 1960—see s. 2 (2) (*a*). Nor will a disposition by such a registered charity of land which does not require an order under s. 29 be subject to the control of the corporation under s. 1, if the land is not grant-aided—see s. 2 (2) (*b*).

If a registered charity is an unregistered association its dispositions will be subject to the Corporation's control only if the land is grant-aided—s. 2 (1) (*b*). Even then the disposal will not be subject to control by the Corporation if it is one which requires an order under s. 29 of the Charities Act 1960—s. 2 (2) (*a*).

The Charity Commissioners are required to consult the Corporation before making an order of the kind referred to in s. 2 (2) (*a*). See Sch. 2 for the definition of "grant-aided".

Dwellings originally provided without grant, subsidy or loans from Government or local authority funds may become "grant-aided' because they have been converted or modernised with the aid of grants or loans.

See Circular 133/74 in Appendix II.

DEFINITIONS

"Land" includes any estate or interest in or right over land—s. 12
"Registered charity",—see s. 129 (1)
"Registered housing association"—see s. 129 (1) and (2)

3. Acquisition of land

(1) The Corporation may acquire land, whether by way of purchase, lease, exchange or gift—

(*a*) for the purpose of selling or leasing it to a registered housing association or an unregistered self-build society; or

(*b*) for the purpose of their general functions under section 1 (2) (*d*) above.

(2) For the purpose of the purchase of land in Scotland by agreement by the Corporation, the Lands Clauses Acts (except so much thereof as relates to the acquisition of land otherwise than by agreement, and the provisions relating to access to the special Act, and except sections 120 to 125 of the Lands Clauses Consolidation (Scotland) Act 1845), and section 6 and sections 70 to 78 of the Railways Clauses Consolidation (Scotland) Act 1845 (as originally enacted and not as amended by section 15 of the Mines (Working Facilities and Support) Act 1923) are hereby incorporated with this section, and, in construing those Acts for the purposes of this section, this section shall be deemed to be the special Act and the Corporation shall be deemed to be the promoters of the undertaking or company, as the case may require.

(3) The Corporation may be authorised by the Secretary of State to purchase land compulsorily for any purpose for which they could acquire it by agreement under subsection (1) above.

(4) The Acquisition of Land (Authorisation Procedure) Act 1946, or, as the case may be, the Acquisition of Land (Authorisation Procedure) (Scotland) Act

1947 shall apply in relation to a compulsory purchase of land by the Corporation under subsection (3) above as if the Corporation were a local authority and as if that subsection were contained in an Act in force immediately before the commencement of that Act.

(5) In Scotland the Corporation (without prejudice to their own power to acquire land compulsorily) may request the Scottish Special Housing Association to acquire land compulsorily on their behalf for any purpose for which the Corporation may purchase land compulsorily as provided in section 175 (2) of the Housing (Scotland) Act 1966.

(6) The powers of acquisition conferred by this section may be exercised as respects any land notwithstanding that it is not immediately required for selling or leasing as mentioned in subsection (1) (*a*) above or for the purpose of any of the Corporation's general functions under section 1 (2) (*d*) above. **[256]**

GENERAL

The Corporation had a power under s. 3 of the Housing Act 1964 to acquire land for sale or lease to a housing society. This is repealed by Sch. 15 and replaced by the wider power in s. 3, which enables them also to acquire and use land for direct development, and sale or lease, by the Corporation themselves. The Corporation could develop land themselves under s. 5 of the Housing Act 1964, but only if there were no society to whom the land could suitably be sold or leased for development. Each such transaction required the consent of the Minister. They could acquire land only for sale or lease to a housing society. See also s. 4 of the Housing Act 1964 as to powers of compulsory purchase, now repealed and replaced by s. 3 above.

DEFINITIONS

"Land"—see s. 12
"Local authority"—see s. 129 (1) and (2)
"Registered housing association"—see s. 129 (1) and (2)
"Self-build society"—see s. 12, and also Chapter 1 above at page 6.

4. Provision of dwellings or hostels and clearance, management and development of land

(1) The Corporation may undertake the provision or improvement of dwellings or hostels on any land belonging to them.

(2) The Corporation may clear any land belonging to them and carry out any other work on the land to prepare it as a building site or estate, including the laying out and construction of streets or roads and open spaces and the provision of sewerage facilities and supplies of electricity, gas and water.

(3) The Corporation shall have power to repair, maintain and insure any buildings or works for the time being on any land belonging to them and generally to deal in the proper course of management with any such land and any such buildings or works and to charge for the tenancy or occupation thereof.

(4) Without prejudice to subsection (3) above, the Corporation may carry out such operations on, and do any other such things in relation to, land belonging to them as appear to them to be conducive to facilitating the provision or improvement of dwellings or hostels on the land, whether by the Corporation themselves, by a registered housing association or by an unregistered self-build society.

(5) In the exercise of their powers under subsection (4) above, the Corporation may carry out any development ancillary to or in connection with the provision of dwellings or hostels, including development which makes pro-

vision for any building or land intended for use for commercial, recreational or other non-domestic purposes. **[257]**

GENERAL

This makes more explicit the power of the Corporation to provide and improve dwellings or hostels on land belonging to them; to clear land and construct streets, roads, open spaces, sewerage facilities; and to provide services. In sub-s. (5) there is a power to carry-out ancillary developments, such as the provision of shops or recreational facilities. This may be compared with the powers of a local authority under s. 93 of the Housing Act 1957 to make similar provisions, but only with the specific consent of the Minister. However, the Corporation's power to dispose of land on which they have exercised these powers is firmly limited by s. 5 which governs all dispositions by the Corporation.

DEFINITIONS

"Dwelling"—see s. 129 (1) and (2)
"Hostel"—see s. 129 (1) and (2)
"Land"—see s. 12
"Registered housing association"—see s. 129 (1) and (2)
"Self-build society"—see s. 12

5. Disposal of land

(1) The Corporation may not dispose of any land except in accordance with the provisions of this section.

(2) The Corporation may dispose of any land in respect of which they have not exercised their powers under subsection (1) of section 4 above and on which they have not carried out any such development as is mentioned in subsection (5) of that section to—

(*a*) a registered housing association; or
(*b*) an unregistered self-build society; or
(*c*) a subsidiary of the Corporation; or
(*d*) any other body in which the Corporation hold an interest.

(3) The Corporation may dispose of any land on which dwellings or hostels have been provided or improved in exercise of their powers under section 4 above to—

(*a*) a registered housing association, or
(*b*) the council of a county, district or London borough, the Greater London Council or the Common Council of the City of London, or
(*c*) a housing authority as defined in section 78 (1) of the Housing (Financial Provisions) (Scotland) Act 1972, or
(*d*) the Commission for the New Towns or a development corporation within the meaning of the New Towns Act 1965, or
(*e*) a subsidiary of the Corporation,

and may sell or lease individual dwellings to persons for their own occupation.

(4) The Corporation may dispose of any building or land intended for use for commercial, recreational or other non-domestic purposes in respect of which development has been carried out by virtue of section 4 (5) above; but no such building or land may be disposed of for less than the best consideration it commands except with the consent in writing of the Secretary of State.

(5) The Corporation may dispose of any land which is not required for the purposes for which it was acquired but, subject to subsection (6) below, if the land—

(*a*) was acquired compulsorily by, or on behalf of, the Corporation or by a local authority who transferred the land to the Corporation, or (*b*) is not disposed of for the best consideration it commands,

the Corporation shall not dispose of the land except with the consent in writing of the Secretary of State.

(6) The consent of the Secretary of State shall not be required under subsection (5) above to the disposal of land for less than the best consideration it commands if the land is to be used as, or in connection with, a highway or a street not being a highway.

(7) For the purposes of subsection (5) above "local authority", in relation to England and Wales, means—

(*a*) the council of a district or, in the case of an acquisition before 1st April 1974, the council of a county borough or county district; and

(*b*) the council of a London borough or the Common Council of the City of London. **[258]**

GENERAL

This governs all disposals by the Corporation and the latter's freedom of action depends to a considerable extent upon the degree to which they have exercised their powers under s. 4.

For instance, where they have not exercised their power to provide or improve dwellings or hostels they may dispose only to bodies of the type named in sub-s. (2). Where they have provided or improved any dwellings or hostels the field is somewhat wider, but does not include an unregistered self-build society (sub-s. 3). This subsection also empowers them to sell or lease individual dwellings for owner-occupation.

Land which has been developed under s. 4 (5) for commercial, recreational, or non-domestic use is subject to s. 5 (4). There is a special definition of "local authority" applicable to sub-s. (5).

DEFINITION

"Dwelling"—see s. 129 (1) and (2)
"Land"—see s. 12
"Registered housing association"—see s. 129 (1) and (2)
"Self-build society"—see s. 12
"subsidiary" has the same meaning as in the Companies Act 1948—see s. 12 and s. 129

6. Acquisition of securities and control of subsidiaries

(1) The Corporation may with the consent of the Secretary of State subscribe for or acquire any securities of a body corporate and promote or participate in the promotion of any such body.

(2) The Corporation shall exercise their control over any subsidiary of theirs so as to secure that the subsidiary does not—

(*a*) engage in any activity which the Corporation are not empowered to carry on;

(*b*) engage in any activity in a manner in which the Corporation themselves could not engage, by reason of any direction given to the Corporation under section 1 (2) of the 1964 Act;

(*c*) except with the consent of the Secretary of State, borrow money from any person other than the Corporation; or

(*d*) except with the consent of the Secretary of State, raise money by the issue of shares or stock to any person other than the Corporation.

(3) In this section "securities" means shares, stock, debentures, debenture stock and any securities of a like nature. **[259]**

GENERAL

The terms of this section are not so wide as might at first appear. The subsidiary must not engage in any activity which the Corporation themselves are not empowered to carry on, and the Corporation must not act *ultra vires*.

DEFINITIONS
"Subsidiary"—see s. 12

7. Borrowing powers

(1) Subject to subsection (9) below, the borrowing powers of the Corporation shall be those, and only those, conferred by subsections (2) to (4) below; and the powers conferred by those subsections are subject to subsection (5) below.

(2) The Corporation may borrow from the Secretary of State, and the Secretary of State may lend to the Corporation, by way of temporary loan or otherwise, such sums in sterling as the Corporation may require.

(3) Without prejudice to subsection (2) above, the Corporation may, with the consent of the Secretary of State or in accordance with a general authorisation given by him, borrow temporarily by overdraft or otherwise such sums in sterling as the Corporation may require.

(4) The Corporation may, with the consent of the Secretary of State, borrow on such terms as the Secretary of State may from time to time specify,—

(*a*) from such persons as he may so specify, sums in a currency other than sterling; and

(*b*) from the European Investment Bank or the Commission of the European Communities, sums in any currency.

(5) The aggregate amount outstanding by way of the principal of—

(*a*) advances made to the Corporation under section 9 of the 1964 Act before the day appointed for the coming into operation of this Part of this Act,

(*b*) advances made to housing associations, before the day appointed for the coming into force of section 34 of this Act, under section 7 of the Housing Act 1961, section 11 of the Housing (Scotland) Act 1962 and section 23 of the Housing (Financial Provisions) (Scotland) Act 1968 (being advances in respect of which the functions of the Secretary of State are by the said section 34 transferred to the Corporation),

(*c*) any money borrowed by the Corporation under this section, and

(*d*) any money borrowed by a subsidiary of the Corporation, otherwise than from the Corporation,

shall not exceed £400 million or such greater sum not exceeding £750 million as the Secretary of State may by order specify, and no such order shall be made unless a draft of it has been laid before and approved by the Commons House of Parliament.

(6) Any loan made by the Secretary of State in pursuance of this section shall be repaid to him at such times and by such methods, and interest on the loan shall be paid to him at such rates and at such times, as he may from time to time determine.

(7) References in the preceding provisions of this section to the Secretary of State are references to him acting with the approval of the Treasury.

(8) The Treasury may issue out of the National Loans Fund to the Secretary of State such sums as are necessary to enable him to make loans in pursuance of subsection (2) above and any sums received by the Secretary of State in pursuance of subsection (6) above shall be paid into that Fund.

(9) References in this section to borrowing do not include any borrowing from a subsidiary of the Corporation. **[260]**

GENERAL

All the Corporation's borrowing powers are subject to the consent of the Secretary of State. It is expected that the bulk of its borrowing will be from the Secretary of State, either temporarily or otherwise, but he may authorise the Corporation to borrow temporarily by way of overdraft or otherwise. They may borrow in currency other than sterling.

All the Corporation's borrowing is subject to the aggregation limit in sub.s (5). The previous limits under the Housing Act 1964, as amended by the Housing Finance Act 1972, were £150 m or £300 m.

DEFINITIONS

"Housing association"—see s. 129
"Subsidiary"—see s. 12

8. Treasury guarantees

(1) The Treasury may guarantee, in such manner and on such conditions as they think fit, the repayment of the principal of and the payment of interest on any sums which the Corporation borrow from a person other than the Secretary of State.

(2) Immediately after a guarantee is given under this section the Treasury shall lay a statement of the guarantee before each House of Parliament; and where any sum is issued for fulfilling the guarantee so given the Treasury shall, as soon as possible after the end of each financial year (beginning with that in which the sum is issued and ending with that in which all liability in respect of the principal of the sum and in respect of interest thereon is finally discharged), lay before each House of Parliament a statement relating to that sum.

(3) Any sums required by the Treasury for fulfilling a guarantee under this section shall be charged on and issued out of the Consolidated Fund.

(4) If any sums are issued in fulfilment of a guarantee given under this section, the Corporation shall make to the Treasury, at such times and in such manner as the Treasury may from time to time direct, payments of such amounts as the Treasury so direct in or towards repayment of the sums so issued and payments of interest, at such rate as the Treasury so direct, on what is outstanding for the time being in respect of sums so issued.

(5) Any sums received by the Treasury in pursuance of subsection (4) above shall be paid into the Consolidated Fund. **[261]**

GENERAL

This section is self-explanatory.

9. Lending powers

(1) The Corporation may, by way of temporary loan or otherwise, lend to—

(*a*) a registered housing association,
(*b*) an unregistered self-build society,
(*c*) a subsidiary of the Corporation, and
(*d*) any other body in which the Corporation hold an interest,

for the purpose of enabling any of those bodies to meet the whole or any part of any expenditure incurred or to be incurred by it in carrying out its objects.

(2) The Corporation may, by way of temporary loan or otherwise, lend to an individual for the purpose of assisting him to acquire from the Corporation or from any of the bodies specified in paragraphs (*a*) to (*d*) of subsection (1) above a legal estate or interest in a dwelling which he intends to occupy.

(3) Any directions given to the Corporation under section 1 (2) of the 1964 Act with respect to the terms of any loan made under subsection (1) or subsection (2) above shall require the consent of the Treasury and, subject to any such directions and to subsection (4) below, the terms on which any such loan is made shall be such as the Corporation may determine, either generally or in any particular case.

(4) The terms of any loan made under subsection (1) above may, and the terms of any loan made under subsection (2) above may not, include terms for preventing repayment of the loan or any part of it before a specified date without the consent of the Corporation.

(5) In any case where—

(*a*) the Corporation make a loan to an unregistered self-build society under subsection (1) (*b*) above, and

(*b*) under a mortgage or heritable security entered into by the society to secure the loan the Corporation have an interest as mortgagee or, as the case may be, as creditor in any land belonging to the society,

the Corporation may, with the written consent of the Secretary of State, give to the society directions with respect to the disposal of that land, and it shall be the duty of the society to comply with the directions so long as the Corporation continue to have such an interest in that land; and any directions given under this subsection with such consent may be varied or revoked by subsequent directions given thereunder with the like consent.

(6) Where the Corporation propose, under subsection (5) above, to give directions to an unregistered self-build society requiring it to transfer its interest in any land to the Corporation or any other person, the Secretary of State shall not consent to the giving of the directions unless he is satisfied that arrangements have been made which, if the directions are given, will secure that the members of the society receive fair treatment in connection with the transfer. **[262]**

GENERAL

This section replaces s. 2 of the Housing Act 1964. The Corporation have no powers to lend to an unregistered housing association. They can, however, lend to an individual to enable him to acquire a dwelling for his own occupation.

It should be noted that the terms of any loan to a body of the kind listed in s. 9 (1) may include terms for preventing early repayment. But the Corporation may not include such a term in any case where they lend to an individual under sub.s (2).

Under sub.s (5) and (6) the Corporation may, in spite of the fact that they are mortgagees, direct the unregistered self-build society to transfer its land to the Corporation. A somewhat similar power was contained in s. 2 of the Housing Act 1964, but the safeguards in sub-s. (6) should be adequate to prevent misuse.

DEFINITIONS

See s. 12 and s. 129.

10. Miscellaneous financial provisions

(1) With the consent of the Secretary of State, given with the approval of the Treasury, the Corporation may guarantee the repayment of the principal of and the payment of interest on any sums borrowed (otherwise than from the Corporation)—

(*a*) by registered housing associations,

(*b*) by unregistered self-build societies, and

(*c*) by other bodies in which the Corporation hold an interest, and in any case where the Corporation give a guarantee under this subsection they may impose such terms and conditions as they think fit.

(2) The aggregate amount outstanding in respect of—

(*a*) loans for which the Corporation have given a guarantee under sub-section (1) above, and

(*b*) any payments which have been made by the Corporation in meeting any obligation arising by virtue of such a guarantee and have not been repaid to the Corporation,

shall not exceed £100 million.

(3) The Corporation may turn their resources to account so far as they are not required for the exercise of the Corporation's functions.

(4) Any excess of the revenues of the Corporation for any accounting year over the total sums properly chargeable to revenue account for that year shall be applied by the Corporation in such manner as the Secretary of State may, after consultation with the Corporation and with the approval of the Treasury, direct; and such a direction may require the whole or part of the excess to be paid to the Secretary of State.

(5) The Secretary of State may, with the approval of the Treasury, give to the Corporation directions as to any matter relating to the establishment or management of reserves or the carrying of sums to the credit of any reserves or the application of any reserves for the purposes of the Corporation's functions.

(6) The Secretary of State may, with the approval of the Treasury and after consultation with the Corporation, direct the Corporation to pay to the Secretary of State the whole or part of any sums for the time being standing to the credit of any reserves of the Corporation or being of a capital nature and not required for the exercise of the Corporation's functions. **[263]**

GENERAL

The Corporation may give guarantees in respect of sums borrowed by any of the bodies listed in sub-s. 1, except for sums borrowed from the Corporation. The aggregate outstanding is limited to £100 million at any time.

The Corporation may "turn their resources to account" so far as they are not required for the exercise of the Councils functions, but this is presumably subject to the controls contained in sub-ss. 4 and 5. The Secretary of State has power to direct the Corporation to pay him any capital sums standing to their credit and not required for the exercise of their functions.

DEFINITIONS

"Registered housing association"— see s. 129 (1) and (2)
"Self-build society"—see s. 12

11. Exclusion of certain disposals of land from tax on chargeable gains

After section 342 of the Income and Corporation Taxes Act 1970 there shall be inserted the following section:—

"342A. Disposals by Housing Corporation and certain housing associations

(1) In any case where—

(*a*) the Housing Corporation dispose of any land to a registered housing association, or

(*b*) a registered housing association disposes of any land to another registered housing association, or

(*c*) in pursuance of a direction of the Housing Corporation given under Part II of the Housing Act 1974 requiring it to do so, a registered housing association disposes of any of its property, other than land, to another registered housing association, or

(*d*) a registered housing association or an unregistered self-build society disposes of any land to the Housing Corporation,

both parties to the disposal shall be treated for the purposes of corporation tax in respect of chargeable gains or, as the case may require, capital gains tax as if the land or property disposed of were acquired from the Housing Corporation, registered housing association or unregistered self-build society making the disposal for a consideration of such an amount as would secure that on the disposal neither a gain nor a loss accrued to the Corporation or, as the case may be, that association or society.

(2) In this section 'registered housing association' and 'unregistered self-build society' have the same meanings as in Part I of the Housing Act 1974". [**264**]

GENERAL

This provides that certain transfers of land shall, in effect, be exempt from corporation tax in respect of chargeable gains, and from capital gains tax.

12. Interpretation of Part I

In this Part of this Act—

"heritable security" means a heritable security within the meaning of section 9 (8) (*a*) of the Conveyancing and Feudal Reform (Scotland) Act 1970;

"highway", in relation to Scotland, includes a public right of way;

"land" includes any estate or interest in or right over land;

"self-build society" means a housing association whose object is to provide, for sale to, or occupation by, its members, dwellings built or improved principally with the use of its members' own labour and "unregistered self-build society" means a self-build society which is not a registered housing association;

"subsidiary" has the same meaning as in the Companies Act 1948; and

"the 1964 Act" means the Housing Act 1964. [**265**]

Part II

Registration of Housing Associations

13. The register of housing associations

(1) There shall be a register of housing associations which shall be established and maintained by the Corporation and in which the Corporation may register any housing association which—

(*a*) is a registered charity and not an exempt charity; or

(*b*) is a society registered under the Industrial and Provident Societies Act 1965 (in this Part of this Act referred to as "the 1965 Act") and fulfils the conditions in subsection (2) below.

(2) The conditions referred to in subsection (1) (*b*) above are that the housing association does not trade for profit and is established for the purpose of, or has among its objects or powers those of, providing, constructing, improving or managing—

(*a*) houses to be kept available for letting, or

(*b*) where the rules of the association restrict membership of the association to persons entitled or prospectively entitled (whether as tenants or otherwise) to occupy a house provided or managed by the association, houses for occupation by members of the association, or

(*c*) hostels,

and that, if the association has any additional purposes or objects, it has none which are not mentioned in subsection (3) below.

(3) The additional purposes or objects referred to in subsection (2) above are those—

(*a*) of providing land or buildings for purposes connected with the requirements of the persons occupying the houses or hostels provided or managed by the association;

(*b*) of providing amenities or services for the benefit of those persons, either exclusively or together with other persons;

(*c*) of encouraging and giving advice on the formation of other housing associations which would be eligible for registration by the Corporation; and

(*d*) of providing services for, and giving advice on the running of, registered housing associations.

(4) The Corporation shall, after consultation with the committee established under section 14 below, establish criteria which should be satisfied by a housing association seeking registration, and may from time to time, after such consultation, vary those criteria.

(5) In deciding whether to register a housing association, the Corporation shall have regard—

(*a*) to any advice given to them by the committee established under section 14 below, and

(*b*) to the question whether the association satisfies the criteria established in accordance with subsection (4) above.

(6) For all purposes other than rectification of the register, a body shall be conclusively presumed to be a housing association falling within subsection (1) above at any time when it is or was on the register of housing associations.

(7) The register of housing associations shall be open to inspection at the head office of the Corporation at all reasonable times. **[266]**

GENERAL

This lays down the general conditions as to eligibility for registration. One of the Corporation's most important functions, as set out in s. 1, is to promote and assist the development of

(*a*) registered housing associations, and

(*b*) unregistered self-build societies.

The latter do not need to register because there is no question of their being eligible for grants or subsidies from public funds, and their efforts are entirely directed to building houses for their own occupation.

Section 13 (1) divides category (*a*) above into two-parts. The position of the first group, *i.e.* registered charities is comparatively clear-cut, but the second type of registered housing association, *i.e.* that described in s. 13 (1) (*b*), is less so.

Such Associations must meet the requirements of sub-s. (2) and (3). Sub-s. (2) and (3) do not apply to a registered charity. See also s. 25.

The Corporation are required, after consultation as laid down in s. 14, to establish criteria which must be satisfied by housing associations seeking to register.

DEFINITIONS

"Charity"—see s. 28. See also s. 129 for "registered charity"

"Hostel—see s. 129 (1) and (2)

"House"—see s. 27
"Housing association"—see s. 129 (1) and (2)
"Land"—see s. 12

14. The Housing Associations Registration Advisory Committee

(1) There shall be a committee which shall be called the Housing Associations Registration Advisory Committee and shall have the function of advising the Corporation—

(*a*) generally on the exercise of the Corporation's powers with respect to the registration of housing associations; and

(*b*) when consulted in accordance with subsection (4) of section 13 above, on the establishment and variation of the criteria referred to in that subsection; and

(*c*) on the question whether any particular housing association whose application for registration is referred to the Committee by the Corporation should be registered.

(2) The Committee shall consist of a chairman appointed by the Secretary of State and such number of other members so appointed as the Secretary of State may from time to time determine; and every member shall hold and vacate office in accordance with the terms of his appointment.

(3) The Committee shall consist of persons whom the Secretary of State considers to be qualified to advise the Corporation on the matters referred to in subsection (1) above.

(4) The Secretary of State may, out of money provided by Parliament, pay to all or any of the members of the Committee such salaries or other remuneration as he may with the consent of the Minister for the Civil Service determine.

(5) The Corporation may pay,—

(*a*) to all or any of the members of the Committee, such travelling and other expenses, and

(*b*) to persons attending their meetings at the request of the Committee, such travelling and other allowances (including compensation for loss of remunerative time),

as the Secretary of State may with the consent of the Minister for the Civil Service determine. **[267]**

GENERAL

This section is self-explanatory. There was some criticism during the passage of the Bill about the fact that it contained no provision for an association to appeal against refusal by the Corporation to register it. There is still no specific provision but the strengthening of the Advisory Committee's functions with regard to criteria should go a long way to meet the criticism.

15. Removal of bodies from the register

(1) Where a body has been registered in the register of housing associations, that body shall not be removed from the register except by the Corporation in accordance with the provisions of this section.

(2) If it appears to the Corporation that any body which is registered—

(*a*) is no longer a housing association falling within paragraph (*a*) or paragraph (*b*) of section 13 (1) above, or

(*b*) has ceased to exist or does not operate,

the Corporation shall, on giving not less than 14 days' notice to that body, remove it from the register; and in a case where paragraph (*b*) above applies, any such notice shall be deemed to be given to a body if it is served at the address last known to the Corporation to be the principal place of business of that body.

(3) A body which is aggrieved by a decision of the Corporation to remove it from the register of housing associations may appeal against the decision to the High Court or, as the case may be, the Court of Session.

(4) If an appeal is brought under subsection (3) above and is not withdrawn the Corporation shall not remove the body concerned from the register of housing associations until the appeal has been finally determined.

(5) No sum shall be paid in respect of a grant under section 29, section 32 or section 33 of this Act to a body which has been removed under this section from the register of housing associations.

(6) Where, at the time of its removal under this section from the register of housing associations, a body owns any land, section 2 of this Act shall continue to apply to that land after the removal as if the body concerned continued to be a registered housing association. **[268]**

GENERAL

It will be noted that if there is no provision for voluntary de-registration. There are provisions for appeal against a decision by the Corporation to remove an association from the register. On de-registration the association ceases to be entitled to any grant under Part III of this Act. Where a body is removed from the register and it owns any land, disposal of that land will still be subject to the Corporation's consent under s. 2.

16. Notifications to and by other bodies

(1) As soon as may be after registering a housing association or removing a body from the register the Corporation shall give notice of the registration or removal—

(*a*) if the association or body is a registered charity and not an exempt charity, to the Charity Commissioners; and

(*b*) if the association or body is a society registered under the 1965 Act, to the appropriate registrar.

(2) Where notice is given to the Charity Commissioners or to the appropriate registrar as mentioned in subsection (1) above, the Commissioners or the registrar, as the case may be, shall record the registration or removal from the register by the Corporation.

(3) As soon as may be after an appeal is brought under section 15 (3) above, the Corporation shall give notice of the appeal,—

(*a*) if the body appealing is a registered charity and not an exempt charity, to the Charity Commissioners; and

(*b*) if the body appealing is a society registered under the 1965 Act, to the appropriate registrar. **[269]**

GENERAL

This provides for notifications of registration or de-registration by the Corporation to the Charity Commissioners in respect of an association as defined in s. 13 (1) (*a*), and to the appropriate registrar in respect of an association registered under 13 (1) (*b*).

DEFINITIONS

"Appropriate registrar"—see s. 28
"charity" and "registered charity"—see s. 28 and s. 129

17. Certain loans and grants limited to registered housing associations

(1) Subject to subsections (3) and (4) below, on and after 1st April 1975 or such later date as the Secretary of State may by order specify for the purposes of this subsection—

(*a*) no such loan as is specified in sub-paragraphs (*b*) and (*c*) of paragraph 3 of Schedule 2 to this Act shall be made to a housing association unless, at the time the loan is made, the association is a registered housing association; and

(*b*) the powers of a local authority, including a county council, under paragraphs (*a*) and (*c*) of subsection (3) of section 119 of the Housing Act 1957 or under paragraphs (*a*) and (*c*) of subsection (2) of section 152 of the Housing (Scotland) Act 1966 (to make grants and loans to, and to guarantee payments in respect of money borrowed by, housing associations) shall not be exercisable unless, at the time the grant or loan is made or, as the case may be, the guarantee is given, the housing association is a registered housing association.

(2) Subject to subsection (3) below, the power of the Secretary of State to make grants under section 93 of the Finance Act 1965 (grants to housing associations for affording relief from tax) shall not be exercisable on a claim made by a housing association under that section in respect of a period beginning on or after 6th April 1975 or such later date as the Secretary of State may by order specify for the purposes of this subsection unless, throughout that period, the housing association is a registered housing association.

(3) Subsections (1) and (2) above shall not apply in relation to a housing association if—

(*a*) it is for the time being specified in an order made by the Secretary of State under section 80 of the Housing Finance Act 1972 (power to apply to certain housing associations provisions of that Act relating to local authorities); or

(*b*) before the operative date, the association has made an application for registration to the Corporation and the application has not yet been disposed of by the Corporation.

(4) Nothing in subsection (1) (*b*) above shall prevent a local authority, including a county council, from making loans under section 119 (3) (*a*) of the Housing Act 1957 or section 152 (2) (*a*) of the Housing (Scotland) Act 1966 to an unregistered housing association for the assistance of the association—

(*a*) in connection with any works required to be carried out in pursuance of, or the acquisition of any estate or interest in a dwelling or other building for the purposes of, any arrangements under section 121 of the said Act of 1957 or under section 155 of the said Act of 1966 which, before the operative date, have been approved by the Secretary of State; or

(*b*) in connection with the provision of dwellings which are relevant dwellings, within the meaning of section 73 of the Housing Finance Act 1972 (dwellings taken into account for the purposes of special residual subsidy); or

(*c*) in connection with the provision of works which are relevant works, approved for subsidy, within the meaning of section 53 of the Housing (Financial Provisions) (Scotland) Act 1972 (works taken into account for the purposes of special residual subsidy); or (*d*) in connection with a building scheme, within the meaning of section 75 of the Housing Finance Act 1972, which, before the operative date, has been approved by the Secretary of State for the purposes of that section; or

(*e*) in connection with a building scheme or improvement scheme, within the meaning of sections 55 and 57 of the Housing (Financial Provisions) (Scotland) Act 1972, which before the operative date has been approved by the Secretary of State for the purposes of those sections. **[270]**

GENERAL

This contains the strongest compulsion to register, in that, as from 1st April 1975, loans and grants under the various existing enactments listed in Sch. 2 will be restricted to registered housing associations. As the financial assistance to be provided for housing associations under Part III of this Act is also limited to registered housing associations, there will be little hope of any association being able to progress at all unless it is registered.

Similarly the power of the Secretary of State to make grants under s. 93 of the Finance Act 1965 (grants for affording tax relief) will be limited in respect of any period after 6 April 1975, to registered associations.

Sub-s. (3) refers to the North Eastern Housing Association and any similar body which may be specified under s. 80 of the Housing Finance Act 1972.

Loans for schemes in the transitional stages are dealt with in sub-s. (4), apart from this no further grants may be made to unregistered associations.

DEFINITIONS

"Dwelling"—see s. 129 (1) and (2)
"Housing association" and "registered"—see s. 129 (1) and (2)

18. Special rules applicable to tenancies of registered and certain other housing associations

(1) On and after the operative date, the reference in subsection (5) of section 5 of the Rent Act 1968 or in subsection (4) of section 5 of the Rent (Scotland) Act 1971 to a housing association shall be construed as not extending to an unregistered housing association unless—

(*a*) the association is for the time being specified in an order made by the Secretary of State under section 80 of the Housing Finance Act 1972; or

(*b*) the association is a society registered under the 1965 Act and its rules restrict membership to persons who are tenants or prospective tenants of the association and preclude the granting or assignment of tenancies to persons other than members; or

(*c*) the association has made an application for registration to the Corporation before the operative date and the application has not been disposed of by the Corporation.

(2) If at any time, by virtue of subsection (1) above, a tenancy ceases to be one to which Part VIII of the Housing Finance Act 1972 applies, or sections 60 to 66 of the Housing (Financial Provisions) (Scotland) Act 1972 apply, and becomes a protected tenancy for the purposes of the Rent Act 1968, or of the Rent (Scotland) Act 1971, that tenancy shall be a regulated tenancy and the housing association which is the landlord under that tenancy shall give notice in writing to the tenant, in such form as may be prescribed, informing him that his tenancy is no longer excluded from protection under the Rent Act 1968 or the Rent (Scotland) Act 1971.

(3) If, without reasonable excuse, a housing association fails to give notice to a tenant under subsection (2) above within the period of 21 days beginning

on the day on which his tenancy becomes a protected tenancy, the association shall be liable on summary conviction to a fine not exceeding £100.

(4) Where an offence under subsection (3) above committed by a body corporate is proved to have been committed with the consent or connivance of, or to be attributable to any neglect on the part of, any director, manager or secretary or other similar officer of the body corporate or any person who was purporting to act in any such capacity, he as well as the body corporate shall be guilty of that offence and shall be liable to be proceeded against and punished accordingly.

(5) In this section "prescribed" means prescribed by order made by the Secretary of State.

(6) The provisions of Schedule 3 to this Act shall have effect for supplementing this section, and Part I of that Schedule shall come into force on the passing of this Act. [**271**]

GENERAL

The special position of housing association tenancies which are excluded from protection under the Rent Acts is preserved only for tenancies of registered associations; tenancies of the exceptional North Eastern Housing Association; 1965 Act associations by whose rules tenancies are restricted to members only; and cases where registration has been applied for but not completed. However, it should be noted that this section refers only to tenancies which are not "protected" because they are excluded under sub-ss. (5) and (6) of s. 5 of the Rent Act 1968. Sub-ss. (1) to (3) of s. 5 remain, and therefore any tenancies of a housing trust which are not "protected" under the Rent Act 1968 will remain unprotected.

Any tenancy which ceases to be in this special position will become a normal protected regulated tenancy. The Association which is the landlord must give the tenant notice in the prescribed form. Penalties for failure to do so are dealt with in sub-ss (3) and (4).

This section is supplemented by Sch. 3 of the Act, Part 1 of which deals with interim protection, Part II with the longer term, and Part III with the Rent (Scotland) Act 1971.

See Sch. 3 below and the Notes thereon, and Circular 133/74 in Appendix II.

DEFINITIONS

"Registered housing association"—see s. 129
"The 1965 Act"—see s. 28

HOUSING ASSOCIATION TENANCIES

As to the effect on the "fair rent" under the Rent Act 1968 of differing degrees of security of tenure as between tenants protected under that Act and housing association tenancies not protected, see *Palmer* v. *Peabody Trust* [1974] 3 All E.R. 355; [1974] 3 W.L.R. 575.

19. Inquiries into affairs of registered 1965 Act associations

(1) The Corporation may appoint a person (who may or may not be a member of the Corporation's staff) to conduct an inquiry into the affairs of any registered 1965 Act association.

(2) For the purposes of an inquiry under subsection (1) above, the person appointed to conduct the inquiry may, by notice in writing served on the association concerned or on any person who is or has been an officer or member of the association, require the association or that person to produce to the person appointed to conduct the inquiry such books, accounts and other documents relating to the association's business, and to furnish to him such other information relating to that business, as he considers necessary for the purposes of the inquiry.

(3) Any association or other person who without reasonable excuse fails to comply with the requirements of a notice under subsection (2) above shall be liable on summary conviction to a fine not exceeding £400.

(4) For the purposes of an inquiry under subsection (1) above the Corporation may require the accounts and balance sheet of the association concerned, or such of them as the Corporation may specify, to be audited by an auditor appointed by the Corporation being a person who,—

(*a*) under section 7 (1) of the Friendly and Industrial and Provident Societies Act 1968, is a qualified auditor for the purposes of that Act, or

(*b*) under section 7 (2) of that Act, is a qualified auditor in relation to the particular association whose accounts are required to be audited under this subsection.

(5) Any person appointed to conduct an inquiry under subsection (1) above and any person appointed to make an audit under subsection (4) above shall, on completion of the inquiry or, as the case may be, the audit, make a report to the Corporation on such matters and in such form as the Corporation may specify.

(6) The expenses of an audit under subsection (4) above, including the remuneration of the auditor, shall be paid by the Corporation.

(7) An audit under subsection (4) above shall be additional to, and shall not affect, any audit made or to be made under any other enactment. **[272]**

GENERAL

The Corporation have considerable powers under this section to conduct an inquiry into the affairs of any registered 1965 Act association *i.e.* an association as defined in s. 13 (1) (*b*), and there are penalties for obstructing the Corporation's requirements. In connection with an inquiry under this section the Corporation may require an audit of the accounts and balance sheet of the association. If so, they will meet the expenses.

20. Corporation's power to act for protection of registered 1965 Act associations

(1) Where the Corporation are satisfied, as the result of an inquiry or an audit under section 19 above, that there has been in the administration of a registered 1965 Act association any misconduct or mismanagement, the Corporation may do all or any of the following, namely,—

(*a*) by order remove any member of the committee of the association, or any officer, agent or servant of the association, who has been responsible for or privy to the misconduct or mismanagement or has by his conduct contributed to it or facilitated it;

(*b*) order any bank or other person who holds money or securities on behalf of the association not to part with the money or securities without the approval of the Corporation;

(*c*) by order restrict the transactions which may be entered into, or the nature or amount of the payments which may be made, in the administration of the association without the approval of the Corporation.

(2) The Corporation may also by order remove a member of the committee of a registered 1965 Act association where that member—

(*a*) is a bankrupt or, in Scotland, is insolvent within the meaning of paragraph 9 (2) of Schedule 3 to the Conveyancing and Feudal Reform (Scotland) Act 1970 or is incapable of acting by reason of mental disorder within the meaning of the Mental Health Act 1959 or the Mental Health (Scotland) Act 1960;

(*b*) has not acted; or

(*c*) cannot be found or does not act and his absence or failure to act impedes the committee's proper management of the association's affairs.

(3) The Corporation may by order appoint a person to be a member of the committee of a registered 1965 Act association (whether or not he is a member of the association and, if he is not, notwithstanding that the rules of the association restrict membership of the committee to members of the association)—

(*a*) in place of a member of the committee removed by them under this section or otherwise;

(*b*) where there are no members of the committee; or

(*c*) where the Corporation are of opinion that it is necessary for the proper management of the association's affairs to have an additional member of its committee.

(4) A person appointed to be a member of the committee of a registered 1965 Act association under subsection (3) above shall hold office for such period and on such terms as the Corporation may specify and, on the expiry of any such period, the Corporation may renew the appointment for such period as they may specify; but nothing in this subsection shall prevent any such person from retiring from the appointment in accordance with the rules of the association.

(5) Any member of the committee of a registered 1965 Act association or any officer, agent or servant of the association who is ordered by the Corporation to be removed under subsection (1) (*a*) or subsection (2) above may appeal against the order to the High Court or, as the case may be, the Court of Session.

(6) Before making an order under subsection (1) (*a*) or subsection (2) above the Corporation shall give not less than 14 days' notice of their intention to do so—

(*a*) to the person whom they intend to remove, and

(*b*) to the registered 1965 Act association concerned,

and any such notice may be given by post and, if so given to the person whom the Corporation intend to remove, may be addressed to the recipient's last known address in the United Kingdom.

(7) If any person contravenes an order under subsection (1) (*b*) above, he shall be liable on summary conviction to a fine not exceeding £400, or to imprisonment for a term not exceeding 3 months, or to both; but no proceedings for an offence punishable under this subsection shall be instituted in England and Wales except by or with the consent of the Corporation. [**273**]

GENERAL

The Corporation have sweeping powers under this section but they arise only after the Corporation have held an inquiry or audit under s. 19, and are satisfied that there has been misconduct or mismanagement. They may remove any member of the association's committee and appoint other members, either in replacement, or to strengthen the committee. The Corporation may also remove any officer, agent or servant. They may impose controls on money and securities belonging to the association and control the transactions which may be entered into.

A right of appeal is given in sub-s. 5.

Further powers are given in s. 21.

DEFINITIONS

"Committee"—see s. 28

"Registered 1965 Act association"—see s. 28

21. Corporation's power to require transfer of land of registered 1965 Act associations

(1) Where the Corporation are satisfied, as the result of an inquiry or an audit under section 19 above, that—

(*a*) there has been in the administration of a registered 1965 Act association any misconduct or mismanagement, or

(*b*) the management of the land belonging to any such association would be improved if the land were to be transferred in accordance with the provisions of this section,

the Corporation may, with the consent of the Secretary of State, direct the association to transfer the land belonging to it to another body in accordance with subsection (2) below.

(2) A direction under subsection (1) above may require the association concerned to transfer the land belonging to it,—

(*a*) in a case where that association is a charity, to another registered housing association which is a charity and the objects of which appear to the Corporation to be, as nearly as practicable, akin to those of the association directed to make the transfer; and

(*b*) in any other case, to the Corporation or to another registered housing association.

(3) A transfer in pursuance of a direction under subsection (1) above shall be made on the terms that the Corporation or, as the case may be, the association to which the land is transferred will pay or undertake to pay to the association making the transfer such sum, if any, as will be necessary to defray all its proper debts and liabilities (including any debts and liabilities secured on the land to be transferred) after taking into account any money or other assets belonging to the association.

(4) If it appears to the Corporation to be likely that, as a result of a transfer in pursuance of a direction under subsection (1) above, the association making the transfer will be dissolved as mentioned in paragraph (*a*) or paragraph (*b*) of section 55 of the 1965 Act, the Corporation shall secure that the costs of such a dissolution are taken into account in determining the sum payable to the association under subsection (3) above. **[274]**

GENERAL

In addition to their powers under s. 20, the Corporation may deal with misconduct or mismanagement by requiring the transfer of land belonging to any registered 1965 Act association which is not a charity. Again this power can only arise as the result of an inquiry under s. 19. The consent of the Secretary of State to the proposed transfer is required. These powers may be compared with those originally given to the Corporation under s. 5 of the Housing Act 1964.

DEFINITIONS

"Charity"—see s. 28
"Registered 1965 Act association"—see s. 28

22. Corporation's power to petition for winding up of certain registered housing associations

(1) Without prejudice to the power of any person under any other enactment to petition for the winding up of a registered housing association which is a company incorporated under the Companies Act 1948, the Corporation may present a petition for the winding up under that Act of any such registered housing

association on the ground that the association is failing properly to carry out its purposes or objects.

(2) Subject to section 55 (*a*) of the 1965 Act, subsection (1) above shall also apply in relation to a registered housing association which is not such a company as is mentioned in that subsection but which is a registered 1965 Act association. **[275]**

GENERAL

This is a further power, not linked with the holding of an audit or inquiry under s. 19.

23. Transfer of net assets on dissolution of registered 1965 Act associations

(1) If a registered 1965 Act association is dissolved as mentioned in paragraph (*a*) or paragraph (*b*) of section 55 of the 1965 Act then, notwithstanding anything in that Act or in the rules of the association, there shall be transferred to the Corporation, or, if the Corporation so directs, to such registered housing association as may be specified in the direction, so much of the property of the association as remains after meeting the claims of its creditors and any other liabilities arising on or before the dissolution.

(2) If it appears to the Corporation to be appropriate to do so in order to avoid the necessity for the sale of any land belonging to a registered 1965 Act association which is being dissolved as mentioned in subsection (1) above and thereby secure the transfer of the land under that subsection, the Corporation may make payments to discharge any such claims or liabilities as are referred to in that subsection.

(3) The Corporation may not dispose of any property transferred to them by virtue of subsection (1) above otherwise than to a registered housing association or a subsidiary of the Corporation, and in any case where the property so transferred to the Corporation includes land subject to an existing mortgage or charge, whether in favour of the Corporation or otherwise, the Corporation may, in exercise of their powers under Part I of this Act, dispose of the land subject to that mortgage or charge or subject to a new mortgage or charge in favour of the Corporation, and the amount secured by any such new mortgage or charge shall be such as appears to the Corporation to be appropriate in the circumstances.

(4) Notwithstanding anything in subsection (3) above, where property is transferred to the Corporation by virtue of subsection (1) above on the dissolution of a registered 1965 Act association which is a charity, the Corporation may not dispose of that property except to another registered housing association which is a charity and the objects of which appear to the Corporation to be, as nearly as practicable, akin to those of the association which was dissolved. **[276]**

GENERAL

The net assets are to be transferred to the Corporation, or, if they so direct, to a specified housing association.

To avoid difficulties which might arise if land had to be sold to meet the liabilities of an association about to be dissolved, the Corporation may make payments to discharge liabilities or claims upon the association. The powers of the Corporation to dispose of land transferred to them under this section are limited by sub ss. (3) and (4).

DEFINITIONS

"Charity"—see s. 28
"Registered 1965 Act association"—see s. 28
"Subsidiary"—see s. 12

24. Restrictions on exercise of certain powers by registered 1965 Act associations

(1) The provisions of this section apply in relation to a registered 1965 Act association, the registration of which by the Corporation has been recorded by the appropriate registrar under section 16 (2) above, and references in the following provisions of this section to a registered 1965 Act association shall be construed accordingly.

(2) The appropriate registrar shall not register a special resolution, as defined in section 50 (2) of the 1965 Act, which is passed by a registered 1965 Act association for the purposes of section 50 or section 51 of that Act (amalgamation of societies and transfer of engagements between societies) unless, together with the copy of the special resolution sent to him as mentioned in section 50 (4) of that Act, there is sent a copy of the Corporation's consent to the amalgamation or transfer concerned.

(3) Section 52 of the 1965 Act (power of registered society to convert itself into, to amalgamate with, or to transfer its engagements to, a company registered under the Companies Acts) shall not apply to a registered 1965 Act association.

(4) If, in pursuance of section 55 (*a*) of the 1965 Act, a registered 1965 Act association resolves by special resolution, as defined in section 141 of the Companies Act 1948, that it be wound up voluntarily, the resolution shall not have effect for the purposes of that Act as a resolution for voluntary winding up unless—

(*a*) before the passing of the resolution the Corporation have given their consent to the passing of the resolution, and

(*b*) together with the copy of the resolution required to be forwarded to the appropriate registrar under section 143 of the Companies Act 1948 (as that section has effect by virtue of the said section 55 (*a*)) there is forwarded a copy of the Corporation's consent.

(5) If, in pursuance of section 55 (*b*) of the 1965 Act, a registered 1965 Act association is to be dissolved by an instrument of dissolution, the appropriate registrar shall neither register that instrument, as required by subsection (5) of section 58 of that Act, nor cause notice of the dissolution to be advertised as mentioned in subsection (6) of that section unless, together with the instrument of dissolution required to be sent to him under subsection (4) of that section, there is sent a copy of the Corporation's consent to the making of that instrument.

(6) Any reference in the preceding provisions of this section to the Corporation's consent is a reference to an order under the seal of the Corporation giving their consent. **[277]**

GENERAL

Once a registered 1965 Act association has registered under s. 13 and the fact has been recorded by the "appropriate registrar" there are restrictions on its power to amalgamate with other societies, or to transfer engagements. The appropriate registrar cannot proceed unless the Corporation have given consent to the proposal. Similarly any such association which wishes to pass a resolution that it be wound up voluntarily must obtain the Corporation's consent before doing so.

DEFINITIONS

"Appropriate registrar"—see s. 28
"Registered 1965 Act association"—see s. 28

25. Change of objects of certain charities to require consent

(1) If, in the case of a registered charity which is a registered housing association,—

(*a*) the charity is neither a company incorporated under the Companies Act 1948 nor an exempt charity, and

(*b*) its registration by the Corporation has been recorded by the Charity Commissioners under section 16 (2) above,

no power contained in the trusts of the charity and permitting any variation of or addition to the objects of the charity may be exercised without the consent of the Charity Commissioners.

(2) Before giving any consent under subsection (1) above, the Charity Commissioners shall consult the Corporation.

(3) In subsection (1) above "trusts" has the same meaning as in the Charities Act 1960. [**278**]

GENERAL

This provides that the consent of the Charity Commissioners to any variation in the objects of a charity can be given only after consultation with the Corporation. See also Notes on s. 13.

DEFINITIONS

"Registered charity"—see s.129

26. Payments by registered housing associations to members, etc.

(1) Subject to subsection (2) below, a registered housing association shall not make a gift or pay any sum by way of dividend or bonus—

(*a*) to any person who is or has been a member of the association; or

(*b*) to any person who is a member of the family of any such person as is referred to in paragraph (*a*) above; or

(*c*) to any company of which a person falling within paragraph (*a*) or paragraph (*b*) above is a director or any Scottish firm of which such a person is a member.

(2) Subsection (1) above does not apply to—

(*a*) any sum paid, in accordance with the rules of the association concerned, as interest on capital lent to the association or subscribed by way of shares in the association; or

(*b*) any sum which—

(i) is paid by an association whose rules restrict membership to persons who are tenants or prospective tenants of the association and preclude the granting or assignment of tenancies to persons other than members; and

(ii) is paid to a person who has ceased to be a member of the association; and

(iii) is due to that person under the terms of the agreement under which he became a member of the association.

(3) The Corporation may from time to time specify the maximum amounts which may be paid by a registered housing association, other than a registered charity which is not an exempt charity, by way of fees or other remuneration or by way of expenses to a person who is a member of the association, and different amounts may be so specified for different purposes.

(4) Where a sum which exceeds any maximum amount for the time being specified under subsection (3) above is paid to a person who is a member of the association by a registered housing association to which that subsection applies, the amount by which that sum exceeds that maximum amount shall be recoverable by the association.

(5) The Corporation may from time to time specify the conditions subject to which a member of the committee of a registered 1965 Act association may enter into a contract with the association for the provision by that member, directly or indirectly, of goods or services to the association in return for payment; and any such conditions may be so specified as to apply to particular associations, contracts or sums payable thereunder, or as to apply generally.

(6) Any sum paid to a person under a contract in contravention of any condition specified under subsection (5) above shall be recoverable by the association making the payment. [**279**]

GENERAL

This prohibits the making of any gift, or the payment of any dividend or bonus, except as provided in sub-s. (2), to any of the persons described in sub-s. (1).

The section gives the Corporation power to specify the maximum amounts which may be paid by way of fees etc. This does not apply to a registered housing association which is a registered charity.

The Corporation are also given a power to lay down conditions governing contracts between any member of the committee of a registered 1965 Act association and the association.

DEFINITIONS

"Committee"—see s. 28
"Housing association", and "registered"—see s. 129
"Registered charity"—see s. 129
"Registered 1965 Act association"—see s. 28

27. Disclosure of interest by members of committees of registered 1965 Act associations

(1) Subject to the provisions of this section, it shall be the duty of a member of the committee of a registered 1965 Act association who is in any way, whether directly or indirectly, interested in a contract or proposed contract with the association to declare the nature of his interest to the committee in accordance with this section.

(2) In the case of a proposed contract, the declaration required by this section to be made by a member of a committee shall be made at the meeting of the committee at which the question of entering into the contract is first taken into consideration, or, if the member was not at the date of that meeting interested in the proposed contract, at the next meeting of the committee held after he becomes interested in the proposed contract.

(3) Where a member of a committee becomes interested in a contract with the association after it is made, the declaration required by this section shall be made at the first meeting of the committee held after he becomes interested in the contract.

(4) For the purposes of this section, a general notice given at a meeting of the committee of an association by a member of the committee to the effect that he is a member of a specified company or firm, and is to be regarded as interested in any contract which may, after the date of the notice, be made with that company or firm, is a sufficient declaration of interest in relation to any contract made after that date with that company or firm.

(5) A member of a committee need not make a declaration or give a notice under this section by attending in person at a meeting of the committee if he takes reasonable steps to secure that the declaration or notice is brought up and read at the meeting.

(6) A member of a committee who fails to comply with the provisions of this section shall be liable on summary conviction to a fine not exceeding £200.

(7) Nothing in this section shall be taken to prejudice the operation of any rule of law restricting members of the committee of a registered 1965 Act association from having any interest in contracts with the association. **[280]**

GENERAL

This section, which requires no comment, was added during the passage of the Bill through the Lords.

28. Interpretation of Part II

Except in so far as the context otherwise requires, in this Part of this Act—

"appropriate registrar" has the same meaning as in the 1965 Act;

"charity" and "exempt charity" have the same meanings as in the Charities Act 1960;

"committee", in relation to a society registered under the 1965 Act, has the same meaning as in that Act;

"house" has the same meaning as in Part I of the Housing Act 1964;

"registered 1965 Act association" means a registered housing association which is a society registered under the 1965 Act; and

"the 1965 Act" has the meaning assigned to it by section 13 (1) (*b*) above. **[281]**

PART III

FINANCIAL ASSISTANCE FOR HOUSING ASSOCIATIONS

29. Housing association grants

(1) The Secretary of State may, in accordance with the provisions of section 30 below, make grants (in this Part of this Act referred to as "housing association grants") to registered housing associations, other than associations falling within section 18 (1) (*b*) of this Act, in respect of their expenditure in connection with housing projects approved by him.

(2) For the purposes of this Part of this Act a project is a housing project if it is undertaken for all or any of the following purposes, namely,—

(*a*) providing housing or residential accommodation,

(*b*) improving such accommodation,

(*c*) repairing such accommodation,

(*d*) providing land or buildings for purposes which, in the opinion of the Secretary of State, will be for the benefit of persons for whom any housing or residential accommodation is or is to be provided, and

(*e*) improving or repairing any such buildings as are referred to in paragraph (*d*) above,

and in this subsection "housing or residential accommodation" means dwellings which are or are to be let or available for letting or a building or part of a building used or for use as a hostel or part of a hostel and for this purpose the grant of a licence to occupy shall be treated as a letting.

(3) No housing association grant shall be paid in respect of any project unless an application therefor is submitted to the appropriate body, that is to say,—

(*a*) in England and Wales, if the registered housing association concerned makes an application to a council for a loan under section 119 of the Housing Act 1957 in connection with the project, to that council, and in any other case to the Corporation, and

(*b*) in Scotland, to a local authority, the Corporation or the Secretary of State,

and where a council in England and Wales, a local authority in Scotland or the Corporation receive an application under this subsection, they shall forward it to the Secretary of State together with their own assessment of the project.

(4) Subject to subsection (5) below, the housing association grant payable to a registered housing association in respect of a housing project approved by the Secretary of State shall be equal to the net cost of the project to the association.

(5) The Secretary of State may, with the consent of the Treasury, determine maximum levels of cost or of grant applicable to housing projects generally, to any particular housing project or to any description of housing project, and the amount of the housing association grant payable in respect of a project to which any such determination applies shall be limited in accordance with the determination.

(6) Subject to subsection (7) below, for the purposes of this section the net cost of a housing project to a registered housing association means the difference between—

(*a*) the estimated expenditure of the association which, in the opinion of the Secretary of State, is attributable to the project and reasonable and appropriate, having regard to all the circumstances, and

(*b*) the estimated income which, in the opinion of the Secretary of State, the association might reasonably be expected to receive in respect of the project, including any sums received or to be received by way of grant or subsidy under any enactment, other than this section,

and for this purpose estimated expenditure and estimated income shall be calculated in such manner as the Secretary of State may, with the consent of the Treasury, from time to time determine, and any such calculation may take account of expenditure likely to be incurred and income likely to be received after the completion of the project in connection with the premises to which the project relates.

(7) If, in the case of an application for a housing association grant in respect of a particular project, it appears to the Secretary of State that it would be appropriate to do so, he may for the purposes of this section determine the net cost of the project to the association in such manner as he considers appropriate instead of in accordance with subsection (6) above.

(8) Before making any general determination for the purposes of subsection (5) or subsection (6) above, the Secretary of State shall consult such bodies appearing to him to be representative of housing associations as he considers appropriate. [**282**]

GENERAL

This section creates an entirely new grant system for housing associations for the carrying out of any of the types of housing project listed in s. 29 (2). In England and

Wales application for grant must be made to a council if the registered association is seeking a loan from that council under s. 119 of the Housing Act 1957. If it is not seeking such a loan, application is to be made to the Corporation. Whether the application is made in the first instance to the local Council, or to the Corporation, the receiving body must forward it to the Secretary of State, with their own assessment of the project.

The procedure in Scotland is slightly different, as will be seen.

The general approach is that "housing association" grant is payable project by project, and will be "equal to the net cost of the project to the association". However, the Secretary of State has firm control, under sub-ss. (4) to (7), of the method of computing the net cost.

The Secretary of State is required to consult representative bodies before making any general determinations.

See Chapter 3 and also s. 31 as to management grants, s. 32 as to revenue deficit grants, and s. 33 as to hostel deficit grants. See also Circular 133/74 in Appendix II.

Ss. 29 to 33 came into operation on 18th September 1974.

DEFINITIONS

"Hostel"—see s. 129

"Housing association" and "registered"—see s. 129

30. Payments of housing association grant

(1) According as the Secretary of State may determine, a housing association grant in respect of a housing project shall be payable—

(*a*) in a single sum at such time as, in the opinion of the Secretary of State, the project is completed, or

(*b*) in annual instalments beginning in the financial year in which, in his opinion, the project is completed and continuing over such number of years as he may determine, either generally or in relation to the particular project,

but, in either case, the Secretary of State may, if he considers it appropriate to do so, make payments on account of the grant before the project is completed.

(2) In giving his approval to a housing project for the purposes of a housing association grant, the Secretary of State may provide that payment of the grant is conditional upon compliance by the housing association concerned with such conditions as he may specify, including (in a case where the project has not yet been completed) conditions as to the period within which it is to be completed.

(3) The Secretary of State may reduce the amount of, or of any payment in respect of, a housing association grant or suspend or discontinue any instalments of such a grant—

(*a*) if he imposed any conditions under subsection (2) above and any of those conditions have not been complied with; or

(*b*) if he is satisfied that the whole or any part of a building to which the project relates and which comprises or is intended to comprise housing or residential accommodation as defined in section 29 (2) above—

(i) has been converted, demolished or destroyed; or

(ii) is not fit to be used or is not being used for the purpose for which it was intended; or

(iii) has been sold or leased; or

(iv) has ceased for any reason whatsoever to be vested in the housing association concerned or in trustees for that association.

(4) If at any time any dwelling or hostel or part thereof to which a housing project relates is leased to or becomes vested in a registered housing association or trustees for a registered housing association, other than the association by whom the application for the housing association grant relating to that project

was made, the Secretary of State may pay to that other association the whole or any part of the grant or any instalment thereof which would otherwise have been paid after that time to the association by whom the application for the grant was made.

(5) If, at any time after a housing association grant or any payment in respect of such a grant has been made to a registered housing association, it appears to the Secretary of State that any building to which the housing project concerned relates has ceased to be available for use for the purpose for which, at the time the project was approved, it was intended that it should be used, he may direct the association to pay to him an amount equal to the whole or such proportion as he may determine of that grant or, as the case may be, of any payment made in respect of it; and any amount which a registered housing association is directed to repay to the Secretary of State under this subsection shall be recoverable as a simple contract debt, or in Scotland as a debt due under a contract, in any court of competent jurisdiction.

(6) For the purposes of this section, the whole or any part of any building is leased if and only if it is leased for a term exceeding 7 years, or for a term not exceeding 7 years granted by a lease which confers on the lessee an option for renewal for a term which, together with the original term, exceeds 7 years.

(7) No housing association grant (or payment in respect of such a grant) may be made before the operative date, but applications for such grants may be submitted in accordance with section 29 (3) above before that date and may be so submitted by a housing association notwithstanding that it is not then registered.

(8) On such terms as he may with the approval of the Treasury specify, the Secretary of State may appoint the Corporation, the Greater London Council, a district council, a London borough council, the Common Council of the City of London or a local authority within the meaning of section 1 of the Housing (Scotland) Act 1966 to act as his agent in connection with the making, in such cases as he may specify, of payments in respect of housing association grant; and where such an appointment is made the Corporation, council or local authority, as the case may be, shall act as such an agent in accordance with the terms of their appointment. [**283**]

GENERAL

There is considerable flexibility as to the ways in which grants may be paid. Payment may (*a*) be a single sum payable on completion, or (*b*) a series of annual instalments beginning in the year of completion and spread over such number of years as the Secretary of State may determine. In either case, payments may be made on account before a project is completed. The Secretary of State may lay down conditions and reduce, suspend or discontinue payments if his conditions are not complied with, or in the event of any of the situations in sub-s. 3 (*b*) arising.

There is provision for the switching of grants in whole or in part if the dwelling or hostel is leased to, or becomes vested in, another registered housing association.

The Secretary of State may appoint the Corporation or certain councils his agents for the payment of grant.

DEFINITIONS

"Dwelling"—see s. 129 (1) and (2)
"Hostel"—see s. 129 (1) and (2)
"Housing association" and "registered"—see s. 129 (1) and (2)

31. Management grants for certain housing associations

(1) If it appears to the Secretary of State that—

(*a*) before 1st January 1973 a housing association provided any dwellings without the assistance of any grant, subsidy or contribution from the

Secretary of State or a local authority under any enactment, other than section 93 of the Finance Act 1965 (grants for affording relief from tax), and

(*b*) during the whole or any part of an accounting year of the association beginning on or after that date the dwellings were subject to tenancies to which Part VIII of the Housing Finance Act 1972 or sections 60 to 66 of the Housing (Financial Provisions) (Scotland) Act 1972 applied, being tenancies under which the interest of the landlord belonged to the association, and

(*c*) by reason of the operation of the said Part VIII, or of the said sections 60 to 66, and the association's lack of any other funds, the association has incurred a deficit in that accounting year as a result of its expenditure in connection with those dwellings,

the Secretary of State may, in accordance with the provisions of this section, pay to the association a grant towards the difference between the income arising to the association from those dwellings in that year and so much of the expenditure incurred by the association in that year as, in the opinion of the Secretary of State, was necessary for the proper management of those dwellings.

(2) No grant shall be payable under this section in respect of an accounting year of a housing association unless—

(*a*) an application in respect of that year is made by the association to the Secretary of State not later than the expiry of the period of 15 months beginning immediately after the end of that year and that application is approved by him; and

(*b*) the application is made with the consent of the Corporation; and

(*c*) both at the time the application is made and at the time the grant is paid the association is a registered housing association.

(3) An application under subsection (2) above shall be in such form and contain such information as the Secretary of State may from time to time determine.

(4) A grant to a housing association under this section shall be paid in a single sum in respect of the year to which it relates; and the amount of any such grant shall be calculated in such manner as the Secretary of State may, with the agreement of the Treasury, determine.

(5) No grant shall be paid under this section before the operative date, but an application for such a grant may be made before that date. [**284**]

GENERAL

This is a new type of grant applicable only to associations which provided dwellings prior to 1st January 1973, without any grant, subsidy etc., other than a grant for affording tax relief. The dwellings must be ones which were subject to either of the two Housing Finance Acts mentioned in sub-s. (1) (*b*); and the deficit must have arisen because of the operation of those Acts.

Part VIII of the Housing Finance Act 1972 brought housing association dwellings into the "fair rent" provisions of the Rent Act 1968 but provided for phased progression towards such fair rents. It also made provision for reducing rents chargeable which were above the fair rents determined as a result of the Act. This could have caused a loss of rent revenue in some cases, though there were transitional provisions. It is more likely that the associations have suffered losses due to the Government's freeze which operated from 8th March 1974, but it is difficult to see how such a loss could be wholly ascribed to the operation of Part VIII of the Housing Act 1972.

This section enables the Secretary of State to pay a grant towards the deficit in any year. There is no precise formula in the Act for computing the deficit, and the calculation is very much in the hands of the Secretary of State and the Treasury.

Only registered housing associations which provided unsubsidised housing are eligible to apply. The consent of the Corporation is necessary to any application. Application for the grant may be made as soon as an association has registered but will not be paid before the operative date. It will be paid as a single sum.

DEFINITIONS
"Dwelling"—see s. 129 (1) and (2)
"Housing association" and "registered"—see s. 129 (1) and (2)
"Operative date"—see s. 129

32. Revenue deficit grants for registered housing associations

(1) The Secretary of State may, in accordance with the provisions of this section, pay a grant (in this section referred to as a "revenue deficit grant") to a registered housing association, other than an association falling within paragraph (*a*) or paragraph (*b*) of section 18 (1) above, if the association incurs a deficit on its annual revenue account for an accounting year of the association ending on or after 1st January 1974.

(2) No revenue deficit grant shall be payable in respect of an accounting year of a registered housing association unless—

(*a*) an application in respect of that year is made by the association to the Secretary of State not later than the expiry of the period of 15 months beginning immediately after the end of that year and that application is approved by him; and

(*b*) the application is in such form and contains such information as the Secretary of State may from time to time determine; and

(*c*) the application is accompanied by the audited accounts of the association for the accounting year to which the application relates.

(3) Subject to subsection (4) below, for the purposes of this section, a registered housing association shall be treated as incurring a deficit on its annual revenue account for an accounting year of the association if—

(*a*) the expenditure of the association for that year which, in the opinion of the Secretary of State, is attributable to dwellings provided by the association and any related property and is reasonable and appropriate, having regard to all the circumstances,

exceeds

(*b*) the income which, in the opinion of the Secretary of State, the association might reasonably be expected to receive in respect of those dwellings and any related property in that year, including any sums received or to be received in respect of that year by way of grant or subsidy under any enactment, other than this section,

and for this purpose expenditure and income shall be calculated in such manner as the Secretary of State may, with the consent of the Treasury, from time to time determine.

(4) Notwithstanding anything in subsection (3) above, no account shall be taken for the purposes of this section of so much of any deficit as, in the opinion of the Secretary of State, arises by virtue of any such difference between income and expenditure as is specified in section 31 (1) above.

(5) The revenue deficit grant payable to a registered housing association in respect of any accounting year shall be of such amount as the Secretary of State may determine in relation to that association but shall not be greater than the amount of the excess determined for that year under subsection (3) above.

(6) If he considers it appropriate to do so the Secretary of State may make payments on account of any revenue deficit grant which he considers is likely to become payable to a registered housing association in respect of any accounting year but, subject thereto, any such grant shall be paid in a single sum in respect of the accounting year to which it relates.

(7) No revenue deficit grant shall be paid before the operative date but applications for such a grant may be made before that date and such an application may be so made by a housing association notwithstanding that it is not then registered.

(8) In subsection (3) above "related property", in relation to dwellings provided by a housing association, means property of the association which is provided for the benefit of the persons occupying those dwellings. [**285**]

GENERAL

This is a new provision inserted during the later stages of the Bill's passage through the house. Revenue deficit grant may be payable to a registered housing association, other than the North Eastern Housing Association, or a 1965 Act society whose membership is restricted to its own tenants or prospective tenants. It is payable only in respect of an accounting year ending after 1st January 1974. Application may be made at once and must in any case be made within 15 months of the end of the accounting year in which the deficit occurred. The broad basis of calculation is set out in the section. Grants will normally be paid as a single sum, but the Secretary of State has power to make advance payments on account.

DEFINITIONS

As for s. 31

33. Hostel deficit grants

(1) The Secretary of State may, in accordance with the provisions of this section, make a grant (in this section referred to as a "hostel deficit grant") to any registered housing association which, in relation to a hostel managed by the association, incurs a revenue deficit in respect of an accounting year of the association ending on or after the operative date.

(2) No hostel deficit grant shall be payable to a registered housing association in respect of any accounting year of the association unless an application in respect of that year is made by the association to the Secretary of State not later than the expiry of the period of 15 months beginning immediately after the end of that year and that application is approved by him.

(3) For the purposes of this section, a registered housing association shall be treated as incurring, in relation to any hostel managed by them, a revenue deficit in respect of an accounting year of the association if—

(*a*) the expenditure of the association for that year which, in the opinion of the Secretary of State, is attributable to the hostel and reasonable and appropriate having regard to all the circumstances

exceeds

(*b*) the income which, in the opinion of the Secretary of State, the association might reasonably be expected to receive in respect of the hostel in that year, including any sums received or to be received in respect of that year by way of grant or subsidy under any enactment, other than this section, and so much as is reasonably attributable to the hostel of any sums received or to be received by the association in respect of that year otherwise than by reference to a specific hostel or purpose, and for this purpose expenditure and income shall be calculated in such manner as the Secretary of State may, with the consent of the Treasury, from time to time determine.

(4) In any case where more than one hostel is managed by the same registered housing association and that association makes an application for a hostel deficit grant in respect of any accounting year of the association, the Secretary of State may, if he considers it appropriate to do so, treat all the hostels managed by the association, or any two or more of them, as a single hostel for the purpose of determining whether the association incurs a revenue deficit in respect of that year in relation to those hostels.

(5) The hostel deficit grant payable to a registered housing association in respect of any accounting year shall be of such amount as the Secretary of State may determine in relation to that association but shall not be greater than the amount of the excess determined for that year under subsection (3) above.

(6) According as the Secretary of State may determine, a hostel deficit grant payable to a registered housing association in respect of any accounting year shall be payable—

(*a*) in a single sum, or

(*b*) in instalments payable at such times and in such manner as the Treasury may direct,

but, in either case, if the Secretary of State considers that a registered housing association is likely to be entitled to a hostel deficit grant in respect of any accounting year, he may make payments on account of such a grant before the expiry of that year.

(7) An application under subsection (2) above shall be in such form and contain such information as the Secretary of State may from time to time determine. **[286]**

GENERAL

Hostel deficit grants are another new form of financial aid. The Secretary of State may pay hostel deficit grant to a registered housing association which incurs a revenue deficit in relation to a hostel in respect of any accounting year ending on or after the operative date. The grant is payable only in relation to a hostel, *i.e.* any other activities of the association do not come into the calculation. Where an association has more than one hostel the Secretary of State may treat two or more as a single hostel for the purpose of determining the revenue deficit.

Grant may be paid in a single sum or by instalments and there may be payments on account before the accounting year has ended. Contributions and subsidies under s. 92 of the Housing Finance Act 1972 and s. 21 of the Housing (Financial Provisions) (Scotland) Act 1968 will continue to be payable to both registered and unregistered housing associations, unless they are affected by the transitional arrangements in s. 35 of this Act. Ss. 29 to 33 came into operation on 18 September, 1974.

DEFINITIONS

"Housing association" and "registered"—see s. 129 (1) and (2)
"Hostel"—see s. 129 (1) and (2)
"Operative date"—see s. 129

34. Transfer to Corporation of rights and obligations of Secretary of State in relation to certain advances

(1) On and after the appointed day, any rights or obligations of the Secretary of State under an agreement in force immediately before that day under section 7 of the Housing Act 1961 or section 23 of the Housing (Financial Provisions) (Scotland) Act 1968 (in this section referred to respectively as "the principal

section" and "the principal Scottish section") shall, by virtue of this section, become rights or obligations of the Corporation.

(2) In accordance with subsection (1) above, on and after the appointed day—

(*a*) any reference in any such agreement as is referred to in subsection (1) above to the Secretary of State and any reference in any such agreement which immediately before the appointed day falls to be construed as a reference to the Secretary of State shall be construed as a reference to the Corporation;

(*b*) in subsections (4), (6) and (7) of the principal section for the word "Minister" there shall be substituted the words "Housing Corporation" and in subsections (3), (6) and (7) of the principal Scottish section for the words "Secretary of State" there shall be substituted the words "Housing Corporation"; and

(*c*) any rights and obligations of the Secretary of State in relation to advances made under those sections (whether or not arising by virtue of any such agreement as is referred to in subsection (1) above) shall become rights and obligations of the Corporation.

(3) In any case where an advance under the principal section is, immediately before the appointed day, secured by a mortgage of any property in favour of the Secretary of State, the interest of the Secretary of State as mortgagee shall, by virtue of this section (and without any transfer or conveyance), on that day vest in the Corporation.

(4) In this section "the appointed day" means the day appointed for the coming into operation of this section. **[287]**

GENERAL

This relates to advances made to certain housing associations who have provided, under agreements in force immediately before the appointed day, dwellings let at cost-rents, or by co-ownership schemes. The dwellings may have been provided by new construction, conversion or improvement. The obligations of the Secretary of State are now transferred to the Corporation.

35. Existing subsidies and grants for housing associations: transition to housing association grants

(1) After the operative date, no approval may be given by the Secretary of State—

(*a*) for the purposes of section 75 of the Housing Finance Act 1972 (the new building subsidy) in respect of any building scheme; or

(*b*) for the purposes of sections 55 and 57 of the Housing (Financial Provisions) (Scotland) Act 1972 (new building subsidy and improvement subsidy) in respect of any building scheme or improvement scheme; or

(*c*) for the purposes of section 92 of the Housing Finance Act 1972 (hostel subsidy) in respect of a hostel scheme; or

(*d*) for the purposes of section 21 of the Housing (Financial Provisions) (Scotland) Act 1968 (exchequer contributions for hostels) in respect of the provision of hostels.

(2) If, before the expiry of the period of one year beginning on the operative date, a registered housing association makes an application for housing association grant in respect of a housing project which is or includes a building scheme or improvement scheme which has been previously approved for the purposes

of the said section 75 or, as the case may be, the said sections 55 and 57 and the Secretary of State gives his approval to that project for the purposes of housing association grant,—

(*a*) no further payments of new building subsidy or improvement subsidy shall be made in respect of that approved scheme;

(*b*) the Secretary of State may, under section 30 (2) above, impose a condition requiring the repayment by the association of all or any payments of new building subsidy or improvement subsidy already made in respect of that approved scheme; and

(*c*) where any such condition as is referred to in paragraph (*b*) above is so imposed, no account shall be taken under section 29 (6) (*b*) above of any payments received by way of new building subsidy or improvement subsidy which are required to be so repaid.

(3) If, before the operative date, a registered housing association has applied for the approval of the Secretary of State under the said section 75 or the said sections 55 and 57 in respect of a building scheme or improvement scheme or under section 92 of the Housing Finance Act 1972 in respect of a hostel scheme or under section 21 of the Housing (Financial Provisions) (Scotland) Act 1968 in respect of the provision of hostels, and no such approval has been given before that date, then, for the purposes of section 29 above, the application shall be treated—

(*a*) as an application for housing association grant in respect of a housing project consisting of that building scheme, improvement scheme or hostel scheme (in England and Wales) or, as the case may be, the provision of hostels (in Scotland), and

(*b*) as having been submitted to the appropriate body referred to in section 29 (3) above and forwarded by that body to the Secretary of State,

and for the purpose of his consideration of the application for housing association grant, the Secretary of State may require the registered housing association to furnish to him such additional information as he may determine.

(4) A registered housing association may not make an application for housing association grant in respect of a housing project which consists of or includes—

(*a*) the carrying out of works comprised in a hostel scheme which, before the operative date, has been approved by the Secretary of State for the purposes of section 92 of the Housing Finance Act 1972, or

(*b*) the carrying out of works for the provision of hostels which, before the operative date, have been approved by the Secretary of State for the purposes of section 21 of the Housing (Financial Provisions) (Scotland) Act 1968, or

(*c*) the provision or conversion of a building for use as a hostel or part of a hostel in accordance with any such arrangements as are referred to in subsection (2) of section 15 of the Housing (Financial Provisions) Act 1958 or of section 9 of the Housing Act 1961 (grants for hostels),

if, before the operative date, any payment of subsidy under the said section 92 has been made in respect of that hostel scheme or any contribution has been made in respect of the provision of hostels under the said section 21 or, as the case may be, any contribution has been paid in respect of that building under the said section 15.

(5) If, in a case where subsection (4) above does not prevent the making of such an application, a registered housing association makes an application for

housing association grant in respect of a housing project falling within that subsection and the Secretary of State gives his approval to that project for the purposes of housing association grant, then, according to the nature of the housing project,—

(*a*) section 92 of the Housing Finance Act 1972 shall cease to have effect with respect to the hostel scheme referred to in paragraph (*a*) of that subsection; or

(*b*) section 21 of the Housing (Financial Provisions) (Scotland) Act 1968 shall cease to have effect with respect to the provision of hostels referred to in paragraph (*b*) of that subsection; or

(*c*) section 15 of the Housing (Financial Provisions) Act 1958 shall cease to apply to the building referred to in paragraph (*c*) of that subsection.

(6) In any case where—

(*a*) a registered housing association is a party to any such arrangements as are referred to in subsection (1) of section 21 of the Housing Act 1969 or, in Scotland, subsection (1) of section 16 or section 17 of the Housing (Financial Provisions) (Scotland) Act 1968 (contributions for dwellings provided or improved by housing associations under arrangements with local authorities and, in Scotland, the Secretary of State), and

(*b*) before the operative date approval has been given in accordance with subsection (2) of the said section 21 or in accordance with section 14 of the said Act of 1968, as applied by section 17 (1) (ii) of that Act, to the making and terms of those arrangements, and

(*c*) before the operative date particulars and estimates in respect of works to which those arrangements relate (in this section referred to as a "related project") have been submitted in an application made under subsection (3) of the said section 21 or, as the case may require, have been furnished under section 18 of the said Act of 1968,

the registered housing association may not make an application for housing association grant in respect of a housing project which consists of or includes the carrying out of any of the works comprised in the related project if any contribution under the said section 21 or the said section 16 and 17 has been paid in relation to the related project before the operative date.

(7) If, in a case falling within paragraphs (*a*) to (*c*) of subsection (6) above,—

(*a*) the registered housing association concerned makes an application (permitted by that subsection) for housing association grant in respect of a related project, and

(*b*) the Secretary of State gives his approval to the related project for the purposes of housing association grant,

section 21 of the Housing Act 1969 or, as the case may be, sections 16 and 17 of the Housing (Financial Provisions) (Scotland) Act 1968 shall cease to have effect with respect to so much of the arrangements concerned as relates to the carrying out of the related project.

(8) In this section—

"building scheme" has the same meaning as in section 75 of the Housing Finance Act 1972 or, in Scotland, section 55 of the Housing (Financial Provisions) (Scotland) Act 1972; and

"hostel scheme" has the same meaning as in section 92 of the Housing Finance Act 1972; and "improvement scheme" has the same meaning as in section 57 of the Housing (Financial Provisions) (Scotland) Act 1972. **[288]**

GENERAL

These transitional arrangements appear rather complicated until broken down into their component parts, as follows:

(1) After the operative date no further approvals may be given by the Secretary of State to—
  (*a*) Schemes involving new building subsidy under s. 75 of the Housing Finance Act 1972, or
  (*b*) Schemes involving new building subsidy or improvement subsidy under ss. 55 and 57 of the Housing (Financial Provisions) (Scotland) Act 1972, or
  (*c*) Hostel schemes under s. 92 of the Housing Finance Act 1972, or
  (*d*) Hostel provision under s. 21 of the Housing (Financial Provisions) Scotland Act 1968.

(2) It is to be noted that sub-s. (2) applies only to classes (*a*) and (*b*) above. Where the Secretary of State has already approved a building scheme or improvement scheme, and a registered housing association makes application for the new housing association grant within one year of the operative date under the new Act, and the Secretary of State gives his approval to the changeover to "housing association grant", the conditions in sub-s. (2) (*a*) (*b*) and (*c*) will apply.

(3) Sub-s. (3) applies to ALL the classes enumerated under (1) above, but only where the Secretary of State has not given approval to a scheme already submitted under any of these earlier enactments. Here the position is simple—he may treat the application as one for housing association grant under s. 29 of the new Act.

(4) Reference has already been made to the fact that sub-s. (2) does not apply to hostel schemes under earlier Acts relating to England and Scotland. The point here is that the switch to housing association grant under s. 29 can be made under s. (2) even though payments have been made, if the schemes fall within sub-s. 1 (*a*) or 1 (*b*). But for hostel schemes the switch is barred by sub-s. (4) if any payment has been made.

(5) If no payment has been made it is possible to switch over earlier hostel schemes to housing association grants under the 1974 Act; and the conditions of sub-s. (5) will apply.

(6) The position with regard to improvements under s. 21 of the Housing Act 1969, or under ss. 16 and 17 of the Scottish 1968 Act, is parallel to that for hostels under sub-s. (4) and (5). Under sub-s. (6) no application for a change to housing association grant under the new Act may be made if any contribution has already been paid.

(7) If an application is not barred by sub-s. (6) because no contribution has been paid, the way is open to an association to apply for housing association grant under the new Act. If the Secretary of State approves the application the earlier enactments, *i.e.*, s. 21 of the Housing Act 1969, or s. 16 and s. 17 of the Housing (Financial Provisions) (Scotland) Act 1968, will cease to have effect "with respect to so much of the arrangements—as relates to the carrying out of the related project".

See Circular 133/74 in Appendix II.

DEFINITIONS

"Building scheme"—see sub-s. (8)
"Hostel"—see s. 129 (1) and (2)
"Hostel scheme"—see sub-s. (8)
"Improvement scheme"—see sub-s. (8)
"Operative date"—see s. 129

PART IV

HOUSING ACTION AREAS

36. Declaration of housing action areas

(1) Where a report with respect to an area consisting primarily of housing accommodation is submitted to the local authority within whose district the

area lies by a person or persons appearing to the authority to be suitably qualified (whether or not that person is or those persons include an officer of the authority) and, upon consideration of the report and of any other information in their possession, the authority are satisfied that, having regard to—

(*a*) the physical state of the housing accommodation in the area as a whole, and

(*b*) social conditions in the area,

the requirement in subsection (2) below is fulfilled with respect to the area, the authority may cause the area to be defined on a map and by resolution declare it to be a housing action area.

(2) The requirement referred to in subsection (1) above is that the living conditions in the area are unsatisfactory and can most effectively be dealt with within a period of 5 years so as to secure—

(*a*) the improvement of the housing accommodation in the area as a whole, and

(*b*) the well-being of the persons for the time being residing in the area, and

(*c*) the proper and effective management and use of that accommodation,

by declaring the area to be a housing action area.

(3) In considering whether to take action under subsection (1) above with respect to any area, a local authority shall have regard to such guidance as may from time to time be given by the Secretary of State, either generally or with respect to a particular authority or description of authority or in any particular case, with regard to the identification of areas suitable to be declared as housing action areas.

(4) As soon as may be after passing a resolution declaring an area to be a housing action area, a local authority shall—

(*a*) publish in two or more newspapers circulating in the locality (of which at least one shall, if practicable, be a local newspaper) a notice of the resolution identifying the area and naming a place or places where a copy of the resolution, a map on which the area is defined and of the report referred to in subsection (1) above may be inspected at all reasonable times;

(*b*) take such further steps as may appear to them best designed to secure that the resolution and the obligations imposed by section 47 below are brought to the attention of persons residing or owning property in the area and that those persons are informed of the name and address of the person to whom should be addressed any inquiries and representations concerning any action to be taken with respect to the area or, as the case may be, any inquiries concerning the obligations so imposed;

(*c*) send to the Secretary of State a copy of the resolution, the map and a copy of the report mentioned in paragraph (*a*) above, a statement of the numbers of dwellings, houses in multiple occupation and hostels in the area and a statement containing such information as the Secretary of State may for the time being require, either generally or with respect to a particular authority or description of authority or in any particular case, to show the basis on which the local authority satisfied themselves that the area was suitable to be declared a housing action area, having regard to the matters specified in paragraphs (*a*) and (*b*) of subsection (1) above and any relevant guidance given under subsection (3) above; and

(*d*) send to the Secretary of State a statement of their proposals, whether general or specific, for the participation of registered housing associations in dealing with the living conditions in the area.

(5) As soon as may be after a resolution has been passed declaring an area to be a housing action area, the resolution shall be registered in the register of local land charges—

(*a*) by the proper officer, for the purposes of section 15 of the Land Charges Act 1925, of the local authority in whose area the housing action area is situated; and

(*b*) in such manner as may be prescribed by rules under section 19 of that Act.

(6) In this Part of this Act "housing accommodation" means dwellings, houses in multiple occupation and hostels. **[289]**

GENERAL

Housing action areas are somewhat similar in character to general improvement areas under the Housing Act 1969, but more emphasis is laid on the existence of housing stress factors, and the object is to eradicate the bad conditions by urgent action within a period of 5 years, or, at most, 7 years.

The report which gives rise to the resolution declaring the area to be a housing action area need not be prepared by, or wholly by, an officer of the authority. The local authority must be satisfied that the requirements of both sub-ss. (1) and (2) are fulfilled. Local authorities are required to have regard to such guidance on these matters as may be given to local authorities from time to time by the Secretary of State.

Instructions for publicising the declaration are given in sub-s. (4). Declaration takes place before submission of the proposals to the Secretary of State; and the resolution must be registered in the register of local land charges.

DEFINITIONS

"Dwellings"—see s. 129
"Local authority"—see s. 49
"House in multiple-occupation"—see s. 129
"Housing association"—see s. 129

37. Functions of Secretary of State

(1) When a local authority have declared an area to be a housing action area and have sent to the Secretary of State the documents referred to in section 36 (4) (*c*) above, he shall send to the authority a written acknowledgement of the receipt of those documents.

(2) If it appears to the Secretary of State to be appropriate to do so, he may, at any time within the period of 28 days beginning with the day on which he sent an acknowledgement under subsection (1) above, send a notification to the local authority concerned—

(*a*) that the area declared by the authority to be a housing action area is no longer to be such an area; or

(*b*) that land which is within the area declared by the authority to be a housing action area and which is defined on a map accompanying the notification is to be excluded from that area; or

(*c*) that the Secretary of State requires more time to consider the authority's declaration of the area as a housing action area.

(3) In any case where—

(*a*) the Secretary of State notifies a local authority as mentioned in paragraph (*c*) of subsection (2) above, and

(*b*) by a direction given with respect to the particular area declared by the authority to be a housing action area, he so requires,

the authority shall send to him such information and documents, in addition to the information and documents mentioned in section 36 (4) (*c*) above, as may be specified in the direction.

(4) Where the Secretary of State notifies a local authority as mentioned in paragraph (*c*) of subsection (2) above, he shall, on completion of his consideration of the matter, send a further notification to the authority—

(*a*) as mentioned in paragraph (*a*) or paragraph (*b*) of that subsection; or

(*b*) that he does not propose to take any further action with respect to the local authority's declaration.

(5) With effect from the date on which a local authority is notified as mentioned in paragraph (*a*) or paragraph (*b*) of subsection (2) above (whether the notification is sent under that subsection or subsection (4) above) the area concerned shall cease to be a housing action area or, according to the nature of the notification, the land defined on the map accompanying the notification shall be excluded from the housing action area.

(6) Where subsection (5) above applies, the local authority concerned shall, as soon as may be after receipt of the notification,—

(*a*) publish in two or more newspapers circulating in the locality (of which at least one shall, if practicable, be a local newspaper) a notice of the effect of the Secretary of State's notification and naming a place or places where a copy of the notification and, in the case of such a notification as is mentioned in subsection (2) (*b*) above, a copy of the amended map of the housing action area may be inspected at all reasonable times; and

(*b*) take such further steps as may appear to them best designed to secure that the effect of the notification is brought to the attention of persons residing or owning property in the area declared by the local authority to be a housing action area. [**290**]

GENERAL

The Secretary of State may, within 28 days of receiving the documents relating to the declaration of a housing action area, send a notification to the local authority that it is no longer such an area. Or he may exclude certain land from the area. Thirdly, he may say that he needs more time to consider the matter. He has the right to direct them to supply further information. Having done this he may notify the local authority that he has decided that the area is no longer to be a housing action area, or that certain land is to be excluded from it. See Circular 160/74 in Appendix II.

Again, there is a requirement to publicise these decisions.

38. Incorporation of general improvement areas, priority neighbourhoods, or parts thereof into housing action areas

(1) If a local authority propose, by a resolution under section 36 above, to declare as a housing action area an area which consists of or includes land which, immediately prior to the declaration,

(*a*) is comprised in a general improvement area declared under Part II of the Housing Act 1969, or

(*b*) is comprised in a priority neighbourhood declared under section 52 below they shall indicate on the map referred to in section 36 (1) above the land which is so comprised (in this section referred to as "the relevant land").

(2) Subject to the following provisions of this section, with effect from the date on which such a resolution as is referred to in subsection (1) above is passed, the relevant land shall be deemed (according to its status) either—

(*a*) to have been excluded from the general improvement area or, as the case may be, to have ceased to be a general improvement area by virtue of a resolution under section 30 (1) of the Housing Act 1969 passed on that date and approved by the Secretary of State; or

(*b*) to have been excluded from the priority neighbourhood by virtue of a resolution passed on that date under section 40 (1) below, as that section applies in relation to priority neighbourhoods by virtue of section 54 below or, as the case may be, to have ceased to be a priority neighbourhood by virtue of a resolution passed on that date under section 39 (3) below (as that section so applies).

(3) If the Secretary of State notifies the local authority concerned under section 37 above that the area declared by them to be a housing action area is no longer to be such an area, subsection (2) above shall be treated as never having applied in relation to the relevant land.

(4) If the Secretary of State notifies the local authority concerned under section 37 above that any land which—

(*a*) is within the area declared by the authority to be a housing action area, and

(*b*) consists of or includes any of the relevant land,

is to be excluded from the housing action area, subsection (2) above shall be treated as never having applied in relation to so much of the relevant land as is comprised in the land so excluded. [**291**]

GENERAL

The local authority may, by resolution, declare all or part of a general improvement area (under Part II of the Housing Act 1969), or all or part of a priority neighbourhood, to be a housing action area. The "relevant land" will be excluded from the general improvement area, or priority neighbourhood, immediately the resolution is passed. However, the Secretary of State may decide to the contrary, or exclude some parts of the land from the housing action area. Such action will restore the status of the general improvement area, or priority neighbourhood, as it was before the resolution was passed.

A "priority neighbourhood" is a new type of area as described in Part VI of this Act.

39. Duration of housing action areas

(1) Where a local authority have passed a resolution with respect to any area under section 36 (1) above, then, subject to section 37 (5) above and the following provisions of this section, the area shall be a housing action area throughout the period of 5 years beginning on the date on which the resolution was passed.

(2) If, not less than 3 months before the date on which, apart from any extension, or further extension, under this subsection, a housing action area would cease to exist, the local authority concerned notify the Secretary of State in writing that they have passed a resolution under this subsection, the duration of the housing action area shall be extended, subject to subsections (3) and (6) below, by the addition of a further period of 2 years.

(3) Notwithstanding anything in subsections (1) and (2) above, if a local

authority by resolution under this subsection so declare, an area which they had previously declared to be a housing action area shall cease to be such an area on the date on which the resolution under this subsection is passed; and as soon as may be after passing such a resolution the local authority shall send a copy of it to the Secretary of State.

(4) On receipt of any notification sent to him under subsection (2) above the Secretary of State shall send a written acknowledgment to the local authority by whom the notification was sent and, if it appears to him to be appropriate to do so, he may, at any time within the period of 28 days beginning with the day on which he sent an acknowledgment under this subsection, send a notification to the local authority concerned—

(*a*) that the duration of the housing action area is not to be extended in accordance with the authority's resolution; or

(*b*) that the Secretary of State requires more time to consider the authority's extension of the duration of the housing action area.

(5) Where the Secretary of State notifies a local authority as mentioned in paragraph (*b*) of subsection (4) above, he shall, on completion of his consideration of the matter, send a further notification to the authority—

(*a*) as mentioned in paragraph (*a*) of that subsection; or

(*b*) if, at the time of the notification, the 2 years' extension of the duration of the housing action area by virtue of the authority's resolution under subsection (2) above has begun to run, that the area concerned is to cease to be a housing action area on such date as may be specified in the notification; or

(*c*) that he does not propose to take any further action with respect to the authority's resolution.

(6) Where the Secretary of State notifies a local authority as mentioned in subsection (4) (*a*) above or subsection (5) (*b*) above (whether, in the former case, the notification is given under subsection (4) or subsection (5) above) the duration of the housing action area shall not be extended by virtue of the authority's resolution under subsection (2) above or, in the case of a notification under subsection (5) (*b*) above, the extension by virtue of that resolution shall be for a period expiring on the date specified in the notification.

(7) As soon as may be after passing a resolution under subsection (2) or subsection (3) above or, if subsection (6) above applies, as soon as may be after receipt of the notification from the Secretary of State, a local authority shall—

(*a*) publish in two or more newspapers circulating in the locality (of which at least one shall, if practicable, be a local newspaper) a notice of the resolution or, as the case may be, of the effect of the Secretary of State's notification and naming a place or places where a copy of the resolution or notification, as the case may be, may be inspected at all reasonable times; and

(*b*) take such further steps as may appear to the authority best designed to secure that the resolution or, as the case may be, the effect of the notification, is brought to the attention of persons residing or owning property in the housing action area concerned. **[292]**

GENERAL

Normally the housing action area continues as such for 5 years, but the local authority may resolve, before the expiry of that period, upon a 2-year extension, under sub-s. (2). This is subject to the approval of the Secretary of State.

On the other hand, a local authority may bring the life of a housing action area to an end before the expiry of 5 years, by taking action under sub-s. (3).

Where the local authority make application for an extension of time under sub-s. (2) the Secretary of State may refuse it, or fix a shorter extension than 2 years, or acquiesce in the 2 year extension.

All these various steps must be publicised.

40. Reduction of housing action area

(1) A local authority may at any time by resolution exclude from a housing action area any land for the time being included therein.

(2) As soon as may be after passing a resolution under this section, the local authority shall—

(*a*) publish in two or more newspapers circulating in the locality (of which one at least shall, if practicable, be a local newspaper) a notice of the resolution, identifying the housing action area concerned and the land excluded from it;

(*b*) take such further steps as may appear to the authority best designed to secure that the resolution is brought to the attention of persons residing or owning property in the housing action area; and

(*c*) send to the Secretary of State a copy of the resolution. **[293]**

GENERAL

This is self-explanatory. The local authority's decision appears to be final.

41. Duty to publish information

Where a local authority have declared an area to be a housing action area, it shall be their duty to bring to the attention of persons residing or owning property in the area—

(*a*) the action which they propose to take in relation to the housing action area, and

(*b*) the assistance available for the improvement of the housing accommodation in the area,

by publishing from time to time, in such manner as appears to them appropriate, such information as is in their opinion best designed to further the purpose for which the area was declared a housing action area. **[294]**

GENERAL

This provides for publicity additional to that required by s. 36, s. 37, s. 38 and s. 39 of the Act.

42. Duty to inform Secretary of State of action taken

(1) If at any time they are directed by the Secretary of State to do so, a local authority who have declared an area to be a housing action area shall furnish the Secretary of State with such information as may be specified in the direction with respect to the action taken by the authority for the purpose of securing all or any of the objectives specified in paragraphs (*a*) to (*c*) of subsection (2) of section 36 above.

(2) A direction for the purposes of subsection (1) above—

(*a*) may require the information concerned to be furnished within a time specified in the direction or within such further time as the Secretary of State may allow; and

(*b*) may be given to local authorities generally or to a particular authority or description of authority or in any particular case. **[295]**

GENERAL

This gives the Secretary of State power to monitor progress in each housing action area.

43. Acquisition of land in housing action areas

(1) Where a local authority have declared an area to be a housing action area then, for the purpose of securing or assisting in securing all or any of the objectives specified in paragraphs (*a*) to (*c*) of subsection (2) of section 36 above,—

(*a*) they may be authorised by the Secretary of State to acquire compulsorily any land in the area on which are situated premises which consist of or include housing accommodation; and

(*b*) to the extent that they could not do so apart from this subsection, they may acquire any such land by agreement.

(2) The Acquisition of Land (Authorisation Procedure) Act 1946 shall apply in relation to a compulsory acquisition of land under subsection (1) above as if that subsection were contained in an Act in force immediately before the commencement of that Act.

(3) If at any time after—

(*a*) a local authority have entered into a contract for the acquisition of land falling within subsection (1) above, or

(*b*) a compulsory purchase order authorising the acquisition of any such land has been confirmed,

the housing action area concerned ceases to be such an area or the land concerned is excluded from the area, the provisions of this section shall continue to apply as if the land continued to be in a housing action area.

(4) If, at any time after a compulsory purchase order authorising the acquisition of land falling within subsection (1) above has been made but before it is confirmed, the housing action area concerned ceases to be such an area by virtue of paragraph (*a*) of subsection (2) of section 53 below or the land concerned is excluded from the area by virtue of that paragraph, the provisions of this section shall continue to apply as if the land continued to be in a housing action area.

(5) Section 72 of the Housing Act 1964 (restriction on recovery of possession after making of compulsory purchase order) shall apply in relation to the compulsory acquisition of land under this section as if—

(*a*) the reference in that section to the Housing Act 1957 were a reference to this section; and

(*b*) the reference in that section to a house which is occupied by persons who do not form a single household were a reference to the land proposed to be acquired under this section.

(6) In subsection (2) of section 131 of the Local Government Act 1972 (enactments which relate to dealings in land by local authorities and which override the provisions of Part VII of that Act relating to land transactions) after paragraph (*j*) there shall be inserted the following paragraph:—

"(*jj*) section 43 of the Housing Act 1974".

(7) In this section "land" includes any estate or interest in land and "local authority" includes the Greater London Council and a county council. [**296**]

GENERAL

This gives the local authority certain powers to acquire land by agreement or compulsory purchase but it has to be land on which are situated premises which consist of, or include, housing accommodation. In view of the very wide powers local authorities already have under ss. 92, 96 and 97 of the Housing Act 1957 it is difficult to see why this new power is necessary, but it may prove useful. Land, with or without such premises as described above can be acquired under Part V of the Housing Act 1957 for the provision of accommodation in any of the several ways described in s. 92 of that Act.

Section 72 of the Housing Act 1964 is intended to protect occupants of houses in multiple occupation from eviction by owners until twelve months have elapsed since the making of the compulsory purchase order, or during the period between the making of the order and the Minister's refusal to confirm it, or its being quashed by a court.

As to the width of a local authority's powers of acquisition under s. 96 of the Housing Act 1957, see *H. E. Green & Sons* v. *Minister of Health*, [1948] 1 K.B. 34, [1947] 2 All E.R. 469, which relates to land already partially developed. Also see *Andresier* v. *Minister of Housing and Local Government* (1965), 109 Sol. Jo. 594. The latter case confirms that s. 96 of the 1957 Act enables a local authority to acquire houses with the object of improving them, notwithstanding the fact that no additional accommodation will result.

44. Provision, improvement etc., of housing accommodation by local authorities

(1) The provisions of this section apply to land in a housing action area—

(*a*) on which are situated premises which consist of or include housing accommodation; and

(*b*) which was acquired (by agreement or compulsorily) by the local authority and for the purpose specified in section 43 (1) above; and

(*c*) which was so acquired after the date on which the housing action area was declared.

(2) Subject to section 105 of this Act, the local authority referred to in subsection (1) above may, for the purpose specified in section 43 (1) above, undertake on land to which this section applies all or any of the following activities—

(*a*) the provision of housing accommodation, by the construction, conversion or improvement of buildings or otherwise;

(*b*) the carrying out of works required for the improvement or repair of housing accommodation, including works to the exterior, or on land within the curtilage, of buildings containing housing accommodation;

(*c*) the management of housing accommodation; and

(*d*) the provision of furniture, fittings or services in or in relation to housing accommodation. **[297]**

GENERAL

The powers given under this section for dealing with land in a housing action do not appear to differ materially from the powers of a local authority under ss. 92, 94, 96 and 111 of the Housing Act 1957. Section 105 of this Act gives the Secretary of State control over expenditure under this Act on the provision and improvement of houses by housing authorities. It may be that the desire to establish more control is the reason for not relying on the provisicns of the Housing Act 1957. Nevertheless this seems to be unnecessary duplication.

45. Assistance for carrying out environmental works

(1) For the purpose of effecting or assisting the improvement of living conditions in a housing action area, the local authority may, in accordance with the following provisions of this section, give assistance towards the carrying out of works (in this section referred to as "environmental works")—

(*a*) to the exterior, or on land within the curtilage, of buildings containing housing accommodation, not being works in respect of which an application for a grant under Part VII of this Act has been approved; or

(*b*) on land not falling within paragraph (*a*) above for the purpose of improving the amenities of the area.

(2) Subject to subsection (3) below, assistance under subsection (1) above may be given to any person having an interest in the building or land concerned and shall consist of all or any of the following, namely—

(*a*) a grant in respect of expenditure which appears to the local authority to have been properly incurred in the carrying out of environmental works;

(*b*) the provision of materials for the carrying out of environmental works; and

(*c*) by agreement with the person concerned, the execution of environmental works at his expense, at the expense of the local authority, or partly, at his expense and partly at the expense of the local authority.

(3) No assistance may be given under subsection (1) above in respect of a building or land in which the local authority have such a freehold or leasehold interest as would enable the authority themselves to carry out environmental works in relation thereto.

(4) A grant under subsection (2) (*a*) above may be paid after the completion of the works towards the cost of which it is payable or part of it may be paid in instalments as the works progress and the balance after the completion of the works; and where part of any such grant is paid in instalments the aggregate of the instalments paid shall not at any time before the completion of the works exceed one-half of the aggregate cost of the works executed up to that time. [298]

GENERAL

This enables a local authority to improve the amenities and environment within a housing action area. They can assist by making grants for environmental works, executing such works themselves, or providing materials, by arrangement with any person having an interest in the land. The scope of the works was enlarged by the addition of (*b*) to sub-s. (1) during the passage of the Bill. There is a comparable power to incur expense on works to improve the environment in "general improvement areas" contained in s. 32 of the Housing Act 1969.

46. Contributions towards expenditure under section 45

(1) Subject to the following provisions of this section, the Secretary of State may pay contributions to local authorities in respect of expenditure incurred or to be incurred by them in giving assistance under section 45 (1) above.

(2) No contribution shall be paid to a local authority under subsection (1) above unless an application therefor is made by the authority and approved by the Secretary of State; and any such application—

(*a*) shall be in such form and contain such information as the Secretary of State may from time to time determine; and

(*b*) may be made before the expenditure concerned is incurred by the local authority.

(3) Subject to subsection (4) below, the amount of any contribution under subsection (1) above shall be 50 per cent. of the expenditure incurred or to be incurred by the local authority concerned in giving assistance under section 45 (1) above.

(4) The aggregate amount of the expenditure in respect of which applications for contributions may be approved under this section shall not exceed the sum

arrived at by multiplying £50 by the aggregate of the number of dwellings, houses in multiple occupation and hostels stated by the local authority, in accordance with section 36 (4) (*c*) above, to be in the area.

(5) A contribution under subsection (1) above shall be payable in a single sum in the financial year in which are completed the external works to which the local authority's expenditure relates.

(6) The Secretary of State may by order made with the consent of the Treasury vary the sum of £50 specified in subsection (4) above and any such variation—

(*a*) may be made generally or by reference to housing action areas declared by any particular authority or description of authority or by reference to any particular housing action area or description of housing action area; and

(*b*) shall have effect with respect to applications for contributions under subsection (1) above approved after such date as may be specified in the order.

(7) A statutory instrument containing an order under subsection (6) above shall be subject to annulment in pursuance of a resolution of the Commons House of Parliament. **[299]**

GENERAL

Contributions may be paid by the Secretary of State towards expenditure by local authorities in giving assistance for the carrying out of environmental works. Normally his contribution will be 50 per cent. of the local authority's expenditure but his maximum contribution is limited to 50 per cent. of an aggregate amount of expenditure calculated by multiplying £50 by the number of dwellings, houses in multiple occupation and hostels stated to be in the area when it was declared.

The Secretary of State has power to vary the unit figure of £50 and may fix differing amounts for different areas, and for different types of local authority.

This may be compared with the provisions of s. 37 of the Housing Act 1969 which relates to environmental works in general improvement areas. See also s. 51 of this Act and Sch. 5.

DEFINITIONS

"Dwelling"—see s. 129
"Hostel"—see s. 129
"Local authority"—see s. 49
"Multiple occupation"—see s. 129

47. Notification of notices to quit and disposals of housing accommodation etc.

(1) Within the period of 7 days beginning with the day on which a notice to quit is served—

(*a*) in respect of land consisting of or including housing accommodation in a housing action area, and

(*b*) on a tenant who occupies as a dwelling the whole or any part of that land,

the landlord by or on whose behalf the notice is served shall notify the local authority in accordance with Schedule 4 to this Act, that the notice has been served.

(2) Not less than 4 weeks before the expiry by effluxion of time of any tenancy—

(*a*) which is a tenancy of land consisting of or including housing accommodation in a housing action area, and (*b*) which expires without the service of any notice to quit,

the person who is the landlord under that tenancy shall notify the local authority, in accordance with Schedule 4 to this Act, that the tenancy is about to expire.

(3) Not less than 4 weeks and not more than 6 months before the date on which a person carries out a disposal of land to which this section applies, he shall notify the local authority, in accordance with Schedule 4 to this Act, that the disposal is to take place; and for the purposes of this section a person carries out a disposal of land if he conveys or enters into a contract to convey a legal estate or interest in the land, whether or not that estate or interest is in existence immediately before the date of the conveyance or contract.

(4) Nothing in the preceding provisions of this section shall impose an obligation on any person to notify a local authority of any matter if, apart from this subsection, the obligation would require him to notify the authority at some time before the expiry of the period of 4 weeks beginning with the date on which the housing action area concerned is declared.

(5) A local authority who receive a notification given in compliance with any provision of subsections (1) to (3) above shall,—

(*a*) as soon as practicable after the notification is received, send to the person by whom it was furnished a written acknowledgement of its receipt, stating the day on which it was received; and
(*b*) within the period of 4 weeks beginning with the day on which the notification was received, inform the person by whom it was furnished what action, if any, they propose to take as a result of the notification with respect to the land to which the notification relates.

(6) This section applies to a disposal of land consisting of or including housing accommodation in a housing action area, other than a disposal—

(*a*) by a person who, throughout the period of 6 months ending on the date of the disposal, has been continuously in exclusive occupation (with or without members of his household) of the land to which the disposal relates; or
(*b*) to which the local authority are a party; or
(*c*) consisting of the grant of a protected tenancy, within the meaning of the Rent Act 1968, or of a contract to which Part VI of that Act applies; or
(*d*) consisting of the grant or assignment of a lease (of land or of an interest in land) for a term which expires within the period of 5 years and 3 months beginning on the date of the grant of the lease, where neither the lease nor any other instrument or contract confers on the lessor or the lessee an option (however expressed) to renew or extend the term so that the new term or the extended term would continue beyond the end of that period of 5 years and 3 months; or
(*e*) consisting of the grant of an estate or interest by way of security for a loan; or
(*f*) consisting of the conveyance of an estate or interest where the conveyance gives effect to a contract to convey that estate or interest and the proposal to enter into that contract was notified to the local authority in accordance with subsection (3) above.

(7) Any person who—

(*a*) without reasonable excuse fails to comply with an obligation imposed on him by subsection (1) or subsection (2) above, or

(*b*) without reasonable excuse carries out a disposal of land to which this section applies without having complied with the obligation imposed on him by subsection (3) above, or

(*c*) knowingly or recklessly furnishes a notification which is false in a material particular in purported compliance with any provision of this section, or

(*d*) knowingly or recklessly omits from any such notification any information which is required to be contained therein by virtue of any provision of Schedule 4 to this Act,

shall be guilty of an offence and liable on summary conviction to a fine not exceeding £400.

(8) Where an offence under subsection (7) above which has been committed by a body corporate is proved to have been committed with the consent or connivance of, or to be attributable to any neglect on the part of, a director, manager, secretary or other similar officer of the body corporate, or any person who was purporting to act in any such capacity, he as well as the body corporate shall be guilty of that offence and be liable to be proceeded against and punished accordingly.

(9) Where the affairs of a body corporate are managed by its members, subsection (8) above shall apply in relation to the acts and defaults of a member in connection with his functions of management as if he were a director of the body corporate.

(10) The conviction of any person for an offence under subsection (7) above shall not affect the date on which any tenancy expires (whether by virtue of a notice to quit or otherwise) or the validity of any disposal of land. [**300**]

GENERAL

See Notes in Chapter 4 above on this section.

48. Application of certain provisions of Housing Acts

(1) The following provisions of the Housing Act 1957,—

(*a*) section 159 (power of entry for inspection, etc.),

(*b*) section 160 (penalty for obstructing execution of Act),

(*c*) section 169 (service of notices, etc., on persons other than local authorities), and

(*d*) section 170 (power of local authority to require information as to ownership of premises),

shall apply, subject to subsection (2) below, as if references therein to the Housing Act 1957 included references to this Part of this Act.

(2) In its application, by virtue of subsection (1) above, in relation to this Part of this Act, section 170 of the Housing Act 1957 shall have effect with the insertion after the words "in respect of any premises" of the words "within such period of not less than fourteen days from the date on which the requirement is made as may be specified by the authority" and after the words "that information" of the words "within the period so specified".

(3) In section 70 of the Housing Act 1969 (review of housing conditions by

local authorities with a view to exercising certain statutory functions) for the words "or Part II of this Act" there shall be substituted the words "Part II of this Act or Part IV of the Housing Act 1974". [**301**]

GENERAL

Local authorities are given the necessary powers of entry, and other provisions of the Housing Act 1957 as to notices, requirement of information, and so on are extended to this Part of this Act.

The provisions of s. 70 of the Housing Act 1969 as to reviews of housing conditions by local authorities are extended to this Part of the Act. This places a duty on local authorities to carry out inspections from time to time, and gives the Secretary of State certain powers to ensure that the duty is carried out. As to powers of entry for inspection see *Bedingfield* v. *Jones* (1959), 124 J.P. 11, D.C.

49. Local authorities for the purposes of Part IV

(1) Subject to subsection (2) below, the local authorities for the purposes of this Part of this Act are the councils of districts and London boroughs and the Common Council of the City of London.

(2) The Greater London Council may exercise the powers of a local authority under subsections (1) to (3) of section 36 above with respect to any area in Greater London, but only with the agreement of any local authority in whose district the area or any part of the area is situated; and in relation to, and to any premises in, any area which, in accordance with this subsection, has been declared a housing action area by the Greater London Council, any reference to a local authority in—

- (*a*) section 36 (4) and sections 37 to 42 and 45 to 47 above, or
- (*b*) the provisions of the Housing Act 1957 applied in relation to this Part of this Act by section 48 (1) above, or
- (*c*) Part III of the Housing Finance Act 1972 (rent of dwellings in good repair and provided with standard amenities),

shall be construed, except in so far as the context otherwise requires, as a reference to the Greater London Council, to the exclusion of any other council.

(3) Without prejudice to subsection (2) above, in relation to any premises in a housing action area which, in accordance with that subsection, has been declared by the Greater London Council—

- (*a*) the Greater London Council may exercise the functions of a local authority under Part II or Part IV of the Housing Act 1957, Part II of the Housing Act 1961, Part IV of the Housing Act 1964 or Part IV of the Housing Act 1969, and
- (*b*) any functions exercisable under the enactments referred to in paragraph (*a*) above by the council of a London borough or the Common Council of the City of London shall be so exercisable only after consultation with the Greater London Council. [**302**]

GENERAL

This is simple so far as councils outside Greater London are concerned. In London the local authority will normally be the London borough councils and the Common Council of the City of London. The Greater London Council may exercise the powers of a local authority but only with the consent of the London borough councils concerned.

Under the Bill as drafted it was proposed that the Greater London Council should have concurrent powers with a London borough council and should be able to initiate and deal with housing action areas either with the consent of the London borough concerned, or with the authority of the Secretary of State, but these clauses were amended.

PART V
GENERAL IMPROVEMENT AREAS

50. Consideration by Secretary of State of suitability of general improvement areas

(1) With a view to affording to the Secretary of State an opportunity to consider in advance the suitability of an area as a general improvement area and, where appropriate, to prevent an area which appears to him to be inappropriate to be declared a general improvement area, for section 28 of the Housing Act 1969 there shall be substituted the sections set out in Part I of Schedule 5 to this Act.

(2) In any case where, on or after 12th June 1973 and before the coming into operation of this section, a local authority have,

(*a*) by resolution under section 28 (1) of the Housing Act 1969, declared an area to be a general improvement area, or

(*b*) by resolution under section 30 (2) of that Act, included any land in an existing general improvement area,

the Secretary of State may, if it appears to him appropriate to do so, at any time within the relevant period serve notice on the authority terminating the status of the area as a general improvement area or, as the case may be, excluding the land from the general improvement area in question, with effect from the date on which the notice is served.

(3) In subsection (2) above ,'the relevant period", in relation to a general improvement area or land included in such an area as mentioned in paragraph (*b*) of that subsection, means the period of 42 days beginning on the day appointed for the coming into operation of this section or, if it is later, the day on which the Secretary of State receives, by virtue of any provision of the Housing Act 1969, a copy of the resolution declaring the area referred to in subsection (2) (*a*) above to be a general improvement area or, as the case may be, including the land referred to in subsection (2) (*b*) above in a general improvement area.

(4) As soon as may be after notice has been served on a local authority under subsection (2) above, they shall—

(*a*) publish in two or more newspapers circulating in the locality (of which one at least shall, if practicable, be a local newspaper) a notice identifying the general improvement area concerned and either stating that its status as such an area has been terminated by the Secretary of State and the date on which it was so terminated or, as the case may be, identifying the land excluded from the general improvement area and stating the date on which it was so excluded; and

(*b*) take such further steps as may appear to them best designed to secure that the termination of the general improvement area or, as the case may be, the exclusion of the land from a general improvement area is brought to the attention of persons residing or owning property in the area or, as the case may be, on that land. **[303]**

GENERAL

The Secretary of State is given greater control over the declaration of general improvement areas under the Housing Act 1969. Section 28 of that Act is replaced by new ss. 28 and 28A as set out in Part I of Sch. 5 of this Act.

Transitional powers are given in s. 50 (2), (3) and (4).

The new sections referred to above break the initial process down into two parts. There will, in future, have to be a "preliminary resolution" and, later, if no difficulties arise, a "confirmatory resolution". The local authority must send a copy of the preliminary resolution, with plans and other documents, as listed in the new s. 28 of the

1969 Act within 6 months, to the Secretary of State. He will follow the procedure set out in sub-ss. (4) and (5) of the new s. 28 of the 1969 Act but the local authority cannot pass a confirmatory resolution or proceed to implement the scheme without the approval of the Secretary of State.

51. Further amendments relating to general improvement areas

The provisions of Part II of the Housing Act 1969 (general improvement areas) shall be amended in accordance with Part II of Schedule 5 to this Act. **[304]**

GENERAL

This section and Sch. 5 makes further amendments to the Housing Act 1969. It is made clear that a general improvement area may surround, but may not include, a housing action area. There is an interesting parallel with s. 29 of the Housing Act 1969 which lays down a similar rule that a general improvement area may surround but not include land in a clearance area unless the land has been cleared of buildings. By the same section a clearance area may not include any land in a general improvement area. Where the Minister has not yet confirmed a clearance order he may exclude land from it as being more suitable for inclusion in a general improvement area.

See *Annicola Investments, Ltd.* v. *Minister of Housing and Local Government*, [1968] 1 Q.B. 631; [1965] 3 All E.R. 850.

See also s. 108 as to the future of clearance orders.

PART VI

PRIORITY NEIGHBOURHOODS

52. Declaration of priority neighbourhoods

(1) Where a report with respect to an area which consists primarily of housing accommodation and which, in accordance with subsection (2) below, is appropriate to be declared a priority neighbourhood, is submitted to the local authority within whose district the area lies by a person or persons appearing to the authority to be suitably qualified (whether or not that person is or those persons include an officer of the authority) and, upon consideration of the report and of any other information in their possession, the authority are satisfied that, having regard to—

(*a*) the physical state of the housing accommodation in the area as a whole, and

(*b*) social conditions in the area,

the requirements in subsection (3) below are fulfilled with respect to the area, the authority may cause the area to be defined on a map and by resolution declare it to be a priority neighbourhood.

(2) For the purposes of this section, an area is appropriate to be declared a priority neighbourhood if, immediately before the declaration, it surrounds, or has a common boundary with,—

(*a*) a housing action area other than an area in respect of which the Secretary of State has notified the local authority as mentioned in subsection (2) (*c*) of section 37 above and has not yet sent a further notification under subsection (4) of that section; or

(*b*) a general improvement area in respect of which a confirmatory resolution, within the meaning of section 28 of the Housing Act 1969, has been passed.

(3) The requirements referred to in subsection (1) above are—

(*a*) that the living conditions in the area are unsatisfactory;

(*b*) that it is not, at the date of the resolution, practicable for the local authority to declare the area or any part of it to be a housing action area or a general improvement area or to declare as a housing action area or a general improvement area an area which includes any part of the proposed priority neighbourhood; and

(*c*) that it is necessary to secure in the area all or any of the objectives specified in paragraphs (*a*) to (*c*) of section 36 (2) above and that that need can best be met by declaring the area to be a priority neighbourhood.

(4) In considering whether to take action under subsection (1) above with respect to any area, a local authority shall have regard to such guidance as may from time to time be given by the Secretary of State, either generally or with respect to a particular authority or description of authority or in any particular case, with regard to the identification of areas suitable to be declared as priority neighbourhoods.

(5) As soon as may be after passing a resolution declaring an area to be a priority neighbourhood, a local authority shall—

(*a*) publish in two or more newspapers circulating in the locality (of which at least one shall, if practicable, be a local newspaper) a notice of the resolution identifying the priority neighbourhood and naming a place or places where a copy of the resolution, of the map on which the neighbourhood is defined and of the report referred to in subsection (1) above may be inspected at all reasonable times;

(*b*) take such further steps as may appear to them best designed to secure that the resolution is brought to the attention of persons residing or owning property in the priority neighbourhood and that those persons are informed of the name and address of the person to whom any inquiries and representations concerning any action to be taken with respect to the neighbourhood should be addressed; and

(*c*) send to the Secretary of State a copy of the resolution, the map and a copy of the report mentioned in paragraph (*a*) above and a statement containing such information as the Secretary of State may for the time being require, either generally or with respect to a particular authority or description of authority or in any particular case, to show the basis on which the local authority satisfied themselves that the area concerned was suitable to be declared a priority neighbourhood, having regard to the matters specified in paragraphs (*a*) and (*b*) of subsection (1) above and any relevant guidance given under subsection (4) above.

(6) As soon as may be after a resolution has been passed declaring an area to be a priority neighbourhood, the resolution shall be registered in the register of local land charges—

(*a*) by the proper officer, for the purposes of section 15 of the Land Charges Act 1925, of the local authority in whose area the priority neighbourhood is situated; and

(*b*) in such manner as may be prescribed by rules under section 19 of that Act.

(7) Section 37 above shall apply in relation to the declaration of a priority neighbourhood with the substitution—

(*a*) for any reference to a housing action area of a reference to a priority neighbourhood; and (*b*) for any reference to section 36 (4) (*c*) above of a reference to subsection (5) (*c*) of this section.

(8) In this section "housing accommodation" means dwellings, houses in multiple occupation and hostels. **[305]**

GENERAL

The wording of this section is similar to that of s. 36 except for the changes which arise from the fact that a priority neighbourhood is one which would have been dealt with as a housing action area, or general improvement area, had it been practicable to do so. See Chapters 4 and 6 above, and the Notes in this Appendix on ss. 36 to 49.

When considering whether to take action under sub-s. (1), a local authority is required to have regard to such guidance as may be issued from time to time by the Secretary of State.

The requirements as to publicity, and registration in the register of local land charges are similar to those in Part IV. The proposals will be submitted to the Secretary of State who will follow the same procedure as is adopted in respect of a housing action area (s. 37).

The resolution declaring the priority neighbourhood must be registered in the register of local land charges.

DEFINITIONS

"Local authority"—see s. 55

53. Incorporation into priority neighbourhoods of general improvement areas, housing action areas, or parts thereof

(1) If a local authority propose, by a resolution under section 52 above, to declare as a priority neighbourhood an area which consists of or includes land which, immediately prior to the declaration, is comprised—

(*a*) in a housing action area declared under section 36 above, or

(*b*) in a general improvement area declared under Part II of the Housing Act 1969,

they shall indicate on the map referred to in section 52 above the land which is so comprised (in this section referred to as "the relevant land").

(2) Subject to the following provisions of this section, with effect from the date on which such a resolution as is referred to in subsection (1) above is passed, the relevant land shall be deemed (according to its status) either—

(*a*) to have ceased to be a housing action area by virtue of a resolution passed on that date under section 39 (3) above or, as the case may be, to have been excluded from the housing action area by virtue of a resolution passed on that date under section 40 (1) above; or

(*b*) to have ceased to be a general improvement area or, as the case may be, to have been excluded from the general improvement area by virtue of a resolution under section 30 (1) of the Housing Act 1969 passed on that date and approved by the Secretary of State.

(3) If the Secretary of State notifies the local authority concerned under section 37 above, as that section applies in relation to priority neighbourhoods by virtue of section 52 (7) above, that the area declared by them to be a priority neighbourhood is no longer to be such an area, subsection (2) above shall be treated as never having applied in relation to the relevant land.

(4) If the Secretary of State notifies the local authority concerned under section 37 above, as that section applies in relation to priority neighbourhoods by virtue of section 52 (7) above, that any land which—

(*a*) is within the area declared by the authority to be a priority neighbourhood, and
(*b*) consists of or includes any of the relevant land,

is to be excluded from the priority neighbourhood, subsection (2) above shall be treated as never having applied in relation to so much of the relevant land as is comprised in the land. **[306]**

GENERAL

The objects of this section are obvious. Presumably such steps will be taken where the local authority finds that, because its resources are insufficient, or for other reasons, it is unable to deal with the area so urgently as it would wish, but wishes to safeguard the area. However, if the Secretary of State decides that the area is not to be a priority neighbourhood, it will revert to its former status as a housing action area, or general improvement area, or part thereof.

54. Application to priority neighbourhoods of certain provisions of Part IV

(1) Subject to the provisions of this section, the following provisions of Part IV of this Act shall apply in relation to a priority neighbourhood as they apply in relation to a housing action area, namely—

(*a*) section 39 (duration of housing action areas);
(*b*) section 40 (reduction of housing action areas);
(*c*) section 42 (duty to inform Secretary of State of action taken);
(*d*) section 43 (acquisition of land in housing action areas);
(*e*) section 44 (provision, improvement etc. of housing accommodation by local authorities);
(*f*) section 47 (notification of notices to quit and disposals of housing accommodation etc.); and
(*g*) section 48 (application of certain provisions of Housing Acts).

(2) In the application, by virtue of subsection (1) above, of the provisions of Part IV of this Act specified in that subsection—

(*a*) for any reference in those provisions to a housing action area there shall be substituted a reference to a priority neighbourhood; and
(*b*) any reference in any of those provisions to any other provision of Part IV of this Act shall be construed as a reference to that other provision as it applies in relation to priority neighbourhoods.

(3) Without prejudice to subsection (2) above, in the application, by virtue of subsection (1) above, of section 39 above—

(*a*) for the reference in subsection (1) of that section to section 36 (1) above there shall be substituted a reference to section 52 (1) above; and
(*b*) for any reference in subsection (2) or subsection (5) of that section to 2 years there shall be substituted a reference to 5 years.

(4) A local authority may not exercise the power conferred by section 40 above, as applied by virtue of subsection (1) above, in relation to a priority neighbourhood unless the land which would be left in the priority neighbourhood after the exclusion of the land in question—

(*a*) would then constitute an area which, having regard to subsection (2) of section 52 above, would be appropriate to be declared a priority neighbourhood; or (*b*) would then surround or have a common boundary with an area which, immediately before the priority neighbourhood was declared, constituted or formed part of a housing action area or a general improvement area; or

(*c*) would then consist of or include land which, immediately before the priority neighbourhood was declared, formed part of a housing action area or a general improvement area.

(5) In the application, by virtue of subsection (1) above, of section 43 above, in subsection (4) of that section for the words "paragraph (*a*) of subsection (2) of section 53 below" there shall be substituted the words "paragraph (*b*) of subsection (2) of section 38 above". **[307]**

GENERAL

This section provides the machinery for dealing with priority neighbourhoods on much the same lines as housing action areas. Whereas a housing action area can have its life extended from 5 years to a maximum of 7 years, the life of a priority neighbourhood can be extended from 5 years to a maximum of 10 years.

55. Local authorities for the purposes of Part VI

(1) Subject to subsection (2) below, the local authorities for the purposes of this Part of this Act are the councils of districts and London boroughs and the Common Council of the City of London.

(2) The Greater London Council may exercise the powers of a local authority under subsections (1) to (4) of section 52 above with respect to any area in Greater London, but only with the agreement of any local authority in whose district the area or any part of the area is situated.

(3) In relation to, and to any premises in, an area which, in accordance with subsection (2) above, has been declared a priority neighbourhood by the Greater London Council, any reference to a local authority in—

(*a*) sections 52 (5), 53 and 54 above, or

(*b*) any provision of Part IV of this Act specified in section 52 (7) or section 54 above, as that provision has effect by virtue of either of those sections, or

(*c*) the provisions of the Housing Act 1957 applied in relation to priority neighbourhoods by section 48 (1) above, as that section has effect by virtue of section 54 (1) (*g*) above,

shall be construed, except in so far as the context otherwise requires, as a reference to the Greater London Council, to the exclusion of any other council. **[308]**

GENERAL

This needs little comment. As in the case of general improvement areas and housing action areas, the Greater London Council may take action as if it were a local authority for the purposes of Part VI, but it may do so only with the agreement of the London borough council concerned. Where the Greater London Council is dealing with a priority neighbourhood its powers under other housing legislation will be increased, and those of the local London borough council modified, as indicated in sub-s. (3).

Part VII

Financial Assistance Towards Works of Improvement, Repair and Conversion

Grants by local authorities

56. Grants for provision, improvement and repair of dwellings

(1) Grants of the descriptions specified in subsection (2) below shall be payable

by local authorities in accordance with the following provisions of this Part of this Act towards the cost of works required for—

(*a*) the provision of dwellings by the conversion of houses or other buildings,
(*b*) the improvement of dwellings,
(*c*) the repair of dwellings, and
(*d*) the improvement of houses in multiple occupation by the provision of standard amenities,

where the provision, improvement or repair is by a person other than a housing authority.

(2) The grants referred to in subsection (1) above are—

(*a*) an "improvement grant" in respect of works required for the provision of a dwelling (as mentioned in paragraph (*a*) of that subsection) or for the improvement of a dwelling or, in the case of a registered disabled person, works required for his welfare, accommodation or employment where the existing dwelling is inadequate or unsuitable for those purposes, not being works falling entirely within paragraph (*b*) below;
(*b*) an "intermediate grant" in respect of works required for the improvement of a dwelling by the provision of standard amenities which it lacks or which in the case of a registered disabled person are inaccessible to that person by virtue of his disability;
(*c*) a "special grant" in respect of works required for the improvement of a house in multiple occupation by the provision of standard amenities; and
(*d*) a "repairs grant" in respect of works of repair or replacement relating to a dwelling in a housing action area or a general improvement area, not being works associated with other works required for the provision (as mentioned in subsection (1) (*a*) above) or improvement of the dwelling.

(3) Except in a case where a local authority exercise their power under subsection (4) below, they shall not entertain—

(*a*) an application for an improvement grant in respect of works required for the provision of a dwelling by the conversion of a house or other building which was erected after 2nd October 1961; or
(*b*) an application for any grant for the improvement or repair of a dwelling which was provided after that date.

(4) Notwithstanding the prohibition in subsection (3) above, but subject to such general or special directions as may from time to time be given by the Secretary of State, where an application is made which falls within paragraph (*a*) or paragraph (*b*) of that subsection, the local authority to whom it is made may entertain the application if they consider it appropriate to do so. **[309]**

GENERAL

The pattern of grants under Part VI is discussed in general terms in Chapter 7, and they are summarised in Table 1 on p. 28. They replace the grant provisions in Part I of the Housing Act 1969. Normally applications for improvement grant are not to be entertained where they involve the conversion of a house or other building erected after 2nd October 1961, or the improvement or repair of a dwelling provided after that date; but see sub-s. (4). This same date limit formerly applied to standard grants under s. 8 of the Housing Act 1969—now repealed.

Grants under this section are not payable where the provision, improvement or repair is by a "housing authority" as defined in s. 84. This definition does not include housing associations, who could presumably qualify for grants under this Part of the Act. The grant system has been enlarged to take account of the needs of disabled persons. See Circular 160/74 in Appendix II.

DEFINITIONS
"Dwelling"—see s. 129
"Housing authority"—see s. 84
"Improvement"—see s. 84
"Local authority"—see s. 84
See also Notes to s. 69 below

57. General provisions relating to applications for grants

(1) No grant shall be paid by a local authority unless an application therefor is made to the authority in accordance with the provisions of this Part of this Act.

(2) An application for a grant shall—

(*a*) specify the premises to which the application relates;

(*b*) contain particulars of the works in respect of which the grant is sought (in this Part of this Act referred to as "the relevant works") and an estimate of their cost; and

(*c*) contain such other particulars as may for the time being be specified by the Secretary of State.

(3) Subject to section 83 below, a local authority shall not entertain an application for a grant unless they are satisfied that the applicant has, in every parcel of land on which the relevant works are to be or have have been carried out, an interest which is either an estate in fee simple absolute in possession or a term of years absolute of which not less than 5 years remain unexpired at the date of the application.

(4) If the Secretary of State has given directions for the purposes of this subsection, either to local authorities generally or to a particular local authority, applying to any application for an improvement grant or an intermediate grant which is of a description specified in the directions, a local authority affected by the directions shall not approve an application to which they apply except with the consent of the Secretary of State; and any such consent may be given generally or with respect to a particular authority or with respect to a particular description of application.

(5) A local authority may not approve an application for a grant if the relevant works have been begun unless they are satisfied that there were good reasons for beginning those works before the application was approved.

(6) Except in so far as this Act otherwise provides, a local authority may not entertain an application for a grant if the relevant works are or include—

(*a*) works which were the relevant works in relation to an application which has previously been approved under this Part of this Act; or

(*b*) works which were specified in an application for a grant under Part I of the Housing Act 1969 which was approved,

and the applicant for the grant is, or is the personal representative of, the person who made the earlier application.

(7) If, after an application for a grant has been approved by a local authority, the authority are satisfied that owing to circumstances beyond the control of the applicant the relevant works will not be carried out on the basis of the estimate contained in the application, they may, on receiving a further estimate, redetermine the estimated expense in relation to the grant and make such other

adjustments relating to the amount of the grant as appear to them to be appropriate, but the amount of a grant shall not be increased by virtue of this subsection beyond the amount which could have been notified as the amount of the grant when the application was approved if the estimate contained in the application had been for the same amount as the further estimate. **[310]**

GENERAL

The condition as to the nature of the estate or interest which must be held by the applicant is similar to that laid down in s. 28 of the Housing Act 1969.

The local authority must not approve an application where the works have already begun unless they are satisfied that there were good reasons for this.

There is provision for revising the original estimate of cost submitted with the application (sub-s. (7)).

The Secretary of State has wide powers to issue directions as to conditions to be observed in relation to improvement grants and intermediate grants. See Circular 160/74 in Appendix II.

DEFINITIONS

See s. 84

58. Standard amenities

(1) Subject to subsection (2) below, the "standard amenities" for the purposes of this Part of this Act are the amenities which are described in the first column of Part I of Schedule 6 to this Act and which conform to such of the provisions of Part II of that Schedule as are applicable.

(2) The Secretary of State may by order vary the provisions of Schedule 6 to this Act and any such order may contain such transitional or other supplemental provisions as appear to the Secretary of State to be expedient. **[311]**

GENERAL

This section should be read with ss. 65 to 68 which deal with "intermediate grants", formerly known as "standard grants" payable for the provision of these amenities. The wording of Part 1 of Sch. 6 is almost identical with the wording of Part 1 of Sch. 1 of the Housing Act 1969, but the cash values have been increased.

59. Appropriate percentage

(1) In this Part of this Act "the appropriate percentage" (which is relevant for determining the amount, or the maximum amount, of any grant) shall be determined according to whether, on the date on which the application for the grant concerned is approved, the premises to which the application relates are in a housing action area, a general improvement area or neither and, subject to the following provisions of this section, the appropriate percentage is—

(*a*) in a case where those premises are on that date in a housing action area, 75 per cent.;

(*b*) in a case where those premises are on that date in a general improvement area, 60 per cent.; and

(*c*) in any other case, 50 per cent.

(2) If, in the case of premises which are in a housing action area on the date on which the application for the grant concerned is approved, it appears to the local authority by whom the application is approved that the applicant will not without undue hardship be able to finance the cost of so much of the relevant works as is not met by the grant, they may treat the appropriate percentage as increased to such percentage not exceeding 90 per cent. as they think fit.

(3) If, at any time after an application for a grant has been approved but before the relevant works have been begun, an area which includes the land on

which the premises concerned are situated is declared to be a housing action area or a general improvement area, the local authority by whom the application was approved shall allow the application to be withdrawn with a view to enabling the applicant to make a further application for a grant.

(4) The Secretary of State may by order made with the consent of the Treasury vary all or any of the percentages specified in subsections (1) and (2) above, and any such variation shall have effect with respect to applications for grants approved after such date as may be specified in the order.

(5) An order under subsection (4) above—

(*a*) shall not be made unless a draft thereof has been approved by a resolution of the Commons House of Parliament; and

(*b*) shall not specify a date earlier than the date of the laying of the draft. **[312]**

GENERAL

The percentages laid down in this section are applicable to all the four grants named in s. 56 and vary according to the type of area in which the house is situated. The object of having varying percentages is to give the highest degree of encouragement to improving living conditions in housing action areas, the next priority being work in general improvement areas, and the lowest priority being work outside those areas. Even here, however, grant is at the rate of 50 per cent., and may possibly be increased if the house is later included in a housing action area or a general improvement area. However, repairs grants are not applicable to properties outside housing action areas and general improvement areas.

By sub-s. 2 the local authority is given power to raise the percentage up to a maximum of 90 per cent. in a housing action area, on the grounds of hardship. They already have power to lend the balance of an owner's costs after allowing for whatever grant he has received—see, *inter alia*, s. 74 of the Housing Act 1969.

The Secretary of State has power, by order, to vary the percentages—see Table 1 on p. 28. See Circular 160/74 in Appendix II.

60. Certificates of future occupation

(1) Subject to section 83 below, a local authority shall not entertain an application for a grant other than a special grant unless the application is accompanied by a certificate under this section as to future occupation of the dwelling or, as the case may be, each of the dwellings for the provision, improvement or repair of which the grant is sought.

(2) A certificate of future occupation shall be either a certificate of owner-occupation under subsection (3) or subsection (4) below or a certificate of availability for letting under subsection (5) below.

(3) Subject to subsection (4) below, for the purposes of this Part of this Act a "certificate of owner-occupation" is a certificate stating that the applicant for the grant intends that, on or before the first anniversary of the certified date and throughout the period of 4 years beginning on that first anniversary, the dwelling will be his only or main residence and will be occupied exclusively by himself and members of his household (if any).

(4) For the purposes of this Part of this Act, in a case where an application for a grant is made by the personal representatives of a deceased person or by trustees, a "certificate of owner-occupation" is a certificate stating that the applicants are personal representatives or trustees and intend that, on or before the first anniversary of the certified date and throughout the period of 4 years beginning on that first anniversary, the dwelling will be the only or main residence of, and exclusively occupied by, a person who, under the will or intestacy or, as the case may require, under the terms of the trust, is beneficially entitled

to an interest in the dwelling or the proceeds of sale thereof and members of his household (if any).

(5) For the purposes of this Part of this Act a "certificate of availability for letting" is a certificate stating that the applicant for the grant intends that, throughout the period of 5 years beginning with the certified date,—

(*a*) the dwelling will be let or available for letting as a residence, and not for a holiday, to a person other than a member of the applicant's family; or

(*b*) the dwelling will be occupied or available for occupation by a member of the agricultural population in pursuance of a contract of service and otherwise than as a tenant. **[313]**

GENERAL

This marks a return to the idea of restrictions on sale and letting contained in earlier Acts dealing with improvements, but abolished in 1969. The local authority cannot entertain an application for grant (other than special grant) unless it is accompanied either by a "certificate of owner-occupation" or a "certificate of availability for letting". This is more fully discussed under ss. 73 to 77 below. See Circular 160/74 in Appendix II.

DEFINITIONS

"agricultural population"—see s. 84
"Certified date"—see s. 75 (6)
"Local authority"—see s. 84

Improvement grants

61. Improvement grants

(1) A local authority shall pay an improvement grant if—

(*a*) an application for such a grant, made in accordance with this Part of this Act, is approved by them, and

(*b*) the conditions for the payment of the grant are fulfilled,

and, subject to the provisions of this Part of this Act, a local authority may approve an application for an improvement grant in such circumstances as they think fit.

(2) A local authority shall not approve an application for an improvement grant unless they are satisfied that, on completion of the relevant works, the dwelling or, as the case may be, each of the dwellings to which the application relates will attain the required standard.

(3) For the purposes of this section a dwelling shall be taken, subject to subsections (4) and (5) below, to attain the required standard if the following conditions are fulfilled with respect to it, namely—

(*a*) that it is provided with all the standard amenities for the exclusive use of its occupants; and

(*b*) that it is in good repair (disregarding the state of internal decorative repair) having regard to its age and character and the locality in which it is situated; and

(*c*) that it conforms with such requirements with respect to construction and physical conditions and the provision of services and amenities as may for the time being be specified by the Secretary of State for the purposes of this section; and

(*d*) that it is likely to provide satisfactory housing accommodation for a period of 30 years.

(4) If it appears to a local authority that it is not practicable at reasonable expense for a dwelling to which an application for an improvement grant relates—

(*a*) to be provided with all the standard amenities, or

(*b*) to attain the standard of repair required by the condition in paragraph (*b*) of subsection (3) above, or

(*c*) to conform in every respect with the requirements referred to in paragraph (*c*) of that subsection,

the authority may, in the case of that dwelling, reduce the required standard by dispensing with the condition in question to such extent as will enable them, if they think fit, to approve the application.

(5) If it appears to a local authority reasonable to do so in the case of any dwelling to which an application for an improvement grant relates, they may reduce the required standard by substituting for the period specified in paragraph (*d*) of subsection (3) above such shorter period of not less than 10 years as appears to them to be appropriate in the circumstances. [**314**]

GENERAL

The first sub-section appears to be more mandatory than is really the case. The local authority has a very wide discretion as to whether or not to approve an application, which they may do "in such circumstances as they think fit". Having once approved an application, however, it is mandatory that they pay the grant when the conditions are fulfilled.

Their discretion to approve is governed by sub-s. (2), *i.e.* before giving approval they must be satisfied that, on completion, the dwellings will attain the required standard, as defined in sub-s. (3). However, sub-ss. (4) and (5) give some elasticity both as to physical standards and the expected useful life of the dwelling, which must not be less than 10 years.

There is no definition in the Act of "reasonable expense" in sub-s. (4). See Circular 160/74 in Appendix II.

DEFINITIONS

"Relevant works"—see s. 57 (2) and s. 84
"Standard amenities"—see s. 58
"Dwelling"—see s. 129
"Improvement grant"—see s. 56 (2) (*a*)
"Local authority"—see s. 84

62. Rateable value limit on improvement grants for dwellings for owner occupation

(1) If an application for an improvement grant in respect of works required for the improvement of a dwelling or dwellings is accompanied by a certificate of owner-occupation relating to that dwelling or, as the case may be, one of those dwellings, the local authority shall not approve the application if, on the date of the application, the rateable value of the dwelling to which that certificate relates is in excess of the relevant limit.

(2) If an application for an improvement grant in respect of works required for the provision of a dwelling or dwellings by the conversion of any premises which consist of or include a house or two or more houses is accompanied by a certificate of owner-occupation in respect of that dwelling or, as the case may be, one of those dwellings, the local authority shall not approve the application if, on the date of the application,—

(*a*) the rateable value of that house or, as the case may be, any of those houses, or (*b*) where the certificate relates to a dwelling to be provided by the conversion of premises consisting of or including two or more houses, the aggregate of the rateable values of those houses,

is in excess of the relevant limit.

(3) In this section "the relevant limit" means such limit of rateable value as the Secretary of State may with the consent of the Treasury by order specify; and different limits may be so specified in relation to dwellings falling within subsection (1) above and houses converted as mentioned in subsection (2) above and also in relation to property in different areas.

(4) For the purposes of this section the rateable value on any day of a dwelling or house shall be determined as follows:—

(*a*) if the dwelling or house is a hereditament for which a rateable value is then shown in the valuation list, it shall be that rateable value;

(*b*) if the dwelling or house forms part only of such a hereditament or consists of or forms part of more than one such hereditament, its rateable value shall be taken to be such value as the local authority, after consultation with the applicant as to an appropriate apportionment or aggregation, shall determine. **[315]**

GENERAL

There is now wide acceptance of the principle that grants ought not to be payable out of public funds for the improvement of dwellings for owner-occupation, if the owner is in a position to pay for the improvements himself. See Circular 160/74 in Appendix II which lays down the limits of rateable value.

DEFINITIONS

"Certificate of owner-occupation"—see s. 60.
"Dwelling"—see s. 129
"Improvement grant"—see s. 56 (2)

63. Determination of estimated expense in relation to improvement grant

(1) Where a local authority approve an application for an improvement grant they shall determine the amount of the expenses which, in their opinion, are proper to be incurred for the execution of the relevant works and shall notify the applicant of that amount; and, in relation to an improvement grant which has been approved, the amount so notified is in this section and section 64 below referred to as "the estimated expense" of the relevant works.

(2) Not more than 50 per cent., or such other percentage as may for the time being be prescribed, of the estimated expense of any works shall be allowed or works of repair and replacement.

(3) If the applicant satisfies the local authority that the relevant works cannot be or could not have been carried out without the carrying out of additional works and that this could not have been reasonably foreseen at the time the application was made, the local authority may, subject to subsection (2) above, determine a higher amount as the amount of the estimated expense. **[316]**

GENERAL

The local authority is empowered to determine the "estimated expense" of the relevant works. This governs the maximum amount of the improvement grant, and is, therefore, an important matter. Not more than 50 per cent. of the estimated expense should be for works of repair or replacement.

The figure for "estimated expense" may be adjusted, where this is reasonable, on account of additional works which could not have been foreseen.

DEFINITIONS
"Improvement grant"—see s. 129
"Relevant works"—see s. 84

64. Amount of improvement grant

(1) Subject to the following provisions of this section, the amount of an improvement grant shall be such as may be fixed by the local authority when they approve the application for the grant but shall not exceed the appropriate percentage of the eligible expense.

(2) Together with the notification under section 63 (1) above, the local authority shall send to the applicant a notification of the amount of the grant

(3) Except in a case or description of case in respect of which the Secretary of State approves a higher eligible expense, the eligible expense for the purposes of an improvement grant shall be so much of the estimated expense as does not exceed the relevant limit; and, subject to subsections (4) and (7) below, "the relevant limit", in relation to an improvement grant, is the amount for the dwelling, or if the application for the grant relates to more than one dwelling the total of the amounts for each of the dwellings, applicable under the following paragraphs, that is to say—

(*a*) for a dwelling which is improved by the relevant works or is provided by them otherwise than as mentioned in paragraph (*b*) below, £2,000, or such other amount as the Secretary of State may by order specify; and

(*b*) for a dwelling which is provided by the conversion of a house or other building consisting of three or more storeys, £2,400, or such other amount as the Secretary of State may by order specify.

(4) A statutory instrument containing an order under subsection (3) above shall be subject to annulment in pursuance of a resolution of the Commons House of Parliament.

(5) If the local authority are satisfied in a particular case that there are good reasons for increasing the amount which, apart from this subsection, would constitute the relevant limit, they may substitute for that amount such higher amount as the Secretary of State may approve; and the approval of the Secretary of State may be given either with respect to a particular case or with respect to any description of case.

(6) In any case where, after the amount of an improvement grant has been fixed under subsection (1) above, the local authority, in exercise of their powers under section 63 (3) above, substitute a higher amount as the amount of the estimated expense, the eligible expense shall be re-calculated under subsection (3) above and if, on that re-calculation, the amount of the eligible expense is greater than it was at the time when the application was approved,—

(*a*) the amount of the improvement grant shall be increased accordingly; and

(*b*) the local authority shall notify the applicant of the increased amount of the grant.

(7) In any case where—

(*a*) an intermediate grant, a repairs grant or a standard grant (within the meaning of Part I of the Housing Act 1969) has been made in respect of a dwelling, and (*b*) within the period of 10 years beginning on the date on which that grant was paid or, if it was paid by instalments, the date on which the last instalment was paid, an improvement grant is made in respect of that dwelling,

the amount which, by virtue of subsection (3) above, would otherwise be the relevant limit in relation to the improvement grant shall be reduced by the amount which was the eligible expense for the purposes of the grant referred to in paragraph (*a*) above or, where that grant was a standard grant (within the meaning of Part I of the Housing Act 1969) by an amount determined by reference to the amount of that grant and the rate at which it was made, namely, twice the amount of the grant where that rate was one-half and one and one-third times the amount of the grant where (by virtue of the Housing Act 1971) that rate was 75 per cent.

(8) For the purposes of this section, where an improvement grant is to be paid towards the cost of works required for the provision of a dwelling all or part of which is in the basement of a building, the basement shall count as a storey. [**317**]

GENERAL

The local authority will fix the amount of the grant at the time when they approve the application, but the grant must not exceed the "appropriate percentage" of the "eligible expense". The latter may not exceed the "relevant limit", which is laid down in this section, but may be varied by the Secretary of State.

Thus if the "estimated expense" arrived at under s. 63 for a dwelling is £2,200 and the "relevant limit" is £2,000, the "eligible expense" is limited to £2,000. If the "appropriate percentage" is 60 per cent., because the dwelling is in a general improvement area, then the grant may be up to 60 per cent. of £2,000, *i.e.* £1,200; but the local authority have discretion to adopt a lower percentage, subject to s. 80.

The "relevant limit" may be varied by the Secretary of State.

In a particular case the local authority may seek the approval of the Secretary of State to the fixing of a higher relevant limit.

There is further flexibility in sub-s. (6). Improvement grants must be adjusted in the terms of sub-s. (7) where other grants have already been made in respect of the dwelling. The formula bring the sums to be deducted up to 100 per cent. of the approved expense on which the original grant was based.

See also general comments on s. 63 above, and Circular 160/74 in Appendix II.

DEFINITIONS

"Appropriate percentage"—see s. 59 and s. 84
"estimated expense"—see s. 63
"local authority"—see s. 84
"Improvement grant"—see s. 56 (2) (*a*)
"Intermediate grant"—see s. 56 (2) (*b*)
"Repairs grant"—see s. 56 (2)
"Standard grant"—see Part I, Housing Act 1969

Intermediate grants

65. Intermediate grants

(1) A local authority shall pay an intermediate grant if—

(*a*) an application for such a grant, made in accordance with this Part of this Act, is approved by them; and
(*b*) the conditions for the payment of the grant are fulfilled.

(2) An application for an intermediate grant shall—

(*a*) specify the standard amenity or amenities which it is intended to provide by the relevant works; and (*b*) if some only of the standard amenities are specified as mentioned in paragraph (*a*) above, state whether the dwelling is already provided with the remainder; and

(*c*) contain a statement, with respect to each of the standard amenities specified as mentioned in paragraph (*a*) above, whether, to the best of the knowledge and belief of the applicant, the dwelling has been without that amenity for a period of not less than 12 months ending with the date on which the application is made.

(3) A local authority shall not approve an application for an intermediate grant unless they are satisfied, with respect to each of the standard amenities specified as mentioned in subsection (2) (*a*) above, either—

(*a*) that the dwelling concerned, except in the case of a registered disabled person when this subsection shall not apply, has been without the amenity in question for a period of not less than 12 months ending with the date on which the application is made; or

(*b*) that the dwelling is provided with the amenity in question on the date of the application but the relevant works, exclusive of those for the provision of that amenity, involve interference with or replacement of that amenity and it would not be reasonably practicable to avoid the interference or replacement. [**318**]

GENERAL

The local authority has much less discretion as to whether to approve an application for intermediate grant than it has in respect of improvement grants—see also ss. 66 and 67. This is in line with the policy in respect of grants for standard amenities ever since they were first introduced by the House Purchase and Housing Act 1959. By s. 65 (1) the local authority "shall pay" if the application is approved by them and the conditions of grant are fulfilled; s. 65 (3) debars them from approving an application in certain limited circumstances; s. 66 lays down the physical standards required. But s. 67 (1) requires the local authority to approve any application for intermediate grant, subject to the other sections named therein. See Circular 160/74 in Appendix II.

DEFINITIONS

"Dwelling"—see s. 129
"Intermediate grant"—see s. 56 (2)
"Local authority"—see s. 84
"Standard amenity"—see s. 58

66. Approval of application for intermediate grant conditional on dwelling attaining a particular standard

(1) A local authority shall not approve an application for an intermediate grant unless they are satisfied that, on completion of the relevant works, the dwelling or, as the case may be, each of the dwellings to which the application relates will attain the full standard of, if any of subsections (3) to (5) below applies, the reduced standard.

(2) For the purposes of this section a dwelling shall be taken to attain the full standard if the following conditions are fulfilled with respect to it, namely,—

(*a*) that it is provided with all the standard amenities for the exclusive use of its occupants; and

(*b*) that it is in good repair (disregarding the state of internal decorative repair) having regard to its age and character and the locality in which it is situated; and

(*c*) that it conforms with such requirements with respect to thermal insulation as may for the time being be specified by the Secretary of State for the purposes of this section; and (*d*) that it is in all other respects fit for human habitation, construing that expression in accordance with Part II of the Housing Act 1957; and

(*e*) that it is likely to be available for use as a dwelling for a period of 15 years or such other period as may for the time being be specified by the Secretary of State for the purposes of this subsection.

(3) Where an application for an intermediate grant contains a statement, and the local authority are satisfied, that it is not practicable at reasonable expense for the dwelling to which the application relates to be provided with all the standard amenities, they shall dispense with the condition in paragraph (*a*) of subsection (2) above unless they are satisfied that the dwelling is, or forms part of, a house or building in respect of which they could, by a notice under section 15 of the Housing Act 1961, require the execution of such works as are referred to in subsection (1) of that section.

(4) If it appears to a local authority that it is not practicable at reasonable expense for a dwelling to which an application for an intermediate grant relates—

(*a*) to attain the standard of repair required by the condition in paragraph (*b*) of subsection (2) above, or

(*b*) to conform in every respect with the requirements referred to in paragraph (*c*) of that subsection, or

(*c*) to comply with the condition in paragraph (*d*) of that subsection,

the authority may, in the case of that dwelling, dispense with the condition in question to such extent as will enable them, if they think fit, to approve the application.

(5) If it appears to a local authority reasonable to do so in the case of any dwelling to which an application for an intermediate grant relates, they may in the case of that dwelling vary the condition in paragraph (*e*) of subsection (2) above by substituting for the period of 15 years or such other period as may for the time being be specified as mentioned in that paragraph such shorter period as appears to them to be appropriate in the circumstances.

(6) If, in relation to any dwelling, a local authority by virtue of subsection (3), subsection (4) or subsection (5) above dispense, in whole or in part, with any of the conditions in paragraphs (*a*) to (*d*) of subsection (2) above or vary the condition in paragraph (*e*) of that subsection, then for the purposes of this section the dwelling concerned shall be taken to attain the reduced standard if, subject to any such dispensation or variation, the conditions in subsection (2) above are fulfilled with respect to it. [**319**]

GENERAL

Normally the "relevant works", must result in the dwelling being equipped with all the standard amenities, be in good repair, and be likely to have a life of 15 years. However, some elasticity is provided by the later sub-sections. Early in the history of standard grants conditions were much more rigid but it came to be accepted that it was wrong to deprive an occupant of one or more of the standard amenities simply because physical conditions prevented him from having one of them. The local authority may take "reasonable expense" into account both as regards the provision of amenities and the standard of repair. They may also relax the condition as regards the expected life of the dwelling. Sub-s. 2 (*c*) enables the Secretary of State to specify standards of thermal insulation. See Circular 160/74 in Appendix II.

DEFINITIONS

See under s. 65.

67. Local authority to approve certain applications for intermediate grants

(1) Subject to sections 57, 60, 65 (2), 65 (3) and 66 above, a local authority shall approve an application for an intermediate grant which is duly made in accordance with this Part of this Act.

(2) If an application for an intermediate grant is duly made in accordance with this Part of this Act and the relevant works consist solely of works which the applicant is required to carry out by an improvement notice served or an undertaking accepted under Part VIII of this Act,—

(*a*) subsections (3) to (5) of section 57 and sections 60 and 65 (2) above shall not apply, and
(*b*) if it appears to the local authority to whom the application is made that, on completion of the relevant works, the dwelling concerned will not attain the full standard, they shall be treated as having exercised their powers under subsections (4) and (5) of section 66 above and, where appropriate, as being satisfied as mentioned in subsection (3) of that section, to such extent as is necessary to secure that on completion of the relevant works the dwelling will attain the reduced standard,

and subsection (1) above shall apply accordingly.

(3) Where the relevant works specified in an application for an intermediate grant include works of repair or replacement which go beyond those needed, in the opinion of the local authority, for the purposes of enabling the dwelling concerned to attain the full standard or the reduced standard, as the case may require, the local authority may, with the consent of the applicant, treat the application as varied so that the relevant works—

(*a*) are confined to works other than works of repair or replacement, or
(*b*) include only such works of repair or replacement as (taken with the rest of the relevant works) will secure, in the opinion of the local authority, that the dwelling will attain the full standard or the reduced standard, as the case may require,

and may approve the application as so varied.

(4) In this section "the full standard" and "the reduced standard" have the same meanings as in section 66 above. [**320**]

GENERAL

Reference has already been made in the general comments on s. 65 to the fact that it is mandatory for the local authority to approve an application for intermediate grant, provided certain basic conditions are fulfilled.

Where an application is made for intermediate grant and the relevant works consist solely of works required to comply with a notice under Part VIII (compulsory improvements), or an undertaking under Part VIII, certain basic conditions will not apply—sub-s. (2).

The repairs and replacement element in an application may be reduced in accordance with sub-s. (3). This is important because of the limitation placed upon the amount included for repair and replacement by s. 68 (3). See Circular 160/74 in Appendix 11.

DEFINITIONS

"Full standard", "reduced standard"—see s. 66
"Intermediate grant"—see s. 56 (2)
"Local authority"—see s. 84
"Relevant works"—see s. 57 (2) (*b*)

68. Determination of estimated expense and amount of intermediate grant

(1) Where a local authority approve an application for an intermediate grant they shall determine separately—

(*a*) the amount of the expenses which in their opinion are proper to be incurred for the execution of those of the relevant works which consist of works of repair or replacement, and

(*b*) the amount of the expenses which in their opinion are proper to be incurred for the execution of those of the relevant works which relate solely to the provision of standard amenities,

and shall notify the applicant of the amounts determined by them under this subsection.

(2) If the applicant satisfies the local authority that the relevant works cannot be or could not have been carried out without the carrying out of additional works and that this could not have been reasonably foreseen at the time the application was made, the local authority may determine a higher amount under either or both of paragraphs (*a*) and (*b*) of subsection (1) above.

(3) Except in a case or description of case in respect of which the Secretary of State approves a higher eligible expense, the eligible expense for the purposes of an intermediate grant shall be the aggregate of—

(*a*) so much of the amount determined under subsection (1) (*a*) above as does not exceed £800 or such other amount as may be prescribed; and

(*b*) so much of the amount determined under subsection (1) (*b*) above as does not exceed the total of the amounts specified in the second column of Part I of Schedule 6 to this Act in relation to each of the standard amenities which are to be provided by the relevant works.

(4) In any case where the relevant works make provision for more than one standard amenity of the same description, only one amenity of that description shall be taken into account under subsections (1) to (3) above.

(5) Subject to subsection (6) below, the amount of an intermediate grant shall be the appropriate percentage of the eligible expense and, together with the notification under subsection (1) above, the local authority shall send to the applicant a notification of the amount of the grant.

(6) In any case where, after the amount of an intermediate grant has been notified to the applicant under subsection (5) above, the local authority, in exercise of their powers under subsection (2) above, determine a higher amount under either or both of paragraphs (*a*) and (*b*) of subsection (1) above, the eligible expense shall be re-calculated under subsection (3) above and if, on that re-calculation, the amount of the eligible expense is greater than it was at the time when the application was approved,—

(*a*) the amount of the intermediate grant shall be increased accordingly; and

(*b*) the local authority shall notify the applicant of the increased amount of the grant. [**321**]

GENERAL

The procedure for arriving at the amount of grant is as follows:

(*a*) The local authority determines the "estimated expense", *i.e.* their estimate of the cost of the works as specified in the application. They must separate the figure into two parts:

(i) cost of repairs and replacements, and
(ii) cost of providing whichever standard amenities are now to be provided. They must inform the applicant—s. 68 (1).
(*b*) The local authority then calculates the "eligible expense" in accordance with s. 68 (3). The "eligible expense" limits the amount of the cost of repair and replacement which is eligible for grant to a maximum of £800. The amount of the cost for amenities which is eligible for grant is limited by Part I of Sch. 6. The estimated expense may be whittled down under either of these two headings.
(*c*) Having arrived at the eligible expense" as under (*b*), the local authority then apply, the "appropriate percentage", according to whether the dwelling is in a housing action area, a general improvement area, or neither, and in the light of sub-ss. (1) and (2) of s. 59.

There may be adjustments in respect of additional works if the local authority is satisfied under s. 68 (2). See Circular 160/74 in Appendix II.

DEFINITIONS

"Appropriate percentage"—see s. 59 and s. 84, and Table 1 on p. 28.
"Intermediate grant"—see s. 56 (2)
"Local authority"—see s. 84
"Relevant works"—see s. 57 (2) (*b*).

Special grants

69. Special grants

(1) A local authority shall pay a special grant if—

(*a*) an application for such a grant, made in accordance with this Part of this Act, is approved by them, and
(*b*) the conditions for the payment of the grant are fulfilled,

and, subject to the provisions of this Part of this Act, a local authority may approve an application for a special grant in such circumstances as they think fit.

(2) An application for a special grant shall specify by how many households and individuals the house concerned is occupied and with what standard amenities it is already provided.

(3) In its application in relation to special grants, Part II of Schedule 6 to this Act shall have effect as if paragraphs 2 and 3 and, in paragraph 1, the words "Except as provided by paragraph 2 below" were omitted. [**322**]

GENERAL

The powers and duties of a local authority in respect of special grants are set out in ss. 69 and 70. The grants are intended to encourage the provision of standard amenities in houses let in multiple occupation, as defined in s. 129.

The pattern is very similar to that for intermediate grants, as described in s. 65 to s. 68 above, but adjusted to take account of the fact that multiple occupation may make it desirable to provide more than one amenity of a given kind, and the requirement as to "exclusive use" cannot be applied to houses in multiple occupation.

S. 69 and 70 replace s. 13 of the Housing Act 1969, which together with the remainder of Part I of the Act of 1969 is repealed. See Circular 160/74 in Appendix II.

DEFINITIONS

"House"—no definition is given. See s. 189 of Housing Act 1957. The term could include a house in which each floor is let separately, though the house itself has not been converted—*Kyffin* v. *Simmons* (1903), 67 J.P. 227. A "house" can be a building divided into self-contained flats—*Okereke* v. *Brent London Borough Council*, [1967] 1 Q.B. 42; [1966] 1 All E.R. 150. See also *Quillotex* v. *Minister of Housing and Local Government*, [1965] 2 All E.R. 913; [1966] 1 Q.B. 704.
"Household"—This is not defined. It is not synonymous with "family". See "*Holm* v. *Royal Borough of Kensington and Chelsea*", [1968] 1 Q.B. 646; [1967] 1 All E.R. 289.
House in multiple occupation—see s. 129
"Special grant"—see s. 56 (2) (*c*).

70. Amount of special grant

(1) Where a local authority approve an application for a special grant they shall determine the amount of the expenses which in their opinion are proper to be incurred for the execution of the relevant works and shall notify the applicant of that amount.

(2) If any of the relevant works are not exclusively for the purpose of providing one or more of the standard amenities, only so much of the cost of carrying out those works as is, in the opinion of the local authority, attributable to the provision of the standard amenity or standard amenities shall be taken into account for the purpose of the determination under subsection (1) above.

(3) If the applicant satisfies the local authority that the relevant works cannot be or could not have been carried out without the carrying out of additional works and that this could not have been reasonably foreseen at the time the application was made, the local authority may, subject to subsection (2) above, determine a higher amount under subsection (1) above.

(4) Except in a case or description of case in respect of which the Secretary of State approves a higher eligible expense, the eligible expense for the purposes of a special grant shall be so much of the amount determined under subsection (1) above as does not exceed the aggregate of the amounts specified in the second column of Part I of Schedule 6 to this Act in relation to each of the standard amenities which are to be provided by the relevant works (so that, where the relevant works make provision for more than one standard amenity of the same description, a separate amount shall be aggregated for each of those amenities).

(5) The amount of a special grant shall be such as may be fixed by the local authority when they approve the application for the grant but shall not exceed the appropriate percentage of the eligible expense and, together with the notification under subsection (1) above, the local authority shall send to the applicant a notification of the amount of the grant. **[323]**

GENERAL

The amount of special grant is governed by the local authority's determination of the estimated expense under sub-s. (1). This is limited to the cost of works for providing one or more of the standard amenities, and the "eligible expense" is the estimated expense adjusted to conform with the limits in Part I of Sch. 6 of the Act.

The amount of the grant will be the appropriate percentage of the eligible expense, *i.e.* 75 per cent., 60 per cent., or 50 per cent. See s. 52 and Table 1 in Chapter 7 above.

Unlike "intermediate grants", the special grants do not include any element for repairs.

Under sub-s. (5) the local authority has discretion to make a grant which is less than the appropriate percentage, but this is subject to s. 80.

DEFINITIONS

"Appropriate percentage"—see s. 59
"Local authority"—see s. 84
"multiple occupation"—see s. 129
"Relevant works"—see s. 57 (2) (*b*)
"special grant"—see s. 56 (2)
"standard amenity—see s. 58

Repairs grants

71. Repairs grants

(1) A local authority shall pay a repairs grant if—

(*a*) an application for such a grant, made in accordance with this Part of this Act, is approved by them, and (*b*) the conditions for the payment of the grant are fulfilled,

and, subject to the provisions of this Part of this Act, a local authority may approve an application for a repairs grant in such circumstances as they think fit.

(2) In considering whether or not to exercise their discretion to approve an application for a repairs grant, a local authority shall have regard to the question whether, in their opinion, the applicant would without undue hardship be able to finance the cost of the relevant works without the assistance of a repairs grant.

(3) A local authority shall not approve an application for a repairs grant unless they are satisfied—

(*a*) that the dwelling or, as the case may be, each of the dwellings to which the application relates is situated in a general improvement area or a housing action area, and

(*b*) that on completion of the relevant works the dwelling or, as the case may be, each of the dwellings to which the application relates will attain the relevant standard of repair.

(4) Without prejudice to the discretion of a local authority to approve or decline to approve an application for a repairs grant, if, in the opinion of the authority, the relevant works are more extensive than is necessary for the purpose of securing that the dwelling or, as the case may be, any of the dwellings to which the application relates will attain the relevant standard of repair, the authority may, with the consent of the applicant, treat the application as varied so that the relevant works include only such works as seem to the authority to be necessary for that purpose, and may approve the application as so varied.

(5) For the purposes of this section a dwelling shall be taken to attain the relevant standard of repair if it is in good repair (disregarding the state of internal decorative repair) having regard to its age and character and the locality in which it is situated. [**324**]

GENERAL

These grants are payable only in respect of dwellings in a general improvement area or housing action area. The local authority has a wide discretion as to whether or not to approve a repairs grant. They are to take into account whether the applicant would, in their opinion, be able to finance the works without a grant. The relevant standard is described in sub-s. (5). See also s. 72. The local authority may fix a grant at a figure lower than the appropriate percentage, but this is subject to s. 80.

DEFINITIONS

"Dwelling"—see s. 129
"General improvement area"—s. 50
"Housing action area"—s. 36
"Local authority"—see s. 84
"Relevant works"—see s. 57 (2) (*b*)
"Repairs grant"—see s. 56 (2)

72. Determination of estimated expense and amount of repairs grant

(1) Where a local authority approve an application for a repairs grant they shall determine the amount of the expenses which in their opinion are proper to be incurred for the execution of the relevant works and shall notify the applicant of that amount.

(2) If the applicant satisfies the local authority that the relevant works cannot be or could not have been carried out without the carrying out of additional works and that this could not have been reasonably foreseen at the time

the application was made, the local authority may determine a higher amount under subsection (1) above.

(3) Except in a case or description of case in respect of which the Secretary of State approves a higher eligible expense, the eligible expense for the purposes of a repairs grant shall be so much of the amount determined under subsection (1) above as does not exceed £800 or such other amount as may be prescribed.

(4) The amount of a repairs grant shall be such as may be fixed by the local authority when they approve the application for the grant but, subject to subsection (5) below, shall not exceed the appropriate percentage of the eligible expense and, together with the notification under subsection (1) above, the local authority shall send to the applicant a notification of the amount of the grant.

(5) In any case where, after the amount of a repairs grant has been notified to the applicant under subsection (4) above, the local authority, in exercise of their powers under subsection (2) above, determine a higher amount under subsection (1) above, the eligible expense shall be re-calculated under subsection (3) above, and if, on that re-calculation, the amount of the eligible expense is greater than it was at the time when the application was approved,—

(*a*) the amount of the repairs grant shall be increased accordingly; and
(*b*) the local authority shall notify the applicant of the increased amount of the grant. **[325]**

GENERAL

The local authority will first determine the estimated expense of the relevant works. The amount eligible for grant will then be determined as the amount of the estimated expense with a limit of, at present, £800. The amount of grant will be not more than the appropriate percentage of the eligible expense, and this maximum percentage will be 75 per cent. if it is in a housing action area, or 60 per cent. in a general improvement area. See s. 59 and Table 1 in Chapter 7. If the dwelling is in a housing action area the grant may be up to 90 per cent. s. 59 (2).

DEFINITIONS

See under s. 71

Grant conditions

73. Conditions as to future occupation

(1) Subject to section 83 below, where an application for an improvement grant, an intermediate grant or a repairs grant has been approved by a local authority the provisions of this section shall apply with respect to the occupation, during the period of 5 years beginning with the certified date (in this section referred to as "the initial period"), of the dwelling or, as the case may be, each of the dwellings to which the grant relates.

(2) In any case where the application for the grant was accompanied by a certificate of owner-occupation with respect to the dwelling, it shall be a condition of the grant—

(*a*) that throughout the first year of the initial period the dwelling will, as a residence, be occupied exclusively by, or be available for the exclusive occupation of, a qualifying person and members of his household (if any); and
(*b*) that if, at any time during the second or any subsequent year of the initial period, the dwelling is not occupied exclusively as his only or main residence by a qualifying person and members of his household

(if any), the dwelling will at that time be let or available for letting by a qualifying person as a residence, and not for a holiday, to persons other than members of that person's family.

(3) For the purposes of this section, the following are "qualifying persons" in relation to a dwelling, namely,—

(*a*) the applicant for the grant and any person who derives title to the dwelling through or under the applicant, otherwise than by a conveyance for value; and

(*b*) at any time when personal representatives or trustees as such are the qualifying person by virtue of paragraph (*a*) above, any person who, under the will or intestacy or, as the case may require, under the terms of the trusts concerned, is beneficially entitled to an interest in the dwelling or the proceeds of sale thereof.

(4) In any case where the application for the grant was accompanied by a certificate of availability for letting with respect to the dwelling, it shall be a condition of the grant that, throughout the initial period,—

(*a*) the dwelling will be let or available for letting as a residence, and not for a holiday, by a qualifying person to persons other than members of the family of that qualifying person or any other person who is for the time being a qualifying person in relation to the dwelling; or

(*b*) the dwelling will be occupied or available for occupation by a member of the agricultural population in pursuance of a contract of service and otherwise than as a tenant.

(5) In determining, in a case where subsection (2) above applies, whether there is a breach of the condition specified in that subsection, there shall be disregarded any period of not more than 12 months during which that condition is not fulfilled if—

(*a*) that period begins on the death of a qualifying person who, immediately before his death, was occupying the dwelling concerned as his residence; and

(*b*) throughout that period an interest in the dwelling or the proceeds of sale thereof, being either the interest which belonged to the deceased or an interest which arose or fell into possession on his death, is vested in his personal representatives acting in that capacity or in trustees as such or, by virtue of section 9 of the Administration of Estates Act 1925, in the Probate Judge, within the meaning of that Act.

(6) In any case where subsection (1) above applies, it shall be a condition of the grant that if, at any time within the initial period, the local authority by whom the grant was paid serve notice on the owner of the dwelling requiring him to do so, the owner shall, within the period of 21 days beginning with the date on which the notice is served, furnish to the authority a certificate giving such information as the authority may reasonably require with respect to the occupation of the dwelling, and for this purpose it shall also be a condition of the grant that, if required to do so by the owner of the dwelling, any tenant of the dwelling will furnish the owner with such information as he may reasonably require to enable him to furnish the certificate to the authority. [**326**]

GENERAL

Reference has already been made to the requirement contained in s. 60 that a loca authority shall not entertain an application for an improvement grant, an intermediate grant, or a repairs grant, unless it is accompanied by a certificate of future occupation.

This will be either a certificate of owner-occupation or a certificate of availability for letting. Section 73 amplifies this by setting out the conditions which will apply during the first 5 years after the completion of the works. If there was a certificate of owner-occupation, and the owner ceases to use the dwelling as his only, or main residence, it must be let or available for letting in accordance with sub-s. (2) (3) and (5).

If there was a certificate of availability for letting the dwelling must be let, or genuinely available for letting, on the conditions set out in sub-s. (4) (*a*) or (4) (*b*). This section also arms the local authority with powers to obtain information from the owner, and the owner has power to obtain information from the tenant, to enable him to furnish to the local authority a certificate as to occupancy.

The conditions under s. 73 will apply automatically, but further conditions may be applied, at the discretion of the local authority, under s. 74. See Circular 160/74 in Appendix II.

DEFINITIONS

"Certified date"—see s. 75 (6)
"Dwelling"—see s. 129
"Improvement grant"—see s. 56 (2)
"Intermediate grant"—see s. 56 (2)
"Repairs grant"—see s. 56 (2)

74. Power of local authorities to impose grant conditions

(1) Subject to section 83 below, where an application for an improvement grant, an intermediate grant or a repairs grant is approved by a local authority then, subject to subsection (3) below, the authority may and, in the case of a dwelling or dwellings situated in an area which, on the date on which the application is approved, is a housing action area, a general improvement area or a priority neighbourhood, they shall impose, with respect to the dwelling or, as the case may be, each of the dwellings to which the grant relates, the conditions specified in subsection (2) below as conditions of the grant, but may impose no other condition in relation to the approval or making of the grant, whether the condition purports to operate by way of a condition of the grant, a personal covenant or otherwise.

(2) The conditions referred to in subsection (1) above are—

(*a*) that the dwelling will be let or available for letting on a regulated tenancy or a Part VI contract;

(*b*) that, if the local authority by whom the grant in question was paid serve notice on the owner of the dwelling requiring him to do so, the owner will within the period of 21 days beginning with the date on which the notice is served furnish to the authority a certificate that the condition set out in paragraph (*a*) above is being fulfilled;

(*c*) that, if required to do so by the owner of the dwelling, any tenant of the dwelling will furnish the owner with such information as he may reasonably require for the purpose of enabling him to comply with the condition set out in paragraph (*b*) above;

(*d*) that, if on the certified date there is no registered rent for the dwelling and no such application or reference is pending, an application for the registration of a rent for the dwelling will be made to the rent officer before the expiry of the period of 14 days beginning on the relevant day or, as the case may require, the Part VI contract will be referred to the rent tribunal for the district in question before the expiry of that period;

(*e*) that any such application or reference as is referred to in paragraph (*d*) above which is either pending on the certified date or made as mentioned in that paragraph will be diligently proceeded with and not withdrawn; and (*f*) that no premium shall be required as a condition of the grant, renewal or continuance on or after the certified date of any lease, agreement for a lease or Part VI contract of or relating to the dwelling.

(3) To the extent that a grant relates to a dwelling—

(*a*) in which a registered housing association or an unregistered housing association falling within section 18 (1) (*b*) of this Act has an estate or interest on the date on which the application for the grant is approved (in this subsection referred to as "the approval date"), or

(*b*) in respect of which a certificate of owner-occupation has been given and which has not at any time during the period of 12 months immediately preceding the approval date been let in whole or in part for residential purposes, or

(*c*) which is occupied or available for occupation by a member of the agricultural population in pursuance of a contract of service and otherwise than as a tenant,

no condition may be imposed under this section as a condition of the grant.

(4) In this section—

"Part VI contract" has the same meaning as in Part VI of the Rent Act 1968;

"premium" has the same meaning as in Part VII of that Act;

"registered rent" means,—

(*a*) in relation to a dwelling which is subject to, or available for letting on, a regulated tenancy, a rent registered under Part IV of that Act; and

(*b*) in relation to a dwelling which is let, or available for letting, on a Part VI contract, a rent registered in the register kept under section 74 of that Act;

"regulated tenancy" has the same meaning as in that Act; and

"relevant day", in relation to a dwelling for which there is no registered rent on the certified date, means the first day, not being earlier than the certified date, on which the dwelling is or becomes subject to a regulated tenancy or let on a Part VI contract. [**327**]

GENERAL

This gives the local authority a discretionary power to go beyond s. 73 and impose further conditions when approving a grant for a dwelling covered by a certificate of availability for letting. They can insist that it is not only let but let on either a regulated tenancy at a registered rent or under Part VI contract at a rent approved by the local Rent Tribunal in accordance with the Rent Act 1968. If, on the certified date, there is no registered rent the local authority can insist that an application is made to the rent officer, or the Rent Tribunal, and thus ensure that there is either a rent registered by the rent officer for a protected tenancy or a rent approved by the local Rent Tribunal and registered by the local authority for a furnished letting under Part VI of the Rent Act 1968 as amended by the Rent Act 1974.

No other conditions may be imposed in relation to the approval or making of a grant.

This section is permissive except for dwellings in housing action areas, general improvement areas, or priority neighbourhoods. For dwellings in any of these three types of area the imposition of these conditions is mandatory.

There are powers to obtain information as to whether the conditions are being complied with.

No condition may be imposed under this section where the grant relates to a dwelling falling within any of the descriptions in sub-s. (3).

This section should be read with ss. 60 and 73. See Circular 160/74 in Appendix II.

75. Enforceability and registration of grant conditions

(1) The provisions of this section shall apply in any case where, under or by virtue of any provision of this Part of this Act, a condition (in this section referred to as a "grant condition") is imposed as a condition of a grant.

(2) If and so long as a grant condition remains in force—

(*a*) it shall be binding on any person, other than a housing authority or registered housing association, who is for the time being the owner of the dwelling to which the grant relates; and

(*b*) it shall be enforceable against all other persons having any interest in that dwelling as if it were a condition of the terms of every lease, agreement for a lease or statutory tenancy of, or of property including, that dwelling.

(3) Subject to subsection (4) below, a grant condition shall be in force throughout the period of 5 years beginning on the certified date.

(4) If, on the date on which an application for a grant is approved, the dwelling to which the grant relates is in a housing action area, subsection (3) above shall have effect, except in the case of a grant condition imposed under section 73 above, with the substitution for the words "5 years" of the words "7 years".

(5) A grant condition shall be treated as not being registrable by virtue of section 15 of the Land Charges Act 1925 (either as, or as if it were, a local land charge) but, as soon as may be after an application for a grant has been approved, any condition of that grant shall be registered in the register of local land charges—

(*a*) by the proper officer, for the purposes of section 15 of the Land Charges Act 1925, of the council in whose area the dwelling concerned is situated, and

(*b*) in such manner as may be prescribed by rules under section 19 of that Act,

and in this subsection "council" means a district council, a London borough council or the Common Council of the City of London.

(6) In this Part of this Act "the certified date", in relation to a dwelling in respect of which an application for a grant has been approved, means the date certified by the local authority by whom the application was approved as the date on which the dwelling first becomes fit for occupation after the completion of the relevant works to the satisfaction of the local authority. **[328]**

GENERAL

This specifies the persons upon whom grant conditions are, or will be, binding, and for what period. The period is normally 5 years but, if the dwelling is in a housing action area, the conditions in s. 74 will not only be mandatory but they will be binding for 7 years. See Circular 160/74 in Appendix II.

76. Repayment of grant for breach of condition

(1) The provisions of this section shall have effect in the event of a breach of a condition of a grant (in this section referred to as "the relevant grant") at a time when the condition is binding on the owner of the dwelling concerned by virtue of section 75 (2) above.

(2) Where the relevant grant related to a single dwelling, an amount equal to the amount of the relevant grant, together with compound interest thereon as

from the certified date, calculated at the appropriate rate and with yearly rests, shall, on being demanded by the local authority forthwith become payable to the authority by the owner for the time being of the dwelling.

(3) Where the relevant grant related to two or more dwellings, an amount equal to such part of the relevant grant as appears to the authority to be referable to the dwelling to which the breach relates, together with compound interest on that part as from the certified date, calculated at the appropriate rate and with yearly rests, shall, on being demanded by the local authority, forthwith become payable to the authority by the owner for the time being of that dwelling.

(4) Nothing in subsection (2) or, as the case may be, subsection (3) above shall prevent a local authority from determining not to demand any such amount as is referred to in that subsection or from demanding an amount less than that which they are entitled to demand under that subsection.

(5) Upon satisfaction of the liability of an owner of a dwelling to make a payment under this section to a local authority in respect of a breach of a condition of a grant, the condition shall cease to be in force with respect to that dwelling.

(6) In this section "the appropriate rate" means the rate of interest for the time being fixed by subsection (2) of section 171 of the Local Government Act 1972 for the purposes of the enactments specified in subsection (1) of that section. **[329]**

GENERAL

The discretionary nature of the local authority's powers under this section should be noted—see sub-s. (4). The local authority may demand repayment of the whole amount of the grant, with compound interest, but they may demand a smaller amount, or decide not to make any demand at all.

77. Voluntary repayment of grants

(1) If, at any time while a condition of a grant remains in force, the owner of the dwelling to which the condition relates or a mortgagee of the interest of the owner in that dwelling, being a mortgagee entitled to exercise a power of sale, pays to the local authority by whom the grant was made the like amount as would (on a demand by the local authority) become payable under section 76 above in the event of a breach of that condition, all conditions of the grant shall cease to be in force with respect to that dwelling.

(2) Any amount paid under subsection (1) above by a mortgagee shall be treated as part of the sum secured by the mortgage and may be discharged accordingly.

(3) The purposes authorised for the application of capital money—

(*a*) by section 73 of the Settled Land Act 1925 and by that section as applied by section 28 of the Law of Property Act 1925 in relation to trusts for sale, and

(*b*) by section 26 of the Universities and College Estates Act 1925,

shall include the payment to a local authority under subsection (1) above of the amount mentioned in that subsection in respect of a dwelling. **[330]**

GENERAL

The owner of a dwelling to which a condition of grant is applicable, or a mortgagee of the interest of the owner, may discharge the condition by making voluntary repayment.

Contributions

78. Contributions by Secretary of State towards grants

(1) The Secretary of State may make a contribution towards the expense incurred by a local authority in making a grant.

(2) The contributions shall be a sum payable annually for a period of 20 years beginning with the financial year in which the works towards the cost of which the grant was made were completed, equal to the relevant percentage of the annual loan charges referable to the amount of the grant.

(3) In subsection (2) above "the relevant percentage" means—

(*a*) in a case where, on the date on which the application for the grant concerned is approved, the premises to which the application relates are in a general improvement area or a housing action area, 90 per cent., and

(*b*) in any other case, 75 per cent.

(4) The Secretary of State may by order made with the consent of the Treasury vary either or both of the percentages specified in subsection (3) above, and any such variation shall have effect with respect to applications for grants approved after such date as may be specified in the order.

(5) An order under subsection (4) above—

(*a*) shall not be made unless a draft thereof has been approved by a resolution of the Commons House of Parliament; and

(*b*) shall not specify a date earlier than the date of the laying of the draft.

(6) For the purposes of this section "the annual loan charges" referable to the amount of a grant means the annual sum which, in the opinion of the Secretary of State, would fall to be provided by a housing authority for the payment of interest on, and the repayment of, a loan of that amount repayable over a period of 20 years.

(7) In any case where, on the date on which the application for a grant is approved, the premises to which the application relates are in an area declared by the local authority concerned to be a housing action area and, after that date, the Secretary of State notifies the local authority that the area is no longer to be such an area, or that land on which the premises are situated is to be excluded from the area, he may, without prejudice to his discretion under subsection (1) above not to make a contribution under this section, make such a contribution on the basis that the relevant percentage is 75 per cent. **[331]**

GENERAL

The Secretary of State may make contributions towards the expenditure of a local authority in making grants. His contribution will be the "relevant percentage" of the loan charges on the amount of the grant. The "relevant percentage" is 90 per cent. if the premises are in a general improvement area or a housing action area, on the date when the application is approved; or 75 per cent. if they are elsewhere. The "relevant percentage" should not be confused with the "appropriate percentage" as defined in s. 59.

The Secretary of State has power, by order, to vary the relevant percentages. He may continue the contribution on the 75 per cent. basis even after the premises have ceased to be in a housing action area.

DEFINITIONS

"Grant"—see s. 56 (2)
"Housing authority"—see s. 84
"Local authority"—see s. 84

79. Payment of improvement contributions to housing authorities

(1) The Secretary of State may pay contributions (in this section referred to as "improvement contributions") to housing authorities towards the expenses incurred by them in—

(*a*) the provision of dwellings by the conversion of houses or other buildings, or

(*b*) the improvement of dwellings,

in such circumstances as appear to him to be sufficiently similar to those in which an improvement grant might be paid by a local authority had the provision or improvement been by a person other than a housing authority.

(2) The Secretary of State may pay an improvement contribution with respect to any dwellings if an application therefor containing such estimates and particulars as he may require is made by a housing authority and approved by him.

(3) Where the Secretary of State approves an application for an improvement contribution, he shall determine the amount of the expenses which, in his opinion, are proper to be incurred by the housing authority for the execution of any works required for the provision or improvement of the dwellings.

(4) The eligible expense for the purposes of an improvement contribution shall be so much of the amount determined under subsection (3) above as does not exceed the amount arrived at by taking, for each dwelling provided or improved, £2,000.

(5) The improvement contribution shall be a sum payable annually for a period of 20 years, beginning with the financial year in which the works required for the provision or improvement of the dwellings are completed, equal to 37·5 per cent. of the annual loan charges referable to the eligible expense.

(6) Subsection (6) of section 78 above shall apply for the purposes of this section as it applies for the purposes of that. **[332]**

GENERAL

This covers contributions by the Secretary of State towards the expenses of a "housing authority" in converting and improving its own dwellings.

Application must be made for his approval, and he will determine the expenses which are proper to be incurred. In any case there is a limit of eligible expense, as shown in sub-s. (4).

There is, moreover, an overall policy control resting in the Secretary of State by virtue of s. 105 below.

DEFINITIONS

"Housing authority"—see s. 84
"Local authority"—see s. 84

Supplementary

80. Statement of reasons for refusing application for grant or fixing grant at less than the maximum

If a local authority—

(*a*) do not approve an application for a grant, or

(*b*) fix the amount of an improvement grant, a special grant or a repairs grant at less than the appropriate percentage of the eligible expense within the meaning of section 64, section 70 or, as the case may be, section 72 above,

they shall state to the applicant in writing their reasons for doing so. **[333]**

GENERAL

This is similar to s. 23 of the Housing Act 1969. See also Circular No. 64/69.

81. Grants restricted to applicant and his personal representatives

(1) In relation to a grant or an application therefor, any reference in the preceding provisions of this Part of this Act and in subsection (2) below to the applicant shall be construed, in relation to any time after his death, as a reference to his personal representatives.

(2) If, before the certified date, an applicant for a grant ceases to have such an interest as is referred to in section 57 (3) above,—

(*a*) no grant shall be paid or, if any instalment of the grant was paid before the applicant ceased to have such an interest, no further instalments shall be paid; and

(*b*) any instalment of the grant which has been paid to the applicant shall, on being demanded by the local authority who approved the application for the grant, forthwith become repayable to them by the applicant together with interest thereon from the date on which it was paid until repayment at the rate for the time being fixed by subsection (2) of section 171 of the Local Government Act 1972 for the purposes of the enactments specified in subsection (1) of that section. [**334**]

GENERAL

This is self-explanatory.

82. Payment of grants

(1) In approving an application for a grant a local authority may require as a condition of paying the grant that the relevant works are carried out within such time, not being less than 12 months, as the authority may specify or such further time as they may allow.

(2) Where a local authority are satisfied under section 63 (3), section 68 (2), section 70 (3) or section 72 (2) above that the relevant works cannot be or could not have been carried out without the carrying out of additional works, they may, without prejudice to subsection (1) above, allow further time as the time within which the relevant works and the additional works are to be carried out.

(3) A grant may be paid after the completion of the works towards the cost of which it is payable or part of it may be paid in instalments as the works progress and the balance after the completion of the works.

(4) Where a grant is paid in instalments the aggregate of the instalments paid shall not at any time before the completion of the works exceed one half of the aggregate cost of the works executed up to that time.

(5) The payment of a grant or of any part thereof shall be conditional upon the works or the corresponding part of the works being executed to the satisfaction of the local authority.

(6) If an instalment of a grant is paid before the completion of the works and the works are not completed within the time specified in subsection (7) below, that instalment and any further sums paid by the local authority as part of the grant shall, on being demanded by the authority, forthwith become repayable to them by the person who made the application for the grant or his personal representatives and shall carry interest from the date on which it was paid until repayment at the rate for the time being fixed by subsection (2) of

section 171 of the Local Government Act 1972 for the purposes of the enactments specified in subsection (1) of that section.

(7) Where the local authority have specified no time under subsection (1) above for the completion of the works, the time referred to in subsection (6) above is 12 months from the date on which the instalment is paid or such further time as the authority may allow; and where they have specified a time under subsection (1) above or allowed further time under that subsection or subsection (2) above the time referred to in subsection (6) above is the time so specified or allowed. **[335]**

GENERAL

The provisions of this section are very similar to those of ss. 4 and 6 of the Housing Act 1969. The local authority may pay the grant as a lump sum upon completion of the works, or by instalments provided that the aggregate of the instalments does not at any time before completion exceed half the aggregate cost of the works carried out up to that time and provided that the local authority is satisfied with the work.

DEFINITIONS

"Grant"—see s. 56 (2)
"Relevant works"—see s. 57 (2) (*b*)

83. Special provisions as to parsonages, etc.

(1) Sections 57 (3), 60, 73 and 74 above shall not apply in relation to—

(*a*) an application for a grant in respect of glebe land or the residence house of an ecclesiastical benefice made, during a period when the benefice is vacant, by a sequestrator of the profits thereof; or

(*b*) an application for a grant made by a charity or on behalf of a charity by the charity trustees thereof.

(2) Section 57 (3) above shall not apply in relation to land which is proposed to be sold or leased under section 105 (2) of the Housing Act 1957 (power to dispose of land for the purpose of carrying out works in connection with work on an adjoining house) to the applicant for a grant. **[336]**

GENERAL

The first exclusion, *i.e.* s. 57 (3) and (4), relates to general provisions. Sections 60, 73 and 74 relate to certificates of future occupation, availability for letting and rents. None of these will apply to parsonages, or to applications for grant made on behalf of a charity.

DEFINITIONS

"Charity" and "charity trustees"—see s. 84
"Grant"—see s. 56 (2)

84. Interpretation of Part VII

In this Part of this Act—

"agricultural population" means—

(*a*) persons whose employment or latest employment is or was employment in agriculture or in an industry mainly dependent on agriculture, and

(*b*) the dependants of such persons,

and for this purpose "agriculture" includes dairy-farming and poultry-farming and the use of land as grazing, meadow or pasture land, or orchard or osier land or woodland, or for market gardens or nursery grounds;

"appropriate percentage" has the meaning assigned to it by section 59 above;

"certificate of owner-occupation" and "certificate of availability for letting" have the meanings assigned to them by section 60 above;

"certified date" has the meaning assigned to it by section 75 (6) above;

"charity" and "charity trustees" have the same meanings as in the Charities Act 1960;

"grant" means a grant of a description specified in section 56 (2) above;

"housing authority" means a local authority, the council of a county, the Greater London Council, the Commission for the New Towns or a development corporation within the meaning of the New Towns Act 1965;

"improvement" includes alteration and enlargement, and any reference to works required for the provision or improvement of a dwelling (whether generally or in any particular respect) includes a reference to any works of repair or replacement needed (in the opinion of the person paying any grant or contribution) for the purpose of enabling the dwelling to which the improvement relates to attain the relevant standard;

"let" includes "sub-let";

"local authority",—

(*a*) in relation to premises in a general improvement area or a housing action area, means the council by whom the area was declared to be such an area; and

(*b*) in relation to any other premises, means the council of a district or London borough or the Common Council of the City of London;

"owner", in relation to a dwelling, means the person who—

(*a*) is for the time being entitled to receive from a lessee of the dwelling, or would be so entitled if the dwelling were let, a rent of not less than two-thirds of the net annual value of the dwelling; and

(*b*) is himself not liable, as a lessee of, or of any property which includes, the dwelling, to pay to a superior landlord a rent of not less than two-thirds of the net annual value of the property of which he is such a lessee;

"prescribed" means prescribed by order made by the Secretary of State;

"the relevant standard" means—

(*a*) in relation to an improvement grant, the required standard referred to in section 61 above;

(*b*) in relation to an intermediate grant, the full standard or, as the case may require, the reduced standard referred to in section 66 above; and

(*c*) in relation to a repairs grant, the relevant standard of repair referred to in section 71 above;

"the relevant works" has the meaning assigned to it by section 57 (2) (*b*) above;

"standard amenities" has the meaning assigned to it by section 58 above.

[337]

PART VIII

COMPULSORY IMPROVEMENT OF DWELLINGS

Dwellings in general improvement areas and housing action areas

85. Provisional notice of local authority's proposals for improvement of dwelling

(1) If it appears to the local authority by whom a general improvement area or a housing action area has been declared that a dwelling in that area—

(*a*) is without one or more of the standard amenities, whether or not it is also in a state of disrepair, and

(*b*) is capable at reasonable expense of improvement to the full standard or, failing that, to the reduced standard, and

(*c*) was provided (by erection or by the conversion of a building already in existence) before 3rd October 1961,

then, subject to subsection (3) below, the authority may serve a notice under subsection (2) below on the person having control of the dwelling.

(2) A notice under this subsection (in the following provisions of this Part of this Act referred to as a "provisional notice") shall—

(*a*) specify the works which in the opinion of the local authority are required for the dwelling to be improved to the full standard or, as the case may be, to the reduced standard; and

(*b*) state the date, being a date not less than 21 days after service of the provisional notice, and time and place at which the authority's proposals for the carrying out of the works, any alternative proposals, any proposed housing arrangements, the views and interests of the occupying tenant (if any) and any other matters may be discussed.

(3) A local authority may not serve a provisional notice in respect of a dwelling which is owner-occupied unless it appears to them that the circumstances are such that it is not reasonably practicable for another dwelling—

(*a*) which is in the same building as, or is adjacent to, the dwelling which is owner-occupied, and

(*b*) which is not owner-occupied or in respect of which an application for a grant under Part VII of this Act has been approved,

to be improved to the full standard or, as the case may be, to the reduced standard without effecting the improvement to one of those standards of the dwelling which is owner-occupied.

(4) A local authority shall, not less than 21 days before the date stated in a provisional notice as mentioned in subsection (2) (*b*) above, in addition to serving the notice on the person having control of the dwelling, serve a copy of the notice on the occupying tenant (if any) of the dwelling and on every other person who, to the knowledge of the local authority, is an owner, lessee or mortgagee of the dwelling; and the person having control of the dwelling, the occupying tenant (if any) and every other person who is an owner, lessee or mortgagee of the dwelling shall be entitled to be heard when the authority's proposals are discussed in accordance with the notice.

(5) After the service of a provisional notice and before taking any other action under this Part of this Act, a local authority shall take into consideration all representations made on or before the occasion when their proposals with respect to the dwelling are discussed in accordance with the notice and, in

particular, any representations with respect to the nature of the works proposed by them for improving the dwelling or with respect to any proposed housing arrangements. [**338**]

GENERAL

See Chapter 8 for general comments on compulsory improvements, and s. 89 below as to compulsory improvement of individual dwellings outside general improvement areas and housing action areas. The main energies of local authorities will be devoted to the improvement of conditions in such areas, and they need the powers given by this section to deal with owners who will not carry out improvements voluntarily. The first step is the service of provisional notices under this section. The special position of owner-occupiers under sub-s. (3) should be noted. The occupying tenant, the person having control, and any other person who is an owner, lessee, or mortgagee, are all entitled to be heard, and to have their representations taken into account. See Circular 160/74 in Appendix II.

DEFINITIONS

"Full standard"—see s. 66 and s. 104
"General improvement area"—see s. 50
"Housing action area"—see s. 36
"Housing arrangements"—see s. 86 and Sch. 13, paras. 38 to 41.
For other definitions applicable to Part VIII, see s. 104.

86. Housing arrangements

(1) In this Part of this Act "housing arrangements", in relation to a dwelling falling within section 85 (1) above, means arrangements falling within subsection (2) below and making provision for the housing of an occupying tenant of the dwelling and his household—

(*a*) during the period when improvement works are being carried out, or
(*b*) after the completion of those works, or
(*c*) during that period and after completion of those works,

and for any matters incidental or ancillary thereto.

(2) The arrangements referred to in subsection (1) above are arrangements contained in a written agreement to which the occupying tenant and either or both of his landlord and the local authority concerned are parties. [**339**]

87. Acceptance of undertakings to do works

(1) In any case where an improvement notice has not yet been served in respect of a dwelling falling within subsection (1) of section 85 above, the local authority referred to in that subsection may, subject to subsection (3) below, accept from the person having control of the dwelling or from any other person having an estate or interest in the dwelling an undertaking in writing to improve the dwelling to the full standard or, if in the opinion of the local authority it is not practicable at reasonable expense for the dwelling to be improved to the full standard, to the reduced standard.

(2) The undertaking shall specify the works agreed to be carried out and the period within which (subject to any variation by the local authority as mentioned in subsection (4) (*a*) below) the works are to be carried out, being a period ending not more than 9 months after the date on which the undertaking is accepted.

(3) Before accepting an undertaking under this section with respect to any dwelling, the local authority shall satisfy themselves—

(*a*) that, if there is an occupying tenant, the housing arrangements are satisfactory or no housing arrangements are required and the undertaking incorporates the written consent of the occupying tenant signed by him, to the carrying out of the works specified in the undertaking; and

(*b*) that the person giving the undertaking has a right to carry out the works specified in the undertaking as against all other persons having an estate or interest in the dwelling.

(4) Where a local authority accept an undertaking under this section with respect to any dwelling, they shall serve a notice to that effect on the person by whom the undertaking was given and shall not thereafter serve an improvement notice with respect to that dwelling—

(*a*) unless any works specified in the undertaking are not carried out within the period so specified, or within such longer period as the local authority may by permission in writing have allowed; or

(*b*) unless the local authority are satisfied that, owing to a change of circumstances since the undertaking was accepted by them, the undertaking is unlikely to be fulfilled.

(5) A local authority who have accepted an undertaking under this section—

(*a*) shall discharge the undertaking if at any time they consider that the dwelling no longer falls within paragraph (*a*) or paragraph (*b*) of subsection (1) of section 85 above, and

(*b*) may discharge the undertaking in any other case,

and the discharge of an undertaking under this subsection shall be effected by serving a notice of the discharge on the person by whom the undertaking was given.

(6) Where a local authority serve a notice under subsection (4) or subsection (5) above on the person by whom an undertaking was given, they shall at the same time serve a copy of the notice on the person (if any) who is at that time the occupying tenant of the dwelling and on every other person who, to the knowledge of the authority, is at that time an owner, lessee or mortgagee of the dwelling. [**340**]

GENERAL

Before serving an improvement notice (as distinct from a provisional notice), the local authority may accept an undertaking to improve the dwelling to the required standard. The undertaking must specify the works and the period, not being more than 9 months after acceptance of the undertaking, within which they will be completed.

If they have satisfied themselves on the lines laid down in sub-s. (3) the local authority will serve a notice under sub-s. (4) accepting the undertaking, and shall not thereafter serve an improvement notice except for the reasons in sub-s. (4) (*a*) or (*b*). See Circular 160/74 in Appendix II.

DEFINITIONS

See s. 104.

88. Conditions for service of improvement notices

(1) If a local authority have served a provisional notice in respect of a dwelling and—

(*a*) no undertaking has yet been accepted in respect of the dwelling under section 87 above, or

(*b*) such an undertaking has been accepted but paragraph (*a*) or paragraph (*b*) of subsection (4) of section 87 above applies,

the local authority may, subject to the following provisions of this section, serve an improvement notice on the person having control of the dwelling.

(2) Before serving an improvement notice in respect of any dwelling by virtue of subsection (1) above, a local authority shall satisfy themselves—

(*a*) that the dwelling continues to be in a general improvement area or a housing action area; and

(*b*) that the provisions of paragraphs (*a*) and (*b*) of subsection (1) of section 85 above still apply in relation to the dwelling; and

(*c*) that the dwelling is not for the time being owner-occupied or that the circumstances specified in subsection (3) of that section apply or still apply in relation to it; and

(*d*) if there is an occupying tenant, that the housing arrangements are satisfactory or that no housing arrangements are required or that the occupying tenant has unreasonably refused to enter into any housing arrangements.

(3) An improvement notice may not be served in respect of any dwelling by virtue of subsection (1) above,—

(*a*) if paragraph (*a*) of that subsection applies, more than 9 months after the service of the provisional notice referred to in that subsection; and

(*b*) if paragraph (*b*) of that subsection applies, more than 6 months after the expiry of the period specified in the undertaking mentioned in that paragraph or, as the case may be, such longer period as the local authority may by permission in writing have allowed for the completion of the works specified in the undertaking.

(4) Where, by virtue of subsection (1) above, a local authority serve an improvement notice on the person having control of a dwelling, they shall at the same time serve a copy of the notice on the occupying tenant (if any) of the dwelling and on every other person who, to the knowledge of the authority, is an owner, lessee or mortgagee of the dwelling. **[341]**

GENERAL

An improvement notice may not be served more than 9 months after a provisional notice has been served, unless an undertaking has been accepted, and the works have been unduly delayed.

Before serving the notice the local authority must satisfy themselves that the dwelling is still in a general improvement area or a housing action area, and that the other requirements of s. 88 are satisfied. See Circular 160/74 in Appendix II.

DEFINITIONS

"Dwelling"—see s. 129
"General improvement area"—see s. 50
"Housing action area"—see s. 36
See also s. 104 for other definitions applicable to this Part of the Act.

Dwellings outside general improvement areas and housing action areas

89. Compulsory improvement of dwellings outside general improvement areas and housing action areas

(1) An occupying tenant of a dwelling which—

(*a*) is not in a general improvement area or a housing action area, and

(*b*) is without one or more of the standard amenities, whether or not it is also in a state of disrepair, and

(*c*) was provided (by erection or by the conversion of a building already in existence) before 3rd October 1961,

may make representations in writing to the local authority for the area in which the dwelling is situated with a view to the exercise by the authority of their powers under this section.

(2) A local authority shall notify the person having control of the dwelling of any representations made to them under subsection (1) above.

(3) If, on taking the representations into consideration, the local authority are satisfied—

(*a*) that the person making the representations is an occupying tenant of the dwelling in question, and

(*b*) that the provisions of paragraphs (*a*) to (*c*) of subsection (1) above apply in relation to the dwelling, and

(*c*) that the dwelling is capable at reasonable expense of improvement to the full standard or, failing that, to the reduced standard, and

(*d*) that, having regard to all the circumstances, the dwelling ought to be improved to the full standard or, as the case may be, to the reduced standard, and that it is unlikely that it will be so improved unless the local authority exercise their powers under this section,

the following provisions of this section shall apply.

(4) If the local authority are satisfied as mentioned in subsection (3) above, they shall either—

(*a*) serve a provisional notice on the person having control of the dwelling, or

(*b*) notify the occupying tenant of the dwelling of their decision not to serve a provisional notice and give him a written statement setting out their reasons for making that decision,

and where a provisional notice is served by virtue of paragraph (*a*) above, the provisions of subsections (4) and (5) of section 85 above shall apply accordingly and the dwelling shall be treated for the purposes of section 86 above as being one falling within section 85 (1) above.

(5) Subject to subsection (6) below, in any case where—

(*a*) representations have been made to a local authority under subsection (1) above, and

(*b*) as a result of those representations, a provisional notice has been served by virtue of subsection (4) (*a*) above,

the local authority may, at any time before the expiry of the period of 12 months beginning with the date on which the representations were received by them, serve an improvement notice on the person having control of the dwelling; and subsection (4) of section 88 above shall apply as it applies in relation to an improvement notice served by virtue of subsection (1) of that section.

(6) Before serving an improvement notice in respect of a dwelling by virtue of subsection (5) above, a local authority shall satisfy themselves—

(*a*) that the provisions of paragraphs (*b*) to (*d*) of subsection (3) above still apply in relation to the dwelling; and

(*b*) that the housing arrangements are satisfactory or that no housing arrangements are required or that the occupying tenant has unreasonably refused to enter into any housing arrangements.

(7) The power of serving a provisional notice by virtue of subsection (4) (*a*) above and of taking any further steps authorised under this Part of this Act may be exercised by a local authority notwithstanding that the occupying tenant

who made representations under subsection (1) above quits the dwelling and notwithstanding that, after the occupying tenant has made those representations, the authority pass a resolution declaring an area in which the dwelling is situated to be a general improvement area or a housing action area. **[342]**

GENERAL

Outside general improvement areas and action areas the initiative for compulsory improvement lies wholly with the occupying tenant.

On receiving representations from the occupying tenant the local authority must notify the person having control of the dwelling.

If the local authority are satisfied on the points listed in sub-s. (3), they must either serve a provisional notice on the person having control or notify the tenant that they have decided not to do so, and send him a written statement of their reasons This follows the pattern set by s. 19 of the Housing Act 1964, and the local authority has discretion whether or not to issue a provisional improvement notice.

The service of a provisional notice may, at any time within 12 months of receipt of the tenant's representations, be followed by an improvement notice, but the requirements of sub-s. (6) must first be satisfied.

DEFINITIONS

"Dwelling"—see s. 129

"Standard amenity"—see s. 58

See also s. 104 for other definitions.

General provisions as to improvement notices

90. Improvement notices: content and registration

(1) Subject to the following provisions of this section, a notice under this section (in this Part of this Act referred to as an "improvement notice") shall—

(*a*) specify the works which in the opinion of the local authority are required to improve the dwelling to the full standard or, as the case may be, to the reduced standard;

(*b*) state the authority's estimate of the cost of carrying out those works; and

(*c*) require the person having control of the dwelling to carry out to the authority's satisfaction the works specified in the notice within the period of 12 months beginning with the date when the improvement notice becomes operative or such longer period as the authority may by permission in writing from time to time allow.

(2) The works specified in an improvement notice may be different from the works specified in the provisional notice but shall not require the improvement of a dwelling to the full standard if the provisional notice specified works for improving the dwelling only to the reduced standard.

(3) In an improvement notice which requires the improvement of a dwelling only to the reduced standard the local authority may, if they think fit, substitute for the period of 12 months specified in paragraph (*c*) of subsection (1) above such shorter period as appears to them to be appropriate.

(4) As soon as may be after an improvement notice has been served it shall be registered in the register of local land charges—

(*a*) by the proper officer, for the purposes of section 15 of the Land Charges Act 1925, of the council in whose area the dwelling concerned is situated, and

(*b*) in such manner as may be prescribed by rules under section 19 of that Act, and in this subsection "council" means a district council, a London borough council or the Common Council of the City of London. [**343**]

GENERAL

This is self-explanatory. See Circular 160/74 in Appendix II.

DEFINITIONS

See s. 104.

91. Appeals against improvement notices

(1) Within 6 weeks from the service on the person having control of the dwelling of an improvement notice, that person, the occupying tenant (if any) of the dwelling or any other person having an estate or interest in the dwelling may appeal to the county court against the improvement notice in accordance with the following provisions of this section.

(2) Subject to subsection (3) below, the grounds on which an appeal may be brought under this section are all or any of the following,—

(*a*) that it is not practicable to comply with the requirements of the improvement notice at reasonable expense;

(*b*) that the local authority have refused unreasonably to approve the execution of alternative works, or that the works specified in the notice are otherwise unreasonable in character or extent;

(*c*) that the dwelling is within an area declared to be a clearance area under Part III of the Housing Act 1957 and, having regard to all the circumstances of the case, it would be unreasonable for the local authority to require the works specified in the improvement notice to be carried out;

(*d*) that the dwelling is not, or is no longer, without one or more of the standard amenities;

(*e*) that, in a case where the improvement notice requires the improvement of the dwelling to the full standard, the works specified in the notice are inadequate to secure that the dwelling will attain that standard;

(*f*) that some person other than the appellant will, as the holder of an estate or interest in the dwelling (whether or not that estate or interest entitles him to occupation), derive a benefit from the execution of the works and that that person ought to pay the whole or part of the cost of the execution of the works;

(*g*) that the improvement notice is invalid on the ground that any requirement of this Part of this Act has not been complied with or on the ground of some informality, defect or error in or in connection with the improvement notice.

(3) Without prejudice to the grounds on which he may appeal by virtue of subsection (2) above,—

(*a*) an owner-occupier may bring an appeal under this section on the ground that the local authority are in error in considering that the circumstances specified in section 85 (3) above exist in relation to the dwelling; and

(*b*) the occupying tenant may bring an appeal under this section on the ground that the condition in section 88 (2) (*d*) above or, as the case may be, section 89 (6) (*b*) above for the service of the improvement notice is not fulfilled.

(4) Subject to the following provisions of this section, on an appeal under this section the court may make such order either confirming or quashing or varying the improvement notice as the court thinks fit.

(5) An improvement notice shall not be varied on an appeal under this section—

(*a*) so as to extend the period within which the works specified in the notice are to be carried out; or

(*b*) so as to require the carrying out of works to improve a dwelling to the full standard if the works specified in the notice were works to improve the dwelling to the reduced standard; or

(*c*) so as to require the carrying out of works to improve a dwelling to the reduced standard if the works specified in the notice were works to improve the dwelling to the full standard.

(6) Where an appeal is brought under this section on the ground specified in paragraph (*f*) of subsection (2) above (with or without other grounds), the court may on the hearing of the appeal make such order as it thinks fit with respect to the payment to be made by the other person referred to in that paragraph to the appellant or where, by virtue of section 93 below, the works are carried out by the local authority to the local authority.

(7) In so far as an appeal under this section is based on the ground that the improvement notice is invalid, the court shall confirm the improvement notice unless satisfied that the interests of the appellant have been substantially prejudiced by the facts relied on by him. **[344]**

GENERAL

This section may be compared with s. 27 of the Housing Act 1964.

The grounds on which an appeal may be brought are set out in subs-s. (2) and (3). The county court may confirm, quash, or vary the improvement notice, but the power to vary is subject to sub-s. (5). With regard to "substantially prejudiced" in sub-s. (7), see *De Rothschild* v. *Wing R.D.C.*, [1967] 1 All E.R. 597; [1967] 1 W.L.R. 470. See Circular 160/74 in Appendix II.

DEFINITIONS

See s. 104.

92. Operative effect and withdrawal of improvement notices

(1) If no appeal is brought against an improvement notice under section 91 above, the notice shall become operative at the expiry of the period of 6 weeks beginning with the date of the service of the notice on the person having control of the dwelling, and any improvement notice against which an appeal is so brought shall, if and so far as it is confirmed by the county court, or on appeal from the county court, become operative on the final determination of the appeal.

(2) For the purposes of subsection (1) above the withdrawal of an appeal shall be deemed to be the final determination thereof, having the like effect as a decision confirming the improvement notice or decision appealed against.

(3) An improvement notice shall, subject to the right of appeal conferred by section 91 above, be final and conclusive as to any matters which could be raised on any such appeal.

(4) A local authority may, if they think fit, at any time withdraw an improvement notice by serving notice of the withdrawal on the person having control of the dwelling, and the local authority shall serve a copy of any such notice on the occupier of the dwelling (if different from the person having control

of it) and on every other person who, to the knowledge of the authority, is an owner, lessee or mortgagee of the dwelling. [**345**]

GENERAL

This calls for little comment but it is to be noted that the local authority may withdraw an improvement notice at any time.

93. Enforcement of improvement notices

(1) If the works to be carried out in compliance with an improvement notice have not been carried out in whole or in part within the period specified in the notice, or within such longer period as the local authority by whom the notice was served may by permission in writing have allowed, the authority may themselves carry out so much of the works as has not been completed.

(2) If before the expiry of the period mentioned in subsection (1) above the person who is for the time being the person having control of the dwelling notifies the local authority in writing that he does not intend or is unable to do the works in question, the authority may, if they think fit, do the works before the expiry of that period.

(3) If the local authority by whom an improvement notice was served have reason to believe that the person who is for the time being the person having control of the dwelling does not intend or is unable to do the works in question in compliance with the notice,—

(*a*) the authority may, before the expiry of the period mentioned in subsection (1) above, but not earlier than 6 months after the date on which the improvement notice becomes operative, serve on that person a notice requiring him to furnish them, within 21 days of the service of the notice, with evidence of his intentions with respect to the carrying out of the works; and

(*b*) if, from any evidence furnished to them in pursuance of a notice under paragraph (*a*) above or otherwise, the authority are not satisfied that that person intends to carry out the works in compliance with the notice, they may, if they think fit, do the works before the expiry of the period mentioned in subsection (1) above.

(4) Not less than 21 days before beginning to do the works the local authority shall serve notice of their intention on the occupier of the dwelling, on the person having control of the dwelling and on every other person who, to the knowledge of the authority, is an owner, lessee or mortgagee of the dwelling. [**346**]

GENERAL

The main means of enforcement is the power given by sub-s. (1) for the local authority to carry out the works themselves, if they have not been carried out within the period specified in the notice. They may do the work themselves before the period has expired if the person having control gives notice that he does not intend or is unable to do the works within the specified period.

Thirdly, the local authority may force the issue before the period has expired by taking action under sub-s. (3).

The recovery of expenses incurred by a local authority is dealt with in s. 94.

DEFINITIONS

See s. 104 and s. 129.

94. Recovery of expenses incurred by local authority on default under improvement notice

(1) Subject to subsections (2) and (3) below, any expenses reasonably incurred by a local authority under section 93 above in carrying out any works may, except so far as they are by any direction of the court on appeal recover-

able under an order of the court, be recovered by them by action from the person having control of the dwelling.

(2) A demand for the expenses recoverable by a local authority under subsection (1) above, together with interest thereon in accordance with subsection (3) below, shall be served on the person having control of the dwelling; and on the date on which a demand is so served, the local authority shall serve a copy of the demand on every other person who, to the knowledge of the authority, is an owner, lessee or mortgagee of the dwelling concerned.

(3) Expenses in respect of which a demand is served under subsection (2) above shall carry interest—

(*a*) from the date on which the demand is so served until payment of all sums due thereunder, and

(*b*) at the rate fixed by section 171 (2) of the Local Government Act 1972 (rates of interest in relation to various sums due to local authorities).

(4) The amount of any expenses and interest thereon due to an authority under this section shall, as from the date when the demand under subsection (2) above becomes operative, be a charge on the premises in respect of which the expenses were incurred, and on all estates and interests in those premises, and the authority shall for the purpose of enforcing that charge have all the same powers and remedies under the Law of Property Act 1925 and otherwise as if they were mortgagees by deed having powers of sale and lease, of accepting surrenders of leases and of appointing a receiver; and the power of appointing a receiver under this subsection shall be exercisable at any time after the expiry of one month from the date when the said demand becomes operative.

(5) Within 21 days from the date of service of a demand under subsection (2) above, any person on whom the demand or a copy thereof was so served may appeal to the county court against the demand, but on such an appeal no question may be raised which might have been raised on an appeal against the improvement notice relating to the dwelling in question.

(6) A demand served under subsection (2) above—

(*a*) against which no appeal is brought under subsection (5) above shall become operative on the expiry of 21 days from the date of services of the demand,

(*b*) against which an appeal is so brought shall, if and so far as it is confirmed on appeal, become operative on the final determination of the appeal,

and for the purposes of this subsection the withdrawal of an appeal shall be deemed to be the final determination thereof, having the like effect as a decision confirming the demand appealed against.

(7) A demand served under subsection (2) above shall, subject to the right of appeal conferred by subsection (5) above, be final and conclusive as to any matters which can be raised on such an appeal. [**347**]

GENERAL

Where the local authority itself carries out the works under s. 93 they may recover reasonable expenses, with interest thereon. There is a right of appeal under sub-s. (5).

DEFINITIONS

See ss. 104 and 129.

95. Charging orders in favour of persons carrying out works

Sections 14 and 15 of the Housing Act 1957 (charging orders in favour of owner executing works) shall apply as if any reference to works required to be executed by a notice under Part II of that Act included a reference to works required to be carried out by an improvement notice, and in the application of those sections by virtue of this section any reference to a house or the owner of a house shall be construed as a reference to a dwelling, within the meaning of this Part of this Act, or, as the case may require, the person having control of it, within the meaning of this Part. [**348**]

GENERAL

An owner who has carried out works to the satisfaction of the local authority may apply to them to make a charging order. This will be at the rate of £6 per cent. for 30 years. Any person aggrieved by a charging order may appeal to the Crown Court. There is no appeal against a refusal by the local authority to make a charging order. See *Holborn and Frascati Ltd* v. *London County Council* (1916), 80 J.P. 225, at p. 228.

Supplementary

96. Provisions as to carrying out of works

(1) The person having control of any premises—

(*a*) which consist of or include a dwelling in a general improvement area or a housing action area which is without all or any of the standard amenities, or

(*b*) which consist of or include a dwelling in respect of which representations have been made by the occupying tenant under section 89 above,

shall, as against the occupying tenant of the dwelling and any other person having an estate or interest in the premises, have the right to enter the premises in order to carry out any survey or examination required with a view to providing the dwelling with any of the standard amenities and, where appropriate, of putting it in good repair (disregarding internal decorative repair) having regard to its age and character and the locality in which it is situated.

(2) On and after the date on which an improvement notice in respect of a dwelling becomes operative, the person having control of the dwelling shall have the right, as against the occupying tenant (if any) of the dwelling and any other person having an estate or interest in the premises which consist of or include the dwelling, to take any reasonable steps for the purpose of complying with the improvement notice; and any person bound by an undertaking accepted under this Part of this Act shall have the right as against the occupying tenant (if any) of the dwelling to which the undertaking relates to take any reasonable steps for the purpose of complying with the undertaking.

(3) Section 161 of the Housing Act 1957 (penalty for preventing execution of works) shall apply as if—

(*a*) any reference in that section to Part II of that Act included a reference to this Part of this Act;

(*b*) the reference therein to receiving notice of the intended action included a reference to receiving an improvement notice or a copy thereof; and

(*c*) any reference therein to the owner of any premises included a reference to the person having control thereof.

(4) Without prejudice to subsection (2) above, the carrying out of works in pursuance of an improvement notice or an undertaking accepted under this Part of this Act shall not give rise to any liability on the part of a lessee to reinstate any premises at any time in the condition in which they were before the works were carried out, or to any liability for failure so to reinstate the premises. [**349**]

GENERAL

The person having control is given the right of entry to make a survey or examination with a view to providing the dwelling with any of the standard amenities and putting it into good repair. This applies to any dwelling in the general improvement area or housing action area which is without all or any of the standard amenities; outside such areas it applies only where the occupying tenant has made representations under s. 89 above.

The person having control is given the right to take any reasonable steps to comply with an improvement notice which has become operative, and a similar right is given to any person bound by an undertaking accepted under this Part of the Act. There are penalties for preventing the execution of the works.

DEFINITIONS

See s. 104.

97. Further powers and duties of local authorities

(1) Section 159 of the Housing Act 1957 (powers of entry of local authorities for certain purposes) shall apply to entry for the purpose of survey and examination of any dwelling with a view to ascertaining whether the requirements of an improvement notice served, or undertaking accepted, under this Part of this Act have been complied with, and section 160 of that Act (penalty for obstructing execution of Act) shall apply accordingly.

(2) A local authority may by agreement with a person having control of a dwelling or any other person having an estate or interest in a dwelling execute at his expense any works which that person is required to carry out in the dwelling in pursuance of an improvement notice served, or undertaking accepted, under this Part of this Act, and for that purpose the local authority shall have all such rights as that person would have as against the occupying tenant (if any) of the dwelling and any other person having an interest in the dwelling.

(3) Where under this Part of this Act a local authority are required to serve a copy of a notice on any person who, to their knowledge, is an owner, lessee or mortgagee of any dwelling, any person having an estate or interest in the dwelling who is not served with a copy of the notice shall, on application in writing to the local authority, be entitled to obtain a copy of that notice. [**350**]

GENERAL

The powers of entry of local authorities under s. 159 of the Housing Act 1957 are extended to entry to ascertain whether an improvement notice, or an undertaking, under this Part of this Act, have been complied with.

Sub-s. (2) covers the position of a local authority which by agreement is to execute any works under an improvement notice served, or undertaking accepted, under this Part of this Act.

This section also refers to the duty of a local authority to provide copies of notices to any person who is an owner, lessee, or mortgagee, or any person who has an interest in the dwelling.

98. Consequential modifications of Agricultural Holdings Act 1948

(1) Section 9 of the Agricultural Holdings Act 1948 (increases of rent for improvements carried out by landlord) shall apply, subject to subsection (2) below, as if references in subsection (1) of that section to improvements carried out at the request of the tenant included references to improvements carried out in compliance with an improvement notice or an undertaking accepted under this Part of this Act.

(2) Where a tenant has contributed to the cost incurred by his landlord in carrying out such an improvement as is referred to in subsection (1) above, the increase in rent provided for by the said section 9 shall be reduced proportionately.

(3) Any works carried out in compliance with an improvement notice or an undertaking accepted under this Part of this Act shall be included among the improvements specified in paragraph 8 of Schedule 3 to the Agricultural Holdings Act 1948 (tenant's right to compensation for erection, alteration or enlargement of buildings), but subject to the power conferred by section 78 of that Act to amend that Schedule; and section 49 of that Act (tenant's right to compensation conditional on the landlord consenting to the carrying out of the improvements) shall not apply to any works carried out in compliance with such a notice or undertaking.

(4) Where a person other than the tenant claiming compensation has contributed to the cost of carrying out the works in compliance with an improvement notice or an undertaking accepted under this Part of this Act, compensation in respect of the works, as assessed under section 48 of the Agricultural Holdings Act 1948, shall be reduced proportionately. [**351**]

GENERAL

Increases of rent for improvements carried out by the landlord under an improvement notice or undertaking shall be treated, for the purpose of rent increases under the 1948 Act, as if they were improvements made at the request of the tenant.

Improvements carried out by the tenant under this Part of the Act will affect the tenant's right to compensation under the 1948 Act.

DEFINITIONS

See s. 104 below.

99. Exclusion of dwellings controlled by Crown or a public authority

(1) No provisional notice or improvement notice may be served in respect of a dwelling in which there is a Crown or Duchy interest except with the consent of the appropriate authority and, where a provisional notice or improvement notice is served with the consent of the appropriate authority, this Part of this Act shall apply in relation to the dwelling as it applies in relation to a dwelling in which there is no such interest.

(2) No provisional notice or improvement notice may be served in respect of a dwelling if the person having control of the dwelling is—

(*a*) a local authority;
(*b*) the Commission for the New Towns;
(*c*) the Housing Corporation;
(*d*) a registered housing association;
(*e*) a development corporation within the meaning of the New Towns Act 1965; or
(*f*) a housing trust as defined in section 5 (3) of the Rent Act 1968 which is a charity within the meaning of the Charities Act 1960.

(3) If, after a provisional notice or an improvement notice has been served in respect of any dwelling,—

(*a*) any such body as is mentioned in paragraphs (*a*) to (*f*) of subsection (2) above becomes the person having control of the dwelling, or
(*b*) in the case of a dwelling in which there is a Crown or Duchy interest, the appropriate authority becomes the person having control of the dwelling,

any such notice with respect to the dwelling and any undertaking accepted under this Part of this Act with respect to the dwelling shall cease to have effect.

(4) If, by virtue of subsection (3) above, an improvement notice with respect to any dwelling ceases to have effect, it shall be the duty of the body which or person who has become the person having control of the dwelling as mentioned in that subsection to notify the officer who registered the notice in the register of local land charges and to furnish him with all information required by him for the purpose of cancelling the registration.

(5) In this section "Crown or Duchy interest" means an interest belonging to Her Majesty in right of the Crown or of the Duchy of Lancaster, or belonging to the Duchy of Cornwall or belonging to a government department, or held in trust for Her Majesty for the purposes of a government department, and "the appropriate authority",—

(*a*) in relation to land belonging to Her Majesty in right of the Crown and forming part of the Crown Estate, means the Crown Estate Commissioners, and, in relation to any other land belonging to Her Majesty in right of the Crown, means the government department having the management of that land;

(*b*) in relation to land belonging to Her Majesty in right of the Duchy of Lancaster, means the Chancellor of the Duchy;

(*c*) in relation to land belonging to the Duchy of Cornwall, means such person as the Duke of Cornwall, or the possessor for the time being of the Duchy of Cornwall, appoints; and

(*d*) in relation to land belonging to a government department or held in trust for Her Majesty for the purposes of a government department, means that department;

and if any question arises as to what authority is the appropriate authority in relation to any land, that question shall be referred to the Treasury, whose decision shall be final.

(6) In this section "local authority" includes, in addition to the bodies which, by virtue of section 104 (1) below, are local authorities for the purposes of this Part of this Act,—

(*a*) a county council;
(*b*) the Greater London Council;
(*c*) a parish or community council;
(*d*) the trustees of the Honourable Society of the Inner Temple;
(*e*) the trustees of the Honourable Society of the Middle Temple;
(*f*) the police authority for any police area; and
(*g*) any joint board or joint committee all the constituent members of which are local authorities for the purposes of this section. **[352]**

GENERAL

A provisional notice or improvement notice may only be served in respect of a dwelling in which there is a Crown or Duchy interest where consent has been given on their behalf. Sub-s. (2) lists the types of owner or person having control upon whom no improvement notice may be served.

Sub-s. (3) estends the ban to cases where any of the named bodies becomes the person in control after a notice has been served. The special definition of the term "local authority" in this section is given in sub-s. (6).

DEFINITIONS

See s. 104.

100. Duty of local authority to offer loans to meet expenses of compulsory improvement

(1) Any person who is liable to incur expenditure in complying with an improvement notice served, or undertaking accepted, under this Part of this Act,

or who is liable to make a payment as directed by a court under section 91 (6) above, may apply to the local authority for a loan.

(2) Subject to the following provisions of this section, if the local authority are satisfied that the applicant for a loan can reasonably be expected to meet obligations assumed by him in pursuance of this section in respect of a loan of the amount of the expenditure or payment to which the application relates, the local authority shall offer to enter into a contract with the applicant for a loan by the local authority to the applicant of that amount, to be secured to the local authority by a mortgage of the applicant's interest in the dwelling concerned.

(3) Subject to the following provisions of this section, if the local authority are not satisfied as mentioned in subsection (2) above but consider that the applicant can reasonably be expected to meet obligations assumed by him in pursuance of this section in respect of a loan of a smaller amount, the local authority may, if they think fit, offer to enter into a contract with the applicant for a loan by the local authority to the applicant of that smaller amount, to be secured as mentioned in subsection (2) above.

(4) Any contract entered into by a local authority under this section shall contain a condition to the effect that, if an improvement grant or intermediate grant becomes payable under Part VII of this Act in respect of the expenditure or payment to which the application under this section relates, the local authority shall not be required to lend a sum greater than the amount of the expenditure or payment to which the application relates after deduction of the amount of the improvement grant, or, as the case may be, the intermediate grant.

(5) A local authority shall not make an offer under the preceding provisions of this section unless they are satisfied—

(*a*) that the applicant's interest in the dwelling concerned amounts to an estate in fee simple absolute in possession or an estate for a term of years which will not expire before the date for final repayment of the loan; and

(*b*) that, according to a valuation made on behalf of the local authority, the amount of the principal of the loan does not exceed the value which it is estimated that the mortgaged security will bear after improvement of the dwelling to the full standard or, as the case may be, to the reduced standard.

(6) The rate of interest payable on a loan under this section shall be such as the Secretary of State may direct either generally or in any particular case and the Secretary of State may, if he thinks fit, give directions, either generally or in any particular case, as to the time within which a loan under this section, or any part of such a loan, is to be repaid.

(7) Subject to the preceding provisions of this section, the contract offered by a local authority under this section shall require proof of title and contain such other reasonable terms as the local authority may specify in their offer and, in particular, may provide for the advance being made by instalments from time to time as the works specified in the improvement notice progress.

(8) An application under this section shall be made in writing within the period of 3 months beginning with the date when the improvement notice becomes operative or the undertaking is accepted or the payment is to be made as directed by the court, as the case may be, or such longer period as the local authority by permission given in writing may allow.

(9) Where an improvement grant or intermediate grant is payable under Part VII of this Act partly in respect of expenditure or a payment to which the application under this section relates and partly in respect of other expenditure or another payment, the references in subsection (4) above to an intermediate grant or an improvement grant shall be taken as a reference to the part of the intermediate grant or improvement grant which in the opinion of the local authority is attributable to the expenditure or payment to which the application under this section relates. **[353]**

GENERAL

This creates duties in broadly similar terms to the requirements of s. 57 of the Housing Act 1964. That section is repealed by this Act.

The contract for the loan must contain a condition that the amount is subject to reduction in due course by the amount of any improvement grant on intermediate grant.

Application for a loan must be made in due time—see sub-s. (8). The local authority must not make an offer unless they are satisfied as to the nature and extent of the applicant's interest and the ultimate value of the security.

See Circular 160/74 in Appendix II.

DEFINITIONS

See s. 104 below.

101. Right of person served with improvement notice to serve purchase notice

(1) Where a local authority have served an improvement notice under this Part of this Act on the person having control of a dwelling, that person may, by notice in writing served on the local authority at any time within the period of 6 months beginning with the date on which the improvement notice becomes operative, require the local authority to purchase his interest in the dwelling in accordance with this section.

(2) Where the person having control of a dwelling serves a notice on a local authority under subsection (1) above—

(*a*) the authority shall be deemed to be authorised under and for the purposes of Part V of the Housing Act 1957 to acquire that person's interest in the dwelling compulsorily and to have served a notice to treat in respect of that interest on the date of the service of the notice under subsection (1) above; and

(*b*) the power conferred by section 31 of the Land Compensation Act 1961 to withdraw a notice to treat shall not be exercisable in the case of the notice to treat which is deemed to have been so served.

(3) Within 21 days of the receipt of a notice under subsection (1) above served by the person having control of a dwelling the local authority shall notify every other person who, to their knowledge, is an owner, lessee or mortgagee of the dwelling or who is the occupier thereof. **[354]**

GENERAL

This is on similar lines to s. 59 of the Housing Act 1964, which gave the right to serve a purchase notice where the local authority had taken steps to secure compulsory improvement of a dwelling. S. 59 of the 1964 Act is repealed by this Act.

102. Effect of an area ceasing to be a general improvement area or housing action area after improvement notice is served

If, after an undertaking has been accepted under this Part of this Act in respect of a dwelling or an improvement notice has been served in respect of a dwelling by virtue of section 88 (1) above, the general improvement area or housing action area in which the dwelling is situated ceases to be such an area or the land on which the dwelling is situated is excluded from such an area, the provisions of this Part of this Act shall continue to apply in relation to that undertaking or notice as if the dwelling continued to be in a general improvement area or housing action area declared by the local authority by whom the undertaking was accepted or, as the case may be, the notice was served. **[355]**

GENERAL

Where, after an undertaking has been accepted, or an improvement notice served, the dwelling ceases to be in a general improvement area or a housing action area, this event will have no effect, *i.e.* the provisions of this Part of the Act will continue to apply.

103. Service of notices, etc.

(1) In section 102 (1) of the Housing Act 1964 (where a local authority are under a duty to serve a notice on a person described in a particular way, the local authority are to take reasonable steps to identify the person coming within that description) for the words "or Part II, Part III" there shall be substituted the words "Part VIII of the Housing Act 1974".

(2) In section 103 (1) of the Housing Act 1964 (method of service of notices, etc.) after the words "those Acts" there shall be inserted the words "or under Part VIII of the Housing Act 1974".

(3) In section 103 (2) of the Housing Act 1964 (service of notices, etc. where more than one person comes within the description of the person to be served) for the words "Part II", in the last place where they occur, there shall be substituted the words "Part VIII of the Housing Act 1974". **[356]**

104. Interpretation of Part VIII

(1) In this Part of this Act, unless the context otherwise requires,—

"the full standard" has the same meaning as it has for the purposes of section 66 of this Act (intermediate grants);

"housing arrangements" has the meaning assigned to it by section 86 above;

"improvement" includes alteration and enlargement and, so far as also necessary to enable a dwelling to reach the full standard or the reduced standard, repair, and "improved" shall be construed accordingly;

"improvement notice" means a notice under section 90 above;

"lessee" includes any person entitled, at law or in equity, to a tenancy or any other term of years certain, whether in possession or in reversion;

"local authority", subject to section 99 (6) above, has the same meaning as in Part VII of this Act;

"occupying tenant", in relation to a dwelling, means the person who is not an owner-occupier, but who—

(*a*) occupies or is entitled to occupy the dwelling as a lessee; or

(*b*) is a statutory tenant of the dwelling, within the meaning of the Rent Act 1968; or

(*c*) occupies the dwelling as a residence under a Part VI contract, within the meaning of Part VI of the Rent Act 1968 (furnished lettings); or

(*d*) is employed in agriculture (as defined in section 17 (1) of the

Agricultural Wages Act 1948) and occupies or resides in the dwelling as part of the terms of his employment;

"owner", in relation to a dwelling, means the person who, otherwise than as a mortgagee in possession, is for the time being entitled to dispose of the fee simple in the dwelling;

"owner-occupier", in relation to a dwelling, means the person who, as owner or as lessee under a long tenancy, occupies or is entitled to occupy the dwelling, and "owner-occupied" shall be construed accordingly;

"the person having control", in relation to a dwelling, shall be determined in accordance with subsection (2) below;

"provisional notice" means a notice under section 85 (2) above;

"the reduced standard" has the same meaning as it has for the purposes of section 66 of this Act (intermediate grants);

"standard amenities" has the same meaning as in Part VII of this Act.

(2) References in this Part of this Act to the person having control of a dwelling shall be construed as follows:—

(*a*) if the dwelling is owner-occupied, the person having control of it is the owner-occupier;

(*b*) if there is an occupying tenant of the dwelling and he is a person employed in agriculture (as defined in section 17 (1) of the Agricultural Wages Act 1948) who occupies or resides in the dwelling as part of the terms of his employment, the employer or other person by whose authority the occupying tenant occupies or resides in the dwelling is the person having control of it; and

(*c*) in any other case, the person who has control of a dwelling is the person who is either the owner of it or the lessee of it under a long tenancy and whose interest in the dwelling is not in reversion on that of another person who has a long tenancy.

(3) Section 3 of the Leasehold Reform Act 1967 (meaning of "long tenancy") shall apply for the purposes of subsections (1) and (2) above as it applies for the purposes of Part I of that Act.

(4) References in the following provisions of the Housing Act 1957 to that Act shall be construed as including a reference to this Part of this Act, that is to say—

(*a*) section 169 (service of notices etc. on persons other than local authorities);

(*b*) section 170 (power of local authority to require information as to ownership of premises);

(*c*) section 178 (power of Secretary of State to prescribe information, etc.); and

(*d*) section 179 (dispensation with advertisements and notices). **[357]**

PART IX

MISCELLANEOUS

105. Secretary of State's control over certain expenditure by housing authorities in England and Wales

(1) A housing authority may not incur any expenses in—

(*a*) providing dwellings by the conversion of houses or other buildings, or (*b*) carrying out works required for the improvement of dwellings, with or without associated works of repair,

except in accordance with proposals submitted by the authority to the Secretary of State and for the time being approved by him.

(2) Any approval given by the Secretary of State under subsection (1) above may be given subject to such conditions, and may be varied in such circumstances, as appear to him to be appropriate, but before varying the terms of any such approval the Secretary of State shall consult the housing authority concerned.

(3) In this section "housing authority" and "dwelling" have the same meanings as in Part VII of this Act. **[358]**

GENERAL

The object of this clause was described at the committee stage as "not to introduce detailed interference with local authority expenditure but to establish . . . strategic control over the broad direction of expenditure". There has been a great deal of expenditure over the last few years on the improvement of existing council estates. The object is to direct more resources to the conversion and improvement of acquidre properties. It will be noted that the section refers to consultation with local authorities only where the Secretary of State proposes to vary proposals already approved by him. However, an undertaking was given at committee stage to discuss the exercise of controls "very fully with the local authorities". See Circular 160/74 in Appendix II.

106. Lodging-houses and hostels provided by local authorities and new town corporations in England and Wales

(1) For the year 1975–76 and subsequent years, buildings, or parts of buildings, provided or converted for use as lodging-houses (that is to say, houses not occupied as separate dwellings) or as hostels shall be included among the buildings to which the requirements in subsection (1) of section 12 of the Housing Finance Act 1972 relate and, accordingly, subsection (2) of that section shall cease to have effect except with respect to years prior to the year 1975–76.

(2) No payment shall be made for the year 1975–76 or any subsequent year to a local authority or a new town corporation—

(*a*) under section 40 of the Housing Act 1949 (Exchequer contributions for hostels),

(*b*) under section 15 or section 22 of the Housing (Financial Provisions) Act 1958 (grants for hostels),

(*c*) under section 92 of the Housing Finance Act 1972 (hostel subsidy), or

(*d*) so far as it relates to hostels, under any provision of the New Towns Act 1959 or the New Towns Act 1965,

nor shall any such payment be made by virtue of section 14 (6) of the Housing Subsidies Act 1967; and in this section "local authority" has, in relation to any of the enactments specified in paragraphs (*a*) to (*c*) above, the same meaning as in that enactment and "new town corporation" has the meaning assigned to it by section 106 of the Housing Finance Act 1972.

(3) For the purposes of Part V of the Housing Act 1957 "housing accommodation" shall include, and be deemed always to have included, hostels (within the meaning of this Act), and any reference in that Part to a house shall be, and shall be deemed always to have been, construed accordingly.

(4) In accordance with the preceding provisions of this section, Schedule 1 to the Housing Finance Act 1972 (the Housing Revenue Account) shall be amended in accordance with Schedule 7 to this Act.

(5) In this section "year" means a financial year, and "the year 1975–76" means the financial year beginning in 1975. **[359]**

GENERAL

This is a significant change so far as the Housing Revenue Accounts of local authorities are concerned. For many years transactions relating to hostels have been excluded from the Housing Revenue Account, and the Housing Act 1972 extended this rule to exclude lodging houses also from the HRA. Now the position is reversed and transactions relating to both hostels and lodging houses are to be included in the Housing Revenue Account, in 1975–76 and subsequent years. Until that year the present rule continues.

Subsidies, grants, and contributions for hostels, under the various Acts listed in sub-s. (2) will not be payable in respect of 1975/76 and subsequent years. This affects both local authorities and new town corporations.

Sch. 1 of the Housing Act 1972 is amended accordingly, by Sch. 7 of this Act. The position with regard to rate fund contributions to the Housing Revenue Account is to be noted—see para. 2 of Sch. 7.

107 Hostels provided by housing authorities in Scotland

For the purpose of enabling the Secretary of State to make grants to housing authorities within the meaning of section 5 (3) (*c*) of this Act in respect of their expenditure on housing projects relating to hostels, such an authority shall be treated as a registered housing association, and sections 29 (1) to (7), 30 (1) to (7), 33 and 35 of this Act shall apply accordingly, but otherwise for the said purpose Parts I to III of this Act shall not apply. **[360]**

GENERAL

This is a device to make it possible to make grants under Part III of this Act to "housing authorities" as defined in s. 78 (1) of the Housing (Financial Provisions) (Scotland) Act 1972.

DEFINITIONS

"Hostels"—see s. 129 (2)
"Housing Association"—see s. 129 (2)
"Registered"—see s. 129 (2)

108. Abolition of clearance orders, etc.

(1) The power of a local authority for the purposes of the Housing Act 1957 to make a clearance order under Part III of that Act (clearance and re-development) for the demolition of any building in a clearance area—

(*a*) shall not be available with respect to any clearance area declared on or after the commencement date; and

(*b*) shall cease to be available with respect to any other clearance area after the expiry of the period of 12 months beginning on the commencement date.

(2) In the application of section 60 of the Housing Act 1957 (payments in respect of well-maintained houses in clearance areas) in relation to a house which is the subject of a compulsory purchase order or a clearance order made on or after the commencement date, for subsection (1) of that section there shall be substituted the subsections set out in Schedule 9 to this Act.

(3) This section shall come into operation at the expiry of the period of one month beginning with the date on which this Act is passed, and any reference in subsections (1) and (2) above to the commencement date is a reference to the day on which this section comes into operation. **[361]**

GENERAL

This was added in committee. The effect is to abolish the power of local authorities to deal with unfit houses in a clearance area by making a clearance order instead of by acquisition. The reasons for the change are described in Chapter 9. Unfit houses can be dealt with under Part II of the Housing Act 1957, thus leaving ownership with the present owner.

The current provisions relating to clearance orders will remain in force for the time being to cover clearance orders already made but not executed. This section came into force on 31 August 1974–see sub-s. (1) and (3).

The section also changes the law with regard to payments in respect of well-maintained houses in clearance areas, under Part III of the Housing Act 1957. Local authorities already decide whether an individual house declared unfit under Part II of that Act has been well-maintained, and now they will be responsible for similar decisions in respect of unfit houses in clearance areas declared under Part III of the 1957 Act. This change, it is hoped, will make for speedier decisions and reduce the pressure of work on the Departments inspectors, and on district valuers. The necessary changes are made by Sch. 9, which amends s. 60 of the Housing Act 1957, and by Sch. 13. These changes also affect houses which are the subject of a declaration of unfitness under any of the enactments listed in para. 2 (2) of Sch. 2 to the Land Compensation Act 1961.

See also s. 67 of the Housing Act 1969; the Housing (Payments for Well Maintained Houses) Orders 1972, and 1973, and Circulars No. 69/67 and 40/73. See also Circulars 126/74 and 136/74 in Appendix II.

109. General interpretation of sections 110 to 115 for Scotland

(1) In sections 110 to 115 the reference to an English enactment includes a reference to the corresponding Scottish enactment, and the corresponding Scottish enactments, except where the context otherwise implies or provides, are as follows—

(*a*) the corresponding Scottish enactments to Part III of the Housing Act 1957 are Part III of the Housing (Scotland) Act 1966 and Part I of the Housing (Scotland) Act 1969;

(*b*) the corresponding Scottish enactments to sections 54 and 55 of the Town and Country Planning Act 1971 are respectively sections 52 and 53 of the Town and Country Planning (Scotland) Act 1972;

(*c*) the corresponding Scottish enactment to section 5 of the Compulsory Purchase Act 1965 is section 17 of the Lands Clauses Consolidation (Scotland) Act 1845;

(*d*) the corresponding Scottish enactments to section 9 of the Housing Act 1957 are section 11 of the Housing (Scotland) Act 1966 and section 24 of the Housing (Scotland) Act 1969;

(*e*) the corresponding Scottish enactment to Part V of the Housing Act 1957 is Part VII of the Housing (Scotland) Act 1966;

(*f*) the corresponding Scottish enactment to Part VI of the Town and Country Planning Act 1971 is Part VI of the Town and Country Planning (Scotland) Act 1972;

(*g*) the corresponding Scottish enactments to section 60 of, and Schedule 2 to, the Housing Act 1957 are section 49 of the Housing (Scotland) Act 1966 and section 11 of the Housing (Scotland) Act 1969;

(*h*) the corresponding Scottish enactment to section 8 of the Town and Country Planning (Amendment) Act 1972 is section 9 of that Act;

(*i*) the corresponding Scottish enactment to Schedule 2 to the Town and Country Planning (Amendment) Act 1972 is Schedule 3 to that Act;

(*j*) the corresponding Scottish enactment to Schedule 3 to the Housing Act 1957 is Schedule 3 to the Housing (Scotland) Act 1966 by virtue of section 7 (3) of the Housing (Scotland) Act 1969;

(*k*) the corresponding Scottish enactments to section 43 (2) of the Housing

Act 1957 are section 37 of the Housing (Scotland) Act 1966 and section 6 of the Housing (Scotland) Act 1969;

(*l*) the corresponding Scottish enactments to section 49 of the Housing Act 1957 are section 41 of the Housing (Scotland) Act 1966 and section 9 of the Housing (Scotland) Act 1969;

(*m*) the corresponding Scottish enactments to section 169 of the Housing Act 1957 are section 5 (3) of, and paragraph 19 of Schedule 1 to, the Acquisition of Land (Authorisation Procedure) (Scotland) Act 1947;

(*n*) the corresponding Scottish enactments to Schedule 4 to the Housing Act 1957 are paragraphs 6, 15 and 16 of Schedule 1 to the said Act of 1947, and the corresponding Scottish enactment to paragraph 1 of the said Schedule 4 is the said paragraph 6;

(*o*) the corresponding Scottish enactment to section 30 of the Compulsory Purchase Act 1965 is paragraph 19 of Schedule 1 to the Acquisition of Land (Authorisation Procedure) (Scotland) Act 1947;

(*p*) the corresponding Scottish enactments to section 22 of the Compulsory Purchase Act 1965 are sections 117 and 118 of the Lands Clauses Consolidation (Scotland) Act 1845;

(*q*) the corresponding Scottish enactment to section 32 of the Land Compensation Act 1961 is section 40 of the Land Compensation (Scotland) Act 1963;

(*r*) the corresponding Scottish enactments to the reference to section 68 of and Schedule 5 to the Housing Act 1969 are sections 18 to 20 of the Housing (Scotland) Act 1969.

(*s*) the corresponding Scottish enactment to section 37 of the Land Compensation Act 1973 is section 34 of the Land Compensation (Scotland) Act 1973;

(*t*) the corresponding Scottish enactment to section 30 of the Land Compensation Act 1961 is section 38 of the Land Compensation (Scotland) Act 1963.

(2)

(*a*) The expression "clearance area" includes a housing treatment area which is to be dealt with by securing the demolition of all or some of the buildings in that area under section 4 (2) (*a*) or 4 (2) (*c*) of the Housing (Scotland) Act 1969;

(*b*) "mortgagee" means the creditor in a heritable security. [**362**]

GENERAL

This is part of the mechanics necessary to ensure that ss. 110 to 115, which apply to England and Wales, shall apply also to Scotland.

110. Listed buildings subject to compulsory purchase orders under Part III of the Housing Act 1957

(1) In this section references to a compulsory purchase order are to a compulsory purchase order made (at any time before or after the coming into operation of this section) under Part III of the Housing Act 1957.

(2) Where a building to which a compulsory purchase order applies is (at any time after the making of the order) included in a list of buildings of special architectural or historic interest under section 54 of the Town and Country Planning Act 1971, the authority making the order may, subject to subsection (3) below, apply to the Secretary of State (and only to him) under section 55 of the Act of 1971 for his consent to the demolition of the building.

(3) No such application may be made by virtue of subsection (2) above after the expiry of the period of three months beginning with the date—

(*a*) on which the building is included in the said list, or
(*b*) on which this section comes into force,

whichever is the later.

(4) The following provisions of this section shall have effect where—

(*a*) an application for consent has been made under the said section 55, by virtue of subsection (2) above, and has been refused, or
(*b*) in a case falling within subsection (3) above, the period of three months has expired without the authority having made such an application,

and in this section "relevant date" means the date of the refusal or, as the case may be, of the expiry of the period of three months.

(5) If, at the relevant date—

(*a*) the building has not vested in the authority, and
(*b*) no notice to treat has been served by the authority under section 5 of the Compulsory Purchase Act 1965, in respect of any interest in the building,

the compulsory purchase order shall cease to have effect in relation to the building and, where applicable, the building shall cease to be comprised in a clearance area.

(6) Where a building, which was included in a clearance area solely by reason of its being unfit for human habitation, ceases to be comprised in the clearance area by virtue of subsection (5) above, the authority concerned shall, in respect of the building, forthwith—

(*a*) serve a notice under section 9 of the Act of 1957 (power of local authority to require repair of unfit houses), or
(*b*) make a closing order under Part II of that Act,

whichever is appropriate; and in the application of this subsection to Scotland the words from "solely" to "habitation" shall be omitted.

(7) Where subsection (5) above does not apply, the authority shall cease to be subject to the duty imposed by Part III of the Act of 1957 to demolish the building, and in relation to any interest in the building which at the relevant date has not vested in the authority the compulsory purchase order shall have effect as if—

(*a*) in the case of a house, it had been made and confirmed under Part V of the Act of 1957, and
(*b*) in any other case, it had been made and confirmed under Part VI of the Act of 1971.

(8) If the building, or any interest in the building, was vested in the authority at the relevant date it shall be treated—

(*a*) in the case of a house, as appropriated to the purposes of Part V of the Act of 1957, and
(*b*) in any other case, as appropriated to the purposes of Part VI of the Act of 1971.

(9) As respects a building falling within subsection (2) above, the authority shall not serve notice to treat under section 5 of the Compulsory Purchase Act 1965 in respect of the building until after the relevant date. [363]

GENERAL

This should be read with ss. 111–113, 115 and 116, all of which deal with listed buildings. The local authority may apply for consent to their demolition, but if the Secretary of State refuses consent, or no application is made within the time limit, the effect will be as follows:

(*a*) Where the building has not vested in the authority, and no notice to treat has been served, the compulsory purchase order will cease to apply to the building, and it will no longer be comprised in a clearance area but if it is unfit for human habitation the authority must proceed to take action under Part II of the 1957 Act (individual unfit properties) and secure its repair or closure.

(*b*) Where the building has vested in the authority or a notice to treat has been served the building will remain in the clearance area, but the local authority will no longer be under a duty to demolish it and
(i) if any interest has not vested in the authority the compulsory purchase order will have effect as in sub-s. (7) (*a*) or (*b*);
(ii) if the building or any interest was vested in the authority at the relevant date, it shall be treated as appropriated as indicated in sub-s. (8) (*a*) or (*b*).

Note sub-s. (9) as to restriction in the service of notice to treat.

See Circulars 126/74 and 159/74 in Appendix II.

111. Listed buildings in clearance areas, acquired by agreement

(1) Where Part III of the Housing Act 1957 applies to a building purchased by a local authority by agreement, and at any time (before or after the coming into operation of this section) the building is included in a list of buildings of special architectural or historic interest under section 54 of the Town and Country Planning Act 1971, the authority may, subject to subsection (2) below, apply to the Secretary of State (and only to him) under section 55 of the Act of 1971 for his consent to the demolition of the building.

(2) No such application may be made by virtue of subsection (1) above after the expiry of the period of three months beginning with the date—

(*a*) on which the building is included in the said list, or
(*b*) on which this section comes into force,

whichever is the later.

(3) Where—

(*a*) an application for consent has been made under the said section 55, by virtue of subsection (1) above, and has been refused, or
(*b*) the period of three months mentioned in subsection (2) above has expired without the authority having made such an application,

the authority shall cease to be subject to the duty, imposed by Part III of the Act of 1957, to demolish the building, which shall be treated—

(i) in the case of a house, as appropriated to the purposes of Part V of the Act of 1957, and
(ii) in any other case, as appropriated to the purposes of Part VI of the Act of 1971. [**364**]

GENERAL

Here again, as with s. 110, the local authority may apply for the consent of the Secretary of State to the demolition of the listed building. If he refuses, or the application is out of time, the local authority will no longer be under a duty to demolish it. If it is a house it will be treated as appropriated to the purposes of Part V of the 1957 Act. If it is not a house, it will be treated as appropriated under Part VI of the Town and Country Planning Act 1971. See Circulars 126/74 and 159/74 in Appendix II.

112. Temporary provision for listed buildings subject to clearance orders

(1) In this section references to a "clearance order" are to a clearance order

made (at any time before or after the coming into operation of this section) under Part III of the Housing Act 1957.

(2) Where a building to which a clearance order applies is, at any time after the confirmation of the order, included in a list of buildings of special architectural or historic interest under section 54 of the Town and Country Planning Act 1971, the authority making the order may, subject to subsection (3) below, apply to the Secretary of State (and only to him) under section 55 of the Act of 1971 for his consent to the demolition of the building.

(3) No such application may be made by virtue of subsection (2) above after the expiry of the period of three months beginning with the date—

(*a*) on which the building is included in the said list, or

(*b*) on which this section comes into force,

whichever is the later.

(4) Where—

(*a*) an application for consent has been made under the said section 55, by virtue of subsection (2) above, and has been refused, or

(*b*) the period of three months mentioned in subsection (3) above has expired without the authority having made such an application,

the building shall cease to be comprised in a clearance area or to be subject to the clearance order.

(5) Where a building, which was included in a clearance area solely by reason of its being unfit for human habitation, ceases to be comprised in the clearance area by virtue of subsection (4) above, the authority concerned shall, in respect of the building, forthwith—

(*a*) serve a notice under section 9 of the Act of 1957 (power of local authority to require repair of unfit house), or

(*b*) make a closing order under Part II of that Act,

whichever is appropriate; and in the application of this subsection to Scotland the words from "solely" to "habitation" shall be omitted.

(6) Where a payment in respect of a house has been made by a local authority under section 60 of, or Schedule 2 to, the Act of 1957, or Schedule 5 to the Housing Act 1969, in connection with a clearance order, and by virtue of this section the house is excluded from the clearance area, then, if the person to whom the payment was made is entitled to an interest in the house he shall, subject to subsection (7) below, repay the payment to the authority on demand.

(7) No repayment shall be required by virtue of subsection (6) above in a case where the authority have made a closing order in respect of the house and—

(*a*) no appeal has, within the time allowed, been made against the making of the order, or

(*b*) such an appeal has been made and has failed. [**365**]

GENERAL

The reference to "temporary" presumably arises from the fact that clearance orders will eventually disappear completely as the result of s. 108.

The procedure under this section is broadly similar to that laid down in s. 110. See Notes on s. 112 in Chapter 9. See also Circular 159/74 in Appendix II.

113. Application of provisions about listed buildings to buildings in conservation areas

(1) Sections 110, 111 and 112 above shall, with the modifications mentioned in subsection (2) below, have effect in relation to buildings subject to directions

made and confirmed under section 8 of the Town and Country Planning (Amendment) Act 1972 (control of demolition in conservation areas in England and Wales) as they have effect in relation to listed buildings.

(2) The modifications subject to which those sections are to have effect by virtue of subsection (1) above are—

(*a*) for references to section 55 of the Town and Country Planning Act 1971 there shall be substituted references to that section as applied by Schedule 2 to the Act of 1972; and

(*b*) for references to a building being included in a list under section 54 of the Act of 1971 there shall be substituted references to a building being subject to a direction made and confirmed under section 8 of the Act of 1972. [**366**]

GENERAL

This applies ss. 110, 111 and 112 to buildings in conservation areas and needs no comment. See also s. 116 and Circulars 126/74 and 159/74 in Appendix II.

114. Temporary provision for rehabilitation of unfit houses

(1) This section applies to any building comprised in a clearance area under Part III of the Housing Act 1957 which—

(*a*) at any time before the date on which this section comes into operation has been purchased by agreement by the local authority in whose area the clearance area falls, or

(*b*) is subject to a compulsory purchase order—

(i) made at any time before that date under the said Part III, and

(ii) which, at any time before the expiry of the period of three months beginning with that date, has been confirmed in accordance with Schedule 3 of the Act of 1957.

(2) Where any building to which this section applies—

(*a*) was included in the clearance area solely by reason of its being unfit for human habitation, and

(*b*) in the opinion of the authority concerned is capable of being, and ought to be, improved to the full standard,

the authority may, subject to the provisions of this section and of Schedule 10 to this Act, make and submit to the Secretary of State an order under this section (a "rehabilitation order") in relation to that building.

(3) In subsection (2) above "full standard" in England and Wales means the standard attained by a dwelling in respect of which the conditions mentioned in section 66 (2) of this Act are fulfilled and in Scotland means the standard specified by virtue of section 16 (3) of the Housing (Scotland) Act 1974; and in the application to Scotland of subsection (2) (*a*) above the words "solely" to "habitation" shall be omitted.

(4) Schedule 10 to this Act shall have effect for the purpose of supplementing the provisions of this section. [**367**]

GENERAL

In view of the acute housing shortage in some areas it is desirable to avoid demolishing houses which can, and ought to be, improved to the full standard. The process envisaged in this section has some resemblance to that for the temporary retention of unfit houses under ss. 46 and 48 of the Housing Act 1957. These allowed a local authority to retain an unfit house and to "patch" even though they could not bring it up to the standard of fitness in s. 4 of the 1957 Act. These two sections (46, 48) of the 1957 Act are now repealed. S. 114 requires that any unfit house made subject to a rehabilitation order shall be brought up to the full standard laid down in s. 66 (2) of this Act; or s. 16 (3) of the Housing (Scotland) Act 1974. See also remarks on s. 114 in Chapter 9.

This section makes a temporary provision, and its scope is limited to buildings already purchased by agreement, or those subject to compulsory purchase orders made before the date on which this section came into operation, and confirmed within 3 months thereafter. However, Sch. 10 appears to widen the scope somewhat. See Circulars 126/74 and 159/74 in Appendix II.

115. Compensation

(1) It is hereby declared that where, under section 110 above, or Schedule 10 to this Act, a compulsory purchase order is to be treated as made under Part V of the Housing Act 1957 or Part VI of the Town and Country Planning Act 1971 compensation for the compulsory acquisition of the land comprised in the compulsory purchase order is to be assessed in accordance with the provisions applying to a compulsory acquisition under the said Part V (or, as the case may be, the said Part VI).

(2) Where under section 110 above, or Schedule 10 to this Act, land or any interest in land within a clearance area is to be treated as appropriated by a local authority to the purposes of the said Part V, compensation for its compulsory acquisition shall (where it increases the amount) be assessed or reassessed in accordance with the provisions applying to a compulsory acquisition under the said Part V.

(3) Where under section 111 above or Schedule 10 to this Act, any interest in land acquired by a local authority by agreement (after the declaration of the clearance area) is to be treated as appropriated for the purposes of the said Part V—

(*a*) compensation shall (where subsection (2) above would have increased the amount) be assessed and paid as if the acquisition were a compulsory acquisition, under the said Part III, to which subsection (2) applied, but

(*b*) there shall be deducted from the amount of compensation so payable any amount previously paid in respect of the acquisition of that interest by the authority.

(4) Where subsection (2) or subsection (3) above applies, the local authority shall serve on the person entitled to the compensation a notice in the prescribed form giving particulars of the amount of compensation payable in accordance with the provisions applying to a compulsory acquisition under the said Part V, and if the person served does not within twenty-one days from service of the notice accept the particulars, or if he disputes the amount stated, the question of disputed compensation shall be referred to the Lands Tribunal.

(5) The notice shall be served not later than six months after (as the case may be)—

(*a*) the relevant date as defined in section 110 above, or

(*b*) confirmation of the rehabilitation order,

and section 30 of the Compulsory Purchase Act 1965 (service of notices) shall apply to the notice.

(6) Subsection (2) above shall be left out of account in considering whether under section 22 of the Compulsory Purchase Act 1965 compensation has been

properly paid for the land; and accordingly subsection (2) above shall not prevent an acquiring authority from remaining in undisputed possession of the land.

(7) Where subsection (2) above makes an increase in compensation to be assessed in accordance with Schedule 2 to the Compulsory Purchase Act 1965 (absent and untraced owners)—

(*a*) a deed poll executed under paragraph 2 (2) of that Schedule before the latest date for service of a notice under subsection (5) above shall not be invalid because the increase in compensation had not been paid, and
(*b*) it shall be the duty of the local authority not later than six months after the said date to proceed under the said Schedule 2 and pay the proper additional amount into court.

(8) In Scotland where subsection (2) makes an increase in compensation to be assessed in accordance with sections 56 to 60 and 63 of the Lands Clauses (Consolidation) (Scotland) Act 1845 (provisions dealing with absent and untraced owners)—

(*a*) a notorial instrument executed under section 76 of that Act before the latest date for service of a notice under subsection (4) above shall not be invalid because the increase in compensation had not been paid and
(*b*) it shall be the duty of the local authority not later than six months after the said date to proceed under the said sections and pay the proper additional amount into the Bank.

(9) Any sum payable by virtue of this section shall carry interest at the rate prescribed under section 32 of the Land Compensation Act 1961 from the time of entry by the local authority on the land, or from vesting of the land or interest, whichever is the earlier, until payment.

(10) In this section references to an increase in compensation shall be read as if payments under—

(*a*) sections 60 and 61 of and Schedule 2 to the Act of 1957 (payments in respect of well-maintained houses and payments to owner-occupiers),
(*b*) section 63 (1) of the Act of 1957 or section 30 of the Land Compensation Act 1961 (allowances to persons displaced),
(*c*) section 68 of and Schedule 5 to the Housing Act 1969 (payments to owner-occupiers and others in respect of unfit houses purchased or demolished), and
(*d*) section 37 of the Land Compensation Act 1973 (disturbance payments for persons without compensationable interests),

and any extra-statutory payments made by way of additional compensation were, to the extent that they were made to the person holding the interest in question, compensation in respect of the compulsory purchase.

(11) In this section "prescribed" means prescribed by order made by the Secretary of State for the purposes of this section; and any order under this subsection shall be contained in a statutory instrument which shall be subject to annulment in pursuance of a resolution of either House of Parliament. **[368]**

GENERAL

This deals with compensation problems arising from the change in its basis from Part III to Part V of the Housing Act 1957, resulting from ss. 110, 111 and 114. The term "compensation" covers a variety of payments, as listed in sub-s. (10). See Circulars 126/74 and 159/74 in Appendix II.

116. Amendment of section 4 of the Compulsory Purchase Act 1965

In section 4 of the Compulsory Purchase Act 1965 (time limits for exercising powers under compulsory purchase orders) there shall be added at the end, the following paragraph:—

> "For the purposes of this section no account shall be taken of any period during which an authority are, by virtue of section 110, 113, or 114 of the Housing Act 1974 (which relate among other things to unfit buildings in clearance or conservation areas) prevented from serving notice to treat under section 5 of this Act",

and the same amendment shall be made to section 116 of the Lands Clauses Consolidation (Scotland) Act 1845 with the substitution for the reference to section 5 of the Compulsory Purchase Act 1965 of a reference to section 17 of the said Act of 1845. [**369**]

GENERAL

This is self-explanatory.

See Circular 159/74 in Appendix II.

117. Removal of time limit for completing certain works eligible for higher rates of grants or contributions

(1) In section 1 of the Housing Act 1971 (certain works carried out in local government areas wholly or partly in development areas or intermediate areas to be eligible for increased rates of grants or contributions) paragraph (*b*) of each of subsections (1) and (2) (which requires the works concerned to be completed before the expiration of a period of 3 years beginning with 23rd June 1971) shall not have effect in the case of works falling within subsection (2), subsection (3) or subsection (4) below.

(2) Subsection (1) above applies to works which were the subject of an application to a local authority for an improvement grant, a standard grant or a special grant if the application was approved by the local authority on or before 30th September 1973 and—

(*a*) in the case of an application to a local authority in England and Wales for an improvement grant, if the local authority have, before 23rd June 1974, fixed as the amount of the grant (either originally or by way of variation under subsection (2) of section 2 of the Housing Act 1971) an amount which took account of the amendments of Part I of the Housing Act 1969 effected by subsection (1) of that section (increase of grant or maximum grant from one-half to 75 per cent. of the cost of the works); and

(*b*) in the case of an application to a local authority in Scotland for an improvement grant or a standard grant, if the local authority have, before 23rd June 1974, fixed as the amount of the grant (either originally or by way of variation under subsection (2) of section 3 of the Housing Act 1971) an amount which took account of the amendments of Parts I and II of the Housing (Financial Provisions) (Scotland) Act 1968 effected by subsection (1) of that section (increase of grant or maximum grant from one-half to 75 per cent. of the cost of the works).

(3) Subsection (1) above also applies to works comprised in arrangements to which subsection (1) of section 21 of the Housing Act 1969 applies (contributions for dwellings provided or improved by housing associations under arrangements

with local authorities) if an application for a contribution under that section containing particulars and estimates of those works was received by the Secretary of State on or before 30th September 1973.

(4) Subsection (1) above also applies to works comprised in arrangements to which subsection (1) of section 16 or section 17 (in so far as the latter section applies to housing associations) of the Housing (Financial Provisions) (Scotland) Act 1968 applies (contributions for dwellings provided or improved by housing associations under arrangements with the Secretary of State or local authorities) if the Secretary of State had made arrangements under the said section 16 or had approved improvement proposals made under the said section 17 on or before 30th September 1973.

(5) In this section "local authority", "improvement grant", "standard grant" and "special grant" have, in England and Wales, the same meanings as in Part I of the Housing Act 1969, and in Scotland "local authority" has the same meaning as in section 1 of the Housing (Scotland) Act 1966 and "improvement grant" and "standard grant" have the same meanings as in Part II of the Housing (Financial Provisions) (Scotland) Act 1968. [**370**]

GENERAL

This is a welcome relaxation of the conditions applicable to the higher rates of "improvement grant", "standard grant", and "special grant", where the dwellings are in a development area or intermediate area. The higher rate was 75 per cent. instead of the normal 50 per cent., but one of the conditions was that the work should be completed within 3 years from 23rd June 1971. This condition is now abolished for any of these three grants if the application was approved on a before 30th September 1973, and the local authority have, before 23rd June 1974, fixed the grant at the higher rate. Similar changes are made for Scotland. The time limit is also relaxed for certain housing association improvement schemes—see sub-s. (3) as regards England and Wales and sub-s. (4) with regard to Scotland. This section came into operation on 20 August 1974.

118. Rateable value limits for enfranchisement or extension under Leasehold Reform Act 1967

(1) In section 1 of the Leasehold Reform Act 1967, in subsection (1) (*a*) (certain tenants entitled to enfranchisement or extension of their leaseholds where rateable value is within certain limits on a particular day) after the words "rent and" there shall be inserted the words "subject to subsections (5) and (6) below" and after subsection (4) there shall be added the following subsections:—

"(5) If, in relation to any house and premises, the appropriate day for the purposes of subsection (1) (*a*) above falls on or after 1st April 1973 that subsection shall have effect in relation to the house and premises,—

(*a*) in a case where the tenancy was created on or before 18th February 1966, as if for the sums of £200 and £400 specified in that subsection there were substituted respectively the sums of £750 and £1,500; and

(*b*) in a case where the tenancy was created after 18th February 1966, as if for those sums of £200 and £400 there were substituted respectively the sums of £500 and £1,000.

(6) If, in relation to any house and premises,—

(*a*) the appropriate day for the purposes of subsection (1) (*a*) above falls before 1st April 1973, and

(*b*) the rateable value of the house and premises on the appropriate day was more than £200 or, if it was then in Greater London, £400, and

(c) the tenancy was created on or before 18th February 1966,

subsection (1) (a) above shall have effect in relation to the house and premises as if for the reference to the appropriate day there were substituted a reference to 1st April 1973 and as if for the sums of £200 and £400 specified in that subsection there were substituted respectively the sums of £750 and £1,500."

(2) In any case where, by virtue only of the amendments of section 1 of the Leasehold Reform Act 1967 effected by subsection (1) above, the right specified in subsection (1) of that section is conferred on a tenant, section 19 of that Act (retention of management powers for general benefit of neighbourhood) shall have effect in relation to the house and premises to which the tenant's right applies as if for the reference in subsection (1) of that section to an application made within two years beginning with the commencement of Part I of that Act there were substituted a reference to an application made within two years beginning with the date on which this Act is passed.

(3) After subsection (4) of section 1 of the Leasehold Reform Act 1967 there shall be inserted—

"(4A) At any time the tenant may take the action provided in Schedule 8 to the Housing Act 1974 for his rateable value to be adjusted and in all such cases the agreed rateable value or that determined by the Court or District Valuer shall be the rateable value for the purposes of that Act."

(4) In section 9 of the Leasehold Reform Act 1967 (purchase price of enfranchisement) there shall be inserted after subsection (1):—

"(1A) Notwithstanding, the foregoing subsection, the price payable for a house and premises, the rateable value of which is above £1,000 in Greater London and £500 elsewhere, on a conveyance under section 8 above, shall be the amount which at the relevant time the house and premises, if sold in the open market by a willing seller, might be expected to realise on the following assumptions:—

(a) on the assumption that the vendor was selling for an estate in fee simple, subject to the tenancy, but on the assumption that this Part of this Act conferred no right to acquire the freehold;

(b) on the assumption that at the end of the tenancy the tenant has the right to remain in possession of the house and premises under the provisions of Part I of the Landlord and Tenant Act 1954;

(c) on the assumption that the tenant has no liability to carry out any repairs, maintenance or redecorations under the terms of the tenancy or Part I of the Landlord and Tenant Act 1954;

(d) on the assumption that the price be diminished by the extent to which the value of the house and premises has been increased by any improvement carried out by the tenant or his predecessors in title at their own expense;

(e) on the assumption that (subject to paragraph (a) above) the vendor was selling subject, in respect of rentcharges and other rents to which section 11 (2) below applies, to the same annual charge as the conveyance to the tenant is to be subject to, but the purchaser would otherwise be effectively exonerated until the termination of the tenancy from any liability or charge in respect of tenant's incumbrance; and

(f) on the assumption that (subject to paragraphs (a) and (b) above) the vendor was selling with and subject to the rights and burdens with and subject to which the conveyance to the tenant is to be made, and in particular with and subject to such permanent or extended rights and burdens as are to be created in order to give effect to section 10 below.

(1B) For the purpose of determining whether the rateable value of the house and premises is above £1,000 in Greater London, or £500 elsewhere, the rateable value shall be adjusted to take into account any tenant's improvements in accordance with Schedule 8 to the Housing Act 1974."

[371]

(5) This section shall come into force on the passing of this Act.

GENERAL

This clause as originally drafted merely converted the former limits of £200 and £400 into their approximate equivalents under the 1973 valuation list, *i.e.* £500 and £1,000. During its passage through the Committee stages the section was amended to cover a much wider range of properties, as shown in sub-s. (1) and the new sub-s. to s. 1 of the Leasehold Reform Act 1967.

Sub-s. 3 and Sch. 8 provide the tenant with a means of having the rateable value of his house adjusted.

The purchase price of enfranchisement of a house with a rateable value above £1,000 in London, or £500 elsewhere, is affected by sub-s. (4). This section came into force on 31st July 1974.

119. Option mortgages

(1) Subject to the following provisions of this section, Part II of the Housing Subsidies Act 1967 (assistance for house purchase and improvement) shall be amended in accordance with Schedule 11 to this Act and the amendments of section 28 of that Act contained in paragraph 5 of that Schedule shall be deemed to have taken effect on 18th April 1974.

(2) Until 6th April 1980, nothing in paragraphs 1 (2) and 2 of Schedule 11 to this Act or in paragraphs (ix) to (xi) of section 24 (3) of the said Act of 1967 shall have effect in relation to a loan if—

(*a*) the option notice in respect of the loan was signed on or before 26th June 1974, or

(*b*) the loan was made in pursuance of an offer in writing made by the lender to the borrower on or before 26th June 1974 and the option notice was signed as mentioned in section 24 (3) (*b*) of the said Act of 1967.

(3) Until the expiry of the period of 3 months beginning on the appointed day, nothing in paragraphs 1 (2) and 2 of Schedule 11 to this Act or in paragraphs (ix) to (xi) of section 24 (3) of the said Act of 1967 shall have effect in relation to a loan (being a loan to which subsection (2) above does not apply) if the option notice in respect of the loan was signed after 26th June 1974 and before the day appointed for the coming into operation of this section.

(4) The Secretary of State may by regulations made by statutory instrument make such transitional provisions as he considers appropriate for the purpose of securing the proper application of Part II of the said Act of 1967—

(*a*) on and after 6th April 1980 in relation to a loan to which subsection (2) above applies; and

(*b*) after the expiry of the period specified in subsection (3) above in relation to a loan to which that subsection applies.

(5) Without prejudice to the generality of the power conferred by subsection

(4) above, in relation to a loan to which the power applies, regulations under that subsection—

(*a*) may require things to be done before the date on which the said Part II is to apply to the loan; and

(*b*) may make such modifications of the said Part II as the Secretary of State considers appropriate.

(6) A statutory instrument containing regulations under subsection (4) above shall be subject to annulment in pursuance of a resolution of either House of Parliament. **[372]**

GENERAL

Part II of the Housing Subsidies Act 1967, as amended by s. 78 of the Housing Act 1969, provided subsidies to assist mortgagors buying their own homes. Taxpayers paying the full rate of income tax received, and still receive relief from tax on the interest element in their mortage repayments, but taxpayers paying at a lower level received less tax benefit. The object of the scheme is to ensure that the subsidy under the option mortgage scheme is greater than the value of the tax relief to a person who pays tax at a low rate, but that the reverse is true in the case of a taxpayer who pays the full rate. Hence the option open to a mortgagor.

Interest rates have risen since the scheme was launched and consequently the rates of interest used for calculating the subsidy have been varied from time to time by statutory instrument, the most recent being S.I. 1974 No. 1005. Different rates may be specified for different purposes, *e.g.* one rate for annuity and fixed instalment mortgages and another for endowment and/or standing mortgages.

Sub-s. (1) and Sch. 11 make amendments to the 1967 Act in a number of respects such as the residence condition; spouse's living apart; and cases where the interest due from the borrower for any period is less than the total of the interest which accrues in that period (part of the interest being added to the outstanding debt).

Paragraph 2 of Schedule 11 amends the limit for loans to £25,000. Paragraph 3 makes changes which affect self-build societies. Paragraph 4 amends s. 27 of the 1967 Act and affects the Housing Corporation.

Paragraph 6 deals with recovery in certain circumstances of subsidy already paid. This includes cases where false information has been given.

120. Tax exemptions for self-build societies

After section 341 of the Income and Corporation Taxes Act 1970 there shall be inserted the following section:—

"341A. Self-build societies

(1) Where a self-build society makes a claim in that behalf for any year or part of a year of assessment during which the society was approved for the purposes of this section, rent to which the society was entitled from its members for the year or part shall be disregarded for tax purposes.

(2) Where a claim under subsection (1) of this section has effect, any adjustment of the society's liability to tax which is required in consequence of the claim may be made by an assessment or by repayment or otherwise, as the case may require.

(3) Where a self-build society makes a claim in that behalf for an accounting period or part of an accounting period during which it was approved for the purposes of this section, the society shall be exempt from corporation tax on chargeable gains accruing to it in the accounting period or part thereof on the disposal of any land to a member of the society.

(4) References in this section to the approval of a self-build society are references to its approval by the Secretary of State, and the Secretary of

State shall not approve a self-build society for the purposes of this section unless he is satisfied—

(*a*) that the society is, or is deemed to be, duly registered under the Industrial and Provident Societies Act 1965; and

(*b*) that the society satisfies such other requirements as may be prescribed by or under regulations under subsection (6) below and will comply with such conditions as may for the time being be so prescribed.

(5) An approval given for the purposes of this section shall have effect as from such date (whether before or after the giving of the approval) as may be specified by the Secretary of State and shall cease to have effect if revoked by him.

(6) The Secretary of State may by statutory instrument make regulations for the purpose of carrying out the provisions of this section; and a statutory instrument containing any such regulations shall be subject to annulment in pursuance of a resolution of the Commons House of Parliament.

(7) Section 42 of the Taxes Management Act 1970 (procedure for making claims) shall not apply to a claim under this section, but such a claim shall be made to the inspector and shall be made not later than two years after the end of the year of assessment or accounting period to which, or to a part of which, it relates.

(8) Subject to subsection (9) below, no claim under this section shall have effect unless it is proved that during the year or accounting period, or part thereof, to which the claim relates—

(*a*) no land owned by the society was occupied, in whole or in part and whether solely or as joint occupier, by a person who was not, at the time of his occupation, a member of the society; and

(*b*) the society making the claim satisfies the condition specified in paragraph (*a*) of subsection (4) above and has complied with the conditions prescribed under paragraph (*b*) of that subsection and for the time being in force;

and for the purposes of paragraph (*a*) above, occupation by any other person in accordance with the will, or the provisions applicable on the intestacy, of a deceased member, shall be treated during the first six months after the death as if it were occupation by a member.

(9) Notwithstanding the provisions of subsection (8) above, where, on a claim under this section, the Board are satisfied that the requirements of paragraphs (*a*) and (*b*) of that subsection are substantially complied with, they may direct that the claim shall have effect; but if, subsequently, information comes to the knowledge of the Board which satisfies them that the direction was not justified, they may revoke the direction and thereupon the liability of the society to tax for all relevant years or accounting periods shall be adjusted by the making of assessments or otherwise.

(10) A claim under this section shall be in such form and contain such particulars as may be prescribed by the Board.

(11) In this section—

"self-build society" has the same meaning as in Part I of the Housing Act 1974; and "rent" includes any sums to which a self-build society is entitled in respect of the occupation of any of its land under a licence or otherwise." **[373]**

GENERAL

This amends s. 341 of the Income and Corporation Taxes Act 1970, but only for "approved" self-build societies. "Approved" means approved by the Secretary of State in accordance with sub-s. (4) of the new s. 341A of the 1970 Act. Self-build societies registered under the Industrial and Provident Societies Act 1965 and approved by the Secretary of State will be exempt from Corporation Tax:

(*a*) on income from completed houses occupied by members, and
(*b*) from tax on chargeable gains on the transfer of any house to a member.

121. Disclosure of landlord's identity

(1) If after the coming into operation of this section the tenant of premises occupied as a dwelling makes a written request for the landlord's name and address to any person who demands or to the last person who received rent payable under the tenancy or to any other person for the time being acting as agent for the landlord in relation to the tenancy, and that person fails without reasonable excuse to supply a written statement of the name and address within the period of 21 days beginning with the day on which he receives the tenant's request, that person shall be guilty of an offence and liable on summary conviction to a fine not exceeding £200.

(2) In any case where—

(*a*) in response to a request under subsection (1) above, a tenant is supplied with the name and address of the landlord of the premises concerned; and
(*b*) the landlord is a body corporate; and
(*c*) the tenant makes a further written request to the landlord for information under this subsection,

the landlord shall, within the period of 21 days beginning with the day on which he receives the request under this subsection, supply to the tenant a written statement of the name and address of every director and the secretary of the landlord.

(3) Any reference in subsection (1) or subsection (2) above to a person's address is a reference to his place of abode or his place of business or, in the case of a company, its registered office.

(4) A request under subsection (2) above shall be deemed to be duly made to the landlord if it is made to an agent of the landlord or to a person who demands the rent of the premises concerned, and any such agent or person to whom such a request is made shall as soon as may be forward it to the landlord.

(5) A landlord who fails without reasonable excuse to comply with a request under subsection (2) above within the period mentioned in that subsection and a person who fails without reasonable excuse to comply with any requirement imposed on him by subsection (4) above shall be guilty of an offence and liable on summary conviction to a fine not exceeding £200.

(6) Where an offence under subsection (1) or subsection (5) above which has been committed by a body corporate is proved to have been committed with the consent or connivance of, or to be attributable to any neglect on the part of, a director, manager, secretary or other similar officer of the body corporate, or any person who was purporting to act in any such capacity, he, as well as the body

corporate, shall be guilty of that offence and be liable to be proceeded against and punished accordingly.

(7) Where the affairs of a body corporate are managed by its members, subsection (6) above shall apply in relation to the acts and defaults of a member in connection with his functions of management as if he were a director of the body corporate.

(8) In England and Wales proceedings for an offence under this section may be instituted by any of the following local authorities,—

(*a*) the council of a district or London borough;
(*b*) the Greater London Council; and
(*c*) the Common Council of the City of London.

(9) In this section—

"landlord" means the immediate landlord and, in relation to premises occupied under a right conferred by an enactment, includes the person who, apart from that right, would be entitled to possession of the premises;

"tenant" includes a sub-tenant and a tenant under a right conferred by an enactment, except that it does not include a tenant under a tenancy to which Part II of the Landlord and Tenant Act 1954 (business tenancies) applies.

(10) This section shall come into operation at the expiry of the period of one month beginning with the date on which this Act is passed. **[374]**

GENERAL

This section should be compared with the Landlord and Tenant Act 1962. The latter applies only to tenancies where the rent is "payable weekly". This differs from a "weekly rent". The first requirement of the Act of 1962 is that the landlord shall provide a rent-book. Section 2 of the Act of 1962 goes on to prescribe the information to be contained in a rent-book provided under s. 1, viz:, a notice of the name and address of the landlord, and certain other information in the case of premises protected under the Rent Act 1968, or subject to contracts to which Part VI of 1968 Act applies. Section 1 of the Landlord and Tenant Act 1962 does, however, apply to a wider range of lettings than those covered by the Rent Act 1968.

The Act of 1962 also gives the tenant the right to demand particulars, where the landlord is a company, of the name and address of every director, and of the company secretary.

All the foregoing requirements apply only where the rent is "payable weekly", but an increasing proportion of tenancies are on the basis of a rent which is payable monthly, and the field covered by the Act of 1962 is therefore limited. A stipulation that certain information must be provided in the rent-book is of little value where there is no rent-book and no legal requirement that there should be one.

The new Act gives the tenants of a much wider range of tenancies the right to obtain the landlord's name and address. It applies to the tenant of any premises occupied as a dwelling, regardless of the interval at which rent is payable, and is not confined to tenancies under the Rent Acts. It does not however apply to business tenancies under Part II of the Landlord and Tenant Act 1954.

The terms of this section, which came into operation on 31 August 1974, are quite specific.

See also s. 122 and Sch. 13, para. 10.

122. Duty to inform tenant of a dwelling on assignment of landlord's interest

(1) If the interest of the landlord under a tenancy of premises which consist of or include a dwelling is assigned, the person to whom that interest is assigned (in this section referred to as "the new landlord") shall, within the appropriate

period, give notice in writing to the tenant of the assignment and of the name and address of the new landlord.

(2) In subsection (1) above "the appropriate period" means the period beginning on the date of the assignment in question and ending either two months after that date or, if it is later, on the first day after that date on which rent is payable under the tenancy.

(3) Subject to subsection (4) below, the reference in subsection (1) above to the new landlord's address is a reference to his place of abode or his place of business or, if the new landlord is a company, its registered office.

(4) If trustees as such constitute the new landlord, it shall be a sufficient compliance with the obligation in subsection (1) above to give the name of the new landlord to give a collective description of the trustees as the trustees of the trust in question, and where such a collective description is given—

(*a*) the address of the new landlord for the purpose of that subsection may be given as the address from which the affairs of the trust are conducted; and

(*b*) a change in the persons who are for the time being the trustees of the trust shall not be treated as an assignment of the interest of the landlord.

(5) If any person who is the new landlord under a tenancy falling within subsection (1) above fails, without reasonable excuse, to give the notice required by that subsection, he shall be guilty of an offence and liable on summary conviction to a fine not exceeding £200.

(6) Where an offence under subsection (5) above which has been committed by a body corporate is proved to have been committed with the consent or connivance of, or be attributable to any neglect on the part of, a director, manager, secretary or other similar officer of the body corporate, he, as well as the body corporate, shall be guilty of that offence and be liable to be proceeded against and punished accordingly.

(7) Where the affairs of a body corporate are managed by its members, subsection (6) above shall apply in relation to the acts and defaults of a member in connection with his functions of management as if he were a director of the body corporate.

(8) In this section "tenancy" includes a subtenancy and a statutory tenancy, within the meaning of the Rent Act 1968 or of the Rent (Scotland) Act 1971, but does not include a tenancy to which Part II of the Landlord and Tenant Act 1954 (business tenancies) applies, and "tenant" shall be construed accordingly.

(9) In this section—

(*a*) in relation to England and Wales "assignment" includes any conveyance other than a mortgage or charge; and

(*b*) in relation to Scotland "assignment" means a conveyance or other transfer (other than in security), and any reference to the date of the assignment means the date on which the conveyance or other transfer was granted, delivered or otherwise made effective.

(10) This section shall come into operation at the expiry of the period of one month beginning with the date on which this Act is passed. [**375**]

GENERAL

The new landlord is under a duty to give notice in writing to the tenant of his name and address within 2 months of the date of the assignment or, if it is later, on the first day after the expiry of the 2 months' period on which rent is payable. This section came into operation on 31 August 1974. "Tenancy" is defined in sub-s. (8).

123. Form and content of certain notices to quit

(1) In section 16 of the Rent Act 1957 or, in Scotland, section 131 of the Rent (Scotland) Act 1971 (minimum length of notice to quit) after the words "shall be valid unless it" there shall be inserted the words "is in writing and contains such information as may be prescribed and" and at the end of that section there shall be added the following subsections:—

"(2) In this section "prescribed" means prescribed by regulations made by the Secretary of State by statutory instrument, and a statutory instrument containing any such regulations shall be subject to annulment in pursuance of a resolution of either House of Parliament.

(3) Regulations under this section may make different provision in relation to different descriptions of lettings and different circumstances."

(2) This section does not apply in relation to a notice to quit given before the day appointed for the coming into operation of this section. [**376**]

GENERAL

This amends s. 16 of the Rent Act 1957, which laid down that the minimum length of a notice to quit, even of a weekly tenancy, should be 4 weeks. In future, notices to quit must be in writing and must contain information to be prescribed by the Secretary of State by statutory instrument. This does not apply to notices to quit served before this section came into operation on 2 December 1974.

124. Service charges

(1) After section 91 of the Housing Finance Act 1972 there shall be inserted the following section:—

"91A. Right to challenge service charges

(1) A service charge shall only be recoverable from the tenant of a flat—

(*a*) in respect of the provision of chargeable items to a reasonable standard; and

(*b*) to the extent that the liability incurred or amount defrayed by the landlord in respect of the provision of such items is reasonable; and if any works in respect of which a service charge is claimed are estimated to cost more than £250, at least two estimates of the cost of such works shall be obtained by the landlord or agent and one of the said estimates shall be from a firm wholly unconnected with them, in the manner described in Schedule 12 to this Act;

and if any work in respect of which a service charge is claimed is estimated to cost more than £2,000, there shall be a duty upon the landlord or agent first to discuss it with the tenants' association or if no such body exists or is not wholly independent, then with individual tenants before it is proceeded with (except in cases of emergency) and only after such consultation shall estimates be obtained in accordance with the provisions of this section; and the consultation and expressed views of tenants or their association or both shall be produced to the Court in case of any dispute arising out of the operation of this section.

(2) Any agreement made by a tenant of a flat other than an arbitration agreement within the meaning of section 32 of the Arbitration Act 1950 (whether the agreement is contained in an instrument letting the flat or not and whether it is made before the flat is let or not) shall be void in so far as it purports to provide for determination in a particular manner or on particular evidence (including, without prejudice to the generality of this subsection, determination on the basis of a certificate given by any person) of any question—

(*a*) whether chargeable items have been provided to a reasonable standard; or

(*b*) whether the liability incurred or amount defrayed by the landlord in respect of them was reasonable.

(3) The High Court or the county court, on the application of the landlord or tenant of a flat, may by order, in relation to any chargeable items specified in the order, declare—

(*a*) that they have or have not been provided to a reasonable standard; and

(*b*) that the amount alleged to be payable in respect of them is or is not reasonable,

and may direct the amount to be paid by the tenant in consequence of the declaration.

(4) Where in proceedings brought under the foregoing subsection (3) it is proved to the satisfaction of the Court that an association has been formed to represent the tenants one or more of whom are parties to the application and that the membership of such association comprises not less than 60 per cent. of the tenants eligible to belong thereto the Court may in making any order on the application further declare that the said association shall until further order of the Court be recognised for the purposes of this Act as the tenants' association entitled to exercise the rights conferred by this Act and the term "tenants' association" shall refer to such association so long as it is so recognised.

(5) Regulations relating to the formation of such tenants' association may be made by the Secretary of State.

(6) The county court may make a declaration under this section notwithstanding that the declaration is the only relief sought.

(7) In this section "chargeable items" means any items for which a service charge may be payable, and other expressions used in this section have the meanings assigned to them by section 90 (12) above.

(8) This section does not apply—

(*a*) where the landlord is—

(i) a local authority or a county council, or

(ii) a new town corporation, or

(iii) the Housing Corporation, or

(iv) a housing association falling within paragraph (*d*) of subsection (1) of section 91 above, or

(v) an association or company the membership of which is wholly or mainly restricted to persons who are tenants in the same block or blocks of flats, or (*b*) where the tenant is a protected tenant or a statutory tenant within the meaning of the Rent Act 1968 or a lessee within the meaning of Part VI of that Act (furnished lettings).

(9) This section does not apply in relation to an accounting year ending before 1st August 1974."

(2) The amendments of the Housing Finance Act 1972 specified in Schedule 12 to this Act shall have effect, subject to paragraph 5 of that Schedule.

(3) This section shall come into operation at the expiry of the period of one month beginning with the date on which this Act is passed. **[377]**

GENERAL

This creates a right for tenants to challenge demands for service charges by providing that charges shall be payable only for services carried out to a reasonable standard and at reasonable cost. Either the tenant or the landlord may make application to the High Court or the county court for an order declaring whether the work is or is not, to a reasonable standard, and whether the cost is reasonable—sub-s. 3. In proceedings brought under sub-s. (3) a tenants' association which includes 60 per cent. of the tenants in its membership may be recognised by the Court as entitled to exercise the rights conferred by the Act.

Any works for which service charge is claimed and which are estimated to cost more than £250 must be the subject of at least two estimates, one from a firm totally uncommitted with the landlord or agent. The reference on p. 167 to "Schedule 12 of this Act" is evidently a drafting error as there is no Schedule 12 in the Housing Finance Act 1972.

Where any such works are estimated to cost more than £2,000 the landlord must consult the tenants or their association before he proceeds with the work.

Apparently there have been instances of landlords claiming for services provided at very high cost, and supported by receipts from their own relatives or friends.

The Secretary of State may make regulations relating to the formation of tenants' associations, as referred to in this section. The rights given in this section are additional to those conferred by s. 90 of the Housing Finance Act 1972. Under that Act, where the service charge exceeds £80 per annum per flat, the tenant is entitled to obtain a summary in writing, certified by a qualified accountant, of the costs in the accounting year. This right is modified by s. 90 (3) of that Act where there are not more than five flats in the block, and in other ways. By s. 91 of the Housing Finance Act 1972 the duty under s. 90 to supply information about service charges does not apply where the landlord is a local authority, a new town corporation, the Housing Corporation, or a housing association as defined. Similar exemptions are applied by s. 124 (8) of the new Act. Also exempt are cases where the tenant is protected under the Rent Act 1968 or holds under a contract to which Part VI of that Act applies (furnished tenancies). Such tenants are safeguarded by their rights to apply to the Rent Officer or the Rent Tribunal. See s. 20, 24, 47, 73 and 75 of the Rent Act 1968. See also *Metropolitan Properties Co.* [*F.G.C.*) *Ltd.* v. *Lannon*, [1968] 1 W.L.R. 815, at p. 832.

This section came into operation on 31st August 1974. It does not apply to any accounting year which ended before 1st August 1974.

125. Specific performance of landlord's repairing covenants, etc.

(1) In any proceedings in which a tenant of a dwelling alleges a breach on the part of his landlord of a repairing covenant relating to any part of the premises in which the dwelling is comprised, the court may, in its discretion, order specific performance of that covenant, whether or not the breach relates to a part of the premises let to the tenant and notwithstanding any equitable rule restricting the scope of that remedy, whether on the basis of a lack of mutuality or otherwise.

(2) In this section—

"landlord", in relation to a tenant, includes any person againt whom the tenant has a right to enforce a repairing covenant;

"repairing covenant" means a covenant to repair, maintain, renew, construct or replace any property;

"statutory tenant" has the same meaning as in the Rent Act 1968; and "tenant" includes a sub-tenant and a statutory tenant but does not include a tenant under a tenancy to which Part II of the Landlord and Tenant Act 1954 (business tenancies) applies, and any reference to the premises let to a tenant means, in relation to a statutory tenant, the premises of which he is the statutory tenant.

(3) This section shall come into operation on the passing of this Act. [378]

GENERAL

This makes an important change in the law of landlord and tenant. The award of damages is often a totally inadequate remedy for the landlord's breach of a repairing covenant. This section gives the Court power, at its discretion, to order specific performance. This applies whether or not the breach relates to the part of the premises let to the tenant. The section came into force on 31st July 1974.

126. Enforceability of certain covenants in agreements relating to development of land

(1) The provisions of this section shall apply if a principal council (in the exercise of their powers under section 111 of the Local Government Act 1972 or otherwise) and a person having an interest in land in their area become parties to an instrument under seal executed for the purpose of securing the carrying out of works on that land or of facilitating the development of that land or of other land in which that person has an interest and the instrument is registered in the register of local land charges—

(*a*) by the proper officer, for the purposes of section 15 of the Land Charges Act 1925, of the local authority in whose area the land is situated, and

(*b*) in such manner as may be prescribed by rules under section 19 of that Act,

and in this subsection "local authority" means a district council, a London borough council or the Common Council of the City of London.

(2) If, in a case where this section applies,—

(*a*) the instrument contains a covenant on the part of any person having an interest in land, being a covenant to carry out any works or do any other thing on or in relation to that land, and

(*b*) the instrument defines the land to which the covenant relates, being land in which that person has an interest at the time the instrument is executed, and

(*c*) the covenant is expressed to be one to which this section applies,

the covenant shall be enforceable (without any limit of time) against any person deriving title from the original covenantor in respect of his interest in any of the land defined as mentioned in paragraph (*b*) above and any person deriving title under him in respect of any lesser interest in that land as if that person had also been an original covenanting party in respect of the interest for the time being held by him.

(3) Without prejudice to any other method of enforcement of a covenant falling within subsection (2) above, if there is a breach of the covenant as a result of a failure to carry out any works or to do any other thing on or in relation to any of the land to which the covenant relates, then, subject to subsection (4) below, the principal council who are a party to the instrument in which the covenant is contained may—

(*a*) enter on the land concerned and carry out the works or do any other thing which the covenant requires to be carried out or done; and (*b*) recover from any person against whom the covenant is enforceable (whether by virtue of subsection (2) above or otherwise) any expenses incurred by the council in exercise of their powers under this subsection.

(4) Before a principal council exercise their powers under subsection (3) (*a*) above they shall give not less than 21 days notice of their intention to do so to any person—

(*a*) who has for the time being an interest in the land on or in relation to which the works are to be carried out or other thing is to be done; and
(*b*) against whom the covenant is enforceable (whether by virtue of subsection (2) above or otherwise).

(5) The Public Health Act 1936 shall have effect as if any reference to that Act in—

(*a*) section 277 thereof (power of councils to require information as to ownership of premises),
(*b*) section 283 thereof (notices to be in writing; forms of notices, etc.),
(*c*) section 288 thereof (penalty for obstructing execution of Act), and
(*d*) section 291 thereof (certain expenses recoverable from owners to be a charge on the premises; power to order payment by instalments),

included a reference to subsections (1) to (4) above and as if any reference in those sections of that Act—

(i) to a local authority were a reference to a principal council; and
(ii) to the owner of premises were a reference to the holder of an interest in land.

(6) In its application to a notice or other document authorised to be given or served under subsection (4) above or by virtue of any provision of the Public Health Act 1936 specified in subsection (5) above, section 233 of the Local Government Act 1972 (service of notices by local authorities) shall have effect as if any reference in that section to a local authority included a reference to the Common Council of the City of London.

(7) In this section "principal council" means the council of a county, district or London borough, the Common Council of the City of London or the Greater London Council, and, subject to subsection (8) below, in relation to the Isles of Scilly, the Council of those Isles.

(8) The Secretary of State may, after consultation with the Council of the Isles of Scilly, by order direct that the provisions of subsections (1) to (6) of this section shall apply to the Isles of Scilly subject to such exceptions, adaptations and modifications, if any, as may be specified in the order. [**379**]

GENERAL

See comments on this section in Chapter 9.

127. Expenses and terms of payment of grants, etc.

(1) Except as provided by section 7 of this Act, there shall be defrayed out of money provided by Parliament—

(*a*) any sums required for the payment by the Secretary of State of grants, subsidies or contributions under this Act and any other expenses or outgoings of the Secretary of State under this Act;
(*b*) any increase attributable to the provisions of this Act in the sums payable out of such money under any other Act;

and any sums received by the Secretary of State under this Act shall be paid into the Consolidated Fund.

(2) Any grant, subsidy or contribution payable by the Secretary of State under this Act shall be payable subject to such conditions as to records, certificates, audit or otherwise as the Secretary of State may, with the approval of the Treasury, impose. [**380**]

128. Orders

(1) Any power of the Secretary of State to make an order under any provision of this Act shall be exercisable by statutory instrument.

(2) An order made by the Secretary of State under any provision of this Act may be varied or revoked by a subsequent order made under that provision.

(3) Subject to subsection (4) below, a statutory instrument containing an order made under any of the preceding provisions of this Act shall be subject to annulment in pursuance of a resolution of either House of Parliament.

(4) Subsection (3) above shall not apply to an order made under any of sections 7, 46, 59, 64 or 78 of this Act. [**381**]

GENERAL

The reason for the exceptions under sub-s. 4 is that they all relate to expenditure out of moneys provided by Parliament, and any order made under them is a matter for the Commons and not the Lords.

129. Interpretation

(1) In the application of this Act in England and Wales—

"the Corporation" means the Housing Corporation;

"dwelling" means a building or part of a building occupied or intended to be occupied as a separate dwelling, together with any yard, garden, outhouses and appurtenances belonging to or usually enjoyed with that building or part;

"hostel" means a building wherein is provided, for persons generally or for a class or classes of persons, residential accommodation (otherwise than in separate and self-contained sets of premises) and either board or facilities for the preparation of food adequate to the needs of those persons, or both;

"house in multiple occupation" means a house which is occupied by persons who do not form a single household, exclusive of any part thereof which is occupied as a separate dwelling by persons who do form a single household;

"housing association" has the meaning assigned to it by section 189 (1) of the Housing Act 1957;

"improvement grant" and "intermediate grant" have the meanings assigned to them by section 56 (2) of this Act;

"operative date" means 1st April 1975 or such later date as may be specified under, and for the purposes of, section 17 (1) of this Act;

"registered", except in the expression "registered charity" means registered in the register of housing associations established under section 13 of this Act, and "registration" and "unregistered" shall be construed accordingly;

"registered charity" means a charity of which particulars are entered in the register of charities established under section 4 of the Charities Act 1960;

"repairs grant" and "special grant" have the meanings assigned to them by section 56 (2) above.

(2) In the application of this Act in Scotland—

"charge" includes a heritable security;

"the Corporation" means the Housing Corporation;

"dwelling" means a house within the meaning of section 208 (1) of the Housing (Scotland) Act 1966;

"heritable security" has the meaning assigned to it by section 12 of this Act;

"hostel" has the same meaning as in section 21 (4) of the Housing (Financial Provisions) (Scotland) Act 1968;

"housing association" has the meaning assigned to it by section 208 (1) of the Housing (Scotland) Act 1966;

"local authority" has the meaning assigned to it by section 1 of the Housing (Scotland) Act 1966;

"mortgage" means a heritable security and "mortgagee" means the creditor in such a security;

"operative date" has the same meaning as in subsection (1) above;

"registered" means registered in the register of housing associations established under section 13 of this Act, and "registration" and "unregistered" shall be construed accordingly.

(3) For the purposes of this Act a person is a member of another's family if that person is—

(*a*) the other's wife or husband; or

(*b*) a son or daughter or a son-in-law or daughter-in-law of the other, or of the other's wife or husband; or

(*c*) the father or mother of the other, or of the other's wife or husband.

(4) In paragraph (*b*) of subsection (3) above any reference to a person's son or daughter includes a reference to any step-son or step-daughter, any illegitimate son or daughter, and any adopted son or daughter of that person, and "son-in-law" and "daughter-in-law" shall be construed accordingly.

(5) Any reference in this Act to any other enactment shall be construed as referring to that enactment as amended by or under any other enactment, including this Act. **[382]**

GENERAL

The definition of "dwelling" seems incomplete. A "dwelling" is equated with a dwelling plus any yard garden etc. used or intended to be used as a separate dwelling. The idea of separateness is helpful but to say that a dwelling means a "building . . . occupied as a separate dwelling" seems rather vague. According to *Lewin* v. *End*, [1906] A.C. 299, "dwelling" means "used as a residence". See also *Curl* v. *Angelo*, [1948] 2 All E.R. 189 (C.A.). The term "dwelling" includes a flat—see *Langford Property Co.*, v. *Goldrich*, [1949] 1 K.B. 511.

130. Amendments, transitional provisions, savings and repeals

(1) Schedule 13 to this Act, which contains minor amendments and amendments consequential on the provisions of this Act, shall have effect.

(2) In Schedule 13 to this Act, the amendments of the Land Compensation Act 1973 and the Land Compensation (Scotland) Act 1973 shall have effect in the case of persons displaced on or after the date of the passing of this Act.

(3) The transitional provisions and savings in Schedule 14 to this Act shall have effect.

(4) The enactments specified in Schedule 15 to this Act are hereby repealed to the extent specified in the third column of that Schedule. [**383**]

131. Short title, citation, commencement and extent

(1) This Act may be cited as the Housing Act 1974.

(2) This Act and the Housing Acts 1957 to 1973 may be cited together as the Housing Acts 1957 to 1974.

(3) Except in so far as any provision of this Act otherwise provides, this Act shall come into operation on such day as the Secretary of State may by order appoint, and different days may be so appointed for different provisions and for different purposes.

(4) Without prejudice to any express saving contained in Schedule 14 to this Act, an order under subsection (3) above appointing a day for the coming into operation of any provision of Schedule 13 or Schedule 15 to this Act may contain such savings with respect to the operation of that provision as appear to the Secretary of State to be appropriate.

(5) Parts IV, V, VI, VII, and VIII and, in Part IX, sections 105, 106, 108, 118, 124, 125 and 126 of this Act extend to England and Wales only.

(6) Section 107 of this Act extends to Scotland only.

(7) This Act does not extend to Northern Ireland. [**384**]

SCHEDULES

SCHEDULE 1

Section 1 (1)

AMENDMENTS TO CONSTITUTION ETC. OF HOUSING CORPORATION

1. In sub-paragraph (1) of paragraph 2 of Schedule 1 to the 1964 Act (number of members of Corporation not to exceed nine) for the word "nine" there shall be substituted the word "fifteen". [**385**]

2. At the end of the said paragraph 2 there shall be inserted the following paragraph—

> "2A.—(1) Before appointing a person to be a member of the Corporation the Ministers shall satisfy themselves that that person will have no such financial or other interest as is likely to affect prejudicially the exercise of his functions as a member, and the Ministers shall also satisfy themselves from time to time with respect to every member of the Corporation that he has no such interest; and any person who is, or whom the Ministers propose to appoint, a member of the Corporation shall, whenever requested by them to do so, furnish them with such information as the Ministers consider necessary for the performance of their duties under this paragraph.
>
> (2) A member of the Corporation who is any way directly or indirectly interested in a contract made or proposed to be made by the Corporation shall disclose the nature of his interest at a meeting of the Corporation, and the disclosure shall be recorded in the minutes of the Corporation; and the member shall not take part in any decision of the Corporation with respect to that contract.
>
> (3) For the purposes of sub-paragraph (2) above a general notice given at a meeting of the Corporation by a member of the Corporation to the effect that he is a member of a specified company or firm and is to be regarded as interested in any contract which may, after the date of the notice, be made with

the company or firm shall be regarded as a sufficient disclosure of his interest in relation to any contract so made.

(4) A member of the Corporation need not attend in person at a meeting of the Corporation in order to make any disclosure which he is required to make under this paragraph if he takes reasonable steps to secure that the disclosure is made by a notice which is brought up and read at the meeting.

(5) In sub-paragraph (1) above 'the Ministers' means the persons by whom members of the Corporation are appointed under paragraph 2 (1) above." **[386]**

3. In paragraph 5 of that Schedule after the words "this Act" there shall be inserted the words "or the Housing Act 1974". **[387]**

4. At the end of paragraph 5 of that Schedule there shall be added the following paragraph— **[388]**

"6. The Corporation shall be a public body for the purposes of the Prevention of Corruption Acts 1889 to 1916." **[389]**

GENERAL

This schedule should be read with the s. 1 and the Notes thereon. Background information is given in Chapter 1. The powers and duties of the Corporation are now greatly enlarged and accordingly the number of members is raised from a maximum of nine to a maximum of fifteen members, and additional measures to ensure the probity of its members and officers are contained in paras. 2 to 4.

SCHEDULE 2

Section 2

Grant-Aided Land

1. For the purposes of section 2 of this Act "grant-aided land" means land—

(*a*) in respect of which any such payment as is specified in paragraph 2 below falls or fell to be made in respect of a period ending after 24th January 1974; or

(*b*) on which is or has been secured a loan which is of a description specified in paragraph 3 below and in respect of which any repayment (whether by way of principal or interest or both) falls or fell to be made after that date. **[390]**

2. The payments referred to in paragraph 1 (*a*) above are payments—

(*a*) by way of annual grants under section 31 (3) of the Housing Act 1949 or by way of exchequer contributions under section 19 (3) of the Housing (Scotland) Act 1949 or under section 121 (3) of the Housing (Scotland) Act 1950 (arrangements by local authorities for improvement of housing accommodation);

(*b*) by way of annual grants under section 12 (1) or section 15 of the Housing (Financial Provisions) Act 1958 or by way of exchequer contributions under section 89 (1) of the Housing (Scotland) Act 1950 or under section 12 of the Housing (Scotland) Act 1962 or under section 21 of the Housing (Financial Provisions) (Scotland) Act 1968 (contributions for dwellings improved under arrangements with local authorities and grants for hostels);

(*c*) by way of annual grant under section 12 (6) of the Housing Subsidies Act 1967 or by way of exchequer contributions under section 121 of the Housing (Scotland) Act 1950 or under section 62 of the Housing Act 1964 or under section 17 of the Housing (Financial Provisions) (Scotland) Act 1968 (subsidies for conversions or improvements by housing associations);

(*d*) by way of annual grant under section 21 (8) of the Housing Act 1969 (contributions for dwellings provided or improved by housing associations under arrangements with local authorities);

(*e*) by way of basic residual subsidy, special residual subsidy or new building subsidy under section 72, section 73 or section 75 of the Housing Finance Act 1972 or by way of hostel subsidy under section 92 of that Act; and

(*f*) by way of basic residual subsidy, special residual subsidy, new building subsidy or improvement subsidy under section 52, section 53, section 55 or section 57 of the Housing (Financial Provisions) (Scotland) Act 1972. **[391]**

3. The loans referred to in paragraph 1 (*b*) above are—

(*a*) loans under section 119 of the Housing Act 1957 or under section 152 of the Housing (Scotland) Act 1966 (power of certain local authorities to promote and assist housing associations);

(*b*) loans to housing associations under section 47 of the Housing (Financial Provisions) Act 1958 or under section 78 of the Housing (Scotland) Act 1950 or under section 24 of the Housing (Financial Provisions) (Scotland) Act 1968 (loans by Public Works Loan Commissioners to certain bodies):

(*c*) advances made under section 7 of the Housing Act 1961 or under section 11 of the Housing (Scotland) Act 1962 or under section 23 of the Housing (Financial Provisions) (Scotland) Act 1968 (advances to housing associations providing housing accommodation for letting); and

(*d*) loans made by the Corporation under section 2 of the Housing Act 1964. **[392]**

GENERAL

See notes on s. 2 above. It will be noted that the term "grant-aided" applies only to land in respect of which any payment of grant or subsidy (para. 2), or of loan (para. 3) "falls or fell" to be made after 24th January 1974. The liability to make such payments may be removed by other financial measures in this Act, *e.g.* by s. 35, but that will not alter the classification of the land as "grant-aided" if a payment falls or fell to be made after that date. See Circular 133/74 in Appendix II.

SCHEDULE 3

Section 18

Housing Association Tenancies

Part I

Interim Protection of Housing Association Tenants

1.—(1) The provisions of this Part of this Schedule apply where,—

(*a*) before the passing of this Act, any premises have been let on a tenancy (in this Part of this Schedule referred to as "the former tenancy"); and

(*b*) by reason only of section 5 (5) of the Rent Act 1968 or of section 5 (4) of the Rent (Scotland) Act 1971 (exclusion of housing association tenancies from protection) the former tenancy was not a protected tenancy on the relevant day; and

(*c*) the former tenancy has come to an end before the passing of this Act or comes to an end after the passing of this Act but before the operative date; and

(*d*) at any time after the passing of this Act or the termination of the former tenancy, whichever is the later, any of the persons specified in sub-paragraph (3) below remains in occupation of the premises or part of them and in residence therein. **[393]**

(2) In this Part of this Schedule "the relevant day", in relation to a tenancy, means,—

(*a*) in the case of a tenancy which expired before the passing of this Act, the day on which it expired; and

(*b*) in any other case, the day immediately preceding that on which this Act was passed. **[394]**

(3) The persons referred to in sub-paragraph (1) (*d*) above are—

(*a*) the tenant under the former tenancy;

(*b*) any person to whom the premises or any part thereof has been lawfully sublet as a dwelling; and

(*c*) where any such person as is mentioned in paragraph (*a*) or paragraph (*b*) above has died, any person who, if the deceased had been the original tenant, within the meaning of Schedule 1 to the Rent Act 1968, or to the Rent (Scotland) Act 1971, of the premises or part would have been the first successor, within the meaning of that Schedule, or would have become the statutory tenant on the death of that first successor. **[395]**

2.—(1) In this paragraph "the occupier", in relation to any premises, means the person remaining in occupation and in residence as mentioned in paragraph 1 (1) (*d*) above and "the owner", in relation to any premises, means the person who, as against the occupier, is entitled to possession thereof; and the following provisions of this paragraph shall have effect subject to paragraph 3 below. **[396]**

(2) Without prejudice to any power of the court apart from this Part of this Schedule to postpone the operation or suspend the execution of an order for possession, if in proceedings by the owner against the occupier of any premises the court makes, or has before the passing of this Act made, an order for possession the court may suspend the execution of the order for such period, not exceeding 12 months from the date of the order, as the court thinks reasonable. **[397]**

(3) Where the court by virtue of this paragraph suspends the execution of an order for possession of any premises it may authorise the withdrawal from the occupier of any specified services or furniture and impose such terms and conditions, including conditions as to the payment by the occupier of arrears of rent, rent or mesne profits and otherwise, as the court thinks reasonable. **[398]**

(4) The court may from time to time vary the period of suspension or terminate it and may vary any terms or conditions imposed by virtue of this paragraph, but shall not extend the period of suspension beyond the end of 12 months from the date of the order for possession. **[399]**

(5) In considering whether or how to exercise its powers under this paragraph the court shall have regard to all the circumstances and, in particular, to the following, namely,—

(*a*) whether the occupier has failed (whether before or after the termination of the former tenancy) to observe any terms or conditions thereof;

(*b*) whether he has unreasonably refused an offer of a tenancy of the premises or part of them for a reasonable term; and

(*c*) whether greater hardship would be caused by the suspension of the execution of the order for possession than by its execution without suspension or further suspension. **[400]**

(6) Where in proceedings for the recovery of possession of any premises the court makes an order for possession but suspends the execution of the order by virtue of sub-paragraph (2) above it shall make no order for costs, unless it appears to the court, having regard to the conduct of the owner or of the occupier, that there are special reasons for making such an order. **[401]**

(7) In the application of this paragraph to Scotland—

(*a*) for any reference to an order for possession there shall be substituted a reference to a decree of removing or warrant of ejection,

(*b*) for the reference to mesne profits there shall be substituted a reference to damages arising from unlawful possession, and

(*c*) for the reference to costs there shall be substituted a reference to expenses. **[402]**

3.—(1) If at any time befoie the operative date the interest which, on the relevant day, was the interest of the landlord under the former tenancy (in this paragraph referred to as "the landlord's interest") becomes vested in one of the bodies specified in section 5 (2) of the Rent Act 1968 or of the Rent (Scotland) Act 1971 (bodies whose tenancies are excluded from protection under that Act) the court may not, in exercise of its power under paragraph 2 (4) above, vary the period of suspension otherwise than by shortening it. **[403]**

(2) If on the operative date the landlord's interest belongs to a housing association then, without prejudice to the provisions of Parts II and III below and to the continued operation of any provision made before that date by virtue of paragraph 2 above, the powers of the court under that paragraph shall on that date cease to be exercisable. **[404]**

4.—(1) In this Part of this Schedule "the court",—

(*a*) in relation to premises in England or Wales, means the county court; and
(*b*) in relation to premises in Scotland, means the sheriff. **[405]**

(2) Any powers of a county court in proceedings for the recovery of possession of any premises in circumstances where the powers conferred by this Part of this Schedule are or may be exercisable may be exercised by any registrar of the court, except in so far as rules of court otherwise provide. **[406]**

(3) Except in so far as the context otherwise requires, expressions to which a meaning is assigned by section 113 of the Rent Act 1968 or, in Scotland, section 133 of the Rent (Scotland) Act 1971 have the same meanings in this Part of this Schedule. **[407]**

Part II

Application of Rent Act 1968

5.—(1) The provisions of this paragraph apply on and after the operative date in any case where—

(*a*) a tenancy of a dwelling-house under which the interest of the landlord belonged to a housing association has come to an end at a time before the operative date (whether before or after the passing of this Act), and
(*b*) on the date when it came to an end, the tenancy was one to which Part VIII of the 1972 Act applied, and
(*c*) if the tenancy had come to an end after the operative date it would, by virtue of section 18 (1) of this Act, have then been a protected tenancy. **[408]**

(2) No order for possession of the dwelling-house shall be made which would not be made if the tenancy had been a protected tenancy at the time it came to an end. **[409]**

(3) Where a court has made an order for possession of the dwelling-house before the operative date, but the order has not been executed, the court, if of opinion that the order would not have been made if the tenancy had been a protected tenancy when it came to an end may, on the application of the person against whom it was made, rescind or vary it in such manner as the court thinks fit for the purpose of enabling him to continue in possession. **[410]**

(4) If on the operative date the person who was the tenant under the tenancy which has come to an end duly retains possession of the dwelling-house, he shall be deemed to do so as a statutory tenant under a regulated tenancy and as a person who became a statutory tenant on the termination of a protected tenancy under which he was the tenant. **[411]**

(5) If on the operative date a person duly retains possession of the dwelling-house as being a person who, in the circumstances described in paragraph 1 (3) (*c*) above, would have been the first successor, within the meaning of Schedule 1 to the Rent Act 1968, he shall be deemed to do so as the statutory tenant under a regulated tenancy and as a person who became a statutory tenant by virtue of paragraph 2 or paragraph 3 of that Schedule. **[412]**

(6) If on the operative date a person duly retains possession of the dwelling-house as being a person who, in the circumstances described in paragraph 1 (3) (*c*) above, would have become the statutory tenant on the death of a first successor, he shall be deemed to do so as the statutory tenant under a regulated tenancy and as a person who became a statutory tenant by virtue of paragraph 6 or paragraph 7 of Schedule 1 to the Rent Act 1968. [**413**]

(7) References in the preceding provisions of this paragraph to a person duly retaining possession of a dwelling-house are references to his retaining possession without any order for possession having been made or, where such an order has been made,—

(*a*) during any period while its operation is postponed or its execution is suspended; or

(*b*) after it has been rescinded. [**414**]

(8) Subject to sub-paragraph (9) below, the tenancy referred to in sub-paragraph (1) above shall be treated as the original contract of tenancy for the purposes of section 12 of the Rent Act 1968 (terms and conditions of statutory tenancies) in relation to a statutory tenancy imposed by any of sub-paragraphs (4) to (6) above. [**415**]

(9) The High Court or the county court may by order vary all or any of the terms of a statutory tenancy imposed by any of sub-paragraphs (4) to (6) above in any way appearing to the court to be just and equitable (and whether or not in a way authorised by the provisions of sections 23 and 24 of the Rent Act 1968). [**416**]

6.—(1) If, in a case where either a tenancy becomes a protected tenancy by virtue of section 18 (1) of this Act or a statutory tenancy is imposed by virtue of paragraph 5 above,—

(*a*) a rent was registered for the dwelling-house at a time when Part VIII of the 1972 Act applied to that tenancy or, as the case may be, to the tenancy referred to in paragraph 5 (1) above, and

(*b*) a rent is subsequently registered for the dwelling-house under Part IV of the Rent Act 1968 but the rent so registered is less than the rent registered as mentioned in paragraph (*a*) above,

then, subject to paragraph 8 below, until such time as a rent is registered under Part IV of the Rent Act 1968 which is higher than the rent registered as mentioned in paragraph (*a*) above, the contractual rent limit, or, as the case may be, the maximum rent recoverable during any statutory period of the regulated tenancy concerned shall be the rent registered as mentioned in paragraph (*a*) above. [**417**]

(2) If, in a case falling within sub-paragraph (1) above, the Secretary of State has, in a direction under section 85 of the 1972 Act, specified a rent limit for the dwelling-house higher than the rent registered as mentioned in sub-paragraph (1) (*a*) above, then, during the period for which that direction has effect as mentioned in that section, sub-paragraph (1) above shall have effect with the substitution for any reference to the rent registered as mentioned in paragraph (*a*) of that sub-paragraph of a reference to the rent limit so specified. [**418**]

(3) Nothing in the preceding provisions of this paragraph shall affect the operation of section 48A of the Rent Act 1968 (cancellation of registration of rent) and, accordingly, where the registration of a rent is cancelled in accordance with that section sub-paragraph (1) above shall cease to apply in relation to the rent of the dwelling-house concerned. [**419**]

7.—(1) This paragraph applies for the purposes of the application of Part III of the Rent Act 1968 (rents under regulated tenancies) in relation to—

(*a*) a tenancy which becomes a protected tenancy by virtue of section 18 (1) of this Act,

(*b*) a statutory tenancy arising on the termination of such a tenancy, and

(*c*) a statutory tenancy imposed by virtue of paragraph 5 above, in any case where, at the time when Part VIII of the 1972 Act last applied to the tenancy referred to in paragraph (*a*) above or, as the case may require, paragraph 5 (1) above, subsection (3) of section 83 of the 1972 Act applied (rent limit where no rent is registered). **[420]**

(2) Where this paragraph applies, the rent limit applicable to the tenancy or statutory tenancy referred to in sub-paragraph (1) above shall be deemed to be (or, as the case may be, to have been) the contractual rent limit under the relevant tenancy, but without prejudice to the subsequent registration of a rent for the dwelling-house under Part IV of the Rent Act 1968 or (during the currency of a protected tenancy) the making of an agreement under section 43 of the 1972 Act increasing the rent payable. **[421]**

(3) Sub-paragraph (2) above shall have effect notwithstanding the repeal by the 1972 Act of section 20 (3) of the Rent Act 1968 (contractual rent limit before registration), but nothing in this paragraph shall be taken as applying any provision of section 83 of the 1972 Act to a tenancy at a time when it is a protected tenancy.

(4) In this paragraph "the relevant tenancy" means— **[422]**

(*a*) in the case of a tenancy falling within sub-paragraph (1) (*a*) above, that tenancy;

(*b*) in the case of a statutory tenancy falling within sub-paragraph (1) (*b*) above, the tenancy referred to in sub-paragraph (1) (*a*) above; and

(*c*) in the case of a statutory tenancy falling within sub-paragraph (1) (*c*) above, the protected tenancy referred to in sub-paragraph (4) of paragraph 5 above or, in a case where sub-paragraph (5) or sub-paragraph (6) of that paragraph applies, a notional protected tenancy which, by virtue of section 7 (4) of the Rent Act 1968, would be treated for the purposes of that Act as constituting one regulated tenancy when taken together with the statutory tenancy. **[423]**

8.—(1) The provisions of this paragraph apply where—

(*a*) a tenancy of a dwelling-house becomes a protected tenancy by virtue of section 18 (1) of this Act or a statutory tenancy is imposed by virtue of paragraph 5 above; and

(*b*) immediately before the tenancy became a protected tenancy or, as the case may require, immediately before the tenancy referred to in paragraph 5 (1) above came to an end, section 84 of the 1972 Act (phasing of progression to registered rent) applied to the rent of the dwelling-house let on that tenancy. **[424]**

(2) In the following provisions of this paragraph "the regulated tenancy" means the regulated tenancy consisting of the protected or statutory tenancy referred to in sub-paragraph (1) (*a*) above, together with any subsequent statutory tenancy which, when taken with that regulated tenancy is by virtue of section 7 (4) of the Rent Act 1968 treated for the purposes of that Act as constituting one regulated tenancy. **[425]**

(3) Subject to the following provisions of this paragraph, section 84 of the 1972 Act shall continue to apply or, as the case may require, shall apply to the rent of a dwelling-house subject to the regulated tenancy. **[426]**

(4) Section 84 of the 1972 Act shall cease to apply by virtue of this paragraph to the rent of a dwelling-house—

(*a*) on the date on which a rent is registered for the dwelling-house under Part IV of the Rent Act 1968 if the date of registration, within the meaning of Part VIII of the 1972 Act, is after the operative date; or

(*b*) on the date on which a new regulated tenancy of the dwelling-house is granted to a person who is neither the tenant under the regulated tenancy nor a person who might succeed him as a statutory tenant. **[427]**

(5) If and so long as, by virtue of this paragraph, subsection (2) of section 84 of the 1972 Act imposes for any rental period of a tenancy or statutory tenancy a rent

limit below the rent registered for the dwelling-house as mentioned in subsection (1) of that section,—

(*a*) the contractual rent limit shall be the rent limit so imposed and not the registered rent (as provided by section 20 (2) of the Rent Act 1968) and section 87 of the 1972 Act (increase of rent without notice to quit) shall apply in relation to the tenancy as if it were one to which Part VIII of that Act applied; and

(*b*) a notice of increase under section 22 (2) (*b*) of the Rent Act 1968 (increase of rent for statutory periods) may not increase the rent for any statutory period above the rent limit so imposed, and any such notice which purports to increase it further shall have effect to increase it to that limit but no further. **[428]**

(6) For the purposes of the application on and after the operative date of section 84 of the 1972 Act to the rent of a dwelling-house subject to a regulated tenancy consisting of or beginning with a statutory tenancy which is imposed by virtue of paragraph 5 above, that section shall be deemed to have continued to apply throughout the period between the termination of the tenancy referred to in sub-paragraph (1) of that paragraph and the operative date; but nothing in this paragraph shall affect the rent recoverable for that dwelling-house at any time during that period. **[429]**

9.—(1) This paragraph shall have effect with respect to the application of Schedule 6 to the 1972 Act (restriction on rent increases) in relation to a regulated tenancy consisting of—

(*a*) a tenancy which becomes a protected tenancy by virtue of section 18 (1) of this Act, or

(*b*) a statutory tenancy imposed by virtue of paragraph 5 above,

together with any subsequent statutory tenancy which, when taken with that regulated tenancy, is by virtue of section 7 (4) of the Rent Act 1968 treated for the purposes of that Act as constituting one regulated tenancy. **[430]**

(2) For the purposes of paragraph 1 (1) (*b*) of the said Schedule 6 (application of paragraph 1 to the first registration of rent after completion, during the existence of the regulated tenancy, of certain works), a tenancy falling within sub-paragraph (1) (*a*) above shall be deemed to have been a regulated tenancy throughout the period when Part VIII of the 1972 Act applied to it. **[431]**

(3) In the case of a regulated tenancy falling within sub-paragraph (1) (*b*) above, paragraph 1 (1) (*b*) of the said Schedule 6 shall have effect as if the reference to the completion of works during the existence of the regulated tenancy included a reference to their completion during the period beginning on the day on which Part VIII of the 1972 Act first applied to the tenancy referred to in paragraph 5 (1) above and ending on the day on which the regulated tenancy came into existence. **[432]**

(4) The references in paragraph 3 (1) of the said Schedule 6 to notices of increase authorised by the Rent Act 1968 shall include a reference to notices of increase under section 87 of the 1972 Act.

10. In the application of section 25 of the Rent Act 1968 (increase, on account of improvements, of recoverable rent for statutory periods before registration) in relation to a statutory tenancy arising on the termination of a tenancy which becomes a protected tenancy by virtue of section 18 (1) of this Act and a statutory tenancy imposed by virtue of paragraph 5 above, for the reference to 7th December 1965 (the date after which the improvement must be completed) there shall be substituted a reference to the operative date. **[433]**

11. In the application of section 46 of the Rent Act 1968 in relation to a tenancy which becomes a protected tenancy by virtue of section 18 (1) of this Act or a statutory tenancy which is imposed by virtue of paragraph 5 above, the reference in subsection (3) to a failure to comply with any terms of a regulated tenancy or to

carrying out an improvement includes a reference to a failure occurring or an improvement carried out before the tenancy became a regulated tenancy or, as the case may be, before the statutory tenancy was imposed. **[434]**

12. In this Part of this Schedule "the 1972 Act" means the Housing Finance Act 1972 and sections 38 (1) and 113 (1) of the Rent Act 1968 (interpretation) shall have effect for the purposes of this Schedule as they have effect for the purposes of Part III or, as the case may be, the whole of that Act.

Part III

Application of Rent (Scotland) Act 1971

13.—(1) The provisions of this paragraph apply on and after the operative date in any case where—

(*a*) a tenancy of a dwelling-house under which the interest of the landlord belonged to a housing association has come to an end at a time before the operative date (whether before or after the passing of this Act), and

(*b*) on the date when it came to an end, the tenancy was one to which sections 60 to 66 of the 1972 Act applies, and

(*c*) if the tenancy had come to an end after the operative date it would, by virtue of section 18 (1) of this Act, have then been a protected tenancy. **[435]**

(2) No order for possession of the dwelling-house shall be made which would not be made if the tenancy had been a protected tenancy at the time it came to an end. **[436]**

(3) Where a court has made an order for possession of the dwellinghouse before the operative date, but the order has not been executed, the court, if of opinion that the order would not have been made if the tenancy had been a protected tenancy when it came to an end may, on the application of the person against whom it was made, rescind or vary it in such manner as the court thinks fit for the purpose of enabling him to continue in possession. **[437]**

(4) If on the operative date the person who was the tenant under the tenancy which has come to an end duly retains possession of the dwelling-house, he shall be deemed to do so as a statutory tenant under a regulated tenancy and as a person who became a statutory tenant on the termination of a protected tenancy under which he was the tenant. **[438]**

(5) If on the operative date a person duly retains possession of the dwelling-house as being a person who, in the circumstances described in paragraph 1 (3) (*c*) above, would have been the first successor, within the meaning of Schedule 1 to the 1971 Act he shall be deemed to do so as the statutory tenant under a regulated tenancy and as a person who became a statutory tenant by virtue of paragraph 2 or paragraph 3 of that Schedule. **[439]**

(6) If on the operative date a person duly retains possession of the dwelling-house as being a person who, in the circumstances described in paragraph 1 (3) (*c*) above, would have become the statutory tenant on the death of a first successor, he shall be deemed to do so as the statutory tenant under a regulated tenancy and as a person who became a statutory tenant by virtue of paragraph 6 or paragraph 7 of Schedule 1 to the 1971 Act. **[440]**

(7) References in the preceding provisions of this paragraph to a person duly retaining possession of a dwelling-house are references to his retaining possession without any order for possession having been made or, where such an order has been made,—

(*a*) during any period while its operation is postponed or its execution is suspended; or

(*b*) after it has been rescinded. **[441]**

(8) Subject to sub-paragraph (9) below, the tenancy referred to in sub-paragraph (1) above shall be treated as the original contract of tenancy for the purposes of section 12 of the 1971 Act (terms and conditions of statutory tenancies) in relation to a statutory tenancy imposed by any of sub-paragraphs (4) to (6) above. [**442**]

(9) The court may by order vary all or any of the terms of a statutory tenancy imposed by any of sub-paragraphs (4) to (6) above in any way appearing to the court to be just and equitable (and whether or not in a way authorised by the provisions of sections 22 and 23 of the 1971 Act). [**443**]

14.—(1) This paragraph applies to—

(*a*) a tenancy which becomes a protected tenancy by virtue of section 18 (1) of this Act;

(*b*) a statutory tenancy which is deemed to arise under paragraph 13 above; and

(*c*) a statutory tenancy arising on the termination of any such tenancy as is referred to in head (*a*) or (*b*) of this sub-paragraph. [**444**]

(2) The contractual rent limit for any contractual period of a tenancy to which this paragraph applies or the limit of rent recoverable for any statutory period of that tenancy shall be determined as follows—

(*a*) where no rent has been registered for the dwelling-house under the previous housing association tenancy, the limit for the purposes of section 19 (1) or, subject to sections 22 to 24, of section 21 (1) of the 1971 Act, shall be the rent recoverable for the last rental period of that tenancy determined in accordance with section 62 (3) of the 1972 Act, until either,

(i) a rent is registered for the dwelling-house under Part IV of the 1971 Act, or

(ii) a rent agreement with a tenant having security of tenure is entered into with respect to the dwelling-house; [**445**]

(*b*) where a rent has been registered for the dwelling-house under the previous housing association tenancy and the rent recoverable for the last rental period of that tenancy was that registered rent, the limit, for the purposes of section 19 (2) or section 21 (2) of the 1971 Act, but subject to the provisions of those sections, shall be the registered rent until either—

(i) a new rent is registered for the dwelling-house under Part IV of the 1971 Act, or

(ii) the rent registered for the dwelling-house is cancelled in terms of section 44A of the 1971 Act; [**446**]

(*c*) where a rent has been registered for the dwelling-house under the previous housing association tenancy and the rent recoverable for the last rental period of that tenancy was determined in accordance with section 63 of the 1972 Act, the limit, for the purposes of section 19 (2) or of section 21 (2) of the 1971 Act, shall be the rent limit as determined in accordance with the said section 63 of the 1972 Act and, for this purpose, that registration and the provisions of sections 62 (4), 63 (2) to (4) and 67 of that Act shall subject to the provisions of sub-paragraph (3) of this paragraph, continue to apply or, as the case may require, shall apply to the rent of a dwelling-house under a tenancy to which this paragraph applies as if that tenancy had been a tenancy to which sections 60 to 66 of the 1972 Act applied, until either—

(i) a new rent is registered for the dwelling-house under Part IV of the 1971 Act, or

(ii) the rent registered for the dwelling-house is cancelled in terms of section 44A of the 1971 Act; [**447**]

(*d*) where a rent has been registered for the dwelling-house and the Secretary of State has given a direction under section 64 (4) of the 1972 Act, specifying the rent limit for the dwelling-house under the previous housing association tenancy, the limit, for the purposes of section 19 (2) or of section 21 (2) of the 1971 Act, shall be the rent limit specified in the direction and, for this purpose, the provisions of sections 62 (1), (2), (4) and (5), 64 and 67 of the 1972 Act shall continue to apply or, as the case may require, shall apply to the rent of a dwelling-house under a tenancy to which this paragraph applies as if that tenancy had been a tenancy to which sections 60 to 66 of the 1972 Act applied, until—

(i) the direction ceases to have effect (whether because any condition included in the direction is not complied with or because the period for which the direction has effect ends), or

(ii) a new rent is registered for the dwelling-house under Part IV of the 1971 Act (whether or not the new rent exceeds the rent provisionally registered or the rent specified in the direction),

and where any of the events specified in the foregoing provisions of this sub-paragraph take place the said limits shall be determined in accordance with the provisions of the Rent (Scotland) Acts 1971 and 1972. **[448]**

(3) In the application, by virtue of sub-paragraph (2) (*c*) of this paragraph, of subsection (2) of section 63 of the 1972 Act to the rent of a dwelling-house subject to a statutory tenancy which is deemed to arise under paragraph 13 above, that subsection shall be deemed to have continued to apply throughout the period between the termination of the tenancy referred to in paragraph 13 (1) (*a*) above and the operative date; but nothing in this sub-paragraph shall affect the rent recoverable for that dwelling-house at any time during that period. **[449]**

(4) In the case where sub-paragraph (2) (*c*) of this paragraph applies, and the rent limit therein referred to is the rent limit as determined in accordance with section 63 of the 1972 Act, any notice of increase under section 21 (2) (*b*) of the 1971 Act shall not increase the rent for any statutory period of a tenancy to which this paragraph applies above the rent limit as so determined, and any such notice which purports to increase it further shall have effect to increase it to that limit but no further. **[450]**

(5) In the application of section 24 (1) of the 1971 Act (increase of rent for improvements) to a tenancy to which this paragraph applies, for the reference to 8th December 1965 (the date after which the improvement must be completed) there shall be substituted a reference to the operative date. **[451]**

(6) Section 42 of the 1971 Act (determination of fair rent) shall apply in relation to a tenancy to which this paragraph applies as if the reference in subsection (3) of the said section 42 to the tenant under the regulated tenancy included references to the tenant under the previous housing association tenancy. **[452]**

(7) Any right conferred upon a tenant by section 31 of the 1971 Act, as applied by section 62 (5) of the 1972 Act, to recover any amount by deducting it from rent should be exercisable by deducting it from rent for any rental period beginning after the tenancy has become a tenancy to which this paragraph applies to the same extent as the right would have been exercisable if the tenancy had not become such a tenancy. **[453]**

(8) The fact that the tenancy has become a tenancy to which this paragraph applies should not be taken as affecting any court proceedings which are pending under section 67 (3) of the 1972 Act of the time when the tenancy becomes such a tenancy and a decision on which may affect the recoverable rent for any period before that time or the rent under the tenancy to which this paragraph applies so far as that depends upon the recoverable rent before that time. **[454]**

15. The sheriff shall have jurisdiction, either in the course of any proceedings relating to a dwelling-house or on an application made for the purpose by the landlord or the tenant, to determine any question—

(*a*) as to the application of this Part of this Schedule to any tenancy or as to any matter which is or may become material for determining any such question, or

(*b*) as to the amount of rent recoverable under a tenancy to which paragraph 13 above applies;

and section 123 (1) of the 1971 Act shall apply to any application to the sheriff under this paragraph as it applies to any application under any of the provisions mentioned in section 123 (3) of that Act. [**455**]

16. In this Part of this Schedule—

"the 1971 Act" means the Rent (Scotland) Act 1971;

"the 1972 Act" means the Housing (Financial Provisions) (Scotland) Act 1972:

"the court" means "the sheriff";

"the previous housing association tenancy", in relation to a tenancy to which paragraph 14 above applies, means the tenancy to which sections 60 to 66 of the 1972 Act applied which either became the protected tenancy by virtue of section 18 (1) of this Act or came to an end as mentioned in paragraph 13 (1) (*a*) above; and

other expressions used in this Part of this Schedule which are also used in the Rent (Scotland) Acts 1971 and 1972 shall have the same meanings in this Part as they have in those Acts. [**456**]

GENERAL

See Notes on s. 18 above. The tenancies of housing associations which became registered continue to be excluded from the protection of the Rent Acts, and the same is true of unregistered housing associations whose tenancies are excluded from protection by s. 5 (2) (*g*) of the Rent Act 1968 because they are "housing trusts" as defined in s. 5 (3) of that Act. Tenancies which were excluded from the protection of the Rent Acts by s. 5 (5) of the Rent Act 1968 because the landlord was a housing association, will be brought into protection if the association does not become a registered one.

Part I of this schedule contains measures to give interim protection to persons who remain in occupation of premises after the former tenancy has come to an end before the operative day.

As from the operative day they will, in any case, enjoy the same degree of protection as persons left in occupation at the expiry of a protected tenancy under the Rent Act 1968.

The persons given this relief are described in para. 1 (3).

The Courts may suspend the execution of a Court Order for up to 12 months—para. 2 (2).

The Court may alter the terms and conditions of the tenancy—para. 2 (3). Other powers of the Court are described in para. 2 (4) to 2 (7). Para. 3 provides that, if at any time before the operative date, the interest of landlord becomes vested in one of the bodies specified in para. 5 (2) of the Rent Act 1968 (or the Rent (Scotland) Act 1971) the Court may only vary their suspension of a possession order by shortening it. The bodies in question include local authorities, development corporations for new towns, the Housing Corporation, and housing trusts.

The interim powers under para. 2 come to an end when Part II comes into operation on the operative day.

Part II is, in effect, transitional. It deals with tenancies which come to an end before the operative day, and which would have become protected tenancies had they come to an end after the operative day. The tenancies are treated, from the succession point of view, as if they were protected or statutory tenancies—para. 5.

Para. 6 deals with the rents applicable to tenancies which become protected either by s. 18 or by para. 5 of this Schedule. If a rent was registered for it at a time when Part VIII of the Housing Finance Act 1972 applied, and later a lower rent is registered for it, as a normal protected tenancy under Part IV of the Rent Act 1968, the higher rent will prevail, until such time as there is a new registration of a rent under Part IV, which is higher than the rent registered when Part VIII of the 1972 Act applied.

Similarly, if the Secretary of State has approved a higher rent limit under s. 85 of the Housing Finance Act 1972, that higher rent will prevail as long as his direction remains in force.

Para. 7 deals with the situation where no rent has yet been registered, and it applies the provisions of Part III of the Rent Act 1968 to tenancies which become protected or statutory tenancies under this Act.

The provisions of s. 48A of the Rent Act 1968 (cancellation of registration) and of s. 43 of the Housing Finance Act 1972 are also applicable. Para. 8 deals with tenancies which become protected under s. 18 (1) of this Act or para. 5 of this Schedule, and to which s. 84 of the 1972 Act applied immediately before the non-protected tenancy came to an end. S. 84 deals with the progression to fair rents under Part VIII of the 1972 Act and imposes rent limits. These limits will continue to apply until a fair rent under Part IV of the Rent Act is registered, or until a completely new regulated tenancy is granted. See also para. 8 (5) and (6). Para. 9 links together Sch. 6 of the 1972 Act and the provisions of this Act in relation to tenancies which become protected or statutory tenancies by virtue of s. 18 (1) of the Act or para. 5 of this Schedule, and provides a basis of phasing to replace, in due course, the basis in Part VIII of the 1972 Act.

Para. 10 relates the provisions of s. 25 of the Rent Act 1968 to tenancies which become protected or statutory ones under s. 18 (1) or para. 5 of this Schedule.

Para. 11 relates to the definition of a fair rent under s. 46 of the Rent Act 1968.

As to the possible effect on the fair rent under s. 46 of the difference in security of tenure between protected or regulated tenants and housing association tenants who are not "protected" see *Palmer* v. *Peabody Trust* [1974] 3 All E.R. 355, [1974] 3 W.L.R. 575.

Part III contains broadly similar provisions relating to Scotland.

See Circular 133/74 in Appendix II.

SCHEDULE 4

Section 47

Notification Procedure

1. Where, by virtue of the principal section, a person is under an obligation to notify a local authority of any matter, the obligation shall be fulfilled by furnishing to the local authority a notification in writing containing the information specified in the following provisions of this Schedule. **[457]**

2.—(1) Every such notification shall contain—

(*a*) the name and address of the person by whom it is furnished;
(*b*) the address of, and any further information necessary to identify, the land to which the notification relates; and
(*c*) the estate or interest in that land which the person by whom the notification is furnished has at the time it is furnished.

(2) The reference in sub-paragraph (1) (*a*) above to a person's address is a reference to his place of abode or his place of business or, in the case of a company, its registered office.

(3) To the extent that it is capable of being so given, the information required by sub-paragraph (1) (*b*) above may be given by reference to a plan accompanying the notification. **[458]**

3.—(1) A notification given in compliance with subsection (1) or subsection (2) of the principal section shall also specify—

(*a*) whether the tenancy concerned is periodic or for a term certain;
(*b*) the duration of the period or term; and
(*c*) the date on which the tenancy will come to an end (by virtue of the service of the notice to quit or by effluxion of time).

(2) If the landlord considers it appropriate, he may also, in a notification given in compliance with subsection (1) of the principal section, give his reason for serving the notice to quit. **[459]**

4. A notification given in compliance with subsection (3) of the principal section shall also specify whether, at the time the notification is furnished, the person furnishing it intends to retain any estate or interest in the land specified in the notification in accordance with paragraph 2 (1) (*b*) above and, if he does, the nature of that estate or interest and the land in which he intends that it should subsist. **[460]**

5. In this Schedule "the principal section" means section 47 of this Act. **[461]**

GENERAL

S. 47 and s. 54 of the Act require owners and landlords to notify the local authority of notices to quit and of disposals of housing accommodation in housing action areas and priority neighbourhoods. This Schedule specifies the information to be included in the notification.

SCHEDULE 5

Sections 50 and 52

General Improvement Areas

Part I

Sections to be Substituted for Housing Act 1969, Section 28

28.—(1) Where a report with respect to a predominantly residential area within the district of a local authority is submitted to them by a person or persons appearing to the authority to be suitably qualified (whether or not that person is or those persons include an officer of the authority) and it appears to the authority, upon consideration of the report and of any other information in their possession, that living conditions in the area can most appropriately be improved by the improvement of the amenities of the area or dwellings therein or both and that such an improvement may be effected or assisted by the exercise of their powers under this Act, the authority may cause the area to be defined on a map and by a resolution (in this section referred to as a "preliminary resolution") declare their intention that the area should become a general improvement area in accordance with the provisions of this section. **[462]**

(2) If a local authority have passed a preliminary resolution with respect to any area, they may, subject to the following provisions of this section, proceed by a further resolution (in this section referred to as a "confirmatory resolution") to confirm the preliminary resolution and to declare the area to be a general improvement area; and in relation to a confirmatory resolution or a proposed confirmatory resolution, "the relevant preliminary resolution" means the preliminary resolution confirmed or, as the case may be, proposed to be confirmed, by the confirmatory resolution. **[463]**

(3) A local authority may not proceed to pass a confirmatory resolution with respect to the area to which the relevant preliminary resolution relates (in the following provisions of this section referred to as "the proposed general improvement area") unless, within the period of six months beginning with the date on which the relevant preliminary resolution was passed, they notify the Secretary of State in writing of their intention to do so and send to him—

(*a*) a copy of the relevant preliminary resolution;

(*b*) a copy of the map defining the proposed general improvement area;

(*c*) a copy of the report referred to in subsection (1) above, the consideration of which led to the passing of the relevant preliminary resolution; and

(*d*) such other information and documents as the Secretary of State may direct with respect to general improvement areas generally. **[464]**

(4) On receipt of a notification or of any other document or information sent to him under subsection (3) above with respect to a proposed general improvement area, the Secretary of State shall send a written acknowledgment to the authority by whom the notification or other document was sent and, if it appears to him to be appropriate to do so, he may, at any time within the appropriate period, send a notification to the authority—

(*a*) that they may not pass a confirmatory resolution with respect to the proposed general improvement area; or

(*b*) that he requires more time to consider the proposed declaration of that area as a general improvement area. **[465]**

(5) Where the Secretary of State notifies a local authority as mentioned in

subsection (4) (*b*) above, he shall, on completion of his consideration of the matter, send a further notification to the authority—

(*a*) that they may not pass a confirmatory resolution with respect to the proposed general improvement area; or

(*b*) that they are at liberty to proceed to pass such a resolution. **[466]**

(6) Without prejudice to subsection (3) above, if—

(*a*) a local authority have notified the Secretary of State as mentioned in that subsection with respect to a proposed general improvement area but are not yet able to proceed to pass a confirmatory resolution with respect to it, and

(*b*) the Secretary of State, by a direction given with respect to that particular area, so requires,

the local authority shall send to him such other information and documents with respect to that area as may be specified in the direction. **[467]**

(7) In this section "the appropriate period", in relation to the proposed general improvement area to which a preliminary resolution relates, means the period—

(*a*) of 28 days or such longer period as the Secretary of State may by order made by statutory instrument specify for the purposes of this subsection, and

(*b*) beginning on the date on which the acknowledgment or, as the case may be, the last acknowledgment of any document or information with respect to that proposed general improvement area was sent to the local authority concerned under subsection (4) above. **[468]**

(8) In any case where a local authority have passed a preliminary resolution and, in accordance with subsection (3) above, have sent to the Secretary of State a notification and other documents relating to the proposed general improvement area, they may not proceed to pass a confirmatory resolution with respect to that area—

(*a*) before the expiry of the appropriate period, and

(*b*) if the Secretary of State notifies them as mentioned in subsection (4) (*b*) above, unless and until they are notified as mentioned in subsection (5) (*b*) above,

but if the authority are notified as mentioned in subsection (4) (*a*) or subsection (5) (*a*) above, no resolution confirming that preliminary resolution may be passed with respect to the proposed general improvement area. **[469]**

28A. Publicity for, and information with respect to, general improvement area

As soon as may be after the passing of a confirmatory resolution, within the meaning of section 28 of this Act, declaring an area to be a general improvement area, the local authority shall—

(*a*) publish in two or more newspapers circulating in the locality (of which one at least shall, if practicable, be a local newspaper) a notice of the resolution identifying the area and naming a place or places where a copy of the resolution, of the map on which the area is defined and of the report mentioned in section 28 (1) of this Act may be inspected at all reasonable times;

(*b*) take such further steps as may appear to them best designed to secure that the resolution is brought to the attention of persons residing or owning property within the area and that those persons are informed of the name and address of the person to whom any enquiries and representations concerning any action to be taken in the exercise of the local authority's powers under this Part of this Act should be addressed; and

(*c*) send to the Secretary of State a copy of the resolution and a statement of the number of dwellings in the area. **[470]**

Part II

Other Amendments of Part II of Housing Act 1969

1. After section 29 of the Housing Act 1969 there shall be inserted the following sections:—

"29A. Housing action areas excluded from general improvement areas

A general improvement area shall not be so defined as to include (but may be so defined as to surround) any land which is for the time being comprised in a housing action area declared under Part IV of the Housing Act 1974. [**471**]

29B. Incorporation of priority neighbourhoods into general improvement areas

(1) If a local authority propose, by a preliminary resolution under section 28 (1) of this Act, to declare their intention that an area should become a general improvement area and that area consists of or includes land which, immediately prior to the declaration, is comprised in a priority neighbourhood declared under Part VI of the Housing Act 1974, they shall indicate on the map referred to in the said section 28 (1) the land which is so comprised (in this section referred to as "priority land"). [**472**]

(2) If a local authority, by a confirmatory resolution under section 28 (2) of this Act, confirm a preliminary resolution and declare as a general improvement area an area which, immediately prior to the declaration, consists of or includes priority land, then, with effect from the date on which the confirmatory resolution is passed, the priority land shall be deemed, as the case may require, either—

(*a*) to have ceased to be a priority neighbourhood by virtue of a resolution passed on that date under section 39 (3) of the Housing Act 1974 (as it applies in relation to such a neighbourhood by virtue of section 54 of that Act); or

(*b*) to have been excluded from the priority neighbourhood concerned by virtue of a resolution passed on that date under section 40 (1) of that Act (as it applies in relation to such a neighbourhood by virtue of the said section 54)." [**473**]

2.—(1) In section 30 of that Act (changes with respect to general improvement area) after subsection (1) there shall be inserted the following subsection:—

"(1A) In any case where, by virtue of a resolution under subsection (1) above, any land is excluded from a general improvement area or, as the case may be, an area ceases to be a general improvement area, the resolution shall not affect the continued operation of this Part of this Act and of any other provision relating to general improvement areas in relation to any works which have been begun before the date on which the resolution takes effect, but, subject thereto, the exclusion or cessation shall apply with respect to the approval before that date of any expenditure in respect of works which have not been begun before that date."

(2) Subsections (2) and (3) of that section (power of local authority by resolution to include land adjoining a general improvement area in that area) shall cease to have effect. [**474**]

3. In section 32 of that Act (general powers exercisable by local authority in general improvement area) in subsection (5) (nothing in section 32 to enable a local authority to make any grant where such a grant might be made under Part I of that Act) for the words "Part I of this Act" there shall be substituted the words "Part VII of the Housing Act 1974". [**475**]

4.—(1) After subsection (5) of section 37 of that Act (power of Secretary of State by order to alter the maximum of the aggregate expenditure of local authorities which can be approved for the purposes of his contribution in respect of a general improvement area) there shall be inserted the following subsection:—

"(5A) Without prejudice to subsection (5) above, the Secretary of State may direct that, in the case of a particular general improvement area or any description of general improvement area, subsection (4) above shall have effect as if for the amount of £100 mentioned in that subsection, or such other amount as may for the time being be substituted for that amount under subsection (5) above, there were substituted a greater amount." **[476]**

(2) In subsection (7) of that section (for purposes of contributions by Secretary of State to local authorities towards expenditure in general improvement areas, certain expenditure by housing association to be treated as that of local authority) there shall be inserted before the words "housing association", in the first and third places where they occur, the word "registered" and at the end of that subsection there shall be added the following subsection:—

"(8) In subsection (7) of this section 'registered housing association' means a housing association registered in the register of housing associations established under section 13 of the Housing Act 1974". **[477]**

5. In subsection (2) of section 40 of that Act (in relation to land in a general improvement area declared by them, the Greater London Council is to be deemed to be the local authority for certain purposes and certain functions are to be exerciseable by other authorities only after consultation with the Greater London Council) in paragraph (*a*), for the words "sections 17 to 22 and 74 of this Act", there shall be substituted the words "section 74 of this Act and section 79 of the Housing Act 1974", the words "Part I of this Act other than sections 17 to 22" shall be omitted and for the words "and Part II of the Act of 1957" there shall be substituted the words "Part II of the Act of 1957 and Part VII of the Housing Act 1974 other than section 79"; and in paragraph (*b*), for the words from "section 19" to "that Act" there shall be substituted the words "or Part IV of the Housing Act 1964". **[478]**

GENERAL

Part I of this Schedule gives the Secretary of State greater control over the declaration of general improvement areas. Instead of passing a single resolution declaring it to be a general improvement area, the new procedure requires the local authority to pass a preliminary resolution. They cannot proceed to pass a confirmatory resolution until they have notified the Secretary of State of their intention to do so, sent him a copy of the preliminary resolution and other documents listed in the new s. 28 (3), and received his decision in accordance with s. 28 (4) and (5).

Part II of the schedule should be read with s. 51 of the Act and the Notes thereon. Para. 1 deals with general improvement areas and priority neighbourhoods.

Para. 3 contains an important amendment to s. 32 of the Housing Act 1969, as regards power to make grants under Part VII of this Act.

Para. 4 gives the Secretary of State power to increase the amount of his contribution towards the cost of environmental improvements in relation to any particular general improvement area, or description of area. This is in line with his powers under s. 46 to vary contributions towards expenditure on environmental works in housing action areas.

Para. 4 (2) amends s. 37 of the Housing Act 1969, so that only expenditure by a registered housing association may be treated as if it were expenditure incurred by the local authority for environmental purposes.

This schedule also amends the Housing Act 1969 so far as the declaration of general improvement areas by the Greater London Council is concerned.

SCHEDULE 6

Sections 58, 68 and 70

Standard Amenities

Part I

List of Amenities and Maximum Eligible Amounts

Description of Amenity	*Maximum eligible amount*	
	£	
A fixed bath or shower	100	
A hot and cold water supply at a fixed bath or shower	140	
A wash-hand basin	50	
A hot and cold water supply at a wash-hand basin	70	
A sink	100	
A hot and cold water supply at a sink	90	
A water closet	150	[**479**]

Part II

Provisions Applicable to Certain Amenities

1. Except as provided by paragraph 2 below, a fixed bath or shower must be in a bathroom. [**480**]

2. If it is not reasonably practicable for the fixed bath or shower to be in a bathroom but it is reasonably practicable for it to be provided with a hot and cold water supply it need not be in a bathroom but may be in any part of the dwelling which is not a bedroom. [**481**]

3. The water closet must, if reasonably practicable, be in, and accessible from within, the dwelling or, where the dwelling is part of a larger building, in such a position in that building as to be readily accessible from the dwelling. [**482**]

GENERAL

These are the amenities which it is intended should be available, where practicable, in every house, and for the provision of which improvement, intermediate and special grants, as defined in s. 56 (2), are available. See also ss. 58, 61, 65 to 68, and 70 and the Notes thereon.

SCHEDULE 7

Section 106

Lodging-houses and Hostels: Amendments of Schedule 1 to Housing Finance Act 1972

1. In Part I (credits and debits) in paragraph 1 (1) (*a*) after the word "rents", in the first place where it occurs, there shall be inserted the words "and charges" and after the word "rents", in the second place where it occurs, there shall be inserted the words "or charges". [**483**]

2. In Part II (rate fund contributions to the Housing Revenue Account) after paragraph 9 there shall be added the following paragraph:—

"*Charges for lodging-houses and hostels*

9A.—(1) If for any year the amount received by the local authority by way of charges in respect of lodging-houses (that is to say, houses not occupied as separate dwellings) and hostels within the account is less than the amount which would have been received if those charges had been equal to the reckonable charges, the local authority shall make a rate fund contribution for that year of an amount equal to the deficiency. [**484**]

(2) In this paragraph "the reckonable charges", in relation to any such lodging-houses or hostels, means such charges as, in the opinion of the Secretary of State, are reasonable and appropriate, having regard to all the circumstances. **[485]**

(3) For the purposes of this paragraph the amount of any charges shall be calculated in such manner as the Secretary of State may from time to time determine, either generally or with respect to a particular authority or authorities or in any particular case. **[486]**

(4) Before making a general determination under sub-paragraph (3) above, the Secretary of State shall consult with such associations of housing authorities as appear to him to be concerned and with any housing authority with whom consultation appears to him to be desirable." **[487]**

3. In Part III (limitation of certain subsidies and rate fund contributions) in head E of the Table in paragraph 11, for the words "and 9" there shall be substituted the words "9 and 9A". **[488]**

GENERAL

See Notes on s. 106. This affects local authorities and new town corporations, and the requirements to be observed as regards Housing Revenue Accounts.

SCHEDULE 8

Section 118

Reduction of Rateable Value in Case of Certain Improvements

1.—(1) Where the tenant, or any previous tenant, has made or contributed to the cost of an improvement on the premises comprised in the tenancy and the improvement is one to which this Schedule applies, then, if the tenant serves on the landlord a notice in the prescribed form requiring him to agree to a reduction under this Schedule, their rateable value as ascertained for the purposes of subsection (1) of section 1 of this Act shall be reduced by such amount, if any, as may be agreed or determined in accordance with the following provisions of this Schedule. **[489]**

(2) This Schedule applies to any improvement made by the execution of works amounting to structural alteration, extension or addition. **[490]**

2.—(1) The amount of any such reduction may at any time be agreed in writing between the landlord and the tenant. **[491]**

(2) Where, at the expiration of a period of six weeks from the service of a notice under paragraph 1 of this Schedule any of the following matters has not been agreed in writing between the landlord and the tenant, that is to say,—

(*a*) whether the improvement specified in the notice is an improvement to which this Schedule applies;

(*b*) what works were involved in it;

(*c*) whether the tenant or a previous tenant under the tenancy has made it or contributed to its cost; and

(*d*) what proportion his contribution, if any, bears to the whole cost;

the county court may on the application of the tenant determine that matter, and any such determination shall be final and conclusive. **[492]**

(3) An application under the last foregoing sub-paragraph must be made within six weeks from the expiration of the period mentioned therein or such longer time as the court may allow. **[493]**

3.—(1) Where, after the service of a notice under paragraph 1 of this Schedule, it is agreed in writing between the landlord and tenant or determined by the county court—

(*a*) that the improvement specified in the notice is one to which this Schedule applies, and what works were involved in it, and (*b*) that the tenant or a previous tenant under the tenancy has made it or contributed to its cost, and, in the latter case, what proportion his contribution bears to the whole cost, then if, at the expiration of a period of two weeks from the agreement or determination, it has not been agreed in writing between the landlord and the tenant whether any or what reduction is to be made under this Schedule, and the tenant, within four weeks from the expiration of that period, makes an application to the valuation officer for a certificate under the next following sub-paragraph, that question shall be determined in accordance with the certificate unless the landlord and the tenant otherwise agree in writing. [**494**]

(2) On any such application the valuation officer shall certify—

(*a*) whether or not the improvement has affected the rateable value on the first day of April, nineteen hundred and seventy-three (as ascertained for the purposes of sub-section (1) of section 1 of this Act), of the hereditament of which the premises consist or, as the case may be, in which they are wholly or partly comprised, and

(*b*) if it has, the amount by which the rateable value would have been less if the improvement had not been made. [**495**]

(3) An application for such a certificate shall be in the prescribed form and shall state the name and address of the landlord, and the Valuation Officer shall send a copy of the certificate to the landlord. [**496**]

(4) Where the amount of the reduction under this Schedule falls to be determined in accordance with such a certificate, it shall be equal to the amount specified in pursuance of head (*b*) of sub-paragraph (2) of this paragraph, but proportionately reduced in any case where a proportion only of the cost was contributed by the tenant or a previous tenant under the tenancy. [**497**]

(5) Where at the time of an application for a certificate under this paragraph a proposal for an alteration in the valuation list relating to the hereditament is pending and the alteration would have effect from a date earlier than the second day of April, nineteen hundred and seventy-three, the Valuation Officer shall not issue the certificate until the proposal is settled. [**498**]

FORM ...

LEASEHOLD REFORM ACT 1967

Notice by Tenant to Landlord of Tenant's Improvements affecting Rateable Value

Date ....

To .... landlord of ....

1. [I] [A previous tenant of the above mentioned premises under the tenancy] [made] [contributed to the cost of] the improvement[s] to the above mentioned premises particulars of which are set out in the First Schedule hereto (Note 1).

2. I hereby require you to agree to a reduction in the rateable value of the premises for the purposes of the Leasehold Reform Act 1967.

3. I propose that the rateable value shall be reduced to £ ... (Note 2)

4. If you do not agree to this reduction (Note 3), do you agree that—

(*a*) the improvement[s] [is] [are] [an] improvement[s] made by the execution of works amounting to the structural alteration or extension of the premises or a structural addition thereto:

(*b*) the works set out in the Second Schedule hereto were involved in the making of the improvement[s];

(*c*) [I] [A previous tenant under the tenancy] [made the improvement[s]] [contributed to the cost of the improvement[s];]
(*d*) the proportion of the cost borne by me or a previous tenant is .

Signature of tenant................

[499]

First Schedule

Description of Improvement(s)

Second Schedule

Description of Works

Strike out words in square brackets if inapplicable.

Note 1

The improvement must be one made by the execution of works amounting to the structural alteration or extension of the premises or a structural addition thereto, e.g. the erection of a garage in the grounds. [**500**]

Note 2

If the amount of the reduction is agreed in writing between the landlord and the tenant, the amount of the reduced rateable value as so agreed will be substituted for the purposes of the Leasehold Reform Act 1967, for the rateable value on 1st April, 1973. [**501**]

Note 3

If the amount of the reduction is not agreed in writing between the landlord and the tenant, the Valuation Officer will have to decide whether the improvement has affected the rateable value of the premises, and if so, what that value would have been had the improvement not been made. The name and address of the Valuation Officer can be obtained from the local authority. Before, however, an application is made to the Valuation Officer, the landlord and the tenant must try to agree in writing on the items mentioned at (*a*) to (*d*) of this paragraph, or such of those items as are material. If at the end of a period of six weeks after the service of this notice any of these items have not been agreed, the tenant may, within a further six weeks or so much longer time as the court may allow, apply to the county court to settle the matter. [**502**]

If it has either been agreed or determined by the county court that there has been an improvement of the kind described in Note 1 involving specified works, and that the improvement was carried out by the tenant or a previous tenant, or that the tenant or a previous tenant contributed to its cost, and in the latter case what proportion the contribution bears to the whole cost of the works, then, if within a period of two weeks after the agreement or determination of the county court the landlord and the tenant have still not agreed in writing whether any or what reduction is to be made, the tenant has a further four weeks in which to make an application in the statutory form to the Valuation Officer for a certificate as to whether or not the improvement has affected the rateable value, and if so, the amount by which that value would have been less if the improvement had not been made. [**503**]

FORM ...

LEASEHOLD REFORM ACT 1967

Application by Tenant to Valuation Officer for Certificate as to Reduction for the purposes of the Leasehold Reform Act 1967, in the Rateable Value of premises on account of Tenant's Improvements

Date ....

To the Valuation Officer.

1. I am the tenant of , and my landlord is of

2. It has been [agreed in writing between me and my landlord] [determined by the county court] that the improvement[s] specified in the First Schedule hereto [is an improvement] [are improvements] to which Schedule Seven to the Leasehold Reform Act 1967 applies, and that I or a previous tenant under the tenancy made the improvement[s] or contributed to [its] [their] cost, and that the works specified in the Second Schedule hereto were involved in the improvement[s].
3. It has not been agreed between me and my landlord whether any or what reduction is to be made under said Schedule Seven in the rateable value of the premises for the purposes of the Leasehold Reform Act 1967, and I hereby make application to you for a certificate under paragraph 3 (2) of the said Schedule Seven (Note 4).

Signature of Tenant ....

[504]

First Schedule

Description of Improvement(s)

Second Schedule

Description of Works

Strike out words in square brackets if inapplicable.

Note 4

If the Valuation Officer certifies that the rateable value would have been less but for the improvement by the amounts mentioned in the certificate, the rateable value will be reduced by those amounts for the purposes of the Leasehold Reform Act 1967, except in the case where a proportion only of the cost was contributed by the tenant, in which case the amounts of the reductions will be proportionately reduced accordingly. **[505]**

GENERAL

The Leasehold Reform Act 1967 is amended by s. 118 of this Act, and new limits of rateable value are laid down. Improvements made by a tenant might increase the rateable value of a property above the limits for enfranchisement. This section gives the tenant power to serve a notice on his landlord to have his rateable value adjusted for this purpose. This schedule sets out the procedures to be observed and the forms to be used.

SCHEDULE 9

Section 108

PROVISIONS TO BE SUBSTITUTED FOR SUBSECTION (1) OF SECTION 60 OF THE HOUSING ACT 1957

(1) Where a house is made the subject of a compulsory purchase order under this Part of this Act as being unfit for human habitation or is made the subject of a clearance order, then not later than the date or, if there is more than one, the last date on which they served a notice of the effect of the order under paragraph 2 (1) (*b*) of Schedule 3 or, as the case may be, paragraph 3 (1) (*b*) of Schedule 5 to this Act, the local authority shall—

(*a*) serve on every owner, lessee, mortgagee and occupier of the house, so far as it is reasonably practicable to ascertain those persons, a notification under subsection (1A) of this section with respect to the house; and

(*b*) in the case of a house falling within subsection (2) of section 67 of the Housing Act 1969 (houses comprising more than one dwelling or occupied partly for the purposes of a dwelling and partly for other purposes), serve on every owner, lessee, mortgagee and occupier of each dwelling in the house, so far as it is reasonably practicable to ascertain those persons, a notification under subsection (1A) of this section with respect to that dwelling. **[506]**

(1A) The notification referred to in subsection (1) of this section shall be in the prescribed form and shall state that the local authority are satisfied—

(*a*) that, in the case of a house which does not fall within subsection (1) or subsection (2) of section 67 of the Housing Act 1969 (payments in respect of partially well maintained houses or parts of buildings), both the interior and the exterior of the house have been well maintained; or

(*b*) that, in the case of a house which, apart from section 67 of the Housing Act 1969, would not be treated as well maintained for the purposes of this section, either the exterior or the interior of the house has been well maintained; or

(*c*) that, in the case of a house falling within subsection (2) of the said section 67, the exterior, as defined in that subsection, has been well maintained; or

(*d*) that, in the case of any such dwelling as falls within subsection (2) of the said section 67, the interior of the dwelling has been well maintained; or

(*e*) that no part of the house or dwelling in respect of which a payment might otherwise be made under this section has been well maintained. **[507]**

(1B) Any notification stating that a local authority are satisfied—

(*a*) as mentioned in paragraph (*b*) of subsection (1A) of this section shall also state the reasons why the local authority are not satisfied that the interior or, as the case may be, the exterior of the house concerned has been well maintained;

(*b*) as mentioned in paragraph (*e*) of that subsection shall also state the reasons why the local authority are satisfied that no part of the house or dwelling in respect of which a payment might otherwise be made under this section has been well maintained. **[508]**

(1C) Where a local authority have served a notification under subsection (1A) above, other than a notification falling within paragraph (*e*) thereof, and the house or dwelling to which the notification relates is included in the compulsory purchase order or clearance order as confirmed by the Secretary of State and, in the case of a compulsory purchase order, is so included as being unfit for human habitation, then, according to the nature of the notification, the local authority shall make a payment under this section in respect of the house or dwelling, namely—

(*a*) in the case of a notification falling within paragraph (*a*) of that subsection, a payment of such amount, if any, as is ascertained in accordance with Part I of Schedule 2 to this Act; and

(*b*) in the case of any other notification, a payment of one-half of the amount, if any, so ascertained. **[509]**

(1D) If, in the case of a notification to which subsection (1B) of this section applies, any owner, lessee, mortgagee or occupier of the house or dwelling to which the notification relates is aggrieved at the decision of the local authority that they are not satisfied as mentioned in paragraph (*a*) or paragraph (*b*) of that subsection and makes written representation to that effect to the Secretary of State—

(*a*) in the prescribed manner, and

(*b*) within the period within which an objection may be made to the compulsory order or clearance order concerned,

the Secretary of State may, if he thinks it appropriate to do so and (if he considers it necessary) after causing the house or dwelling concerned to be inspected by an officer of his department, give directions for the making by the local authority of a payment (or, as the case may be, a further payment) in respect of the house or dwelling concerned of such amount, if any, as is ascertained in accordance with Part I of Schedule 2 to this Act or, as the case may require, of one-half of that amount. **[510]**

GENERAL

Clearance orders are to be abolished by s. 108 of this Act. That section also contains an important amendment as regards payments in respect of well-maintained houses in clearance areas, and this schedule sets out that amendment. It should be read with the notes on s. 108 above. The amendment provides, in 1D, for appeals to the Secretary of State by persons aggrieved by the decision of the local authority. See Circulars 126/74 and 136/74 in Appendix II.

SCHEDULE 10

Section 114

Rehabilitation Orders

General

1.—(1) A rehabilitation order may, in addition to applying to any building to which section 114 of this Act applies, be made to apply to—

(*a*) any other building comprised in the clearance area,
(*b*) any land or building which is not comprised in the clearance area but which is subject to the same compulsory purchase order or, as the case may be, has (since being included in the clearance area) been acquired by the authority by agreement under section 43 (2) of the Act of 1957, and
(*c*) any land or building to which the provisions of Part III of the Act of 1957 apply by virtue of section 49 of that Act. **[511]**

(2) Where, by virtue of this Schedule, a local authority are freed from the duty to demolish a house which was included in a clearance area as being unfit for human habitation, the authority shall take such steps as are necessary—

(*a*) to bring the building up to the full standard, or
(*b*) where the building is not vested in the authority, to ensure that it is brought up to that standard. **[512]**

(3) A local authority may, for the purpose of section 114 of this Act, accept undertakings from the owner of a building, or any other person who has or will have an interest in the building, and in particular undertakings concerning the works to be carried out to bring the building up to the full standard, and the time within which the works are to be carried out. **[513]**

2.—(1) A local authority shall not make a rehabilitation order relating to land subject to a compulsory purchase order unless they are satisfied that, after the rehabilitation order comes into force, they can effectively fulfil their duties under Part III of the Act of 1957 as regards the remaining land subject to the compulsory purchase order. **[514]**

(2) Subject to sub-paragraph (1) above, a rehabilitation order may be made notwithstanding that the effect of the order in excluding any building from a clearance area is to sever that area into two or more separate and distinct areas, and in any such case the provisions of Part III of the Act of 1957 relating to the effect of a compulsory purchase order when confirmed, and to the proceedings to be taken after confirmation of the order, shall apply as if those areas formed one clearance area. **[515]**

(3) In exercising his power under this Schedule of confirming a rehabilitation order subject to modifications, the Secretary of State shall have regard to the considerations in sub-paragraphs (1) and (2) above. **[516]**

3.—(1) This paragraph shall have effect in relation to any land or building in respect of which a local authority have made a rehabilitation order which has been confirmed in accordance with the provisions of this Schedule; and in this Schedule "relevant date" means the date on which the rehabilitation order was confirmed or, as the case may be, on which confirmation was refused. **[517]**

(2) If, at the relevant date (in the case of any land or building subject to a compulsory purchase order)—

(*a*) no interest in the land or building has, after the date on which the compulsory purchase order concerned was made, vested in the authority, and

(*b*) no notice to treat has been served by the authority under section 5 of the Compulsory Purchase Act 1965, in respect of any interest in the land or building,

the compulsory purchase order shall cease to have effect and, where applicable, the building shall cease to be comprised in a clearance area. [**518**]

(3) Where sub-paragraph (2) above does not apply, the authority shall, where applicable, cease to be subject to the duty, imposed by Part III of the Act of 1957, to demolish the building, and in relation to any interest in the land or building which at the relevant date has not vested in the authority (being land or a building subject to a compulsory purchase order) the compulsory purchase order shall have effect as if—

(*a*) in the case of a house, it had been made and confirmed under Part V of the Act of 1957, and

(*b*) in any other case, it had been made and confirmed under Part VI of the Act of 1971. [**519**]

(4) If the land or building, or any interest therein, was vested in the authority at the relevant date it should be treated—

(*a*) in the case of a house, as appropriated to the purposes of Part V of the Act of 1957, and

(*b*) in any other case, as appropriated to the purposes of Part VI of the Act of 1971. [**520**]

(5) Where a local authority have made a rehabilitation order they shall not—

(*a*) serve notice to treat under section 5 of the Compulsory Purchase Act 1965 in respect of any land or building subject to the relevant compulsory purchase order, or

(*b*) demolish any such building,

until after the relevant date. [**521**]

(6) Where the owner of any building in respect of which a rehabilitation order could be made applies to the local authority concerned for such an order to be made in respect of the building, and the authority refuse to make the order, they shall give their reasons for so refusing in writing to the owner. [**522**]

(7) Where a rehabilitation order is confirmed in accordance with this Schedule and the effect of the order is to exclude from a clearance area any land adjoining a general improvement area in England and Wales (within the meaning of Part II of the Housing Act 1969), that land shall, unless the Secretary of State otherwise directs, be included in the general improvement area. [**523**]

Procedure for making and confirming rehabilitation orders

4. A rehabilitation order shall be made in the prescribed form and shall describe, by reference to a map—

(*a*) the land and buildings to which it applies,

(*b*) the boundaries of the clearance area to which it applies,

(*c*) the boundaries of the land comprised in any relevant compulsory purchase order, and

(*d*) the parts (if any) of the land to which the rehabilitation order applies which will remain subject to a compulsory purchase order. [**524**]

5.—(1) Before submitting the rehabilitation order to the Secretary of State the local authority shall—

(*a*) publish in one or more newspapers circulating within their district a notice in the prescribed form stating that an order has been made and describing the land and buildings to which it applies and naming a place where a copy of the order and its accompanying map may be seen at all reasonable hours, and

(*b*) serve—

(i) on every person on whom notice of the making of any relevant compulsory purchase order was served, or

(ii) on the person from whom the land or building was purchased by agreement, as the case may be, or

(iii) on their successors in title, where appropriate, a notice in the prescribed form stating the effect of the rehabilitation order and that it is about to be submitted to the Secretary of State for confirmation and specifying the time within, and the manner in which, objections thereto can be made. [**525**]

(2) A notice which is to be served on any person under this paragraph shall be served in accordance with the provisions of section 169 of the Act of 1957; and any notice served in accordance with this paragraph shall be accompanied by a statement of the grounds on which the authority are seeking confirmation of the rehabilitation order. [**526**]

6.—(1) If no objection is duly made by any of the persons on whom notices are required to be served in accordance with paragraph 5 above, or if all objections so made are withdrawn, then, subject to the provisions of this Schedule, the Secretary of State may if he thinks fit confirm the order with or without modifications. [**527**]

(2) If any objection duly made is not withdrawn, the Secretary of State shall, before confirming the order, either cause a public local inquiry to be held or afford to a person by whom an objection has been duly made and not withdrawn an opportunity of appearing before and being heard by a person appointed by the Secretary of State for the purpose. [**528**]

(3) After considering any objection not withdrawn and the report of the person who held the inquiry or of the person appointed under sub-paragraph (2) above, the Secretary of State may, subject to the provisions of this Schedule, confirm the order with or without modification. [**529**]

(4) Notwithstanding anything in the provisions of this paragraph, the Secretary of State may require any person who has made an objection to state in writing the grounds thereof and may disregard the objection for the purposes of this paragraph if he is satisfied that the objection relates exclusively to matters which can be dealt with by the tribunal by whom the compensation is to be assessed. [**530**]

(5) The Secretary of State may modify a rehabilitation order by extending its application to any other land or building to which the order could have been made to apply by the authority making it, but shall not do so unless—

(*a*) he is satisfied that any unfit house which he proposes to include in the rehabilitation order should be improved to the full standard, instead of being demolished,

(*b*) he is satisfied, in respect of any land or building which he proposes to include in the rehabilitation order (being land or a building which is not comprised in the clearance area concerned) that its acquisition by the local authority is unnecessary, and

(*c*) he has served on every owner, lessee and occupier (except tenants for a month or a lesser period than a month) and, so far as it is reasonably practical to ascertain such persons, on every mortgagee, of the land or building a notice in the prescribed form stating the effect of his proposals and has afforded them an opportunity to make their views known. [**531**]

7.—(1) The provisions of Schedule 4 to the Act of 1957 shall have effect, subject to the necessary modifications, in relation to the validity and date of operation of a rehabilitation order as they have effect in relation to the validity and date of operation of a compulsory purchase order made under section 43 of that Act. [532]

(2) The modifications subject to which the provisions of Schedule 4 are to have effect by virtue of this paragraph shall include the addition, at the end of paragraph 1, of the words—

"and every person on whom the Secretary of State served notice under paragraph 6 (5) (*c*) of Schedule 10 to the Housing Act 1974." [533]

8.—(1) In this Schedule "prescribed" means prescribed by order made by the Secretary of State for the purposes of this Schedule; and "full standard" has the same meaning as in section 114 (3) of this Act. [534]

(2) An order under this paragraph shall be contained in a statutory instrument which shall be subject to annulment in pursuance of a resolution of either House of Parliament. [535]

(3) In the application of this Schedule to Scotland the words "as being unfit for human habitation" shall be omitted. [536]

GENERAL

This deals with the temporary provision for rehabilitating unfit houses.

S. 114 relates only to houses acquired by agreement before the date on which this section comes into operation, or subject to a compulsory purchase order made before that date and confirmed within 3 months of that date.

See s. 114 and the notes thereon.

The Secretary of State shall either hold a public local inquiry or afford an objector the opportunity of being heard—see para. 6 (2). The Secretary of State may modify a rehabilitation order, subject to the provisions of para. 6 (5).

SCHEDULE 11

Section 119

Option Mortgages: Amendments of Part II of Housing Subsidies Act 1967

1.—(1) In section 24 (right to opt for subsidy for certain loans in connection with dwellings) at the end of subsection (1) there shall be added the words "and

(*d*) the loan is not one to which a direction under subsection (3A) of this section for the time being applies". [537]

(2) In paragraph (*c*) of subsection (3) of that section (declaration by borrower as to use of land, etc.),—

(*a*) for the words "and the land" there shall be substituted the words "that the amount of the loan will not exceed the appropriate limit determined under section 24A of this Act and that, before the expiry of the period of 12 months beginning on the date referred to in paragraph (*b*) of this subsection, the land"; and

(*b*) for the words from "being the borrower" to "one of them)", in the second place where those words occur, there shall be substituted the words "or persons in such circumstances that the residence condition in section 24B of this Act is fulfilled";

and at the end of that paragraph there shall be added the words "and

(*d*) in a case where the specified person or persons named in a declaration under paragraph (*c*) above is, are or include the borrower or all or any of the joint borrowers, that, if the borrower or, in the case of joint borrowers, any of them is married and is not treated for income tax purposes as living apart from his spouse, the borrower or, as the case may be, each of those joint borrowers and (in either case) his spouse have signed and delivered to the lender a declaration either that there is no existing loan—

(i) the whole or any part of the interest on which is payable (whether alone or jointly with any other person) by the spouse, and

(ii) in respect of which an option notice for the time being has effect or in respect of which a claim for relief has been or is to be made under section 75 of the Finance Act 1972 (relief for payment of interest), and

(iii) which relates to, or was made with a view to the repayment of a previous loan which related to, land used wholly or mainly for the purposes of a dwelling (not being the dwelling to which the declaration under paragraph (*c*) above relates) which is that spouse's only or main residence or a caravan so used,

or that such a loan does exist but the spouse intends that, within the period of 12 months beginning on the date referred to in paragraph (*b*) above, the dwelling referred to in sub-paragraph (iii) above will cease to be the spouse's only or main residence". **[538]**

(3) At the end of subsection (3) of that section there shall be added the following paragraphs—

"(viii) the taking effect of a direction under subsection (3A) of this section with respect to the loan;

(ix) if subsection (5) of section 24B of this Act applies, the expiry of the period of one month beginning with the date on which the lender receives a notification (or, if he receives more than one notification, the first notification) under that subsection or, if he does not receive such a notification, the date on which the lender first becomes aware that the residence condition is not fulfilled as mentioned in that subsection;

(x) if subsection (6) of section 24B of this Act applies and the lender receives a notification in accordance with that subsection, the expiry of the period of twelve months beginning with the date specified in that notification, and if that subsection applies but the lender does not receive such a notification, the expiry of the period of one month beginning with the date on which the lender first becomes aware that the residence condition is not fulfilled as mentioned in that subsection;

(xi) if the lender becomes aware that a declaration under paragraph (*c*) or paragraph (*d*) of this subsection is false in a material particular, the expiry of the period of one month beginning with the date on which the lender first becomes so aware." **[539]**

(4) After subsection (3) of that section there shall be inserted the following subsections:—

"(3A) The Secretary of State may, after consultation with such qualifying lenders or bodies representative of qualifying lenders of any description as may appear to him appropriate, direct that subsidy in accordance with this Part of this Act shall not be available in the case of any loan to which the direction applies, being a loan falling within subsection (3B) below. **[540]**

(3B) A loan is one in respect of which a direction may be made under subsection (3A) above if the terms of the repayment contract (as originally entered into or as subsequently varied) are such that the amount due from the borrower for any period by way of interest under the repayment contract is less than the total of the interest which accrues in respect of that period, so that part of the interest is treated as an addition to the capital outstanding or is otherwise carried forward. **[541]**

(3C) In considering whether to make a direction under subsection (3A) above with respect to any loan, the Secretary of State shall follow such principles, and take account of such matters, as he may from time to time decide after the like consultation as is specified in that subsection. **[542]**

(3D) A direction under subsection (3A) above may be made with respect to a particular loan or loans or any description of loans, and, in so far as the direction relates to a loan in respect of which an option notice has already been given, the direction shall specify a date (being a date after the giving of the direction) with effect from which the direction is to take effect with respect to any such loan. [543]

(3E) Any provision of subsection (3A) or subsection (3C) above which imposes on the Secretary of State a duty to consult any persons or bodies appearing to him to be appropriate shall not be taken as implying that further consultation is required by the provision where the Secretary of State is satisfied that there was consultation before the coming into force of that subsection and in his opinion that consultation was sufficient for the purpose". [544]

(5) In subsection (4) of that section for the words from "conditions specified in subsection (3) (c)" to the end of the subsection there shall be substituted the words "conditions specified in paragraphs (*c*) and (*d*) of subsection (3) of this section there are satisfied such other conditions as may be specified in the direction; and where any such direction has effect in relation to an option notice, the provisions of subsections (5) and (6) of section 24B of this Act shall apply as if the reference therein to the residence condition were a reference to such a condition as may be so specified". [545]

(6) After subsection (5) of that section there shall be inserted the following subsection:—

"(5A) In the case of an option notice to which a direction under subsection (5) of this section applies, paragraph (*c*) of subsection (3) of this section shall have effect as if for the words from "before the expiry" to "to be occupied" there were substituted the words "the land in question is being and will continue to be used wholly or partly for the purposes of a dwelling occupied". [546]

2. After section 24 there shall be inserted the following sections:—

"24A. The appropriate limit for loans

(1) In relation to a loan in respect of which an option notice has been signed (in this section referred to as "the relevant loan") the appropriate limit referred to in paragraph (*c*) of subsection (3) of section 24 of this Act is £25,000 reduced by the amount or, as the case may require, the aggregate amount outstanding by way of capital on the date referred to in paragraph (*b*) of that subsection in respect of every loan—

(*a*) the whole or any part of the interest on which is payable (whether alone or jointly with any other person) by the borrower who signed the declaration under the said paragraph (*c*) or, in the case of joint borrowers, by any of the borrowers who signed that declaration or, where that borrower or any of those joint borrowers is married and is not treated for income tax purposes as living apart from his spouse, that spouse; and

(*b*) which falls to be taken into account by virtue of subsection (2) below and is not to be disregarded by virtue of subsection (4) below. [547]

(2) Subject to subsections (3) and (4) below, a loan falls to be taken into account under subsection (1) above if—

(*a*) it is a loan in respect of which an option notice for the time being has effect; or

(*b*) it is a loan to which Part I of Schedule 9 to the Finance Act 1972 (loans for purchase or improvement of land on which interest is eligible for relief in full) for the time being applies (either in respect of the whole loan or subject to any limit of amount), and the land or caravan referred to in that Part is not used in such circumstances that it falls within paragraph 4 (1) (*b*) of Schedule 1 to the Finance Act 1974 (commercial lettings). [548]

(3) Without prejudice to section 34 (2) of this Act, the reference in subsection (2) (*b*) above to Schedule 9 to the Finance Act 1972 is a reference to

that Schedule either as amended by Schedule 1 to the Finance Act 1974 (restrictions on relief for interest) or (if interest on the loan is excepted from section 19 (3) of that Act) as originally enacted; and in the case of a loan to which the said Schedule 9 applies as originally enacted, the reference in subsection (2) (*b*) above to the use of land or a caravan in circumstances falling within paragraph 4 (1) (*b*) of the said Schedule 1 shall be construed as a reference to use which would fall within that paragraph if that Schedule applied in relation to interest on the loan in question. **[549]**

(4) Notwithstanding anything in subsection (2) above, a loan (in this subsection referred to as a "previous loan") which falls within paragraph (*a*) or paragraph (*b*) of that subsection shall be disregarded in determining the appropriate limit in relation to the relevant loan if—

(*a*) the relevant loan is made with a view to the repayment by means of the relevant loan of the amount outstanding on the previous loan; or

(*b*) the previous loan is an existing loan which is specified in a declaration made for the purpose of satisfying, in relation to the relevant loan, the condition in section 24 (3) (*d*) of this Act; or

(*c*) the previous loan was in connection with the only or main residence of a person who is, or is a qualifying relative of, the borrower or any of the joint borrowers under the relevant loan and the relevant loan is made for or in connection with any one or more of the purposes specified in section 24 (1) (*b*) of this Act in such circumstances that the dwelling referred to in that section is to be used instead as that person's only or main residence. **[550]**

(5) In any case where the option notice in respect of the relevant loan is one to which a direction under section 24 (5) of this Act applies, the preceding provisions of this section shall have effect subject to such modifications as may be prescribed. **[551]**

24B. The residence condition

(1) For the purposes of this Part of this Act, the residence condition is fulfilled with respect to a dwelling to which a declaration under section 24 (3) (*c*) of this Act relates if and so long as—

(*a*) the dwelling is occupied wholly or partly as his only or main residence by the borrower himself or, in the case of joint borrowers, by each of them; or

(*b*) at any time when the borrower or any joint borrower does not occupy the dwelling as mentioned in paragraph (*a*) above, the dwelling is so occupied by a qualifying relative of his. **[552]**

(2) For the purposes of this Part of this Act a person is a qualifying relative of a borrower (or a joint borrower) if he or she is—

(*a*) the borrower's spouse and is living apart from the borrower;
(*b*) the borrower's former spouse;
(*c*) the mother of either the borrower or his spouse and is widowed or living apart from her husband or, in consequence of dissolution or annulment of marriage, is a single woman; or
(*d*) such a relative of the borrower or his spouse as is specified in subsection (3) below and is either over the age of 65 or incapacitated by infirmity from maintaining himself, in whole or in part. **[553]**

(3) The relatives referred to in subsection (2) (*d*) above are—

(*a*) a parent or grandparent;
(*b*) a brother or sister who is over the age of 16; and

(*c*) a child or grandchild (in either case whether legitimate, adopted or illegitimate) who is over the age of 16. **[554]**

(4) A person shall be treated for the purposes of this section as living apart from his or her spouse if he or she would be so treated for income tax purposes. **[555]**

(5) If, after the delivery of a declaration under paragraph (*c*) of subsection (3) of section 24 of this Act (other than a declaration delivered in respect of an option notice to which a direction under subsection (5) of that section applies, the residence condition is not, within the period of 12 months specified in that paragraph, fulfilled with respect to the dwelling concerned, then, within the period of one month beginning on the day following the expiry of that period of 12 months, the borrower or, in the case of joint borrowers, each of them shall notify the lender in writing to that effect. **[556]**

(6) If, at any time after—

(*a*) the delivery of a declaration under paragraph (*c*) of section 24 (3) of this Act, and

(*b*) the residence condition has been fulfilled with respect to the dwelling concerned,

the residence condition ceases to be so fulfilled, then, within the period of one month beginning on the date on which that condition first ceased to be so fulfilled, the borrower or, in the case of joint borrowers, each of them shall notify the lender in writing of the date on which the condition ceased, and of the fact that it has ceased, to be so fulfilled. **[557]**

(7) Any person who knowingly fails to notify the lender as required by subsection (5) or subsection (6) above shall, on conviction on indictment, be liable to imprisonment for a term not exceeding 2 years". **[558]**

3.—(1). In section 26 (extension of right to opt for subsidy to certain other cases) in subsection (2) (*b*) after the words "this section" there shall be inserted the words "and to such modifications as may be prescribed". **[559]**

(2) After subsection (4) of that section there shall be inserted the following subsection:—

"(4A) In relation to a case where a self-build society, within the meaning of Part I of the Housing Act 1974, which is for the time being approved for the purposes of section 341A of the Income and Corporation Taxes Act 1970 borrows or has borrowed from a qualifying lender on the security of a freehold or leasehold estate of that society in Great Britain, the Secretary of State by regulations provide that this Part of this Act shall have effect with such adaptations and modifications of the provisions thereof (other than section 24 (2) (*b*) and (*c*)), appearing to him to be appropriate or expedient, and subject to such special conditions appearing to him to be necessary or expedient, as may be prescribed by the regulations; and in relation to such a society, the said section 24 (2) (*b*) shall have effect as if—

(*a*) the reference therein to the Income Tax Acts included a reference to the Corporation Tax Acts; and

(*b*) in sub-paragraph (ii) thereof, for the reference to income tax there were substituted a reference to corporation tax." **[560]**

4. In subsection (1) of section 27 (qualifying lenders) at the end of paragraph (*e*) there shall be inserted the following paragraph:—

"(*f*) the Housing Corporation";

and the words from "and for the purposes" to the end of the subsection shall be omitted. **[561]**

5.—(1) In paragraph (*a*) of subsection (1) of section 28 (calculation of the aggregate amount which, apart from Part II of the Housing Subsidies Act 1967, would have become due from the borrower) after the words "the aggregate sum which" there shall be inserted the words "taking account of subsection (1A) of this section but otherwise". **[562]**

(2) After subsection (1) of that section there shall be inserted the following subsection:—

"(1A) In any case where, under the terms of a repayment contract (as originally entered into or as subsequently varied) the amount due from the borrower for any period by way of interest under the repayment contract is less than the total of the interest which accrues in respect of that period so that part of the interest is treated as an addition to the capital outstanding or is otherwise carried forward then, for the purpose of determining the aggregate amount of the subsidy in respect of the loan, there shall be treated as becoming due from the borrower in any period the whole of the interest which accrues in that period." **[563]**

6. After section 28 there shall be inserted the following section:—

"28A. Recovery of subsidy in certain cases

(1) If a declaration under paragraph (*c*) or paragraph (*d*) of subsection (3) of section 24 of this Act is false in a material particular, the Secretary of State may recover from the borrower or, as the case may be, jointly and severally from the borrowers an amount equal to the total of the payments received by the lender by virtue of subsection (2) (*a*) (ii) of that section in relation to the loan in respect of which the declaration was made. **[564]**

(2) If, in a case where subsection (5) of section 24B of this Act applies, the lender does not receive a notification under that subsection, the Secretary of State may recover from the borrower or, as the case may be, jointly and severally from the borrowers, an amount equal to the total of the payments received by the lender as mentioned in sub-section (1) above after the expiry of the period of 2 months beginning on the day following the expiry of the period of 12 months specified in the said subsection (5). **[565]**

(3) If, in a case where subsection (6) of section 24B of this Act applies, the lender does not receive a notification under that subsection, the Secretary of State may recover from the borrower or, as the case may be, jointly and severally from the borrowers, an amount equal to the total of the payments received by the lender as mentioned in subsection (1) above after the expiry of the period of 2 months beginning with the date on which the condition specified in the said subsection (6) first ceased to be fulfilled." **[566]**

7. At the end of section 32 (1) (interpretation) there shall be inserted the following definition:—

" 'prescribed' means prescribed by regulations made by statutory instrument by the Secretary of State; and a statutory instrument containing any such regulations shall be subject to annulment in pursuance of a resolution of either House of Parliament". **[567]**

GENERAL

The provisions of s. 119 with regard to option mortgages are discussed in Chapter 9 and in the Notes on s. 119 above.

SCHEDULE 12

Section 124

SERVICE CHARGES: AMENDMENTS OF SECTIONS 90 AND 91 OF HOUSING FINANCE ACT 1972

1. After section 90 (1) there shall be inserted:—

"(1A) A qualified accountant shall have a right of access to such accounts, receipts and other documents, and shall be entitled to require from the landlord such information and explanation, as appear to him to be necessary to enable him to decide whether to give a certificate under subsection (1) above." [**568**]

2. After section 90 (10) there shall be inserted:—

"(10A) Where an offence under subsection (10) above which has been committed by a body corporate is proved to have been committed with the consent or connivance of, or to be attributable to any neglect on the part of, a director, manager, secretary or other similar officer of the body corporate, or any person who was purporting to act in any such capacity, he, as well as the body corporate, shall be guilty of that offence and be liable to be proceeded against and punished accordingly.

(10B) Where the affairs of a body corporate are managed by its members, subsection (10A) above shall apply in relation to the acts and defaults of a member in connection with his functions of management as if he were a director of the body corporate." [**569**]

3. In section 90 (12):—

(*a*) in the definition of "landlord", after that word there shall be inserted "includes any person who has a right to enforce payment of a service charge, and also";

(*b*) in the definition of "qualified accountant", after "excludes" there shall be inserted "any person mentioned in subsection (12A) below, and also". [**570**]

4. After section 90 (12) there shall be inserted:—

"(12A) None of the following persons is a qualified accountant—

(*a*) an officer or employee of the landlord or, where the landlord is a company, of a company which is the landlord's holding company or subsidiary, or a subsidiary of the landlord's holding company;

(*b*) a person who is a partner or employee of any such officer or employee;

and in this subsection "holding company" and "subsidiary" have the meanings given to them by section 154 of the Companies Act 1948." [**571**]

5. Paragraph 2 above shall not have effect in relation to an offence committed before the coming into operation of section 124 of this Act and paragraphs 3 and 4 above shall not have effect in relation to an accounting year (within the meaning of section 90 (12) of the Housing Finance Act 1972) ending before 1st August 1974. [**572**]

GENERAL

The rights of tenants with regard to service charges are considerably strengthened by this schedule and s. 124. See Notes on the latter at p. 169.

SCHEDULE 13

Section 130

Minor and Consequential Amendments

The Sheriff Courts (Scotland) Act 1907

1. In the Sheriff Courts (Scotland) Act 1907, after section 38 there shall be inserted the following section—

"38A. Notice of termination in respect of dwelling-houses

Any notice of termination of tenancy or notice of removal given under sections 37 or 38 above in respect of a dwelling-house, on or after the date of the coming into operation of section 123 of the Housing Act 1974, shall be in writing and shall contain such information as may be prescribed by virtue of section 131 of the Rent (Scotland) Act 1971, and Rule 112 of Schedule 1 to this Act shall no longer apply to any such notice under section 37 above." [**573**]

The Magistrates' Courts Act 1952

2. In Schedule 1 to the Magistrates' Courts Act 1952 (indictable offences by adults which may be dealt with summarily with consent of accused) the following paragraph shall be inserted after paragraph 14:—

"14A. Offences under section 24B (7) of the Housing Subsidies Act 1967". **[574]**

The Housing Act 1957

3. In section 70 of the Housing Act 1957 (provisions as to re-development, improvement or structural alteration by owners not to have effect in certain cases) in subsection (1) for the words from "clearance order" to "so confirmed" there shall be substituted the words "compulsory purchase order confirmed by the Minister". **[575]**

4. In section 105 of that Act (local authority's powers of dealing with land acquired for provision of housing accommodation) after subsection (4) there shall be inserted the following subsection:—

"(4A) Where a local authority acquire a house or building which may be made suitable as a house (or an estate or interest therein) and, in the case of such a building, themselves carry out any necessary work as mentioned in the last foregoing subsection, they shall, as soon as practicable after the acquisition or, as the case may be, after the completion of the necessary work, secure that the house or building is used as housing accommodation." **[576]**

5. Section 121 of that Act (arrangements with housing associations for improvement of housing) shall cease to have effect, but without prejudice to the continuation of any arrangements made before the day appointed for the coming into operation of this paragraph. **[577]**

6. In section 189 (1) of that Act, in the definition of "housing association" after the words "those of" there shall be inserted the word "providing" and after the word "houses" there shall be inserted the words "or hostels, as defined in section 129 (1) of the Housing Act 1974". **[578]**

7. In Schedule 2 to that Act (payments in respect of unfit houses) in the proviso to paragraph 4 (4) for the words "demolition or closing order or clearance order" there shall be substituted the words "or demolition or closing order" and in paragraph 5 (1) (*b*) for the words "closing order or clearance order" there shall be substituted the words "or closing order". **[579]**

The Land Compensation Act 1961

8.—(1) In Schedule 2 to the Land Compensation Act 1961 (acquisition of houses as being unfit for human habitation) in sub-paragraph (2) of paragraph 2 (application of certain provisions of Housing Act 1957) for the words "sections sixty and sixty-one of that Act, and" there shall be substituted the words "section 61 of that Act, and Part II of" and for the words "that Schedule" there shall be substituted the words "that Part of that Schedule". **[580]**

(2) After the said sub-paragraph (2) there shall be inserted the following sub-paragraphs:—

"(2A) Where the local authority make and submit an order under sub-paragraph (2) of this paragraph in relation to a house, the provisions of section 60 of the Act of 1957 and Part I of Schedule 2 thereto shall apply, subject to sub-paragraph (2B) of this paragraph, as if—

(*a*) the house had been made the subject of a compulsory purchase order under Part III of that Act as being unfit for human habitation; and

(*b*) any reference in those provisions to a local authority, other than a provision requiring, or enabling the Secretary of State to direct, a local authority to make a payment, were a reference to the appropriate authority. **[581]**

(2B) In the application of section 60 of the Act of 1957 by virtue of sub-paragraph (2A) of this paragraph—

(*a*) for the reference in subsection (1) to a notice under paragraph 2 (1) (*b*) of Schedule 3 or, as the case may be, paragraph 3 (1) (*b*) of Schedule 5 to that Act there shall be substituted a reference to a notice under sub-paragraph (3) of this paragraph;

(*b*) in so far as any provision of subsection (1C) or subsection (1D) of that section requires, or enables the Secretary of State to direct, a local authority to make a payment, the reference to a local authority shall be construed as a reference to the acquiring authority;

(*c*) the reference in subsection (1C) of that section to the compulsory purchase order being confirmed by the Secretary of State shall be construed as a reference to the condition in either paragraph (*a*) or paragraph (*b*) of sub-paragraph (2) of this paragraph being fulfilled; and

(*d*) for the reference in subsection (1D) (*b*) of that section to the compulsory purchase order or clearance order concerned there shall be substituted a reference to the order under sub-paragraph (2) of this paragraph." **[582]**

(3) The amendments effected by sub-paragraphs (1) and (2) above shall have effect with respect to orders under paragraph 2 (2) of Schedule 2 to the Land Compensation Act 1961 made on or after the day on which section 108 of this Act comes into operation. **[583]**

The Landlord and Tenant Act 1962

9. At the end of section 6 of the Landlord and Tenant Act 1962 (interpretation) there shall be added the following subsection:—

"(2) Any reference in section 2 (1) (*a*) or section 3 (1) of this Act to a person's address is a reference to his place of abode or his place of business or, in the case of a company, its registered office." **[584]**

The Housing Act 1964

10.—(1) In section 5 (1) of the Housing Act 1964 (schemes for Corporation to provide housing accommodation in place of housing society) after the words "housing society", in the first place where they occur, there shall be inserted the words "which is not a registered housing association, within the meaning of the Housing Act 1974, and to which a loan has been made under section 2 of this Act before the operative date". **[585]**

(2) In section 8 of that Act (building society advances to housing societies to which Corporation have made loans) for the words "housing society" or "housing societies", in each place where they occur, there shall be substituted respectively the words "housing association" or "housing associations". **[586]**

(3) In section 10 (4) of that Act (account to be prepared of certain sums advanced to and repaid by the Corporation) after the words "this Act" there shall be inserted the words "or Part I of the Housing Act 1974". **[587]**

(4) In subsection (1) of section 11 of that Act (power of Corporation to authorise Scottish Special Housing Association to act in Scotland as Corporation's agents for certain purposes) the words "section 3" and "section 6" shall be omitted and at the end of that subsection there shall be added the words "or under section 3 (1), section 4 or section 5 of the Housing Act 1974". **[588]**

(5) Section 72 of that Act (restriction on recovery of possession after making of compulsory purchase order) shall be amended as follows:—

(*a*) in subsection (1) in the definition of "the relevant period" the words "of twelve months", in each case where they occur, shall be omitted and after the words "making of the said order" there shall be inserted the words "and ending on the third anniversary of the date on which the order becomes operative"; **[589]**

(*b*) in subsection (2) in paragraph (*a*) for the words from "not exceeding" to "said compulsory purchase order" there shall be substituted the words "not extending beyond the end of the period of three years beginning on the relevant date" and in paragraph (*b*) for the words "twelve months" there shall be substituted the words "three years"; and **[590]**

(*c*) after subsection (2) there shall be inserted the following subsection:—

"(2A) for the purposes of subsection (2) above "the relevant date" means—

(*a*) if the compulsory purchase order concerned has become operative before the date on which the court exercises its power under that subsection, the date on which the order became operative; and

(*b*) in any other case the date on which the court exercises or, as the case may be, exercised its power under paragraph (*a*) of that subsection in relation to the order for possession in question". **[591]**

The Housing (*Slum Clearance Compensation*) *Act* 1965

11. In section 2 of the Housing (Slum Clearance Compensation) Act 1965 (money borrowed by owner-occupier to purchase unfit house or on security of an unfit house) in subsection (2) for the words "closing order or clearance order" there shall be substituted the words "or closing order". **[592]**

The Housing (*Scotland*) *Act* 1966

12. In section 135 of the Housing (Scotland) Act 1966, the same amendments shall be made as are set out in paragraph 10 (5) above with the substitution for the reference to an order for possession of a reference to a decree of removing or warrant of ejection or other like order. **[593]**

13. Sections 153 to 155 and 159 of the Housing (Scotland) Act 1966 shall cease to have effect. **[594]**

14. In section 175 of that Act (compulsory purchase of land by Scottish Special Housing Association) in subsection (2) (power of Association to acquire land compulsorily for selling it or leasing it to a housing society) for the words from "section 4 (1) of the Housing Act 1964" to the end of the subsection there shall be substituted the words "section 3 (5) of the Housing Act 1974, acquire land compulsorily" and in subsection (3) (application of Acquisition of Land (Authorisation Procedure) (Scotland) Act 1947) after the word "and", in the second place where it occurs, there shall be inserted the words "in relation to the exercise of the Association's powers under subsection (1) of this section". **[595]**

15. In section 208 (1) of that Act, in the definition of "housing association" after the words "those of" there shall be inserted the word "providing" and after the words "housing accommodation" there shall be inserted the words "including hostels, as defined in section 21 (4) of the Housing (Financial Provisions) (Scotland) Act 1968". **[596]**

The Rent Act 1968

16. In section 5 (6) of the Rent Act 1968 (conditions for a housing association tenancy to be excluded from that Act) after paragraph (*cc*) there shall be inserted the following paragraph:—

"(*ccc*) that the dwelling was comprised in a housing project approved for the purposes of section 29 of the Housing Act 1974". **[597]**

17.—(1) In section 57 of that Act (grant-aided improvements, etc.) in paragraph (*a*) of subsection (1) (amount of certain grants to be disregarded in increasing rent limit) after the words "(improvement grants and standard grants)" there shall be inserted the words "section 61 of section 65 of the Housing Act 1974 (improvement grants and intermediate grants)". **[598]**

(2) In subsection (2) of that section (amount of certain grants obtainable but not obtained to be disregarded in increasing rent limit) after the words "the Housing Act 1964" there shall be inserted the words "or an improvement notice within the meaning of Part VIII of the Housing Act 1974", for the words "that Part of that Act" there shall be substituted the words "either of those Parts", after the words "the Housing Act 1969" there shall be inserted the words "or an intermediate grant under section 65 of the Housing Act 1974" and after the words "the standard grant" there shall be inserted the words "or intermediate grant". **[599]**

The Housing (Financial Provisions) (Scotland) Act 1968

18.—(1) Sections 16 and 17 of the Housing (Financial Provisions) (Scotland) Act 1968 shall cease to have effect. **[600]**

(2) In section 18 (1) of that Act (local authority to furnish certain particulars to Secretary of State for purpose of determining the amount of certain Exchequer contributions) the words from "or any such" to "section 16 of this Act" and the words "or arrangements" shall be omitted. **[601]**

The Housing Act 1969

19. In section 69 of the Housing Act 1969 (repayment of certain payments made under the Housing Act 1957 or that Act), for the words "closing order or clearance order" there shall be substituted the words "or closing order". **[602]**

20.—(1) In section 75 of that Act (power of local authority to carry out works of improvement by agreement with and at expense of owner, etc.) in subsection (1) for the words "Part I of this Act", in the first place where they occur, there shall be substituted the words "Part VII of the Housing Act 1974" and for the words "Part I of this Act", in the second place where they occur, there shall be substituted the words "that Part". **[603]**

(2) In subsection (2) of that section, paragraph (*b*) shall be omitted and, in paragraph (*c*), for the words "section 27 of this Act" there shall be substituted the words "section 84 of the Housing Act 1974". **[604]**

21. In Schedule 5 to that Act (payments to owner-occupiers and others in respect of unfit houses purchased or demolished) in paragraph 1 (1) for the words "a closing order under section 17 of that Act or a clearance order" there shall be substituted the words "or a closing order under section 17 of that Act". **[605]**

The Rent (Scotland) Act 1971

22. In section 5 (5) of the Rent (Scotland) Act 1971 (conditions for a housing association tenancy to be excluded from that Act) after paragraph (*f*) there shall be inserted the following paragraph:—

"(*g*) that the dwelling-house was comprised in a housing project approved for the purposes of section 29 of the Housing Act 1974". **[606]**

The Housing (Financial Provisions) (Scotland) Act 1972

23.—(1) In section 23 (3) (*a*) of the Housing (Financial Provisions) (Scotland) Act 1972 (certain buildings not to be included among those in respect of which local authority are required to keep a housing revenue account) after the words "the Act of 1968" there shall be inserted the words "or section 107 of the Housing Act 1974". **[607]**

(2) In section 52 of that Act (the basic residual subsidy), at the beginning of subsection (8) (the withdrawal factor for years subsequent to 1972–73) there shall be inserted the words "Subject to subsection (9) below" and after that subsection there shall be added the following subsection:—

"(9) For the year 1974–75, the withdrawal factor is zero". **[608]**

(3) In section 53 of that Act (the special residual subsidy), at the beginning of subsection (9) (the reduction factor for houses completed during any specified year) there shall be inserted the words "Subject to subsection (10) below" and after that subsection there shall be added the following subsection:—

"(10) For the purposes of subsections (6) (*b*) and (7) above the reduction factor for houses completed during the year 1972–73, or, as the case may be, 1973–74 is zero." **[609]**

(4) In sections 54 (1) and 55 (12) of that Act (power of Secretary of State to modify basis of calculation of certain subsidies where a housing association's income for any year will be inadequate to meet the expenditure which it would be reasonable for them to incur in that year in exercise of their housing functions) after the words "will be" there shall be inserted the words "or was" and after the words "would be" there shall be inserted the words "or, as the case may be, was". **[610]**

(5) In section 61 (2) of that Act (rents to be registrable under Part IV of the Rent (Scotland) Act 1971) after the words "the Act of 1971" there shall be inserted the words "(and no other provisions of that Act) shall apply to a tenancy to which the said sections 60 to 66 apply and in their application to such tenancies". **[611]**

(6) After subsection (3) of section 62 of that Act (rent limit where no rent is registered) there shall be inserted the following sub-section—

"(3A) The reference in paragraph (*b*) of subsection (3) above to another tenancy includes, in addition to a tenancy to which sections 62 to 66 of this Act apply, a regulated tenancy within the meaning of the Act of 1971—

(*a*) which subsisted at any time after the operative date, within the meaning of the Housing Act 1974; and

(*b*) under which, immediately before it came to an end, the interest of the landlord belonged to a housing association". **[612]**

(7) In section 66 of that Act (increase of rent without notice to quit), the reference to a housing association shall, on and after the operative date, be construed as not extending to an unregistered housing association unless the provisions of section 18 (1) (*b*) or (*c*) of this Act apply to that association. **[613]**

The Housing Finance Act 1972

24. In the Housing Finance Act 1972 (in this Schedule referred to as "the 1972 Act"), in paragraph (*e*) of section 12 (1) (with the consent of the Secretary of State, a local authority may include in their Housing Revenue Account income and expenditure in respect of houses and buildings not specifically referred to in paragraphs (*a*) to (*d*) of that section) after the word "such" there shall be inserted the word "land" and at the end of that paragraph there shall be added the words "and any consent given by the Secretary of State for the purposes of this paragraph may be given either generally to local authorities or to any local authority or description of local authority or in any particular case". **[614]**

25.—(1) In section 28 of the 1972 Act (application for qualification certificate) in subsection (1) (application may be combined with application for a grant under Part I of the Housing Act 1969) for the words "Part I of the Housing Act 1969" there shall be substituted the words "Part VII of the Housing Act 1974". **[615]**

(2) In subsection (4) of that section (local authority need not serve notice on tenant where they approved an application for a grant under section 2 (1) or section 9 (1) of the Housing Act 1969 and work has been carried out) after the words "section

2 (1) or section 9 (1) of the Housing Act 1969" there shall be inserted the words "or section 61 (1) or section 65 (1) of the Housing Act 1974". **[616]**

26.—(1) In section 33 of the 1972 Act (if one of two conditions is satisfied, county court may by order empower landlord to carry out certain works to which tenant does not consent) in subsection (2) (*a*) (one of the conditions is that the works were specified in an application for a grant under Part I of the Housing Act 1969 and the application has been approved) after the words "Part I of the Housing Act 1969" there shall be inserted the words "or Part VII of the Housing Act 1974". **[617]**

(2) At the end of subsection (3) of that section (order under subsection (1) may impose conditions as to time for carrying out works) there shall be added the words "or section 82 (1) of the Housing Act 1974". **[618]**

27. In section 34 (3) of the 1972 Act (definitions for purposes of Part III of the Act: "standard amenities" has the meaning assigned to it by section 7 of the Housing Act 1969) for the words "section 7 of the Housing Act 1969" there shall be substituted the words "section 58 of the Housing Act 1974". **[619]**

28. In section 38 (2) of the 1972 Act (section 25 (1) of the Rent Act 1968, which provides for increase in recoverable rent for improvements, not to apply to improvements with respect to which a grant under Part I of the Housing Act 1969 is payable or has been paid) after the words "Part I of the Housing Act 1969" there shall be inserted the words "or Part VII of the Housing Act 1974". **[620]**

29. In section 45 of the 1972 Act (protection of tenant with security of tenure where grant-aided improvement is carried out) in subsection (1) after the words "Part I of the Housing Act 1969" there shall be inserted the words "or Part VII of the Housing Act 1974". **[621]**

30. In section 72 of the 1972 Act (the basic residual subsidy) at the beginning of subsection (9) (the withdrawal factor for years subsequent to 1972–73) there shall be inserted the words "Subject to subsection (10) below" and after that subsection there shall be added the following subsection:—

"(10) For the year 1974–5, the withdrawal factor is zero". **[622]**

31. In section 73 of the 1972 Act (the special residual subsidy) at the beginning of subsection (7) (the reduction factor for dwellings completed during any specified year) there shall be inserted the words "Subject to subsection (8) below" and after that subsection there shall be added the following subsection:—

"(8) For the purposes of subsections (4) (*b*) and (5) above, the reduction factor for dwellings completed during the year 1972–73 or, as the case may be, 1973–74 is zero". **[623]**

32. In sections 74 (1) and 75 (12) of the 1972 Act (power of Secretary of State to modify basis of calculation of certain subsidies where a housing association's income for any year will be inadequate to meet the expenditure which it would be reasonable for them to incur in that year in exercise of their housing functions) after the words "will be" there shall be inserted the words "or was" and after the words "would be" there shall be inserted the words "or, as the case may be, was". **[624]**

33.—(1) In subsection (2) of section 82 of the 1972 Act (application of certain provisions of Part IV of Rent Act 1968 in relation to tenancies to which Part VIII of the 1972 Act applies),—

(*a*) after the words "the following" there shall be inserted the words "and no other"; and
(*b*) after the word "shall" there shall be inserted the words "apply in relation to tenancies to which this Part of this Act applies, and in their application to such tenancies shall". **[625]**

(2) If, pursuant to an application by a local authority under section 44A of the Rent Act 1968, a rent has, at any time before the appointed day, been registered

in the part of the register under Part IV of that Act which is provided for by subsection (1) of section 82 of the 1972 Act, that registration—

(*a*) shall be as valid as if section 44A of the Rent Act 1968 had, before the appointed day, been specified in subsection (2) of section 82 of the 1972 Act; and

(*b*) shall be treated on and after the appointed day as if it had been effected pursuant to an application under section 44 of the Rent Act 1968. **[626]**

(3) In this paragraph "the appointed day" means the day appointed for the coming into operation of this paragraph. **[627]**

34. After subsection (3) of section 83 of the 1972 Act (rent limit where no rent is registered) there shall be inserted the following subsection—

"(3A) The reference in paragraph (*b*) of subsection (3) above to another tenancy includes, in addition to a tenancy to which this Part of this Act applies, a regulated tenancy, within the meaning of the Rent Act 1968—

(*a*) which subsisted at any time after the operative date, within the meaning of the Housing Act 1974; and

(*b*) under which, immediately before it came to an end, the interest of the landlord belonged to a housing association". **[628]**

35.—(1) In section 91 (1) of the 1972 Act (exceptions from duty to give information about service charges) at the end of paragraph (*d*) there shall be added the words "which either is registered under section 13 of the Housing Act 1974 or falls within any of paragraphs (*a*) to (*c*) of section 18 (1) of that Act."

(2) This paragraph shall come into operation on the operative date. **[629]**

36. In Schedule 1 to the 1972 Act (the Housing Revenue Account) in paragraph (*d*) of paragraph 1 (1) (amounts to be carried to the credit of the account to include contributions towards costs of improvements and conversions) the word "or" at the end of subparagraph (iii) shall be omitted and, after sub-paragraph (iv), there shall be inserted the words "or

(*v*) section 79 of the Housing Act 1974". **[630]**

37. In Schedule 6 to the 1972 Act (restriction on rent increases) in paragraph 1 (1) and, in paragraph 2, in Case F in the Table, after the words "Part I of the Housing Act 1969" there shall be inserted the words "or Part VII of the Housing Act 1974". **[631]**

The Land Compensation Act 1973

38.—(1) In the Land Compensation Act 1973 (in this Schedule referred to as "the 1973 Act"), in section 29 (right to home loss payment where person displaced from dwelling) subsection (1) shall be amended as follows:—

(*a*) at the end of paragraph (*b*) there shall be added the words "or the service of an improvement notice, within the meaning of Part VIII of the Housing Act 1974, in respect of the dwelling";

(*b*) in paragraph (*c*) after the words "the carrying out of" there shall be inserted the words "any improvement to the dwelling or of" and at the end of that paragraph there shall be added the following paragraph:—

"(*d*) where the land has previously been acquired by a registered housing association, within the meaning of the Housing Act 1974, or by an unregistered housing association which falls within section 18 (1) (*a*) of that Act, the carrying out by that association of any improvement to the dwelling or of redevelopment on the land"; and

(*c*) for the words from "the acquiring authority" to the end of the subsection there shall be substituted the following paragraphs:—

"(i) where paragraph (*a*) above applies, the acquiring authority;

(ii) where paragraph (*b*) above applies, the authority who made the order, passed the resolution, accepted the undertaking or served the notice;

(iii) where paragraph (*c*) above applies, the authority carrying out the improvement or redevelopment; and

(iv) where paragraph (*d*) above applies, the housing association carrying out the improvement or redevelopment. [**632**]

(2) After subsection (3) of that section there shall be inserted the following subsection:—

"(3A) For the purposes of this section a person shall not be treated as displaced from a dwelling in consequence of the acceptance of an undertaking, of the service of such an improvement notice as is mentioned in subsection (1) (*b*) above or of the carrying out of any improvement to the dwelling unless he is permanently displaced from it in consequence of the carrying out of the works specified in the undertaking or notice or, as the case may be, of the improvement in question". [**633**]

(3) In subsection (7) of that section for the words "or section 15 (4) (i) of the said Act of 1966" there shall be substituted the words "section 15 (4) (i) of the said Act of 1966 or section 87 of the Housing Act 1974", the words "and 'redevelopment' includes a change of use" shall be omitted and at the end of that subsection there shall be inserted the following subsection:—

"(7A) In this section—

'improvement' includes alteration and enlargement; and
'redevelopment' includes a change of use". [**634**]

39.—(1) In section 37 of the 1973 Act (disturbance payments for persons without compensatable interests) subsection (1) shall be amended—

(*a*) by adding, at the end of paragraph (*b*), the words "or the service of an improvement notice, within the meaning of Part VIII of the Housing Act 1974, in respect of a house on the land";

(*b*) by inserting, in paragraph (*c*), after the words "the carrying out of" the words "any improvement to a house or building on the land or of";

(*c*) by adding, at the end of paragraph (*c*) the following paragraph:—

"(*d*) where the land has previously been acquired by a registered housing association, within the meaning of the Housing Act 1974, or by an unregistered housing association which falls within section 18 (1) (*a*) of that Act, the carrying out by that association of any improvement to a house or building on the land or of redevelopment on that land"; and

(*d*) by making the like amendments as are specified, in relation to section 29 (1) of that Act, in paragraph 38 (1) (*c*) above. [**635**]

(2) Subsection (3) of that section shall be amended as follows:—

(*a*) for the words "or redevelopment as is mentioned in paragraph (*a*) or (*c*)' there shall be substituted the words "improvement or redevelopment as is mentioned in paragraph (*a*), (*c*) or (*d*)";

(*b*) for the words "or undertaking" there shall be substituted the words "undertaking or improvement notice";

(*c*) for the words "or the undertaking was accepted" there shall be substituted the words "the undertaking was accepted or the notice was served".

[**636**]

(3) After subsection (3) of that section there shall be inserted the following subsection:—

"(3A) For the purposes of subsection (1) above a person shall not be treated as displaced in consequence of the acceptance of an undertaking, of the service of such an improvement notice as is mentioned in paragraph (*b*) of that subsection or of the carrying out of any improvement to a house or building unless he is permanently displaced in consequence of the carrying out of the works specified in the undertaking or notice or, as the case may be, of the improvement in question." [**637**]

(4) In subsection (9) of that section after the words "undertaking" there shall be inserted the word " 'improvement' ". [**638**]

40.—(1) In section 39 of the 1973 Act (duty to rehouse residential occupiers) in paragraph (*c*) of subsection (1) after the words "the carrying out of" there shall be inserted the words "any improvement to a house or building on the land or of" and at the end of that paragraph there shall be added the following paragraph:—

"(*d*) the service of an improvement notice, within the meaning of Part VIII of the Housing Act 1974, in respect of premises in which that accommodation is situated". [**639**]

(2) In subsection (3) of that section after the word "demolition" there shall be added the words "or improvement". [**640**]

(3) In subsection (6) of that section after the words "such acquisition" there shall be inserted the word "improvement", after the words "paragraph (*b*) of that subsection" there shall be inserted the words "or of such an improvement notice as is mentioned in paragraph (*d*) of that subsection" and for the words "or the undertaking was accepted" there shall be substituted the words "the undertaking was accepted or the notice was served". [**641**]

(4) After subsection (6) of that section there shall be inserted the following subsection:—

"(6A) For the purposes of subsection (1) above a person shall not be treated as displaced in consequence of the acceptance of an undertaking, of the carrying out of any improvement to a house or building or of the service of such an improvement notice as is mentioned in paragraph (*d*) of that subsection unless he is permanently displaced from the residential accommodation in question in consequence of the carrying out of the works specified in the undertaking, the carrying out of the improvement or, as the case may be, the carrying out of the works specified in the notice." [**642**]

(5) In subsection (7) of that section for the words "subsection (8)" there shall be substituted the words "subsections (8) and (8A)". [**643**]

(6) After subsection (8) there shall be inserted the following subsection:

"(8A) In a case where subsection (1) above applies in consequence of the acceptance of an undertaking under section 87 of the Housing Act 1974 or the service of an improvement notice within the meaning of Part VIII of that Act, the relevant authority for the purposes of this section is the authority which is the local authority, within the meaning of Part VII of that Act, in relation to the premises in which the residential accommodation is situated". [**644**]

(7) In subsection (9) of that section after the word "undertaking" there shall be inserted the word " 'improvement' ". [**645**]

41.—(1) In section 43 of the 1973 Act (power to defray expenses in connection with acquisition of new dwellings) in subsection (1),—

(*a*) for the words "any such acquisition as is mentioned in section 39 (1) (*a*) above", there shall be substituted the words "any of the events specified in paragraphs (*a*) to (*d*) of section 39 (1) above"; and

(*b*) for the words "the acquiring authority" there shall be substituted the words "then, according to the nature of the event in consequence of which he was displaced, the acquiring authority, the authority who made the order, passed the resolution, accepted the undertaking or served the notice or the authority carrying out the improvement or redevelopment". [**646**]

(2) In subsection (4) of that section for the words "and (6)" there shall be substituted the words "(6) and (6A)" and for the words "subsection 1 (*a*)" there shall be substituted the words "any provision of subsection (1)". **[647]**

The Land Compensation (Scotland) Act 1973

42.—(1) In section 27 of the Land Compensation (Scotland) Act 1973 (right to home loss payment where person displaced from dwelling), subsection (1) shall be amended as follows:—

(*a*) In paragraph (*c*) after the words "the carrying out of" there shall be inserted the words "any improvement to the dwelling or of" and at the end of that paragraph there shall be added the following paragraph:—

"(*d*) where the land has previously been acquired by a registered housing association, within the meaning of the Housing Act 1974, the carrying out by that association of any improvement to the dwelling or of development on the land"; and

(*b*) for the words from "the acquiring authority" to the end of the subsection there shall be substituted the following paragraphs:—

"(i) where paragraph (*a*) above applies, the acquiring authority;

(ii) where paragraph (*b*) above applies, the authority who made the order, passed the resolution or accepted the undertaking;

(iii) where paragraph (*c*) above applies, the authority carrying out the improvement or redevelopment; and

(iv) where paragraph (*d*) above applies, the housing association carrying out the improvement or redevelopment." **[648]**

(2) After subsection (3) of that section there shall be inserted the following subsection:—

"(3A) For the purposes of this section a person shall not be treated as displaced from a dwelling in consequence of the carrying out of any improvement to the dwelling unless he is permanently displaced from it in consequence of the carrying out of the improvement in question." **[649]**

(3) In subsection (7) of that section the words "and 'redevelopment' includes a change of use" shall be omitted and at the end of that subsection there shall be inserted the following subsection:—

"(7A) In this section
'improvement' includes alteration and enlargement; and
'redevelopment' includes a change of use". **[650]**

43.—(1) In section 34 of that Act (disturbance payments for persons without compensatable interests), subsection (1) shall be amended—

(*a*) by inserting, in paragraph (*c*), after the words "the carrying out of", the words "any improvement to a house or building on the land or of";

(*b*) by adding, at the end of paragraph (*c*), the following paragraph:—

"(*d*) where the land has previously been acquired by a registered housing association, within the meaning of the Housing Act 1974, the carrying out by that association of any improvement to a house or building on the land or of redevelopment on that land"; and

(*c*) by making the like amendments as are specified, in relation to section 27 (1) of that Act, in paragraph 42 (1) (*b*) above. **[651]**

(2) In subsection (3) of that section for the words "or redevelopment as is mentioned in paragraph (*a*) or (*c*)" there shall be substituted the words "improvement or redevelopment as is mentioned in paragraph (*a*), (*c*) or (*d*)". **[652]**

(3) After subsection (3) of that section, there shall be inserted the following subsection:—

"(3) For the purposes of subsection (1) above a person shall not be treated as displaced in consequence of the carrying out of any improvement to a house or building unless he is permanently displaced in consequence of the carrying out of the improvement in question". [**653**]

(4) In subsection (8) of that section after the word "undertaking" there shall be inserted the word " 'improvement' ". [**654**]

44.—(1) In section 36 of that Act (duty to rehouse residential occupiers) in paragraph (*c*) of subsection (1) after the words "the carrying out of" there shall be inserted the words "any improvement to a house or building on the land or of". [**655**]

(2) In subsection (3) of that section after the word "demolition" there shall be added the words "or improvement". [**656**]

(3) In subsection (6) of that section after the words "such acquisition" there shall be inserted the word "improvement". [**657**]

(4) In subsection (9) of that section after the word "undertaking" there shall be inserted the word " 'improvement' ". [**658**]

45.—(1) In section 40 of that Act (power to defray expenses in connection with acquisition of new dwellings) in subsection (1)—

(*a*) for the words "any such acquisition as is mentioned in section 36 (1) (*a*) above", there shall be substituted the words "any of the events specified in paragraphs (*a*) to (*c*) of section 36 (1) above"; and
(*b*) for the words "the acquiring authority" there shall be substituted the words "then, according to the nature of the event in consequence of which he was displaced, the acquiring authority, the authority who made the order, passed the resolution or accepted the undertaking or the authority carrying out the improvement or re-development". [**659**]

(2) In subsection (4) of that section for the words "subsection (1) (*a*)" there shall be substituted the words "any provision of subsection (1)". [**660**]

Local Government (Scotland) Act 1973

46.—(1) Section 131 (3) shall cease to have effect.

(2) In Schedule 12, in paragraph 6, in the substituted section 1 for the words "sections 152 and 153" there shall be substituted the words "section 152"; and paragraph 11 shall be omitted. [**661**]

GENERAL

Most of the amendments are clear and call for no comment.

Para. 2 relates to option mortgages.

Para. 4 was originally clause 108, and seems somewhat unnecessary. It came into operation on 2nd December 1974. S. 105 (4) of the 1957 Act as amended, applies where a building has been acquired for conversion or improvement. It does not apply where the building has been acquired as part of land to be used for the erection of houses. See *Uttoxeter Urban District Council* v. *Clarke*, [1952] 1 All E.R. 1318.

Moreover where a house is acquired on a site intended for development as a housing estate, s. 105 (4) does not preclude its demolition. See *Attridge* v. *London County Council* [1954] 2 Q.B. 449.

Para. 5 states that s. 121 of the Housing Act 1957 shall cease to have effect. The provisions of s. 21 of the Housing Act 1969 have been repealed. The provisions of Part III of this Act replace them. The amendments listed in paras. 7 and 8 arise from s. 108 which abolishes clearance orders and also changes the procedure for dealing with payments for well-maintained houses. See Circulars 126/74, 136/74 and 160/74 in Appendix II.

The financial position of many housing associations will be eased by paras. 30 to 32 which reduce to "zero" the withdrawal factor (for basic residual subsidy) and reduction factor for special residual subsidy. Para. 32 will also help them. Home-loss payments are referred to in para. 38, which makes important changes so far as both the acquiring authority and housing associations are concerned. The latter will be liable for home loss payments where families are permanently displaced after 31st July 1974 in connection with improvements or redevelopment—see s. 130.

Paras. 38 to 41 deal with disturbance payments, and para. 40 relates to the duty to rehouse residential occupiers. See Circulars 130/74 and 139/74 in Appendix II.

Para. 42 covers comparable provisions for Scotland.

SCHEDULE 14

Section 130

TRANSITIONAL PROVISIONS AND SAVINGS

Transitional provisions

1. Notwithstanding the repeals effected by this Act, in any case where—

(*a*) the Housing Corporation have before the operative date made a loan under section 2 of the Housing Act 1964, and

(*b*) under a mortgage or heritable security, entered into by the body to whom the loan was made, to secure the loan the Housing Corporation have an interest as mortgagee or, as the case may be, as creditor in any land belonging to that body,

then, whether or not that body becomes a registered housing association on or after the operative date, subsections (3) and (4) of that section, as amended by section 77 (2) of the Housing Finance Act 1972, shall continue to apply in relation to that land as if those provisions had not been repealed. [**662**]

2. In any case where—

(*a*) before the operative date, the Corporation agreed to make a loan to a housing association under section 2 of the Housing Act 1964 but no such loan was made before the repeal of that section by this Act took effect, and

(*b*) that loan was to be made for the purpose of assisting the association in connection with any of the matters specified in paragraphs (*a*) to (*c*) of subsection (4) of section 17 of this Act,

section 9 of this Act shall have effect as if subsection (1) of that section permitted the Corporation to make to the association, at a time when they are an unregistered association, a loan of the same amount and for the same purpose as the loan referred to in paragraphs (*a*) and (*b*) above. [**663**]

3. Before the operative date, sections 36 (4) (*d*) and 74 (3) of this Act shall have effect as if the word "registered" in each place where it occurs, were omitted. [**664**]

4.—(1) Without prejudice to section 99 (2) (*d*) of this Act, no provisional notice or improvement notice may be served in respect of a dwelling before the operative date if the person having control of the dwelling is a housing association and the dwelling is a dwelling-house falling within any of paragraphs (*a*) to (*d*) of subsection (6) of section 5 of the Rent Act 1968 (tenancies of certain dwelling houses excluded from protection under that Act). [**665**]

(2) If, after a provisional notice or an improvement notice has been served in respect of any dwelling but before the operative date, a housing association becomes the person having control of the dwelling and, by virtue of sub-paragraph (1) above, no such notice could then be served in respect of the dwelling, any such notice with respect to the dwelling and any undertaking accepted under Part VIII of this Act with respect to the dwelling shall cease to have effect. [**666**]

(3) In this paragraph "provisional notice", "improvement notice" and "person having control" have the same meanings as in Part VIII of this Act. [**667**]

Savings

5.—(1) The repeal by this Act of sections 17 to 20 of the Housing Act 1969 shall not apply in any case where an application for an improvement contribution or a standard contribution has been approved before the day appointed for the coming into operation of that repeal. [**668**]

(2) In sub-paragraph (1) above "improvement contribution" and "standard contribution" have the same meanings as in sections 18 to 20 of the Housing Act 1969. [**669**]

6. Subject to section 35 (7) of this Act, the repeal by this Act of section 21 of the Housing Act 1969 or, as the case may be, section 16 or section 17 of the Housing (Financial Provisions) (Scotland) Act 1968 shall not affect the continued operation of that section in relation to any such arrangements as are referred to in subsection (1) of that section if, before the day appointed for the coming into operation of the repeal, approval has been given in accordance with subsection (2) of the said section 21 or, in Scotland, section 14 of the said Act of 1968 as applied by section 17 (1) (ii) of that Act to the making and terms of those arrangements. [**670**]

7.—(1) Subject to sub-paragraph (2) below, the repeal by this Act of any provision of Part I of the Housing Act 1969 shall not affect the continued operation of that Part in relation to any case where an application for a grant under that Part has been made (whether or not it has been approved) before the day appointed for the coming into operation of that repeal. [**671**]

(2) For the purpose of allowing an application for a grant under Part VII of this Act to be made notwithstanding that all or some of the works in respect of which that grant is to be sought were specified in an application, made before the day appointed as mentioned in sub-paragraph (1) above, for a grant under Part I of the Housing Act 1969, the local authority to whom that application was made shall allow it to be withdrawn (whether or not it has been approved) unless they are satisfied that the works specified in the application have been begun. [**672**]

GENERAL

Paragraph 1 preserves the position of the Housing Corporation as mortgagee where they have made a loan under s. 2 of the Housing Act 1964 to whether or not the body concerned becomes a registered housing association. Under para. 2 there is a transitional provision which relaxes s. 9 of the Act to enable the Corporation to carry out an agreement to make a loan, promised but not made before the Act comes into force. This will be helpful where the loan is required urgently and the association is not yet registered. Presumably arrangements for a loan could also be completed where the association had no intention of becoming registered. Para. 4 affects housing associations. See Circular 160/74 in Appendix II.

SCHEDULE 15

Section 130

ENACTMENTS REPEALED

Chapter	Short Title	Extent of Repeal
5 & 6 Eliz. II c. 56	The Housing Act 1957	In section 43 (1) the words from "in one or other" to "(*b*)". Sections 44 to 46. In section 50 the words from "(*a*)" to "vested in the authority". Section 51. Sections 53 and 54. In section 60 (1) the word "(*a*)" and the words from "or" to "order".

Chapter	Short Title	Extent of Repeal
5 & 6 Eliz. II c. 56 —*cont.*	The Housing Act 1957 —*cont.*	In section 67 (1) the words "a clearance order, or in". In section 70 (2) the words "clearance or", "clearance order or" and "as the case may be". Section 121. In section 159 paragraph (*b*) (iv). In section 162 (1) the words "or a clearance order". In section 163 (1) the words "or a clearance order". In section 166 (1) the words "any clearance order". In Schedule 2, in paragraph 4 (1), paragraph (*c*) and the word "or" immediately preceding it, in paragraph 6 (1) the words "(*a*)" and "or (*b*) a clearance order", and in paragraph 7 (2) the words "clearance order". In Schedule 4 in paragraph 1 the words "or a clearance order" and in paragraph 5 the words "or fifty-one" and "or a clearance order". Schedule 5.
9 & 10 Eliz. II c. 64	The Public Health Act 1961	In section 29 (4) (*b*) the words "or clearance order", in both places where they occur.
9 & 10 Eliz. II c. 65	The Housing Act 1961	Section 24. Schedule 3.
1964 c. 56	The Housing Act 1964	In section 1, in subsection (1) the words from "whose general duty" to the end of the subsection and subsection (1A). Sections 2 to 4. Section 6. In section 8 subsections (6), (7) and (9). Section 9. In section 11 (1) the words "section 3" and "section 6". In section 12, in subsection (1) the definition of "local authority" and subsection (2). Part II. Sections 57 and 59. In section 72 (1) the words "of twelve months" in each place where they occur.
1965 c. 56	The Compulsory Purchase Act 1965	Section 35.

Chapter	Short Title	Extent of Repeal
1965 c. 75	The Rent Act 1965	In section 35 (5) the words "45 (3)". In Schedule 6, in paragraph 10 (2), the words "45 (3)".
1965 c. 81	The Housing (Slum Clearance Compensation) Act 1965	In section 1 (1) the words "or clearance orders".
1966 c. 49	The Housing (Scotland) Act 1966	Sections 153 to 155. Section 159.
1967 c. 29	The Housing Subsidies Act 1967	Section 14. In section 27, in subsection (1) the words from "and for the purposes" to the end of the subsection. Schedule 2.
1968 c. 13	The National Loans Act 1968	In Schedule 1 the entries relating to subsections (1), (3) and (5) of section 9 of the Housing Act 1964.
1968 c. 23	The Rent Act 1968	In Schedule 15 in the entry relating to the Housing Act 1957 the words "45 (6)" and in the entry relating to the Housing Act 1964, the amendments of section 44 (2) (*a*) and Schedule 2.
1968 c. 31	The Housing (Financial Provisions) (Scotland) Act 1968	Sections 16 and 17. In section 18 (1), the words from "or any such" to "section 16 of this Act"; and the words "or arrangements".
1969 c. 33	The Housing Act 1969	Part I (including Schedule 1). In section 29 (2) the words "or a clearance order under Schedule 5 to that Act". In section 30, subsections (2) and (3). Section 36. In section 37 (4), paragraph (*b*) and the word "or" immediately preceding it. In section 40 (2) (*a*) the words "Part I of this Act other than sections 17 to 22". Section 41. In section 69 paragraph (*c*) and the word "or" immediately preceding it. In section 70 the words "section 20 or". Section 75 (2) (*b*). Sections 76 and 77. In section 88 (1) the words "Part I". In Schedule 5, in each of para-

Chapter	Short Title	Extent of Repeal
1969 c. 33 —*cont.*	The Housing Act 1969 —*cont.*	graphs 3 (1) and 5 (2) the words "clearance order". In Schedule 8 paragraphs 25 to 28 and 31.
1971 c. 76	The Housing Act 1971	In section 2, subsections (1) to (3) and (5). In section 3, subsections (1) to (3) and (5).
1972 c. 47	The Housing Finance Act 1972	In section 11 (7) the words "sections 53 and 54 (clearance orders made before 30th August 1954) and other than". In section 36, in subsection (1), paragraph (*c*) and, in subsection (2), in paragraph (*c*) the words "or clearance order" and "or 44". Section 77. In Schedule 1, in paragraph 1 (1) (*d*), the word "or" at the end of sub-paragraph (iii). In Schedule 8, paragaph 9 (2).
1972 c. 70	The Local Government Act 1972	In section 171 (1) the words "section 6 (4) of the Housing Act 1969". In Schedule 22, in paragraph 24 the words "26".
1973 c. 5	The Housing (Amendment) Act 1973	In section 1, subsections (2) to (4).
1973 c. 26	The Land Compensation Act 1973	In section 29 (7) the words "and 'redevelopment' includes a change of use". Section 73(2).
1973 c. 56	The Land Compensation (Scotland) Act 1973	In section 27 (7) the words "and 'redevelopment' includes a change of use".
1973 c. 65	The Local Government (Scotland) Act 1973	Section 131 (3). In Schedule 12, paragraph 11.

[**673**]

APPENDIX II

DEPARTMENT OF THE ENVIRONMENT/ WELSH OFFICE CIRCULARS

HOUSING ACT 1974

CLEARANCE OF UNFIT HOUSES

1. We are directed by the Secretary of State for the Environment and the Secretary of State for Wales to draw attention to those provisions of the Housing Act 1974, which received Royal Assent on 31 July 1974, affecting existing clearance procedures in relation to unfit houses. Section 108 (1) abolishes the power of local authorities to make clearance orders. Section 108 (2) introduces a new procedure for making payments in respect of houses subject to action under Part III of the Housing Act 1957 that have been well maintained and paragraph 8 of Schedule 13 applies the new procedure to unfitness orders made under paragraph 2 (2) of Schedule 2 to the Land Compensation Act 1961. Sections 110, 111, 112 and 113 deal with the situation that arises when a property subject to action under Part III is listed as being of architectural or historic interest. Finally, section 114 empowers local authorities to make rehabilitation orders on property previously included in a Part III CPO. [**674**]

Abolition of Clearance Orders

2. Section 108 (1) abolishes the power of local authorities to make clearance orders under Part III of the Housing Act 1957. Section 108 (3) applies this provision to any clearance area declared on or after 31 August 1974, which is one month after the passing of the Act. Moreover, for clearance areas declared before that date authorities are given only a further 12 months in which to make clearance orders. Thereafter authorities who decide to proceed with clearance will have to buy the properties by agreement or compulsorily and themselves carry out demolition. Authorities whose intention it has been to deal with properties in resolved clearance areas by way of clearance orders should note these dates carefully.

3. Although there are many amendments and repeals in Schedules 13 and 15 of the Act removing the clearance order provisions from the Housing Act 1957 and deleting references to clearance orders in other legislation, it is intended to ensure that authorities will not be debarred from making clearance orders as appropriate up to 31 August 1975, nor from continuing action on duly made clearance orders.

4. The powers contained in Part II of the Housing Act 1957 are unaffected. [**675**]

Procedure for approving well maintained payments

5. Section 108 (2) introduces a new procedure for authorising payments for the good maintenance of unfit houses dealt with by clearance orders and compulsory purchase orders made under Part III of the Housing Act 1957. Under section 60 of that Act such payments could only be made if they were directed by the Secretary of State following inspection by an officer of the Department. The new procedure is set out in Schedule 9 of the 1974 Act which replaces section 60 (1) of the Housing Act 1957, and it applies to any orders made on or after 31 August 1974, which by virtue of section 108 (3) is the date on which the section comes into operation. Paragraph 8 of Schedule 13 relating to unfitness orders will be brought into operation by commencement order. The procedure requires local authorities in the first instance to decide whether an unfit house in a clearance area or in an unfitness order or any dwelling therein has been wholly or partly well maintained.

6. Details of the new procedure are set out in Annex A to this circular; the form to be prescribed will be contained in regulations to be made shortly. It is proposed to issue a further circular giving guidance to authorities on matters arising from the implementation of the new provisions. [**676**]

Retention of houses included in Part III Orders

7. Sections 110, 111, 112 and 113 provide for the resolution of the conflict that arises when property in a confirmed Part III order or held for Part III purposes, and which therefore the local authority are under a duty to demolish, is listed as being of special architectural or historic interest and which therefore may not lawfully be demolished without special consent.

8. Section 114 and Schedule 10 empower a local authority to make a rehabilitation order in respect of property in a confirmed Part III compulsory purchase order or held for Part III purposes which the authority now think should be rehabilitated rather than demolished. This provision applies only to properties in orders confirmed before this section of the Act comes into force or within the subsequent three months.

9. In general terms, section 115 provides that compensation paid or to be paid to owners or previous owners for properties to be retained under the listed building or rehabilitation order provisions referred to in the preceding two paragraphs should, where appropriate, be assessed or re-assessed in effect as if section 59 (2) of the Housing Act 1957 (which provides that compensation shall be the value of the land as a site cleared of buildings) did not apply. There is also provision for compensation and certain payments and allowances, if any, already paid in connection with the acquisition to be adjusted.

10. These provisions relating to retention will be brought into operation by order. The necessary statutory instrument will be laid before Parliament as soon as possible, when a further circular giving more detailed guidance will be issued.

11. A copy of this circular is enclosed for the use of the authority's Chief Financial Officer. [**677**]

ANNEX A

A SUMMARY OF THE CONTENTS OF SCHEDULE 9 OF THE HOUSING ACT 1974, WHICH SETS OUT THE PROVISIONS TO BE SUBSTITUTED FOR SUBSECTION (1) OF SECTION 60 OF THE HOUSING ACT 1957

Procedure for authorising payments for well maintained houses or dwellings

Where a house is included in a clearance order or a compulsory purchase order made under Part III of the Housing Act 1957 because it is unfit for human habitation, the authority must serve a notification on every owner, lessee, mortgagee and occupier of the house, so far as it is reasonably practicable to ascertain them. Where the house comprises more than one dwelling or is occupied partly for dwelling purposes and partly for other purposes (section 67 (2) of the Housing Act 1969), a notification must also be served on every owner, lessee, mortgagee and occupier of each dwelling in the house, so far as it is reasonably practicable to ascertain them.

The notifications must be served not later than the date (or last date if there is more than one) on which notice of the effect of the Part III order is served under paragraph 2 (1) (*b*) of Schedule 3 or paragraph 3 (1) (*b*) of Schedule 5 of the 1957 Act.

The notification, which must be in a form to be prescribed, must state:—

(*a*) that in the case of a house which does not fall within subsections (1) or (2) of section 67 of the 1969 Act (payments in respect of partially well maintained houses or parts of buildings), both the interior and the exterior have been well maintained; or

(*b*) that either the interior or exterior alone has been well maintained; or

(*c*) that in the case of a house falling within section 67 (2) the exterior, as defined in that subsection, has been well maintained; or

(*d*) that the interior of a dwelling has been well maintained; or

(*e*) that no part of the house or dwelling has been well maintained.

A notification under (*b*) must also state why the authority are not satisfied that the exterior or interior, as the case may be, has been well maintained. A notification under (*e*) must also state why the authority are satisfied that no part of the house or dwelling has been well maintained.

Where the authority have served a notification that a house or dwelling or part thereof has been well maintained and the house or dwelling is included as unfit for human habitation in a clearance or compulsory purchase order confirmed by the Secretary of State, the authority must make a payment ascertained in accordance with Part I of Schedule 2 to the 1957 Act (as it has effect by Schedule 4 to the 1969 Act) or, where appropriate, one-half of such an amount.

Where a notification is served under (*b*) or (*e*) stating that the authority are not satisfied that the exterior or the interior or any part of the house or dwelling has been well maintained, any owner, lessee, mortgagee or occupier of the house or dwelling to which the notification relates, and who is aggrieved by that decision, may within the period within which they may make an objection to the relevant compulsory purchase or clearance order make written representations to the Secretary of State in a manner to be prescribed.

If the Secretary of State receives such a representation duly made, he may, if he thinks it necessary, arrange for the house or dwelling to be inspected by an officer of his department, and, if he thinks it appropriate to do so, may direct the authority to make a payment (or further payment) in respect of the house or dwelling, ascertained in accordance with Part I of Schedule 2 to the 1957 Act or, where appropriate, one-half of that amount.

N.B.—The summary in this Annex is neither exhaustive nor authoritative and regard will need to be paid to the terms of the Act itself. **[678]**

HOUSING ACT 1974

HOME LOSS PAYMENTS, DISTURBANCE PAYMENTS, REHOUSING. TERMINAL ARRANGEMENTS FOR PREFERENTIAL GRANTS FOR HOUSE IMPROVEMENT

1. We are directed by the Secretary of State for the Environment and by the Secretary of State for Wales to draw attention, in this, the first of a series of circulars dealing with the Housing Act 1974, which received Royal Assent on 31 July 1974, to the following provisions, which were brought into operation on 20 August by the Housing Act 1974 (Commencement No. 1) Order 1974 (S.I. 1974 No. 1406 (C25)), the first of the commencement orders made under section 131 (3) of the Act

(*a*) new categories of entitlement to home loss and disturbance payments and to rehousing under the Land Compensation Act 1973 (Schedule 13 to the Housing Act 1974);

(*b*) terminal arrangements for preferential grants for house improvement in the development and intermediate areas under the Housing Act 1971, as amended (section 117 of the 1974 Act).

2. These are the only provisions now operative which require direct local authority action. Other provisions in Parts IV–IX of this Act (e.g. powers to declare housing action areas and priority neighbourhoods and to make grants for house improvement under the new scheme) will not become effective until they are brought into operation by subsequent commencement orders. **[679]**

A. NEW CATEGORIES OF ENTITLEMENT TO HOME LOSS AND DISTURBANCE PAYMENTS AND TO REHOUSING UNDER THE LAND COMPENSATION ACT 1973 (SCHEDULE 13 TO THE HOUSING ACT 1974)

3. The provisions in the 1973 Act which are amended by Schedule 13 were described in the circular "Land Compensation Act 1973" (DOE 73/73 and Welsh Office 132/73) issued on 1 June 1973.

4. It is important to note that paragraphs 38 to 41 of Schedule 13 apply to people displaced on or after the date of Royal Assent, 31 July 1974, and the six months claim period provided by section 32 of the Land Compensation Act 1973 will begin *on the date of displacement*, provided that this is on or after 31 July, and not on the date when the paragraphs came into operation. **[680]**

Home loss payments (Following permanent displacement)

5. Section 29 of the Land Compensation Act 1973 provides for home loss payments to be made to people who are compulsorily displaced from their

homes in consequence of certain actions by public authorities. Paragraph 38 of Schedule 13 to the Housing Act 1974 widens the scope of section 29 by including people permanently displaced from a dwelling in consequence of the acceptance of an undertaking under section 87 of the 1974 Act, of the service of an improvement notice within the meaning of Part VIII of the 1974 Act, of the carrying out of any improvement to a dwelling on land acquired in the circumstances mentioned in section 29 (1) (*c*) of the 1973 Act, or of the carrying out of any improvement to a dwelling or redevelopment on the land where the land has been previously acquired by a registered housing association. Paragraph 38 (2) provides that the displacement must be permanent. Subparagraph (3) defines "improvement" as including alteration and enlargement. [**681**]

Disturbance payments and duty to rehouse

6. Section 37 of the 1973 Act providing disturbance payments for persons without compensatable interests, and section 39 of the Act providing a duty in certain circumstances to rehouse residential occupiers, are similarly amended by paragraphs 39 and 40 of Schedule 13 to bring people permanently displaced by an improvement notice or undertaking or by the carrying out of improvement works within the scope of these provisions. The amendments to section 39 do not however apply to housing associations. [**682**]

Power to defray certain expenses in connection with acquisition of new dwellings

7. Paragraph 41 of Schedule 13 amends section 43 of the 1973 Act to provide that where a person having no greater interest than that of a tenant for a year or from year to year is permanently displaced by any of the events mentioned in section 39 (1) (*a*)–(*d*) of the 1973 Act as amended by the Housing Act 1974 the displacing authority may pay any reasonable expenses he incurs, other than the purchase price, in connection with the acquisition of an alternative dwelling. These amendments again do not apply to housing associations. [**683**]

Application to registered housing associations

8. Section 13 of the Housing Act 1974 provides for the registration of housing associations. Where land has previously been acquired by a registered housing association the association will be responsible, subject to the provisions of the Land Compensation Act 1973 as amended, for making home loss and disturbance payments in certain circumstances to people who are permanently displaced as a consequence of the carrying out of an improvement to a dwelling on the land or of redevelopment on the land. Paragraphs 38 and 39 of Schedule 13 to the 1974 Act amend sections 29 and 37 of the Land Compensation Act 1973 accordingly. These provisions will only apply where the land has been acquired and the displacement occurs after the housing association concerned has been registered in accordance with section 13 of the 1974 Act. Advice on the funding of these payments will be given in a further circular dealing with the housing association provisions. [**684**]

Commencement

9. Section 32 of the 1973 Act provides that a person must make a claim in writing for a home loss payment before the expiration of the period of six

months beginning with the date of displacement. Local authorities and registered housing associations are required by the section to make payment within three months of a valid claim being made or on the date of displacement, whichever is the later.

10. The amendments to sections 29, 37, 39 and 43 of the 1973 Act contained in paragraphs 38–41 of Schedule 13 to the 1974 Act have effect in the case of persons displaced on *or after* 31 *July* 1974. Local authorities and housing associations are asked to take all necessary steps to ensure that those concerned are made aware of their rights in ample time to make their claims within the six months period specified in the 1973 Act.

11. Copies of this circular will be distributed by the National Federation of Housing Associations to housing associations who are members of the Federation, and by the Housing Corporation to housing associations with whom they are in contact. Local authorities are requested to draw the circular to the attention of any housing associations known to them who may be affected by the Land Compensation Act 1973 as amended by Schedule 13 to the Housing Act 1974 and who may not have received a copy from another source. **[685]**

B. Terminal Arrangements for Preferential Grants for House Improvement in the Development and Intermediate Areas

12. In DOE Circular 87/74 (Welsh Office Circular 143/74) local authorities in the development and intermediate areas were advised of the Government's intention to include a provision in the Housing Bill to give effect to the concession relating to the payment of 75 per cent grants under the Housing Act 1971 (as amended by the Housing (Amendment) Act 1973) which the Secretaries of State announced on 30 April. The provision is contained in section 117, which was brought into effect by Commencement Order (S.I. 1974 No. 1406 (C25)) on 20 August 1974. Local authorities in the development and intermediate areas are now authorised to pay the full amount of grant in respect of any application approved on or before 30 September 1973, or to make up the balance in any case where grant of 50 per cent in respect of an application similarly approved before that date has already been paid.

13. Similarly, as indicated by paragraph 5 of DOE Circular 93/74 (Welsh Office Circular 143/74), subsection (3) of section 117 provides that the higher rate of contribution to housing associations under section 21 of the Housing Act 1969 is available in respect of applications for contribution which were received by the Secretary of State on or before 30 September 1973. **[686]**

HOUSING ACT 1974

HOUSING CORPORATION AND HOUSING ASSOCIATIONS

1. We are directed by the Secretaries of State to provide the following preliminary information to local authorities and the Housing Corporation about the arrangements for dealing with housing association projects during the interim period before all the provisions of the Housing Act 1974, which received Royal Assent on 31 July 1974, are brought into effect and before the registration

of housing associations by the Housing Corporation under Part II of the Act is effected. This Circular has also been copied to the National Federation of Housing Associations and the National Association of Almshouses for information to their members.

2. The Housing Act 1974 provides for an entirely new system of financial support for housing association projects in furtherance of the Government's belief that these associations have an important part to play in supplementing the work of local authorities, particularly in areas of severe housing stress and in providing flexibly for special housing needs—such as accommodation for the elderly and the disabled. **[687]**

Scope of the circular

3. Very shortly a more comprehensive Circular will be issued explaining in more detail the provisions of the Housing Act 1974, particularly in relation to the loan finance and grants available to registered housing associations. But it is considered that local authorities should be given preliminary guidance, so as to avoid any tendency to delay the handling of urgent and worthwhile housing association projects because of uncertainties about the provisions of the Act. As will be seen there is no reason for such delay or uncertainty. Efficient and reputable housing associations accustomed to meeting urgent housing needs in collaboration with their local authorities should have no difficulty in securing registration and their approved housing projects will then qualify for the new housing association grant. **[688]**

Local authorities defined

4. Throughout this Circular references to "local authority" should be taken as references to a district council, a London Borough council, the Common Council of the City of London or the Greater London Council as appropriate. **[689]**

England and Wales only

5. Whilst the provisions of Parts I, II and III of the Act extend throughout England, Scotland and Wales, the arrangements set out in this Circular apply in England and Wales only. References to the Secretaries of State should be taken as references to the Secretary of State for the Environment or the Secretary of State for Wales as appropriate. References to "the Act" should be taken as references to the Housing Act 1974.

6. Because of printing difficulties it seems likely that copies of the Housing Act 1974 will not be generally available for several weeks and accordingly it has been decided to defer the implementation of most of the provisions of Parts I, II and III which relate to the Housing Corporation and to housing associations. The only provisions of these Parts of the Act which have immediate effect are:

Housing Corporation: Consents to disposal of land

(*a*) *Section 2:* which provides for control by the Housing Corporation over disposals of certain land by housing associations. In particular, a housing association not registered with the Corporation under Part II of the Act will require the consent of the Housing Corporation before disposing by sale, lease, mortgage, charge or otherwise of any "grant" aided land, as defined in Schedule 2 to the Act, which generally means land which, at 24 January 1974 or subsequently, was the subject of continuing subsidies or grants, or on which a loan from public funds was outstanding. Registered associations will require the consent for the disposal of any of their land.

Registration

(*b*) *Sections* 13 and 14: which provide for the registration of housing associations by the Housing Corporation, and the setting up of a Housing Associations Registration Advisory Committee to advise the Corporation on registration and in particular on the criteria to be applied in considering applications.

Security of tenure for tenants of unregistered housing associations

(*c*) *Section* 18 (6): and in consequence Part I of Schedule 3: which provides the transitional arrangements covering the security of tenure of tenants of housing associations which are not registered under Part II of the Act, during the period from Royal Assent on 31 July 1974 to the operative date on 1 April 1975. From the operative date tenancies of unregistered housing associations (with certain exceptions) will no longer be exempt from the protection of the Rent Act 1968 by virtue of Section 5 of that Act. [**690**]

Housing association grant

7. Housing association grant will provide the basis for the new system of financial assistance available to registered housing associations, to be paid in place of the various existing subsidies. The statutory provisions under which subsidies were previously available are generally to be repealed from 1 April 1975 with savings for commitments entered into and with transitional arrangements.

8. Housing association grant will be available only to housing associations registered with the Housing Corporation under Part II of the Act: associations not so registered being eligible for assistance only on the same basis as any private owner once the registration system comes fully into effect on the operative date of 1 April 1975.

9. It is intended that housing association grant should be available for the provision of all housing accommodation, whether in the form of separate dwellings for letting or of hostels. The grant will cover the net deficit arising from any housing project approved by the Secretaries of State and carried out by a registered housing association whether by new building; acquisition of existing housing accommodation; conversion of existing housing accommodation or other buildings; improvement of existing housing accommodation; or repair of existing housing accommodation. [**691**]

Transitional arrangements

10. The transitional arrangements will enable most existing projects of registered housing associations to transfer to housing association grant. Any schemes already approved for new building subsidy under Section 75 of the

Housing Finance Act 1972 may be transferred, although the Secretaries of State will take account of any subsidy already paid. Schemes for conversion or improvement being carried out following arrangements under Section 121 of the Housing Act 1957 may be transferred, in so far as no payment of improvement contribution under Section 21 of the Housing Act 1969 has been made before 1 April 1975. These payments are made periodically to local authorities by the Secretaries of State: advance payments by local authorities to the housing associations will not in themselves prejudice transfer to housing association grant, but such payments will be taken account of in calculating grant.

11. Hostel projects which have been approved for subsidy under Section 92 of the Housing Finance Act 1972 may be transferred to housing association grant so far as no payment of subsidy has been made. Housing associations who have made application under Section 92, but have not yet received payment, should inform the appropriate DOE Regional Officer or Welsh Officer whether they wish that payment to be made or whether subject to registration they would intend to apply for housing association grant.

12. Where an association has already received approval for a project they wish to transfer to housing association grant it will usually not be necessary to make a thorough re-examination although a formal application for housing association grant will be required. No such application should be submitted before the association becomes registered. [**692**]

Interim arrangements: existing grants and subsidies

13. Until Part III of the Act is brought into effect, and until a housing association becomes registered, it will be advisable to use existing subsidy arrangements wherever possible, since as explained above the Act provides the transitional arrangements whereby projects can be transferred to housing association grant following registration. Thus associations with new building projects should continue to apply for approval under Section 75 of the Housing Finance Act 1972, following the instructions detailed in the Memorandum on Housing Associations; improvements projects should continue under Section 21 of the Housing Act 1969 following the existing procedures; and hostel projects should continue under Section 92 of the Housing Finance Act 1972. The association should make it clear whether, subject to registration, it is intended to apply for transfer to housing association grant. [**693**]

Hostels

14. Should an association fail in the event to become registered by the Housing Corporation the new building subsidy or the improvement contribution would continue to be payable in the normal way. But of course an association which becomes registered will be able to apply for transfer to housing association grant.

15. The arrangements for dealing with hostel projects which do not meet the requirements for Section 92 subsidy, but which may qualify for housing association grant, will be dealt with in the later Circular. [**694**]

Acquisition of satisfactory dwellings

16. The acquisition of satisfactory dwellings, as opposed to acquisitions with a view to improvement, have not in the past qualified for subsidy, but will in

due course be covered by housing association grant, available only to registered associations. The criteria which will apply to these acquisition projects have not yet been approved and applications for grant in respect of them cannot yet be entertained. This matter will be dealt with in more detail in the later Circular. **[695]**

Agency arrangements

17. The Secretaries of State intend to appoint local authorities and the Housing Corporation as their agents for certain functions in relation to the payment of housing association grant largely reflecting the existing procedures, and details will be given in the later Circular. Applications for housing association grant must be submitted in the first instance to the local authority, where that body is to provide the loan finance, or to the Housing Corporation in all other cases.

18. In the meantime however the Secretaries of State urge local authorities and the Housing Corporation to make full use of their existing powers and so ensure that there is no unnecessary delay to those housing association projects which are in a position to proceed.

19. The explanatory notes on the Act contained in this Circular are of course neither exhaustive nor authoritative and regard will need to be paid to the terms of the Act itself. **[696]**

HOUSING ACTS 1957, 1969 AND 1974

CLEARANCE OF UNFIT HOUSES—PAYMENTS FOR WELL MAINTAINED HOUSES

1. We are directed by the Secretary of State for the Environment and the Secretary of State for Wales to draw the attention of the Council to the Housing (Prescribed Forms) (Amendment Etc) Regulations 1974 (S.I. 1974 No. 1511) a copy of which is enclosed. **[697]**

2. Circular No. 126/74 (Welsh Office No 205/74) issued on 23 August 1974 drew attention to those provisions of the Housing Act 1974 affecting existing clearance procedures in relation to unfit houses. Section 108 (2) of that Act introduces a new procedure for authorising payments for the good maintenance of unfit houses dealt with by clearance orders or compulsory purchase orders made under Part III of the Housing Act 1957, and paragraph 8 of Schedule 13 to the 1974 Act applies the new procedure to unfitness orders made under paragraph 2 (2) of Schedule 2 to the Land Compensation Act 1961. The new procedure is set out in Schedule 9 to the 1974 Act which replaces the existing section 60 (1) of the Housing Act 1957, and it applies by virtue of section 108 (3) of the Act and the Housing Act 1974 (Commencement No. 1) Order 1974 (S.I. 1974 No. 1406) to all orders made on or after 31 August 1974. **[698]**

3. Local authorities will be required in the first instance to decide whether an unfit house in a clearance, compulsory purchase or unfitness order has been well maintained. The annex to Circular No. 126/74 (Welsh Office No. 205/74) fully summarises the requirements of Schedule 9 and local authorities will have noted that they are required to serve a notification in a prescribed form on every owner,

lessee, occupier or mortgagee, so far as it is reasonably practicable to ascertain them, stating whether they are satisfied that the house (or dwelling where appropriate) has been wholly or partly well maintained. **[699]**

4. The enclosed order prescribes the form in which the notification must be made. In each notification four of the five statements lettered a to e will need to be struck out. These relate to the five categories specified in (*a*) to (*e*) of the new section 60 (1A) of the 1957 Act (as introduced by Schedule 9 of the 1974 Act). A person with an interest in a property falling within section 67 (2) of the Housing Act 1969 may therefore receive more than one notification. Where a person is entitled in different capacities to a notification he should be served with separate notices. **[700]**

5. Section 60 (1B) of the 1957 Act requires authorities to give reasons in any notification informing the recipient that they consider that the whole or any part of the house has not been well maintained. Provision is made in the form for these reasons to be given where required. The reasons should be given in sufficient detail for the recipient to comprehend the authority's grounds for finding the house, or part thereof as the case may be, not to have been well maintained. While it is not thought to be necessary to refer to every minor fault, the reasons should not be given in such broad terms as "general disrepair". Where no part of the house has been well maintained it will normally be desirable to refer separately to the items of exterior and interior disrepair. In an ordinary house "exterior" would cover those external items which a landlord might be expected to keep in repair, for example roofs, outside drains, guttering and main walls. For a house falling within section 67 (2) of the Housing Act 1969 "exterior" would also include any part of the interior not included in the interior of a dwelling, such as common staircases, halls, landings and parts occupied for business purposes. **[701]**

6. Any written representations against the authority's decision on maintenance must be sent to the Secretary of State before the expiry of the period within which objections may be made against the relevant clearance, compulsory purchase or unfitness order. The prescribed forms for the personal notices of the making of these orders require the insertion of a date before which objections should be made. The prescribed form of notification about maintenance requires the insertion of the same date. The minimum period permissible is 14 days from the date of service of the notice. It is however considered that 14 days may be an unduly short period to allow for objections to the order and for representations about maintenance. Accordingly authorities are requested to allow a minimum period of 28 days in every case where this is possible, both for objections to the order and for representations. This extension will not substantially affect the time-scale for dealing with orders. **[702]**

7. Local authorities are asked to assist those who may wish to make representations by providing a form on the lines of S/C55, (see Appendix III to MHLG Circular 44/56) a revised version of which will be provided in due course, and to impress on all inquirers that any representations should be made before the expiry of the closing date for objections to the order. **[703]**

8. Following the introduction of the new procedure, the reference to well maintained payments in the notes on compensation appended to the personal notices of the making of clearance, compulsory purchase and unfitness orders

(prescribed forms 17, 19, 26 and 33 in the Housing (Prescribed Forms) Regulations 1972 (S.I. 1972 No. 228)) are incorrect in respect of orders made on or after 31 August 1974. Paragraph 3 (4) of these Regulations makes consequential amendments to the 1972 Regulations. Authorities are asked to ensure that the necessary amendments are made to any existing forms they may hold that are used for orders made on or after the coming into operation of the 1974 Regulations. **[704]**

HOUSING ACT 1974

SCHEDULE 13 (PARAGRAPHS 38–41): INFORMATION FOR THE PUBLIC ON NEW ENTITLEMENTS TO HOME LOSS AND DISTURBANCE PAYMENTS, REHOUSING ETC

DOE Circular 130/74 (Welsh Office 186/74) outlined the amendments to the Land Compensation Act 1973 contained in Schedule 13 to the Housing Act 1974. As copies of the 1974 Act are not yet available authorities may wish to issue notes of guidance to inform those who may be eligible of their entitlements under the new provisions. Authorities may like to use the attached note for this purpose.

Authorities will wish to note that the provisions referred to in paragraph 5 of the note will be brought into operation by a subsequent commencement order, followed by a further circular. **[705]**

New benefits for people who lose their homes so that improvements can be carried out

[This note is intended for general guidance only. It does not cover every aspect of the new provisions and it is not an authoritative statement of the law.]

1. If you are a local authority/ New Town Development Corporation tenant and have to leave your home so that improvements can be made to it you may now be entitled to a home loss payment because of a change the law brought about by the new Housing Act 1974. To qualify you have to meet the following main conditions:—

(*a*) you must have been displaced permanently (if you merely have to leave your home temporarily and you return after the improvement works have been completed you will not qualify for a payment);

(*b*) you must have been living there for at least five years on the date you finally move out;

(*c*) you must have finally moved out on or after 31 July 1974.

There are other conditions which could affect your entitlement. If in doubt ask the authority which is your landlord. If you are a tenant of any public authority other than a local authority or New Town Development Corporation, you may have an entitlement under these new provisions. You should seek advice on this from the authority which is your landlord. **[706]**

2. The payment will be based on three times the rateable value of your home, but in any case it cannot be less than £150 or more than £1,500. To be eligible for a payment you must make a claim to the authority which is your landlord within six months of the date when you move. **[707]**

3. You may also be entitled to a disturbance payment to help meet your removal costs and to rehousing. Certain categories of short term tenants can get help towards the incidental costs of buying a new home, apart from the actual purchase price. For more details consult the authority which is your landlord. **[708]**

Tenants of registered housing associations

4. If a registered housing association becomes your landlord after 12 August 1974, and if you have to move because your home is to be improved or re-developed, you should ask the landlord about any right you may have to a home loss or disturbance payment. Under provisions in the new Housing Act tenants of dwellings acquired by registered housing associations may be entitled to these payments. These provisions do not have effect however until the new system of registration set up by the Act begins to work, and they do not apply to dwellings owned by an association before it becomes registered. **[709]**

Other provisions of the Act not yet in force

5. The Act gives new powers to local authorities to serve compulsory improvement notices on landlords or to accept binding undertakings that the necessary improvements will be carried out. These are not yet in force. When they are brought into operation people displaced from their homes may be entitled to home loss payments, disturbance payments, rehousing, and help towards the costs of buying a new home, apart from the actual purchase price, if they meet the qualifying conditions. Local authorities will be told when these provisions of the Act are brought into force and they will then be able to give you information about these new rights. **[710]**

HOUSING ACTS 1957 AND 1974

RETENTION OF PROPERTY SUBJECT TO ACTION UNDER PART III OF THE HOUSING ACT 1957

1. We are directed by the Secretary of State for the Environment and the Secretary of State for Wales to refer to Circular No 126/74 (Welsh Office No 205/74) which drew attention to those provisions of the Housing Act 1974 affecting existing slum clearance procedures. **[711]**

2. Paragraphs 7 to 10 of that Circular referred to those sections of the Housing Act 1974 relating to the retention of houses included in confirmed orders under Part III of the Housing Act 1957, and promised detailed guidance when the sections were brought into operation. The Housing Act 1974 (Commencement No 3) Order 1974 (SI 1974 No 1791) a copy of which was sent to local authorities under cover of Circular No 156/74 (Welsh Office No 253/74) brought these provisions other than Section 113 into force with effect from 2 December 1974 and the Appendix to this Circular contains the promised detailed guidance. **[712]**

3. The contents of the Appendix are neither exhaustive nor authoritative, and regard will need to be paid to the terms of the Act itself **[713]**

4. The procedure for making and confirming rehabilitation orders set out in Schedule 10 of the 1974 Act requires that the order itself and a number of notices

should be in a form prescribed by the Secretaries of State. Section 115, which provides for the assessment or re-assessment of compensation in certain circumstances, also provides for the service of a notice in the prescribed form. It is hoped that Regulations prescribing these forms will be available shortly. [**714**]

Appendix

Retention of Houses Subject to Action under Part III of the Housing Act 1957

Listed buildings in Part III compulsory purchase orders

Section 110 empowers local authorities to apply to the Secretary of State under section 55 of the Town and Country Planning Act 1971 for consent to demolish a building included in a Part III compulsory purchase order which, at any time after the making of the order, is listed under section 54 of the 1971 Act as being of special architectural or historic interest (subsection (2)).

It will be necessary when such a building is listed for the authority concerned to give further consideration to their proposals and to decide whether they accept that the property should be retained because of its special interest, or whether they remain of the opinion that despite the listing it should nevertheless be demolished. If their decision favours demolition, the authority *must apply for listed building consent within three months* of the date of listing, or before 2 March 1975 where the building was listed before this section comes into force (subsection (3)). Failure to apply for consent within this period will automatically lead to the retention of the property. [**715**]

Listing before confirmation of the order.—If a building in a Part III order is listed after the order has been *submitted* to the Secretary of State for confirmation but before he has issued his decision, the authority should notify the Secretary of State as soon as possible if they decide in favour of the retention of the building. They should request that it be withdrawn from the order and thus obviate possible delay in consideration of the order. Alternatively, if an application for listed building consent is submitted, a joint inquiry or a second inquiry will be arranged as necessary to enable decisions on the compulsory purchase order and the application for listed building consent to be issued concurrently. [**716**]

Listing after confirmation of the order.—If, on the other hand, a building in a Part III order is listed after the order has been *confirmed* different considerations apply. If listed building consent is granted, acquisition, if not completed, can proceed and demolition can follow. If, however, listed building consent is refused, or if no application is made within the three month period, subsequent action depends on whether or not notice to treat has been served, and, if it has, whether the property is vested in the authority. [**717**]

Action following refusal of listed building consent.—If notice to treat *has not* been served, subsection (9) of section 110 prohibits an authority from doing so until after the decision has been given on any application for listed building consent, or, if there is no application, the expiry of the period of three months within which such application could have been made. Furthermore refusal of listed building consent or failure to apply for it within the specified period will effectively release the building from the compulsory purchase order, and, where applicable, from the clearance area (subsection (5)), but in the latter event the authority must then take appropriate action under Part II of the 1957 Act (subsection (6)).

In cases where notice to treat *has* been served before the listing but where acquisition has not been completed before the refusal of listed building consent or the expiry of the three months period, the compulsory acquisition may continue but under the powers contained in Part V of the 1957 Act for houses or in Part VI of the Town and Country Planning Act 1971 for other buildings (subsection (7)).

In those cases where property is already vested in the authority it will be appropriated to Part V of the 1957 Act or Part VI of the 1971 Act as the case may be (sub-section (8)). **[718]**

Listed buildings in clearance areas acquired by agreement

Section 111 relates to property purchased by an authority by agreement under Part III of the 1957 Act, or under some other power and now held under Part III, and subsequently listed. The authority may apply for listed building consent if they still favour demolition. If consent is refused, or not applied for within the specified period, the authority are no longer subject to the duty to demolish the building imposed by Part III and must appropriate it to Part V of the 1957 Act or Part VI of the 1971 Act as appropriate. **[719]**

Listed buildings in clearance orders

Section 112 relates to buildings in a clearance order which are listed after the confirmation of that order. Authorities are given power, as in the previous two sections, to apply for listed building consent within the specified period of three months of the listing or of the coming into force of this section (subsection (3)). If listed building consent is given the clearance order can be enforced and the building demolished. If consent is refused or not applied for within the specified period the building will be excluded from the clearance area and the clearance order will cease to have effect in relation to that building (subsection (4)). The authority will then have to take appropriate action under Part II of the 1957 Act (subsection (5)).

Subsection (6) provides for the refund of any payment made following confirmation of a clearance order for good maintenance or to a residential or business owner-occupier under Schedule 2 to the Housing Act 1957 or Schedule 5 to the Housing Act 1969 if the recipient has retained an interest in the house. Repayment will not have to be made if the house is subsequently included in an operative closing order (subsection (7)). **[720]**

Buildings subject to Part III action included in conservation areas

Section 113 was designed to apply the provisions of sections 110, 111 and 112, suitably modified, to Part III/1957 Act buildings included in a conservation area and subject to a direction under section 8 of the Town and Country Planning (Amendment) Act 1972. The effect of such a direction was to require listed building consent to be obtained before the building concerned could be demolished.

The Town and Country Amenities Act 1974 which passed through Parliament concurrently with the Housing Act 1974 repealed section 8 of the 1972 Act, effectively replacing it by section 277A of the Town and Country Planning Act 1971 which in general has the effect of preventing demolition of any building in a conservation area without listed building consent. By virtue of subsection (4) of that section a direction has been made by the Secretaries of State in Circular No 147/74 (Welsh Office No. 220/74) excluding certain categories of properties in conservation areas from the requirement to obtain listed building consent before those properties can be demolished. One such category includes buildings in an operative compulsory purchase order or clearance order made under Part III of the 1957 Act. Section 113 has therefore not been brought into effect. [**721**]

Rehabilitation of unfit houses

Section 114 gives local authorities the power to make rehabilitation orders.

Successive Governments have expressed the view that schemes of widespread comprehensive redevelopment are not necessarily the best method of dealing with areas of sub-standard housing and that consideration should be given to the alternative of rehabilitation where this is now recognised to be practicable. Indeed, Parts IV to VIII of the Housing Act 1974 introduced wider powers in the house renovation field. Authorities will no doubt take these new provisions into consideration in reaching their decision in the future whether to clear or to rehabilitate an area of unfit housing. It may be, moreover, that in the light of these new powers an authority may now wish to retain and rehabilitate houses which they are committed to demolish because of action already taken under Part III of the 1957 Act. Section 114 provides for such a change. [**722**]

Scope of rehabilitation order.—A rehabilitation order may be made in respect of any house included in a clearance area because it is unfit to be lived in and which is subject to a compulsory purchase order made under Part III of the 1957 Act before 2 December 1974 and confirmed before the expiry of three months from that date, or which has been purchased by agreement under Part III before that date (subsection (1)). The authority must be satisfied that the house can and ought to be improved to the full standard specified in section 66 (2) of the Act (subsection (2)).

Schedule 10 provides that a rehabilitation order made under section 114 may also include any other building comprised in the clearance area (badly arranged buildings) (paragraph 1 (1) (*a*)) or any property which is not in the clearance area but is subject to the same compulsory purchase order or has been acquired by agreement under section 43 (2) of the 1957 Act (added lands) (paragraph 1 (1) (*b*)). The rehabilitation order may also include any property acquired by the authority and brought within the scope of Part III by virtue of section 49 of the 1957 Act (paragraph 1 (1) (*c*)). [**723**]

Effect of confirmed rehabilitation order.—An authority cannot serve notice to treat nor demolish a property included in a rehabilitation order until after the decision on that order is made (paragraph 3 (5)). Confirmation of an order frees the authority from the duty to demolish the properties concerned but they must ensure that any unfit houses are improved to the full standard (paragraph 1 (2)).

If no interest has been acquired or notice to treat served in respect of a property before it is included in a rehabilitation order, then on confirmation of that order the compulsory purchase order in respect of that property ceases to have effect and the property is, where applicable, excluded from the clearance area (paragraph 3 (2)). In those cases where notice to treat was served before the rehabilitation order was made but the interest has not been vested in the authority, compulsory acquisition can continue following confirmation of the rehabilitation order but as if it had been authorised under Part V of the 1957 Act for houses or Part VI of the Town and Country Planning Act 1971, for other buildings (paragraph 3 (3)). If the property is already vested in the authority it will be appropriated to Part V of the 1957 Act or Part VI of the 1971 Act as the case may be (paragraph 3 (4)). Property excluded from a clearance area by confirmation of a rehabilitation order and which adjoins a general improvement area is included in that general improvement area unless a direction to the contrary is given by the Secretary of State (paragraph 3 (7)).

An authority must give their reasons in writing if, following an approach by an owner of any building in respect of which a rehabilitation order could be made, the authority refuse to make the order (paragraph 3 (6)). [**724**]

Procedure for making and confirming rehabilitation orders.—The procedure for making and confirming a rehabilitation order is set out in paragraphs 4-8 of Schedule 10. Notice of the making of the rehabilitation order must be served on all recipients of the notice of the making of the compulsory purchase order, or their successors in title and, where appropriate, on persons from whom property was purchased by agreement. The recipients will have a right of objection including the right to represent that their property also should be included in the rehabilitation order. A rehabilitation order will be subject to confirmation by the Secretary of State who will normally hold a public local inquiry if there are objections. The exceptional nature of the provision in paragraph 6 (5) will be noted. This provides that the Secretary of State may modify a rehabilitation order on confirmation by adding, subject to certain conditions, any other property which could have been included in the order by the authority making it. [**725**]

Prescribed forms.—Five of the provisions in Schedule 10 necessitate prescribed forms, and these will be prescribed by statutory instrument to be laid before Parliament shortly. The relevant provisions are:—

Paragraph 4 —the rehabilitation order;
Paragraph 5 (1) (*a*)—the public notice of the making of the order;
Paragraph 5 (1) (*b*)—the personal notice of the effect of the order to be served on all owners etc;
Paragraph 6 (5) (*c*)—the notice to be served on owners etc affected stating the effect of any proposed modifications by the Secretary of State extending the order; and
Paragraph 7 (1) —the public and personal notice of the confirmation of the order, by virtue of the application of Schedule 4 of the 1957 Act suitably modified. [**726**]

Adjustment of compensation in consequence of the decision to retain an unfit house

Section 115 recognises that it would be inequitable if owners received only site value for houses which are now not to be demolished as worthless but are to be retained and rehabilitated by the authority.

Properties in confirmed orders.—Subsections (1) and (2) relate to properties in a confirmed Part III compulsory purchase order which are subsequently listed and by virtue of section 110 are not to be demolished, or which are in a confirmed rehabilitation order.

Subsection (1) provides that where the compulsory acquisition of an interest in such a property is to continue, compensation is to be assessed as if the compulsory purchase were under Part V of the 1957 Act in the case of a house or Part VI of the 1971 Act in other cases. Subsection (2) provides that where an interest is vested in the authority in respect of a property in a clearance area which has been appropriated to Part V, compensation is to be assessed or re-assessed as if the compulsory acquisition had been under Part V. **[727]**

Properties acquired by agreement.—Subsection (3) relates to interests in properties acquired by agreement after the declaration of a clearance area which are to be treated as appropriated to Part V. Compensation is to be assessed as if the property had been compulsorily acquired under Part V and an additional payment made if the assessed amount is higher than the amount actually paid to the previous owner of the interest.

In considering whether the assessment or re-assessment under subsections (2) or (3) necessitates an additional payment, account should be taken of any payments made to that owner for good maintenance, supplementary payments under Part II of Schedule 2 to the 1957 Act or Schedule 5 to the Housing Act 1969, disturbance payments, statutory discretionary allowances to displaced persons or extra-statutory payments (subsection (10)). **[728]**

Service of notice of change of compensation.—The local authority must serve a notice in a prescribed form (to be prescribed by statutory instrument) where compensation is assessed or re-assessed under subsections (2) or(3). The notice must be served within six months from the relevant date as defined in section 110 or, where appropriate, from the confirmation of the rehabilitation order. If the recipient does not accept the particulars within 21 days or disputes the amount the matter must be referred for determination to the Lands Tribunal (subsection (4)). To avoid possible unnecessary reference to the Lands Tribunal, in view of the short period allowed for acceptance after service of the notice, authorities should seek to enter into (or where appropriate ask the District Valuer to enter into) negotiations with the owner as soon as possible after the relevant date referred to above or the confirmation of the rehabilitation order, and endeavour to reach agreement before the notice is served. Any additional sum payable will attract interest at the prescribed rate from the time of entry or vesting, whichever is the earlier, until payment is made (sub-section (9)). **[729]**

Time limit for exercise of compulsory purchase powers

Section 116 amends section 4 of the Compulsory Purchase Act 1965 which provides that the powers of a compulsory purchase order cannot be exercised after three years from the date it comes into operation. This amendment in effect extends the three-years period for the relevant Part III compulsory purchase order by a period equivalent to that for which the powers of an authority to serve notice to treat are suspended by sections 110, 113 or 114. **[730]**

HOUSING ACT 1974

IMPROVEMENT OF OLDER HOUSING

Scope of Circular.—1. This circular relates mainly to Parts VII and VIII of the Housing Act 1974 and deals in some detail with:

—house renovation grants; and
—compulsory improvement notices.

Parts VII and VIII of the Act will be brought into operation with effect from 2 December 1974 by virtue of Commencement Order (No 3) 1974, SI No 1791 of 1974.

2. In this circular, references to the "Secretary of State" are to the Secretary of State for the Environment or the Secretary of State for Wales as appropriate; and to "Secretaries of State" are to the Secretary of State for the Environment in respect of England and to the Secretary of State in respect of Wales. References to "The Act" are to the Housing Act 1974. **[731]**

Older housing: Policy objectives

3. We are directed by the Secretaries of State to advise local authorities of their view that it is necessary to regard rehabilitation of existing houses as an integral part of an authority's housing programme. Renewal of residential areas should be based upon a comprehensive strategy consisting of a judicious mixture of essential clearance and redevelopment by a variety of agencies; of appropriate infill schemes; of acquisition and subsequent renovation of houses by a local authority, housing association or housing co-operative society in cases where it is desirable to bring property into community ownership; of voluntary grant-aided improvements and repair; of compulsory improvements and repair in defined circumstances; and of environmental treatment. The crucial tasks for local authorities will be to determine which areas should be tackled as a matter of priority, and how limited resources of manpower and finance (not only those directly controlled by local authorities) should be deployed to produce the most beneficial and effective results in both social and physical terms.

4. The main provisions in the Act, including those codes which are the subject of this circular, are designed to reinforce two basic aims of the Government's housing policy, aims related to the integrated approach to housing renewal recommended in the previous paragraph. **[732]**
These are:

(i) *The need for priority programmes*.—The Act will require local authorities to concentrate resources more positively than hitherto within housing areas most in need of improvement and upon dwellings which are manifestly sub-standard. In the past authorities have tended to give too much attention to areas of housing which were far from having the worst conditions. This has been true of some council estates as well as of improvements to private dwellings. Too high a proportion of public spending on improvement has been on dwellings already satisfactory (*i.e.* at or above the former "12-point" standard). Too many improvement grants have been devoted to replacing or adding to existing amenities in cases where this was desirable but by no means essential. The Act encourages selection of urgent priorities by providing extra powers and preferential rates of house renovation grants in housing action areas and general improvement areas. It also empowers the Secretary of State to prevent the declaration of a general improvement area and to cancel the declaration of a housing action area where he considers such declarations are inappropriate. The Circulars on housing action areas, priority neighbourhoods and general improvement areas, now in preparation, will provide guidance on the selection and declaration of areas, but it is of prime importance that, especially in advance of those circulars being issued, there should be the closest consultation between authorities and the Department's regional offices, or the Welsh Office, as appropriate, during the stages leading up to the declaration.

As part of the drive towards greater selectivity, the Act restructures the grant system to prevent abuses and to direct available help towards the rehabilitation of dwellings still lacking basic amenities or in serious disrepair rather than on houses already at or above that standard. [**733**]

(ii) *The need to see renewal as a continuous process.*—The aim is to transform the run-down residential areas of our towns and cities into decent civilised neighbourhoods by a careful mixture and phasing of re-development and rehabilitation which would result in gradual and continuous urban renewal over the years rather than massive bulldozing and rebuilding. Disturbance and dislocation of resident communities, which is both socially and economically damaging, would thus be minimised.

The new code for house renovation grants lends itself to the implementation of a gradual policy. Grants may henceforth be given over a very wide range of house condition. For example, although the Act specifies requirements as to the standard of work and the estimated life of the dwelling after renovation for both improvement and intermediate grants, authorities are empowered to waive or reduce these requirements in individual cases where they are satisfied that there are good reasons for doing so. Grant-aided renovation has social as well as economic aims. For example, there may not be obvious economic justification for a particular improvement but an overwhelming social case (with subtle but real economic benefit) to install a bath or toilet in a dwelling due to be demolished in the not-too-distant future, thus making life tolerable meanwhile for the family concerned. This is far better than the too-common experience of confirmed clearance areas remaining blighted for many years as development schemes and rehousing arrangements for families are postponed. [**734**]

House renovation grants

5. Part VII of the Act contains the provisions relating to the four types of house renovation grant for which local authorities may now, subject to certain qualifications, entertain applications:

—*improvement grants* available at the discretion of the local authority for works normally of a high all-round standard for the improvement or conversion—plus repair—of properties with a good life ahead of them. Authorities may fix grant up to a maximum appropriate percentage of the eligible expense. The Government has announced its intention to raise, by Order, the limits of eligible expense in section 64 of the Act to £3,200 in normal cases and to £3,700 where a house of three or more storeys is being converted;

—*intermediate grants* generally obtainable by owners as of right for the installation of missing standard amenities and the execution of repairs. The maximum eligible expense for intermediate grants is £700 for the provision of standard amenities and £800 for repairs; grants are fixed by reference to the appropriate percentage of eligible expense;

—*special grants* available at the local authority's discretion, for the installation of standard amenities in houses in multiple occupation at a maximum appropriate percentage of the rates of eligible expense set out in Schedule 6 to the Act;

—*repairs grants* available at the discretion of the local authority for the repair of dwellings (and not being works associated with the improvement or provision by conversion of dwellings) within housing action areas and general improvement areas in cases where the authority thinks it appropriate after taking into account the capacity of the applicant to finance the work without grant aid. This grant may be fixed by the authority up to a maximum appropriate percentage of eligible expense which itself may not exceed £800.

6. These provisions replace those contained in Part I of the Housing Act 1969 which, subject to the transitional arrangements described in paragraph 15 below, is duly repealed by section 130 of, and Schedule 15 to, the Act.

7. Appendix A contains specifications and directions in relation to the revised grant system. Guidance on matters falling within the local authority's discretion under Part VII of the Act is contained in Appendix B. **[735]**

8. *Exchequer contribution to grants.*—Although the Secretary of State's power to make contributions towards grants approved by local authorities is discretionary, the Government contribution towards the cost of grants will be paid in all instances in which the statutory requirements of a grant are met and where the local authority is satisfied that it would be right to pay grant. The Secretary of State reserves the right, however, in cases to which subsection (7) of section 78 of the Housing Act 1974 applies (*i.e.* in cases where he may, under section 37 (2) of the Act, nullify the declaration of a housing action area, or exclude certain land from such an area), not to pay any contribution or to pay a contribution at a relevant percentage of 75% only.

9. The estimates and particulars required by the Secretary of State in support of an application by a housing authority for an improvement contribution are set out in the model form at Appendix D. **[736]**

Compulsory improvement notices

10. Part VIII of the Act contains the new and strengthened provisions relating to compulsory improvement powers exercisable by local authorities in housing action areas and general improvement areas, and otherwise. These provisions replace those contained in the now-repealed Part II of the Housing Act 1964. Appendix E contains guidance on aspects of the new provisions. **[737]**

Miscellaneous provisions

11. *Control over local authority expenditure on improvement or conversion.*—Section 105 of the Act has not yet been brought into operation. Consultation

with local authorities will take place on the way in which the control will be exercised before the provision is given effect by order. It is not the intention of the Secretary of State to seek to authorise local authority expenditure on these programmes on a scheme-by-scheme basis. The aim will be to establish annual spending programmes within which authorities will be free to determine their priorities for the improvement of council dwellings. [**738**]

12. *Records.*—Subsection (2) of section 127 of the Act provides for any grant, subsidy or contribution under this Act to be payable subject to such conditions as to records, certificates, audit or otherwise as the Secretary of State may, with Treasury approval, impose. The relevant conditions are set out in Appendix F. [**739**]

Schedule 13: Use of local authority housing

13. Paragraph 4 of Schedule 13 to the Act imposes a duty on a local authority that has acquired a house, or a building which may be made suitable for use as a house, and undertakes the necessary work, to secure that is it used as housing accommodation as soon as practicable after the acquisition, or, as the case may be, after the completion of the work needed to make it suitable. This duty complements the existing duty under section 105 (4) of the Housing Act 1957 of an authority that has acquired a building which may be made suitable as a house to make it so suitable forthwith.

14. This provision should not be regarded as a reflection on the manner in which authorities have hitherto managed their estates; indeed their vacancy rates have latterly been generally lower than those in the private sector. It should rather serve as one statutory reflection of the need for unoccupied property in areas of housing shortage to be brought into use as soon as practicable. [**740**]

Schedule 14: Transitional arrangements for grants

15. Paragraph 7 (1) provides that, where an application for grant has been made under Part I of the Housing Act 1969 before the date of its repeal under the 1974 Act, that part shall continue to operate in relation to that application, whether or not it has been approved. Paragraph 7 (2) provides that, in order to allow an application for a grant under Part VII to be made, notwithstanding that all or some of the works were specified in an earlier application under Part I of the Housing Act 1969, the local authority concerned shall allow it to be withdrawn (whether or not it has been approved) unless the authority is satisfied that the works have begun.

16. The effect of these provisions is that, provided work has not started, an applicant may choose whether to proceed under the old or the new arrangements. In the case of a grant approved before the new provisions came into force, the onus will be on the applicant to apply, if he so wishes, for withdrawal of the earlier application. In the case of applications made under the earlier legislation but not yet approved, however, local authorities should take early steps to inform the respective applicants of their rights as set out in the previous paragraph and to ask them whether they wish the Council to proceed with the consideration of the existing application or to regard it as withdrawn pending submission of a fresh application. [**741**]

List of Appendices

17. Matters dealt with in detail in the Appendices to this circular are:

Appendix A: Specifications and Directions in respect of house renovation grants
Appendix B: Guidance on house renovation grants
Appendix C: Model forms for house renovation grants including form of grant conditions
Appendix D: Application form for improvement contributions
Appendix E: Guidance on aspects of compulsory improvement
Appendix F: Conditions as to records etc under section 127 of the Housing Act 1974. **[742]**

APPENDIX A

DIRECTIONS AND SPECIFICATIONS RELATING TO PART VII OF THE HOUSING ACT 1974

1. The following paragraphs of this Appendix set out the directions and specifications which the Secretary of State is empowered to issue under various provisions of Part VII of the Housing Act 1974. Unlike the guidance offered in Appendix B to this Circular, these directions and specifications have statutory force. **[743]**

Section 56

2. *Dwellings provided after 2nd October 1961.*—The provision in subsection (3) of Section 56 generally prohibits a local authority from entertaining applications involving the provision of dwellings by conversion of buildings erected after 2 October 1961. Similarly the section prohibits the entertainment of applications relating to the improvement or repair of any dwellings provided after that date. This prohibition extends to all four types of grant the restriction which, by virtue of section 8 (3) of the Housing Act 1969, previously applied only in the case of standard grants. The significance of the date is that since 2 October 1961 a local authority has had the power, under section 33 of the Public Health Act 1961, to reject plans for dwellings that did not have a bathroom, with a fixed bath or shower, and a means of supplying hot and cold water thereto.

3. The provision in subsection (4) of section 56 recognises, however, that there may occasionally be circumstances in which it would be appropriate for a local authority to entertain an application for a grant in respect of a dwelling provided after 2 October 1961, but this discretion is subject to any general or special direction that the Secretary of State may give. In exercise of his powers under subsection (4) of section 56, therefore, the Secretary of State *hereby directs* that local authorities may only entertain applications to which the restriction in paragraphs (*a*) or (*b*) of subsection (3) would otherwise apply, where, as a consequence of the plans for the dwelling having been approved prior to that date, one or more of the standard amenities were not installed in the completed dwelling. **[744]**

Section 57 (2)

4. *Grant applications.*—The Secretary of State, in exercise of his powers under section 57 (2) of the Act, *hereby specifies* that the particulars which an application for improvement grant must contain (in addition to particulars required under section 57 (2) (*a*) and (*b*) and the certificate of future occupation required under section 60) are:

(i) in the case of works of improvement, plans showing the dwelling or dwellings to which the application relates before and after the proposed works of improvement are carried out;

(ii) in the case of works of conversion, plans showing the building or buildings to which the application relates before and after the proposed works of conversion are carried out;

(iii) a specification of the works proposed to be carried out;

(iv) in the case of dwellings in respect of which a certificate of availability for letting has been provided by the applicant, a statement of what housing arrangements, if any, are to be made for any existing tenants and their households during and after improvement;

(v) a statement that the dwelling was provided before 2 October 1961 or in the case of works of conversion, that the house or other building to be converted was erected before that date; and

(vi) a statement of the rateable value or values of the dwelling or dwellings to which the application relates.

For intermediate and repairs grants the specifications set out at sub-paragraphs (i), (iii), (iv) and (v) above apply. For special grants the specifications set out at sub-paragraphs (i), (iii) and (v) apply.

5. Further details about housing arrangements (see paragraph 4 (iv) above) are contained in Appendix E to this Circular. Except in those cases where a dwelling is the subject of a compulsory improvement notice, there is no statutory requirement that a local authority should be satisfied about the temporary or permanent rehousing of tenants in dwellings for which a grant application has been received. However, the Secretary of State advises local authorities to have careful regard to this aspect when deciding whether or not discretionary grants (*i.e.* improvement, special or repairs grants) should be approved.

6. The above-stated requirements have been incorporated in the model forms of application for house renovation grants—see Appendix C. [**745**]

Section 57 (4)

7. *Applications which may not be entertained.*—Subsection (4) of section 57 empowers the Secretary of State to give directions to local authorities, either generally or individually, to prevent them from approving applications for an improvement grant or intermediate grant of a specified description unless they have his consent. This reflects the Government's belief that, whilst local authorities should continue to exercise considerable discretion in assessing the needs of individual applicants, certain matters call for a common approach. In exercise, therefore, of his powers under section 57 (4), the Secretary of State *hereby directs generally* that, insofar as an application for an improvement grant or an intermediate grant is of a description specified below, a local authority

shall not approve such an application unless the consent of the Secretary of State has been obtained under section 57 (4):

(i) an application which includes works for insulating a dwelling against heat loss;

(ii) an application for an improvement grant which relates to a dwelling in respect of which a previous improvement grant (or the final instalment thereof) has been paid during the period of 30 years immediately preceding the date of application and where that previous grant had been intended to bring that dwelling up to the full required standard;

(iii) an application for an improvement grant for the provision of a dwelling by the conversion of premises which do not, at the date of application, comprise at least one house.

8. In relation to paragraph 7 (i) above, the Secretary of State would give sympathetic consideration to any submissions made to him by local authorities only in respect of applications from elderly or disabled persons in circumstances where the local authorities consider that the applicants could not reasonably meet without grant-aid the cost of carrying out works of thermal insulation of roof spaces to the standard set out in paragraph 11 of this Appendix. The Secretary of State would not approve grant towards the cost of insulation in any other circumstances.

9. In relation to paragraph 7 (ii) above, in cases where a previous improvement had *not* been intended to bring a dwelling up to the full required standard, a further improvement grant may be given at the discretion of the local authority. In such cases, the Secretary of State advises authorities that, in fixing the amount of grant, account should be taken of the amount of the earlier grant paid.

10. The restriction in paragraph 7 (iii) above is necessary to cover those cases where the rateable value limitation does not apply—*e.g.* the conversion of barns, oast houses, railway stations etc. Before giving this consent in any individual cases the Secretary of State will expect the local authority to confirm that such a conversion would be of advantage to the housing authority and to explain why, in the authority's view, it is appropriate for the applicant to receive help from public funds, having regard to general evidence as to his financial means. **[746]**

Section 61

11. *Standard of dwellings improved or provided by conversion with aid of improvement grant.*—The Secretary of State, in exercise of his powers under section 61 (3) (*c*) of the Act, *hereby specifies* that the requirements with respect to construction and physical conditions and the provision of services and amenities with which a dwelling must conform on completion of works of improvement or conversion (in addition to the other standards laid down in section 61 (3) but subject to the power of local authorities in section 61 (4) to dispense with any requirement with which it appears to them not practicable for a dwelling to conform), are that the dwelling must:

(i) be substantially free from damp;

(ii) have adequate natural lighting and ventilation in each habitable room;

(iii) have adequate and safe provision throughout for artificial lighting, and have sufficient electric socket outlets for the safe and proper functioning of domestic appliances;
(iv) be provided with adequate drainage facilities;
(v) be in a stable structural condition;
(vi) have satisfactory internal arrangements;
(vii) have satisfactory facilities for preparing and cooking food;
(viii) be provided with adequate facilities for heating;
(ix) have proper provision for the storage of fuel (where necessary) and for the storage of refuse; and
(x) conform with the specifications applicable to the thermal insulation of roof spaces laid down in Part F of the Building Regulations in force at the date of the grant approval.

12. These specifications, which reflect certain changes in the former "12 point" standard, incorporate those matters specified in section 4 of the Housing Act 1957 (which relates to "fitness") that are not covered by the provisions of section 61 (3) (*a*) and (*b*) of the 1974 Act. The references to, for example, structural stability and internal arrangement should be interpreted in accordance with the standard adopted for the purposes of section 4 of the Housing Act 1957.

13. The specification at paragraph 11 (*x*) relating to thermal insulation should be read in conjunction with paragraph 14 of this Appendix, and also paragraph 7 (*i*), which generally rules out grant aid for thermal insulation. [**747**]

Section 66

14. *Intermediate Grant: Thermal insulation.*—In exercise of his powers under subsection 2 (*c*) of this section the Secretary of State *hereby specifies* that the requirements with respect to thermal insulation, with which a dwelling must conform to fulfill one of the conditions for attaining the full standard for intermediate grant, are those applicable to roof spaces in Part F of the Building Regulations in force at the time of the grant approval.

15. Part F of the Building Regulations at present specifies that roof spaces should have a thermal transfer co-efficient of not more that 1·42. Proposals have however been circulated for improving the standard to 0·6—the equivalent of, for instance, 50 mm of insulating quilt. [**748**]

APPENDIX B

Guidance on Grant Approvals

1. The purpose of this Appendix is to discuss some issues of general relevance to the house renovation grant system, and to offer guidance on certain aspects of it. On none of the matters dealt with is it the Secretary of State's intention to impose rules to which local authorities must conform; on the various issues discussed in this Appendix authorities have wide discretion to decide whether or not they will approve grant-aid, and, in certain cases, to what extent. Nevertheless the Secretary of State hopes that the advice

contained herein will be useful, to, and noted by, local authorities. It is not exhaustive, however, and much of the guidance contained in earlier Circulars remains valid. [**749**]

Matters common to all grants

2. *Standard amenities: ancillary works* (*Section 58*).—The intermediate grant, unlike the former standard grant, does not cover ancillary expenditure related to the provision of a standard amenity but beyond the limits specified for the amenity itself—*e.g.* on works to bring a piped supply of cold water to the dwelling for the first time, or the installation of a septic tank or a cesspool (see Part III of Schedule I to the Housing Act 1969). Subject to the relevant provisions of the Act, however, it is open to local authorities to grant aid such works by approving improvement grants for this purpose, to a reduced standard if necessary. The Secretary of State would hope that applications relating to such works would receive no less sympathetic consideration for approval for improvement grant than would have been the case had the former provisions relating to standard grants continued to apply. [**750**]

3. *Appropriate percentage of grant* (*Section 59*).—It should be noted that for improvement, repairs or special grants it is open to local authorities to approve grants at percentages lower than the maximum appropriate percentages specified in section 59 (1) should they so wish. Under section 80 of the Act, however, a local authority fixing grant at less than the appropriate percentage is required to state to the applicant its reasons for so doing. [**751**]

4. *Undue hardship* (*Sections 59* (*2*) *and 71* (*2*).—Section 59 (2) of the Act relates to premises which, on the date of the grant approval, are in a housing action area, and enables the local authority, in determining the amount of grant, to increase the appropriate percentage (beyond the normal limit of 75 per cent.) up to 90 per cent. if the local authority is satisfied that the applicant (including those who are landlords) will not without undue hardship be able to finance his share of the cost of improvement or repairs. Similarly, a local authority in receipt of an application for a repairs grant is required under section 71 (2) to consider whether the applicant would without undue hardship be able to finance the cost of the relevant works without the help of such a grant. Although local authorities may find it helpful to have this guidance on how to assess "undue hardship" for these purposes, it is stressed that there may well be other deserving cases not covered by the following examples; local authorities should, therefore, consider each application carefully on its merits.

5. The onus would usually rest with applicants to show why exceptional help towards the cost of the work is necessary to avoid hardship, and a statement of the financial resources of any such applicant would, therefore, normally be expected. Many people, especially the elderly, are reluctant to divulge their financial resources. Local authorities are advised, therefore, to emphasise that any information they receive will be treated in the strictest confidence—and so to treat it. Favourable consideration should generally be given to applicants whose financial resources would qualify them for supplementary benefit, even if such benefit has not been claimed; and, although criteria related to income, upon which eligibility for rate rebate is assessed, are not necessarily a true reflection of ability to meet capital expenditure, many of those qualifying for

rate rebate are unlikely to have adequate savings to meet their normal share of the cost or have sufficient income to bear without stress the loan charges that would arise if they resorted to borrowing. Finally, very sympathetic consideration should be given to any applicant whose principal source of income consists of a state retirement or disability pension. **[752]**

6. *Certificates of future occupation* (*Section 60*).—Under section 60 of the Act applicants are normally required to submit a certificate of future occupation with their applications for grants other than special grants. (This does not apply to those categories of applicant specified in section 83 of the Act). In general, the effect of this will be that grant applications cannot be entertained by a local authority unless the applicant certifies that he intends to reside in the improved dwelling as an owner-occupier or that he intends to let the dwelling. Special provision is made for dwellings occupied or kept available for occupation by a member of the agricultural population in pursuit of a contract of service. The provisions of sections 73 and 74 relating to grant conditions are, of course, relevant, but local authorities should also note that a person who obtains a grant by signing a false declaration under this section might be guilty of a criminal offence, under section 15 of the Theft Act 1968, punishable by imprisonment for up to ten years.

7. The provisions of this section should in particular prevent grants being approved in respect of dwellings which are to be used as second homes; or which are being improved by property companies prior to being sold for owner-occupation.

8. An applicant who is, or who intends to become, the owner-occupier of a dwelling to be improved would provide a "certificate of owner-occupation". This should certify that the applicant intends that, on or before the first anniversary of the date on which the dwelling is certified by the local authority as being fit for occupation after completion of the relevant works to its satisfaction (the "certified date"—see section 75 (6)), and throughout the next 4 years, the dwelling will be his only or main residence for exclusive occupation by himself and any members of his household. The requirement as to the dwelling being the applicant's *only or main* residence does not necessarily apply during the first year of "the initial period" for the purposes of grant conditions (see section 73), thereby enabling those who wish to improve a dwelling for subsequent use as their principal residence (*e.g.* on retirement) to have one year in which to do so.

9. An applicant who is, or who intends to become, the landlord of a dwelling to be improved would provide a "certificate of availability for letting". This should certify that the applicant intends, throughout the period of 5 years beginning with the certified date, that the dwelling will be let or kept genuinely available for letting as a residence. In all such cases the relevant conditions in section 73 (4) apply automatically. Section 74 (2) contains further conditions, applicable other than to special grants, essentially relating to the letting, or to the availability for letting, of the dwelling.

10. Local authorities should note carefully that certificates of future occupation cannot be regarded as an entirely foolproof means of preventing abuses of the grant system from occurring from time to time. Local authorities should remain vigilant when considering applications for improvement grants and

should not hesitate to exercise their discretion to refuse grant in any case where they judge it likely that the result of the renovation will not contribute towards the alleviation of housing problems in their district. Similarly it will be for local authorities to satisfy themselves that breaches of grant conditions have not taken place, and to take appropriate action under section 76 in the event of such breaches. **[753]**

11. *Grant conditions* (*Section 73 and 74*).—The obligatory conditions set out in section 73 of the Act are essentially a corollary of the certificates of future occupation accompanying grant applications under section 60. Together with sections 75 and 76 they broadly ensure that, if the use made of the improved dwelling throughout the period of the conditions is not consistent with the intention stated in the certificate, the grant is repayable with compound interest. Section 74 sets out further conditions which are obligatory when the dwelling in a housing action area (where they apply, in the case of dwellings in respect of which a certificate of availability for letting was given, for 7 years instead of the normal 5), a general improvement area or a priority neighbourhood, but are elsewhere discretionary. These are the only conditions which a local authority is permitted to attach to the payment of grant. **[754]**

12. "*Certified date*" (*Section 75*).—Part VII introduces for the first time the concept of "the certified date", which is defined in section 75 (6) as the date certified by the local authority which approved a grant as the date on which the dwelling first becomes fit for occupation after the completion of the relevant works to their satisfaction. The "certified date" is of relevance throughout the provisions relating to certificates of future occupation and to grant conditions; and, under section 81, if an applicant or successor ceases before the certified date to have the relevant interest in the property, he forfeits the grant.

13. Local authorities will therefore wish to note that, in addition to satisfying themselves, as under earlier legislation, that the works have been executed to their satisfaction, they are now also thereafter required to decide on what date the dwelling becomes fit for occupation and to certify the same. It would seem appropriate for these two aspects to be dealt with simultaneously, not least to avoid a hiatus between payment of grant and the coming into operation of the grant conditions. **[755]**

14. *Repayment of grant on breach of conditions* (*Section 76*).—Section 76 of the Act provides for the repayment of grant in the event of a breach of condition. Although the amount recoverable is normally a sum equal to the original grant plus compound interest calculated in the manner provided for in section 76 (6), a local authority has discretion under subsection (4) of this section not to demand a payment from the owner of dwelling if a grant condition is breached, or to demand a lesser amount.

15. The two main situations with which the conditions are intended to deal, and in which the Secretary of State would advise local authorities not to exercise their discretion to reduce or waive repayment of grant, would be:—

(i) where an owner-occupier improves a house and then uses it as a second home or sells it in order to realise a profit, and

(ii) where a landlord, having improved a tenanted house, removes the tenants, probably with the intention of selling with vacant possession.

At the other end of the scale there will no doubt be a few instances—for example, where sale is forced on an owner-occupier through circumstances beyond his control, perhaps because he has to move with his job or buy another house because of an increase in family—where local authorities might reasonably decide not to demand any repayment at all. Between the two extremes, however, there are likely to be many cases where breaches of various kinds will occur, especially where owners decide, for any one of a number of reasons, to dispose of their property. Each case ought to be considered on its merits but in most circumstances local authorities may consider it appropriate to demand repayment of an amount which reflects that proportion of the conditions period which remains unexpired. In cases of difficulty the Secretary of State would be prepared to offer advice should local authorities wish to consult the Department. **[756]**

16. *Revision of grant after approval* (*Section 57*).—Section 57 (7) of the Act enables a local authority, after approving a grant application and on receipt of a further estimate, to redetermine the estimated expense provided the authority is satisfied that, due to circumstances beyond the control of the applicant, the relevant works will not be carried out on the basis of the original estimate. This is intended to provide a reasonable degree of flexibility in hard cases where an applicant, through no fault of his own, is unable to proceed with an improvement because his original grant approval is incapable of being acted upon. Local authorities are advised to exercise this power only if:—

(i) the original contractor is no longer prepared to carry out the work on the basis of his tender;

(ii) the failure on the part of the contractor was due entirely to matters beyond the control of the applicant; and

(iii) the further estimate submitted is from a different contractor **[757]**

17. *Grant not payable after property is sold* (*Section 81*).—For the avoidance of doubt, section 81 (2) of the Act makes it clear that no grant shall be paid if an applicant relinquishes his interest in the dwelling before the date certified by the local authority as the date on which the dwelling concerned first became fit for occupation after completion of the works. Accordingly the advice in DOE Circular 81/73 (Welsh Office Circular 151/73) no longer applies. **[758]**

Improvement grants

18. *Disabled persons* (*Section 56*).—As a result of an amendment during House of Lords Report stage the description in section 56 (2) (*a*) of works for which an improvement grant may be given was extended to refer to registered disabled persons. Although the precise effect of the amendment is not altogether clear, it would seem that where the dwelling concerned is *to be occupied by* a registered disabled person (normally either the applicant or a member of his household), the grant can cover, "works required for his welfare, accommodation or employment where the existing dwelling is inadequate or unsuitable for those purposes". **[759]**

19. *Rateable value limits*, (*Section 62*).—The Secretary of State in exercise of his powers under section 62 (3), and with Treasury consent, will be making an Order specifying the limits of rateable value which will determine whether

applications for improvement grant may be approved in respect of dwellings for which a certificate of owner-occupation has been provided. The limits in the Order will be rateable values in excess of £300 for Greater London, and in excess of £175 for the rest of England and Wales. It should be noted that the provisions of section 62 do not apply to dwellings in respect of which a certificate of availability for letting has been given by the applicant; nor do they apply in cases where the application relates to an intermediate, repair or special grant. **[760]**

20. *Enlargements and extensions.*—The enlargement of a house, which is already adequate in other respects (for example, to provide additional living or bedroom space by an extension or loft conversion), cannot be regarded as a high priority in terms of the house renovation programme, even if the house in its original form is too small for the occupants for the time being. The use of public funds for an increase in bedroom space in an otherwise adequate dwelling should be very rare, although it would be reasonable to make an exception in the case of dwellings in isolated positions occupied by families who, because of the nature of their livelihood, cannot be expected to seek alternative accommodation. The extension of a house to provide a first bathroom or a more adequate kitchen is, of course, an entirely different matter. In the view of the Secretary of State, however, grant towards any such extension should be kept to a minimum consistent with the basic requirements of the resident family. **[761]**

21. *Fire escapes.*—The cost of any necessary means of escape from fire may be accepted as part of the eligible cost of the works for improvement grant purposes, notably where the conversion of a property into separate flats is being undertaken with the aid of a grant. Local authorities are free also to exercise their discretion in suitable cases to approve improvement grant to cover a proportion of the cost of fire escapes even where these do not form part of a comprehensive improvement scheme. In dealing with any such applications, local authorities ought to consider whether the absence of the facilities proposed would pose a serious threat to the safety of the occupants in the event of fire. **[762]**

22. *Electrical rewiring.*—The renewal of existing electrical wiring is regarded as replacement and in view of the definition of "improvement" in section 84 of the Act, such works should not, in the Secretary of State's opinion, attract improvement grant unless carried out in conjunction with other improvements and accepted by the local authority as necessary to enable the dwelling to achieve the relevant standard. The installation of electric lighting or a power supply for the first time may, however, properly be regarded as an improvement. **[763]**

23. *Central heating.*—Grant towards the cost of space heating up to Parker Morris standards* may reasonably be given when this forms part of the cost of a scheme for converting a property into flats or for the comprehensive improvement of a dwelling. But in the Secretary of State's opinion grant should not be given for the installation of central heating, either on its own or linked with other inessential improvements. **[764]**

24. *Parker Morris Standards.*—Parker Morris standards are intended for new construction and cannot always be rigidly applied to conversions and

* Appendix 1 of MHLG Circular 36/67 (Welsh Office Circular 28/67).

improvements. If an owner can meet the required standard contained in section 61 of the Act he or she ought to be able to expect sympathetic consideration of the application for grant, subject, of course, to the basic requirements laid down for the payment of grant being satisfied. But the standard set out in section 61 is only a minimum. If owners are prepared to do more, authorities may approve grant towards the cost of any improvements which they consider to be reasonable. For example, an owner, carrying out a comprehensive scheme of improvements, who wished to achieve Parker Morris standards for fittings and equipment, (*e.g.* the scale of water closet and wash hand basin provision, kitchen fitments and electric socket outlets) could be assisted by grant aid, within the maximum eligible expense, if, in the authority's judgment, the result would be worth the cost. It is important, however, that replacement of existing and adequate amenities should be kept to the minimum—see paragraph 26 below. [**765**]

25. *Water and drainage.*—For improvements involving the provision of water and drainage facilities it is particularly important to bear in mind that house renovation grants are available only for works within the curtilage of a dwelling. Within this limitation, improvement grant may be given for the necessary provision of service piping to and from a fitment which is itself an improvement; for the provision of a separate service pipe where a common service pipe exists but where this is inadequate; for the provision for the first time of piped water supply; or for the provision of a septic tank or a cesspool where the local authority is satisfied that connection with main drainage is not reasonably practicable. The replacement of mains supply or internal piping or a change-over from septic tank or cesspool to main drainage ought not, in the Secretary of State's view, to attract grant if it does not form part of a comprehensive scheme of improvement. [**766**]

26. *Repairs and replacements.*—The proportion of *an improvement grant* that may relate to repairs and replacements remains limited to a maximum of 50 per cent. of the estimated expense. These works should consist of repairs and replacements needed, in the opinion of the local authority, for the purpose of enabling the dwelling to attain the relevant standard. The extent of repairs and replacements justified for grant purposes in any individual case is a matter for the judgment of local authorities, especially where a house is having its life extended for a considerable span of years. It can be difficult to strike a balance between the minimum repairs needed to put a house in a reasonable condition and those which could be justified on the grounds that they would substantially reduce the owner's future maintenance liability. As a broad guide, where a house is being improved to the "30 year life" standard, it would be reasonable to allow for grant all repairs that would be likely to arise within a few years of the improvement if not carried out as part of the major scheme. These could include re-roofing, replacement of ineffective damp-proof courses, suspect electrical wiring and defective rainwater pipes and guttering. In all cases, the cost of repairs and redecorations to make good damage occurring as a result of carrying out improvements would normally attract grant as being incidental to those improvements, but any other internal decorative repair ought, in the Secretary of State's view, generally to be excluded.

27. Where the local authority uses its power to substitute a higher amount of estimated expense because unforeseen works arise after approval, the pro-

portion of the cost of repairs and replacements should be calculated on the basis of the revised estimated expense. For example, if the original estimate was £1,000, made up of £200 of repairs and £800 of other improvements, and if unforeseen works cost another £900 of which £800 were for repairs and £100 for improvements, the final eligible expense would be £1,800 made up of £900 improvements and a matching £900 of repair costs. **[767]**

28. *Higher amounts of improvement grant* (*Section 64*).—Section 64 (5) of the Act gives the Secretary of State power to substitute a higher amount than the relevant limit of the eligible expense if he is satisfied that there are good reasons for doing so with respect to a particular case or description of case. Applications for higher limits to be approved in individual cases may be submitted to the appropriate regional office of the Department of the Environment or the Welsh Office, and will be considered on their merits. However, it should be noted that in view of the increased limits of eligible expense to be introduced by Order, approval by the Secretary of State is likely to be given only in the exceptional circumstances described in the following paragraph. **[768]**

29. *Listed Buildings*.—If, in the course of improvements to a building listed as being of special architectural or historic interest, it is necessary to incur extra expenditure on specific works, materials or architectural detail required to maintain the character or quality of the building concerned, the Secretary of State will be prepared to consider, in respect of cases falling within the aforementioned description, an increase in the normal limit on eligible expense. Attention is, however, drawn to the grants available for repairs under the Historic Buildings Acts and the need to ensure that a historic buildings grant and an improvement grant are not given for the same works of repair. **[769]**

Intermediate grants

30. Intermediate grant replaces the former standard grant, but, in addition to assisting with the cost of providing missing basic amenities, the grant may also provide help towards the cost of repairs and replacements. **[770]**

31. *Disabled persons* (*Section 56*).—Sections 56 (2) (*b*) and 65 (3) incorporate special provisions relating to registered disabled persons. In the case of an application for an intermediate grant the Secretary of State takes the view that where the dwelling is to be occupied by a registered disabled person, the normal requirement that the dwelling should have been without the standard amenity concerned for not less than twelve months need not apply, so long as the existing amenity is inaccessible to that person because of his disability. **[771]**

32. *Estimates* (*Section 57*).—In addition to the particulars required in an application for an intermediate grant set out in section 65 (2) and specified by the Secretary of State under section 57 (2) (*c*), an estimate of the cost will henceforth be required under section 57 (2) (*b*). Intermediate grants—unlike the former standard grants—are not paid on actual costs but are based on estimates. **[772]**

33. *Relevant standard* (*Section 66*).—The conditions to be fulfilled for a dwelling to attain the relevant standard are set out in section 66. Local authorities are placed under a duty to pay grant to an applicant provided various requirements of the Act are satisfied. Under section 65 (3), however, the authority must normally be satisfied that the amenity has either been missing for at least a year or must necessarily be disturbed or replaced. The main purpose of this

requirement is to prevent the payment of grant where standard amenities have been removed in order to claim grant for new ones. [**773**]

34. *Repairs and replacements* (*Section 67*).—The introduction of the cost of repairs or replacements into the grant calculation means that the local authority must make the necessary judgments before the work is carried out, so that the applicant can be fully aware of the grant position before he enters into any commitment with his builder. At this state the local authority will also have to decide on the extent and expense of the works of repair or replacement needed, and to notify the applicant of its decision. For example, the question of whether it is necessary to execute works to put a dwelling into good repair, make it fit and give it a 15 year life, and the extent and proper cost of those works are matters which will warrant full consideration before grant is approved. In the opinion of the Secretary of State, however, intermediate grant should not be approved in respect of any repairs which, in the local authority's estimation, exceed the full standard for intermediate grant. [**774**]

35. *Relationship with compulsory improvement notice* (*Section 67* (*2*)).—It should also be noted that works which are to be required to be carried out in consequence of the service of a compulsory improvement notice automatically qualify for the payment of an intermediate grant, even if those works are to a reduced standard. [**775**]

Special grants

36. *Circumstances in which appropriate.*—Local authorities have power to approve an application for a special grant in such circumstances as they think fit, subject to the statutory provisions about the information to be included in the application (a model application form is at Appendix C). Local authorities have wide discretion to make a special grant towards providing any of the standard amenities or any number or combination of these amenities in a house in multiple occupation. There will usually be no immediate prospect of a thorough-going conversion of such houses into flats. Such amenities as exist will often be shared between two or more families. The object of special grants should be to encourage the provision where required of additional sinks with hot and cold water supplies and more water closets, and perhaps in some cases baths and wash hand basins with hot and cold water supplies. Although some of the amenities will still be shared, life in the house will be more tolerable than previously.

37. The Secretary of State hopes that these powers will be exercised mainly by those local authorities with areas of intensive multiple occupation within which, to a greater or lesser extent, the regulatory powers under the Housing Acts 1961 and 1964 to improve conditions in houses in multiple occupation will be in use. Special grants are in no way a substitute for these powers but should enable local authorities to give help, when appropriate, and thus create a better chance of enlisting the co-operation of the person in charge of the property. The grants are not intended to assist in creating multi-occupation, but to relieve bad conditions where multi-occupation already exists.

38. The improvements to be aided by grant should at least achieve the standard which the local authority would require under its regulatory powers. In appropriate circumstances an owner might be encouraged by the prospect

of a grant to make provision above that basic level. The authority could also help in cases where it is known that an owner occupier has heavy mortgage commitments and where the authority intends to limit the number of persons who may live in the house while, at the same time, requiring the installation of more amenities.

39. The provisions of Part I of Schedule 6 to the Act apply to special grants but the concessions in Part II do not. For special grants, a fixed bath or shower must be in a bathroom; no requirement is made about the location of the water closet.

40. As in the case of intermediate grant, an estimate of the cost will be required with an application for a special grant.

41. In section 129, "house in multiple occupation" is defined as a house which is occupied by persons who do not form a single household, exclusive of any part thereof which is occupied as a separate dwelling by persons who do form a single household. Local authorities should seek to distinguish which parts of a house are capable of being improved as separate entities, and which, on the basis of separate occupation, would as a minimum be eligible for intermediate grant for the provision of standard amenities and associated repairs. It should be noted that special grants do not cover the cost of repairs or replacement arising in respect of houses in multiple occupation. **[776]**

Repair grants

42. These grants, available only in housing action areas and general improvement areas, are intended to help owners with limited means to carry out basic repairs that they would not otherwise be able to finance. Repairs grants are entirely discretionary. In deciding whether to approve an application a local authority is, however, required to take into account the capacity of the applicant to finance, without undue hardship, the cost of the works without a grant. Guidance on how to assess hardship in relation to the award of 90 per cent. grants in housing action areas (see paragraphs 4 and 5 of this Appendix) applies equally in this context.

43. It is for local authorities to determine what standard of repairs might be grant-aided in these circumstances, but the grant could, for example, appropriately be used to help meet the cost of essential repairs such as might be the subject of a compulsory repairs notice under section 9 of the Housing Act 1957 (as amended). **[777]**

General questions on administration

44. Local authorities have been asked in previous circulars to review their internal arrangements with a view to handling grant applications with due efficiency and despatch. Nevertheless complaints continue to be received in both Departments about delays both in approving grants and in making payments when the work has been completed. Undue delays wherever they occur often discourage house owners from proceeding with improvements or lead builders to lose enthusiasm for this type of work. The aim should be to reach a decision on approvals within 6 weeks of a full application being received. Local authorities are also urged to ensure that when improvements have been completed the work is promptly and thoroughly inspected. On being satisfied

as to the quality of the improvement, the local authority should make every effort to expedite payment of grant. [**778**]

45. *Estimates.*—Many authorities are normally willing to accept one estimate and to rely on the knowledge and experience of their officers to assess its reasonableness. The Secretary of State commends this practice. Indeed, it is doubtful whether it would be proper, in the case of an intermediate grant application, for a local authority to insist on more than one estimate. A stipulation that more than two estimates must be provided inevitably slows down the process of making application. In addition the uncertainty of getting work for which they have estimated creates a reluctance on the part of local builders to estimate for individual jobs and to interest themselves in improvement work generally. [**779**]

46. *Value Added Tax.*—Since works of repair and maintenance are taxable at the standard rate, whereas alterations are zero-rated, it is desirable that, to avoid the possibility of VAT being charged on the whole of an improvement scheme, separate estimates of taxable and non-taxable work should be provided by builders. Local authorities will doubtless take suitable steps, as part of the liaison arrangements referred to in paragraph 49 below, to inform those concerned of the correct position. [**780**]

47. *Co-ordinated handling of applications.*—Most applications have to be referred to several departments of the authority, but arrangements should be made to enable them to be considered concurrently. It is particularly important that once a formal application has been made to the authority no responsibility should rest upon the applicant himself for ensuring that the application is cleared by all the departments involved. Many authorities have made the co-ordinated handling of applications a responsibility either of a specially appointed improvement officer or of another suitable nominated officer. Proper co-ordination should ensure that, once the application has been checked, consideration and action by the individual departments may proceed simultaneously and that, if committee decision is needed, it is taken as early as possible. [**781**]

48. *Committee machinery.*—It is important that, where processing of an application has moved quickly to a favourable recommendation at official level, delay should be avoided if the matter has then to be referred to a council committee. The committee machinery and the extent of authority delegated to officers will vary from council to council, but in the interests of efficiency it is desirable that where grant applications come before a committee or sub-committee they should not require scrutiny by more than one such body, and that every effort should be made to reach a decision on first presentation of the case. [**782**]

49. *Liaison with local bodies.*—A continuing liaison and exchange of views with local bodies representing builders, builders' merchants, architects, estate agents, building societies and others who may advise clients and in some cases submit grant applications on their behalf can help to ensure the smooth and efficient handling of applications. Since applications which fail to include all the necessary information are a source of delay, it is important that these local interests should be aware of the current requirements and the normal timetable of the authority for processing a properly completed application. Local branches of the building trade organisations are increasingly active in helping to

publicise the scheme and their experience in advising clients and submitting applications on their behalf can be a great help to the authority. **[783]**

50. *Applications from builders.*—Where a firm of builders carry out works to properties which they own, the Secretary of State considers that it would be reasonable to treat their application in the normal way. The authority should, however, consider carefully whether it should approve a discretionary grant in circumstances where the only effect of so doing would be to add to the profits of a builder who would go ahead with the scheme as a commercial venture even without grant. **[784]**

51. *"Do-it-yourself" applicants.*—In cases where an applicant who is not a builder himself carries out works to his own dwelling, many local authorities regard it is appropriate to exclude from the estimated expense any notional charge for the applicant's own labour. The Secretary of State commends this approach. **[785]**

52. *Payment of grant direct to builders.*—There is nothing to prevent an applicant arranging with the local authority for grant to be paid at his request direct to the person or firm carrying out the work. Authorities may wish to give sympathetic consideration to requests of this kind. It should be made plain, however, that it is entirely for the applicant to decide whether he wants payment to be made in this way.

53. Attention is drawn to the two forms of contract which have been issued by the Joint Contracts Tribunal for use in grant aided improvement works. One is for use where an architect or superintending officer is acting for the employer and the other is for use where the employer has not engaged an architect or supervising officer. Under both forms the local authority can be authorised by the building owner to pay grant direct to the builder. The Secretary of State would like local authorities to accept freely any of these completed authorisation forms. Where applicants make use of these forms authorities are not expected to suggest that legal advice should be obtained. But if there were any possibility of payment of grant by instalments the local authority should make sure that the applicant understands that he, and not the builder, would be responsible for repaying to the authority any instalments already paid if the works were not completed within the specified time. **[786]**

54. *Power to make advances.*—Authorities are encouraged to make full use of their powers to make advances to house owners on mortgage terms for the improvement or repair of houses, under section 43 of the Housing (Financial Provisions) Act 1958. This section was clarified and strengthened by section 37 of the Local Government Act 1974 which enables authorities to make an advance for the repayment of a previous loan issued for any of the purposes specified in section 43 of the 1958 Act, provided that the advance will be used primarily to meet the housing needs of the applicant. Authorities may find this power useful where an owner-occupier wants to borrow money for house improvements but is unable to get a further advance from the original lender, since an authority will be able to make a loan which is large enough to pay off the subsisting mortgage and to cover the cost of the improvements.

55. Section 37 of the Local Government Act 1974 also gives local authorities a general power to grant maturity mortgages in place of the previous power in

section 74 of the Housing Act 1969. Under this type of advance the capital sum need not be repayable until the end of a fixed period (with or without provision for the period to be extended) or on the happening of a specified event before the end of that period. This type of loan can be particularly helpful to elderly people, and moreover the periodic payment of interest may in certain circumstances attract social security benefits. **[787]**

APPENDIX C

Model Forms of Application and Approval and of Grant Conditions

Model forms as under have been prepared for the guidance of local authorities:

Form No. 1 —Application for improvement grant
1A—Combined application for improvement grant and for qualification certificate
2 —Approval of application for improvement grant
3 —Application for intermediate grant
3A—Combined application for intermediate grant and for qualification certificate
4 —Approval of application for intermediate grant
5 —Application for special grant
6 —Approval of application for special grant
7 —Application for repairs grant
8 —Approval of application for repairs grant
9 —Certificate of owner-occupation
10 —Certificate of availability for letting

The following forms relate to grant conditions:

Form A—Conditions as to future occupation where a certificate of owner-occupation applies
B—Conditions as to future occupation where a certificate of availability for letting applies
C—Other conditions relating to the letting of dwellings improved with grant
D—Notes on grant conditions

Form A or form B (or forms B and C if appropriate), together with form D, should be attached by the local authority to the notice of approval.

These forms may be freely reproduced for the purposes described in this circular provided that the following legend appears on each copy:

> "Reproduced from Department of the Environment Circular 160/74 and Welsh Office Circular 266/74. Crown copyright."

Application must be made to the Controller of Her Majesty's Stationery Office for permission to reproduce for any other purpose. **[788]**

Form No. 1

HOUSING ACT 1974

APPLICATION FOR IMPROVEMENT GRANT

.... COUNCIL

Please complete and return this form to the Chief Executive of the Council.

DO NOT START ANY WORKS OF IMPROVEMENT OR CONVERSION BEFORE YOU HAVE RECEIVED NOTICE OF APPROVAL OF THIS APPLICATION, OTHERWISE A GRANT MAY NOT BE PAID. A CONSENT GIVEN FOR PLANNING OR BUILDING REGULATION PURPOSES IS NOT SUFFICIENT. YOU SHOULD THEREFORE WARN ANY PERSON ACTING FOR YOU IN THESE MATTERS NOT TO START WORK WITHOUT YOUR CONSENT.

---

1. (a) Address of the property to be improved or converted.

   (b) Was the building erected or dwelling provided by conversion before 3 October, 1961? If so, say when.

---

2. Name of applicant and address if different from 1.

---

3. (a) Are you the freeholder or leaseholder?

   (b) If leaseholder, how long has the lease to run?

---

4. Are you the occupier?

   (a) If so, state the current rateable value of the hereditament.

   (b) If not—

   (i) has any occupying tenant consented to the proposals?

   (ii) what housing arrangements, if any, are to be made for any occupying tenants and their households during and after improvements?

---

5. (a) Name and address of mortgagee (building society, etc.) if any.

   (b) Has the mortgagee consented to the making of this application?

   See note

---

6. Has any kind of house renovation grant ever been paid in respect of the property under this or earlier legislation? If so, give details.

---

7. Particulars of work to be carried out by you and estimated cost, indicating whether any of the works are for the welfare, accommodation or employment of a registered disabled person.

---

8. ENCLOSURES: Tick as enclosed

(a) Plans showing, in the case of improvements, the dwelling or dwellings (or, in the case of conversion, the building or buildings) to which the application relates before and after the proposed works are carried out.

(b) Specification of the works to be carried out with an estimate of the cost, distinguishing between

(i) grant-aided works of conversion/improvement, showing separately the works of replacement and repair on which grant is being claimed,

(ii) other works (if any),

(iii) professional fees.

(c) Certificate of future occupation.

---

9. Has any necessary permission been obtained (if so give dates):

(a) for planning purposes?

(b) for building regulation purposes?

I declare that to the best of my knowledge and belief the particulars in this application are correct.

Date .... Signature of applicant ....

Note: A mortgagor should always notify his building society or other mortgagee that he had applied for grant. Otherwise he may be breaking the terms of his mortgage deed. [**789**]

Form No. 1A

HOUSING ACT 1974/HOUSING FINANCE ACT 1972

COMBINED APPLICATION FOR IMPROVEMENT GRANT AND FOR QUALIFICATION CERTIFICATE

(where dwelling subject to a controlled tenancy does not have all the standard amenities)

.... COUNCIL

After reading the notes carefully please complete and return this form to the Chief Executive of the Council. A separate form must be completed for each dwelling subject to a controlled tenancy.

GRANT MAY NOT BE PAID IF YOU START WORK BEFORE GETTING THE NECESSARY CONSENT. A CONSENT GIVEN FOR PLANNING OR BUILDING REGULATION PURPOSES IS NOT SUFFICENT. YOU SHOULD THEREFORE WARN ANY PERSON ACTING FOR YOU IN THESE MATTERS NOT TO START WORK WITHOUT YOUR CONSENT.

---

1. (a) Address of the property to be improved or converted.

   (b) Was the building erected or dwelling provided by conversion before 3 October 1961?

---

2. Name of applicant and address if different from 1.

---

3. Address of the dwelling for which qualification certificate is sought if different from 1.

---

4. (a) Are you the freeholder or leaseholder?

   (b) If leaseholder, how long has the lease to run?

---

5. (a) Name of your tenant under the controlled tenancy of the dwelling.

   (b) Has he consented to the proposals?

   (c) What housing arrangements, if any, are to be made for him and his household during and after improvement?

---

6. Is the dwelling occupied partly for business and partly as living accommodation?

---

7. (a) Name and address of mortgagee (building society, etc.) if any.

   (b) Has the mortgagee consented to the making of this application?

   See note (i)

---

8. Has any kind of house renovation grant ever been paid in respect of the property under the Housing Act 1974 or earlier legislation? If so, give details.

---

9. Which standard amenities are at present lacking in the dwelling?

---

10. Particulars of works to be carried out by you and estimated cost, indicating whether any of the works are for the welfare, accommodation or employment of a registered disabled person.

---

11. ENCLOSURES: Tick as enclosed

(a) Plans showing, in the case of improvement, the dwelling or dwellings (or, in the case of conversion, the building or buildings) to which the application relates before and after the proposed works are carried out.

(b) Specification of the works to be carried out with an estimate of the cost, distinguishing between

(i) grant-aided works of conversion/improvement, showing separately the works of replacement and repair on which grant is being claimed.

(ii) other works (if any),

(iii) professional fees.

(c) Certificate of availability for letting.

---

12. Are all the works described under question 10 required in order to make the dwelling satisfy the qualifying conditions?

If the answer is "No" state which of these works are required for this purpose.

See note (*v*)

---

13. When the works are completed will the dwelling have all the standard amenities for the exclusive use of the occupants?

See note (*v*)

---

14. Has any necessary permission been obtained (if so give dates):

(a) for planning purposes?

(b) for building regulation purposes?

---

15. Date of commencement of tenancy (if before 6 July, 1957, it will be sufficient to say so).

I declare that to the best of my knowledge and belief the particulars in this application are correct.

Date .... Signature of applicant ....

Notes: (i) A mortgagor should always notify his building society or other mortgagee that he has applied for grant. Otherwise he may be breaking the terms of his mortgage deed.

(ii) An application for a qualification certificate should not be made on this form where the dwelling has all the standard amenities. *There is a separate form of application for that situation.*

(iii) The standard amenities are:

(a) A fixed bath or shower which must be in a bathroom unless this is not reasonably practicable (but must not be in a bedroom).

(b) A wash-hand basin.

(c) A sink.

(d) A water closet must be in, and accessible from within, the dwelling unless this is not reasonably practicable.

(e) A hot and cold water supply at the fixed bath or shower, at the wash-hand basin and at the sink.

(iv) The application may include works in addition to those needed to make the dwelling satisfy the qualifying conditions (note v); but the works needed for those conditions to be satisfied must be stated (question 12). A landlord will no doubt discuss his proposals with his tenant before submitting this application and he should bear in mind that, at a later stage in the procedure, he will need to obtain the tenant's consent in order to carry out improvements. If the tenant then withholds his consent, the landlord may in certain circumstances apply to the county court for an order authorising him to carry out works required to make a dwelling satisfy the qualifying conditions.

(v) The qualifying conditions are:

(a) that all the standard amenities are provided for the exclusive use of the occupants of the dwelling;

(b) that the dwelling is in good repair having regard to its age, character and locality and disregarding internal decorative repair; and

(c) that the dwelling is in all other respects fit for human habitation.

The standard of fitness for human habitation is laid down in section 4 of the Housing Act 1957 as amended by section 71 of the Housing Act 1969. A dwelling is "fit for human habitation" if it is reasonably suitable for occupation having regard to repairs, stability, freedom from damp, internal arrangement, natural lighting, ventilation, water supply, drainage and sanitary conveniences, and facilities for preparation and cooking of food and for the disposal of waste water.

(vi) A copy of the application will be sent by the Council to the tenant.

(vii) If the Council are satisfied that the qualifying conditions will be satisfied when the proposed works have been completed they will issue a certificate of provisional approval.

(viii) If the Council refuse to issue a certificate of provisional approval or a qualification certificate, the landlord will be sent a written statement of their reasons for doing so.

[(ix) Advice to both landlord and tenant on the procedure and on what happens as regards the rent, if the tenancy becomes regulated is contained in the booklet "Controlled Rents to Fair Rents" obtainable from the Council.] **[790]**

HOUSING ACT 1974 *Form No. 2*

APPROVAL OF APPLICATION FOR IMPROVEMENT GRANT

.... COUNCIL

To .... Reference No. ....
of ....

1. The Council have approved your application dated .... for improvement grant for the provision/improvement of .... dwellings by the conversion of/at ....

2. The Council have determined £............................ as being the amount of the expenses which, in their opinion, are proper to be incurred by you for the execution of the relevant works specified in the application. [This sum is made up as follows:

Brief description of dwelling/works	Estimated expense
....	....
....	....
....	......................]

3. The grant will be £................., representing ....% of the eligible expense of £.................

4. Subject to conditions referred to below, the grant will be paid to you on completion of the works to the Council's satisfaction, in accordance with the particulars, plans and specifications approved by them for the purpose [within .... months or such further time as the Council may allow].
See note (i)

5. The Council have decided to reduce the required standard by dispensing with the conditions to the following extent:

....
....

6. As from the date certified by the Council as the date on which the dwelling first becomes fit for occupation after the completion of the relevant work to their satisfaction, the conditions as to future occupation set out in section 73 [and section 74] of the Housing Act 1974 will have to be observed for a period. Details of the conditions, indicating the periods involved, are attached.

Dated this .... day of .... 19..............

....

Signature of authorised officer

Notes: (i) The Council may require that the works be carried out within such time (not being less than twelve months) as they may specify.

(ii) If you require any further information you should get in touch with Mr. .... at ...., telephone No. ...., quoting the above reference. **[791]**

Housing Act 1974 — *Form No.* 3

Application for Intermediate Grant

.... COUNCIL

Please complete and return this form to the Chief Executive of the Council. A separate form must be completed for each dwelling.

DO NOT START ANY OF THE WORK TO PROVIDE THE STANDARD AMENITIES LISTED IN PARAGRAPH 8 BEFORE YOU HAVE RECEIVED NOTICE OF APPROVAL OF THIS APPLICATION OTHERWISE A GRANT MAY NOT BE PAID. A CONSENT GIVEN FOR PLANNING OR BUILDING REGULATION PURPOSES IS NOT SUFFICIENT. YOU SHOULD THEREFORE WARN ANY PERSON ACTING FOR YOU IN THESE MATTERS NOT TO START WORK WITHOUT YOUR CONSENT.

1. Address of dwelling to be improved.

2. Name of applicant and address if different from 1.

3. (a) Are you the freeholder or leaseholder?
   (b) If leaseholder, how long has the lease to run?

4. (a) Are you the occupier?
   (b) If not—
      (i) has the occupier consented to the proposals?
      (ii) what housing arrangements, if any, are to be made for any existing tenant and his household during and after improvement?

5. (a) Name and address of mortgagee (building society, etc.) if any.
(b) Has the mortgagee consented to the making of this application?
See note (iv)

6. Was the dwelling provided before 3 October, 1961? If so, say when.

7. Particulars of works to be carried out by you and estimated cost.

8. The standard amenities are listed at (a) to (g) below.

The fixed bath or shower must be in a bathroom where this is reasonably practicable, but must not be in a bedroom.

Complete columns A and B

Standard amenities	*Col. A* *Tick those already available*	*Col. B* *Tick those to be provided*
(a) (i) A fixed bath or shower in a bathroom		
(ii) A fixed bath or shower elsewhere in the dwelling		
(b) A hot and cold water supply at a fixed bath or shower		
(c) A wash-hand basin		
(d) A hot and cold water supply at a wash-hand basin		
(e) A sink		
(f) A hot and cold water supply at a sink		
(g) A water closet (i) in and accessible from within the dwelling; or		
(ii) where the dwelling is part of a larger building, in such a position as to be readily accessible from the dwelling.		

9. In order to provide the amenities you have ticked in Column B is it necessary to interfere with or replace any of the amenities ticked in Column A? If so, give details.

---

10. (a) Has the dwelling, to the best of your knowledge and belief, been without the amenities ticked in Column B for a period of not less than 12 months ending with the date of this application?

(b) In the case of a registered disabled person, indicate which standard amenities are inaccessible because of his disability.

---

11. Will all the amenities be for the exclusive use of the occupants of the dwelling? If not, say how they will be shared.
See note (i)

---

12. Do you claim that it is not practicable at reasonable expense to provide the dwelling with all the standard amenities?
See note (ii)

---

13. ENCLOSURES: Tick as enclosed

(a) Plans showing the dwelling before and after the proposed works of improvement are carried out.

(b) Specification of the works to be carried out, with an estimate of the cost, distinguishing between

(i) grant-aided works for the provision of standard amenities,

(ii) works of replacement and repair on which grant is being claimed,
See note (iii)

(iii) other works (if any),

(iv) professional fees.

(c) Certificate of future occupation.

---

14. Has any necessary permission been obtained (if so give dates)

(a) for planning purposes?

(b) for building regulation purposes?

I declare that to the best of my knowledge and belief the particulars in this application are correct.

Date .... Signature of applicant ....

Notes: (i) The Council must approve an application for an intermediate grant which is made in accordance with the relevant provisions. These include the necessity for the dwelling, after improvement, to be provided with all the standard amenities (see question 8) for the exclusive use of its occupants (see question 11), to be in good repair, having regard to its age, character and locality (disregarding internal decorative repair), to be in all other respects fit for human habitation, conform with specified requirements for thermal insulation, and likely to remain fit and available for use as a dwelling for a period of not less than fifteen years.

(ii) In cases where the above requirements are not met the Council nevertheless may, at their discretion, approve (and in certain circumstances are obliged to approve) an application for intermediate grant.

(iii) In addition to grant for standard amenities, the Council may also make a grant towards the cost of repairs and replacements needed in their opinion to enable the dwelling to attain the relevant standard.

(iv) A mortgagor should always notify his building society, or other mortgagee that he has applied for grant. Otherwise he may be breaking the terms of his mortgage deed. [**792**]

Form No. 3A

HOUSING ACT 1974/HOUSING FINANCE ACT 1972

COMBINED APPLICATION FOR INTERMEDIATE GRANT AND FOR QUALIFICATION CERTIFICATE

(where dwelling subject to a controlled tenancy does not have all the standard amenities)

.... COUNCIL

After reading the notes carefully please complete and return this form to the Chief Executive of the Council. A separate form must be completed for each dwelling subject to a controlled tenancy.

GRANT MAY NOT BE PAID IF YOU START WORK BEFORE GETTING THE NECESSARY CONSENT. A CONSENT GIVEN FOR PLANNING OR BUILDING REGULATION PURPOSES IS NOT SUFFICENT. YOU SHOULD THEREFORE WARN ANY PERSON ACTING FOR YOU IN THESE MATTERS NOT TO START WORK WITHOUT YOUR CONSENT.

1. Address of dwelling to be improved.

---

2. Name of applicant and address if different from 1.

---

3. Address of the dwelling for which qualification certificate is sought if different from 1.

---

4. (a) Are you the freeholder or leaseholder?

   (b) If leaseholder, how long has the lease to run?

---

5. (a) Name of your tenant under the controlled tenancy of the dwelling.

   (b) Has he consented to the proposals?

   (c) What housing arrangements, if any, are to be made for him and his household during and after improvement?

---

6. Is the dwelling occupied partly for business and partly as living accommodation?

---

7. (a) Name and address of mortgagee (building society, etc.) if any.

   (b) Has the mortgagee consented to the making of this application?
   See note (iii)

---

8. Was the dwelling provided before 3 October, 1961? If so, say when.

---

9. Particulars of works to be carried out by you and estimated cost.

---

10. The standard amenities are listed at (a) to (g) below. The fixed bath or shower must be in a bathroom where this is reasonably practicable, but must not be in a bedroom.

Complete columns A and B

Standard amenities	*Col. A* *Tick those already available*	*Col. B* *Tick those to be provided*
(a) (i) A fixed bath or shower in a bathroom		
(ii) A fixed bath or shower elsewhere in the dwelling		
(b) A hot and cold water supply at a fixed bath or shower		
(c) A wash-hand basin		
(d) A hot and cold water supply at a wash-hand basin		
(e) A sink		
(f) A hot and cold water supply at a sink		
(g) A water closet (i) in and accessible from within the dwelling; or		
(ii) where the dwelling is part of a larger building, in such a position as to be readily accessible from the dwelling.		

11. In order to provide the amenities you have ticked in Column B is it necessary to interfere with or replace any of the amenities ticked in Column A? If so, give details.

12. (a) Has the dwelling, to the best of your knowledge and belief, been without the amenities ticked in Column B for a period of not less than 12 months ending with the date of this application?

(b) In the case of a registered disabled person, indicate which standard amenities are inaccessible because of his disability.

13. When the works are completed will the dwelling have all the standard amenities for the exclusive use of the occupants?
See notes (i) and (vii)

---

14. ENCLOSURES: Tick as enclosed

(a) Plans showing the dwelling before and after the proposed works of improvement are carried out.

(b) Specification of the works to be carried out, with an estimate of the cost, distinguishing between

(i) grant-aided works for the provision of standard amenities,

(ii) works of replacement and repair on which grant is being claimed,

(iii) other works (if any),

(iv) professional fees.

(*c*) Certificate of availability for letting.

---

15. Are all the works listed in answer to question 10 required in order to make the dwelling satisfy the qualifying conditions?
If the answer is "No" state which of the works are required for this purpose.
See note (vii)

---

16. Has any necessary permission been obtained (if so give dates)

(a) for planning purposes?

(b) for building regulation purposes?

---

17. Date of commencement of tenancy (if before 6th July 1957, it will be sufficient to say so).

I declare that to the best of my knowledge and belief the particulars in this application are correct.

Date .... Signature of applicant ....

Notes: (i) The Council must approve an application for an intermediate grant which is made in accordance with the relevant provisions. These include the necessity for the dwelling, after improvement, to be provided with all the standard amenities (see question 10) for the exclusive use of its occupants (see question 12); that the improved dwelling will be in good repair, having regard to its age, character and locality (disregarding internal decorative repair), will in all other respects be fit for human habitation, and conform with specified requirements for thermal insulation. There is a further requirement for intermediate grant that the dwelling will be likely to remain fit and available for use as a dwelling for a period of not less than fifteen years.

(ii) In addition to grant for standard amenities, the Council may also make a grant towards the cost of repairs and replacements needed in their opinion to enable the dwelling to attain the relevant standard.

(iii) A mortgagor should always notify his building society, or other mortgagee that he has applied for grant. Otherwise he may be breaking the terms of his mortgage deed.

(iv) An application for a qualification certificate should not be made on this form where the dwelling has all the standard amenities. There is a separate form of application for that situation.

(v) The standard amenities are:

(a) A fixed bath or shower which must be in a bathroom unless this is not reasonably practicable.

(b) A wash-hand basin.

(c) A sink.

(d) A water closet which must be in, and accessible from within, the dwelling unless this is not reasonably practicable.

(e) A hot and cold water supply at the fixed bath or shower, at the wash-hand basin and at the sink.

(vi) The application may include works in addition to those needed to make the dwelling satisfy the qualifying conditions (note (vii)); but the works needed for those conditions to be satisfied must be stated (question 15). A landlord will no doubt discuss his proposals with his tenant before submitting this application and he should bear in mind that, at a later stage in the procedure, he will need to obtain the tenant's consent, in order to carry out improvements. If the tenant then withholds his consent, the landlord may in certain circumstances apply to the county court for an order authorising him to carry out works required to make a dwelling satisfy the qualifying conditions.

(vii) The qualifying conditions are:

(a) that all the standard amenities are provided for the exclusive use of the occupants of the dwelling;

(b) that the dwelling is in good repair having regard to its age, character and locality and disregarding internal decorative repair; and

(*c*) that the dwelling is in all other respects fit for human habitation.

The standard of fitness for human habitation is laid down in section 4 of the Housing Act 1957 as amended by section 71 of the Housing Act 1969. A dwelling is "fit for human habitation" if it is reasonably suitable for occupation having regard to repairs, stability, freedom from damp, internal arrangement, natural lighting, ventilation, water supply, drainage and sanitary conveniences, and facilities for preparation and cooking of food and for the disposal of waste water.

(viii) A copy of the application will be sent by the Council to the tenant.

(ix) If the Council are satisfied that the qualifying conditions will be satisfied when the proposed works have been completed they will issue a certificate of provisional approval.

(x) If the Council refuse to issue a certificate of provisional approval or a qualification certificate, the landlord will be sent a written statement of their reasons for doing so.

[(xi) Advice to both landlord and tenant on the procedure and on what happens as regards the rent, if the tenancy becomes regulated is contained in the booklet "Controlled Rents to Fair Rents" obtainable from the Council.] **[793]**

HOUSING ACT 1974 *Form No.* 4

APPROVAL OF APPLICATION FOR INTERMEDIATE GRANT

.... COUNCIL

To .... Reference No. ....

of ....

1. The Council have approved your application dated .... for an intermediate grant for the improvement of ....

2. The Council have determined the following as being the amounts of the expenses which, in their opinion, are proper to be incurred by you for the execution of the relevant works:

(a) Works of repair or replacement Estimated expense

....

....

....

(b) Provision of the following amenities

....

....

....

3. The grant will be £................., representing .... % of the eligible expense of £................. made up of £................. for repairs and replacements and £................. for standard amenities.

4. Subject to the conditions referred to below, the grant will be paid to you on completion of the works to the Council's satisfaction, in accordance with the particulars, plans and specifications approved by them for the purpose [within .... months or such further time as the Council may allow].

See note (*i*)

5. The Council have decided to reduce the required standard by dispensing with the conditions to the following extent:

....

....

6. As from the date certified by the Council as the date on which the dwelling first becomes fit for occupation after the completion of the relevant works to their satisfaction, the conditions as to future occupation set out in section 73 [and section 74] of the Housing Act 1974 will have to be observed for a period. Details of the conditions, indicating the periods involved, are attached.

Dated this .... day of .... 19..............

....

Signature of authorised officer

Notes: (i) The Council may require that the works be carried out within such time (not being less than twelve months) as they may specify.

(ii) If you require any further information you should get in touch with Mr. .... at ...., telephone No. ...., quoting the above reference. [**794**]

HOUSING ACT 1974 *Form No.* 5

APPLICATION FOR SPECIAL GRANT

.... COUNCIL

Please complete and return this form to the Chief Executive of the Council. A separate form must be completed for each house.

DO NOT START ANY OF THE WORK TO PROVIDE THE STANDARD AMENITIES LISTED IN PARAGRAPH 7 BEFORE YOU HAVE RECEIVED NOTICE OF APPROVAL OF THIS APPLICATION OTHERWISE A GRANT MAY NOT BE PAID. A CONSENT GIVEN FOR PLANNING OR BUILDING REGULATION PURPOSES IS NOT SUFFICIENT. YOU SHOULD THEREFORE WARN ANY PERSON ACTING FOR YOU IN THESE MATTERS NOT TO START WORK WITHOUT YOUR CONSENT.

---

1. (a) Address of house to be improved.
   (b) Was the house built before 3 October 1961? If so, say when,

---

2. (a) Number of households in the house.
   (b) Number of individuals occupying the house.

---

3. Name of applicant and address if different from 1.

---

4. (a) Are you the freeholder or leaseholder?
   (b) If leaseholder, how long has the lease to run?

---

5. (a) Name and address of mortgagee (building society, etc.) if any.
(b) Has the mortgagee consented to the making of this application?
See note

6. Particulars of works to be carried out by you and estimated cost.

7. The standard amenities are listed at (a) to (g) below.

Standard amenities	*Col. A* *Say how many amenities are already in the house*	*Col. B* *Say how many are to be provided*
(a) A fixed bath or shower in a bathroom.		
(b) A hot and cold water supply at a fixed bath or shower.		
(c) A wash-hand basin.		
(d) A hot and cold water supply at a wash-hand basin.		
(e) A sink.		
(f) A hot and cold water supply at a sink.		
(g) A water closet.		

8. ENCLOSURES: Tick as enclosed
(a) Plans showing the house before and after the proposed works of improvement are carried out.
(b) Specification of the works to be carried out, with an estimate of the cost.

9. Has any necessary permission been obtained (if so give dates)
(a) for planning purposes?
(b) for building regulation purposes?

I declare that to the best of my knowledge and belief the particulars in this application are correct.

Date .... Signature of applicant ....

Note: A mortgagor should always notify his building society or other mortgagee that he has applied for grant. Otherwise he may be breaking the terms of his mortgage deed. [**795**]

HOUSING ACT 1974 *Form No.* 6

APPROVAL OF APPLICATION FOR SPECIAL GRANT

.... COUNCIL

To .... Reference No. ....
of ....
....

1. The Council have approved your application dated .... for a special grant for the improvement of ....
....

2. The Council have determined the following as being the amounts of the expenses which, in their opinion, are proper to be incurred by you for the execution of the relevant works:

	Estimated expense
....	....
....	....
....	....

3. The grant will be £................, representing .... % of the eligible expense of £................

4. Grant will be paid to you on completion of the works to the Council's satisfaction, in accordance with the particulars, plans and specifications approved by them for the purpose [within .... months or such further time as the Council may allow].
See note (*i*)

Dated this .... date of .... 19........

....
Signature of authorised officer

Notes: (i) The Council may require that the works be carried out within such time (not being less than twelve months) as they may specify.
(ii) If you require any further information you should get in touch with Mr. .... at ...., telephone No. ...., quoting the above reference. [**796**]

HOUSING ACT 1974 *Form No.* 7

APPLICATION FOR REPAIRS GRANT RELATING TO DWELLINGS IN HOUSING ACTION AREA OR GENERAL IMPROVEMENT AREA

.... COUNCIL

Please complete and return this form to the Chief Executive of the Council.

DO NOT START ANY WORKS OF REPAIR BEFORE YOU HAVE RECEIVED NOTICE OF APPROVAL OF THIS APPLICATION, OTHERWISE A GRANT MAY NOT BE PAID. YOU SHOULD THEREFORE WARN ANY PERSON ACTING FOR YOU IN THESE MATTERS NOT TO START WORK WITHOUT YOUR CONSENT.

---

1. (a) Address of dwelling to be repaired.
(b) Was it built before 3 October 1961?
If so, say when.

---

2. Name of applicant and address if different from 1.

---

3. (a) Are you the freeholder or leaseholder?
(b) If leaseholder, how long has the lease to run?

---

4. (a) Are you the occupier?
(b) If not:
(i) has the occupier consented to the proposals?
(ii) what housing arrangements, if any, are to be made for any existing tenants and their households during and after repairs?

---

5. (a) Name and address of mortgagee (building society, etc), if any.
(b) Has the mortgagee consented to the making of this application?
See note (i)

---

6. Particulars of works to be carried out by you and estimated cost.

---

7. ENCLOSURES: Tick as enclosed
(a) Plan of the dwelling showing the works to be carried out.
(b) Specification of the works to be carried out with an estimate of the cost, distinguishing between

(i) works of replacement and repair on which grant is being claimed,

(ii) other works (if any),

(iii) professional fees.

(c) Certificate of future occupation.

(d) A statement that you cannot finance, without undue hardship, the cost of the works without a grant.

See note (ii)

I declare that to the best of my knowledge and belief the particulars in this application are correct.

Date .... Signature of applicant ....

Notes: (i) A mortgagor should always notify his building society or other mortgagee that he has applied for grant. Otherwise he may be breaking the terms of his mortgage deed.

(ii) The grant is intended to help owners on a low income to carry out certain basic repairs or replacements that would not otherwise be within their means, to enable the dwelling to reach the "relevant standard of repair". To achieve this standard a dwelling has to be in good repair having regard to its age and character and the locality in which it is situated (and disregarding internal decorative repair). [797]

HOUSING ACT 1974 *Form No.* 8

APPROVAL OF APPLICATION FOR REPAIRS GRANT

.... COUNCIL

To .... Reference No. ......
of ....
....

1. The Council have approved your application dated .... for grant for the repair of ....
....

2. The Council have determined £.............. as being the amount of the expenses which, in their opinion, are proper to be incurred by you for the execution of the relevant works specified in the application. [This sum is made up as follows:

	Estimated expense
....	....
....	....
....	..................]

3. The grant will be £................, representing .... % of the eligible expense of £................

4. Subject to the conditions referred to below, the grant will be paid to you on completion of the works to the Council's satisfaction, in accordance with the particulars, plans and specifications approved by them for the purpose [within .... months or such further time as the Council may allow].
See note (i)

5. As from the date certified by the Council as the date on which the dwelling first becomes fit for occupation after the completion of the relevant works to their satisfaction, the conditions as to future occupation set out in section 73 [and section 74] of the Housing Act 1974 will have to be observed for a period. Details of the conditions, indicating the periods involved, are attached.

Dated this .... day of .... 19 ....

....

Signature of authorised officer

Notes: (i) The Council may require that the works carried out within such time (not being less than twelve months) as they may specify.

(ii) If you require any further information you should get in touch with Mr. .... at ...., telephone No. ...., quoting the above reference. [**798**]

HOUSING ACT 1974—Section 60 *Form No.* 9

CERTIFICATE OF OWNER-OCCUPATION (TO ACCOMPANY APPLICATION FOR HOUSE RENOVATION GRANT)

To: The Chief Executive,

.... COUNCIL

1. *(a) In connection with my application dated ....
for .... grant in respect of ....
........................., I HEREBY CERTIFY that I intend that, on or before the first anniversary of the certified date and throughout the period of 4 years beginning on that first anniversary, the dwelling will be my only or main residence and will be occupied exclusively be me and members of my household (if any).
See note (i)

*(b) (IF THE APPLICATION IS MADE BY PERSONAL REPRESENTATIVES OR TRUSTEES). In connection with my/our application dated .... for ....
grant in respect of ....
I/WE HEREBY CERTIFY that I/we are personal representatives or trustees and intend that, on or before the first anniversary of the certified date and throughout the period of 4 years beginning on that first anniversary, the dwelling will be the only or main residence of, and exclusively occupied by, a person who [under the will or intestacy] [under the terms of the trust]† is beneficially entitled to an interest in the dwelling or the proceeds of sale thereof and members of his household (if any).

2. I understand that, if a grant is approved, conditions as to future occupation of the dwelling will apply and that, in the event of a breach of those conditions, the grant and interest thereon from the certified date will be repayable to the local authority on demand.

(Signed) ....
Address ....
Date ....

* Complete appropriate paragraph and delete the other.
† Delete words in square brackets, as appropriate.

Notes: (i) "Certified date" means the date certified by the local authority as the date on which the dwelling first becomes fit for occupation after completion of the relevant works to their satisfaction.

(ii) Anyone who knowingly signs a false declaration may be guilty of an offence and might be prosecuted if the local authority has evidence of an intention to obtain a grant by deception. **[799]**

HOUSING ACT 1974—Section 60 *Form No.* 10

CERTIFICATE OF AVAILABILITY FOR LETTING (TO ACCOMPANY APPLICATION FOR HOUSE RENOVATION GRANT)

To: The Chief Executive,
.... COUNCIL

1. In connection with my application dated .... for .... grant in respect of ....

I HEREBY CERTIFY that I intend that, throughout the period of 5 years beginning with the certified date *see notes* (*i*) *and* (*ii*),

* (a) the dwelling will be let or available for letting as a residence, and not for a holiday, to a person other than a member of my family *see note* (*iii*), or

* (b) the dwelling will be occupied or available for occupation by a member of the agricultural population in pursuance of a contract of service and otherwise than as a tenant.

2. I understand that, if a grant is approved, conditions as to future occupation of the dwelling will apply and that, in the event of a breach of those conditions, the grant and interest thereon from the certified date will be repayable to the local authority on demand.

(Signed) ....
Address ....
Date ....

* Delete as appropriate.

Notes: (i) A separate certificate of availability for letting must be supplied for each dwelling comprised in a composite application.

(ii) "Certified date" means the date certified by the local authority as the date on which the dwelling first becomes fit for occupation after completion of the relevant works to their satisfaction.

(iii) A person is a member of another's family if that person is:

(a) the other's wife or husband; or

(b) a son or daughter or a son-in-law or daughter-in-law of the other, or of the other's wife or husband ("son" or "daughter" includes any step-son or step-daughter, any illegitimate son or daughter, any adopted son or daughter of that person, and "son-in-law" and "daughter-in-law" are to be construed accordingly); or

(c) a father or mother of the other, or of the other's wife or husband.

(iv) Anyone who knowingly signs a false declaration may be guilty of an offence and might be prosecuted if the local authority have evidence of an intention to obtain a grant by deception. **[800]**

GRANT CONDITIONS *Form A*

SECTION 73 OF THE HOUSING ACT 1974—CONDITIONS AS TO FUTURE OCCUPATION

A. WHERE A CERTIFICATE OF OWNER-OCCUPATION APPLIES

1. The following conditions apply throughout the period of 5 years beginning with the certified date:

(a) throughout the first year the dwelling shall, as a residence, be occupied exclusively by, or be available for the exclusive occupation of, a qualifying person and members of his household (if any); and

(b) if, at any time during the second or any subsequent year, the dwelling is not occupied exclusively as his only or main residence by a qualifying person and members of his household (if any), the dwelling shall at that time be let or available for letting by a qualifying person as a residence and not for a holiday to persons other than members of that person's family.

2. In determining whether a breach of these conditions has occurred, any period of 12 months during which the condition is not fulfilled shall be disregarded if:

(a) that period begins on the death of a qualifying person who, immediately before his death, was occupying the dwelling concerned as his residence; and

(b) throughout that period an interest in the dwelling or the proceeds of sale thereof, being either the interest which belonged to the deceased or an interest which arose or fell into possession at his death, is vested in his personal representatives acting in that capacity or in trustees as such or, by virtue of section 9 of the Administration of Estates Act 1925, in the Probate Judge, within the meaning of that Act.

3. It is a condition of grant that if, at any time within the relevant period, the local authority by whom the grant was paid serve notice on the owner of the dwelling requiring him to do so, the owner shall, within the period of 21 days beginning with the date on which the notice is served, furnish to the authority

a certificate giving such information as the authority may reasonably require with respect to the occupation of the dwelling.

Definitions:

(i) "Certified date" means the date certified by the local authority as the date on which the dwelling first becomes fit for occupation after the completion of the relevant works to their satisfaction.

(ii) "Qualifying persons" are as follows:

(a) the applicant for grant and any person who derives title to the dwelling through or under the applicant, otherwise than by a conveyance for value; and

(b) at any time when personal representatives or trustees as such are the qualifying person by virtue of paragraph (a) above, any person who, under the will or intestacy or, as the case may require, under the terms of the trusts concerned, is beneficially entitled to an interest in the dwelling or the proceeds of sale thereof.

(*Note*: Sale of a dwelling therefore represents a breach of the conditions but not its demise under a will or trust.)

(iii) A person is a member of another's family if that person is:

(a) the other's wife or husband; or

(b) a son or daughter or a son-in-law or daughter-in-law of the other, or of the other's wife or husband ("son" or "daughter" includes any step-son or step-daughter, any illegitimate son or daughter, any adopted son or daughter of that person, and "son-in-law" and "daughter-in-law" are to be construed accordingly); or

(c) a father or mother of the other, or of the other's wife or husband. **[801]**

GRANT CONDITIONS *Form B*

SECTION 73 OF THE HOUSING ACT 1974—CONDITIONS AS TO FUTURE OCCUPATION

B. WHERE A CERTIFICATE OF AVAILABILITY FOR LETTING APPLIES

1. The following conditions apply throughout the period of 5 years beginning with the certified date:

(a) the dwelling shall be let or available for letting as a residence, and not for a holiday, by a qualifying person to persons other than members of the family of that qualifying person or any other person who is for the time being a qualifying person in relation to the dwelling; or

(b) the dwelling shall be occupied or available for occupation by a member of the agricultural population in pursuance of a contract of service otherwise than as a tenant.

2. It is a condition of grant that if, at any time within the relevant period, the local authority by whom the grant was paid serve notice on the owner of the dwelling requiring him to do so, the owner shall, within the period of 21 days beginning with the date on which the notice is served, furnish to the authority

a certificate giving such information as the authority may reasonably require with respect to the occupation of the dwelling, and for this purpose it shall also be a condition of the grant that, if required to do so by the owner of the dwelling, any tenant of the dwelling shall furnish the owner with such information as he may reasonably require to enable him to furnish the certificate to the authority.

Definitions:

(i) "Certified date" means the date certified by the local authority as the date on which the dwelling first becomes fit for occupation after the completion of the relevant works to their satisfaction.

(ii) "Qualifying persons" are as follows:

(a) the applicant for grant and any person who derives title to the dwelling through or under the applicant otherwise than by a conveyance for value; and

(b) at any time when personal representatives or trustees as such are the qualifying person by virtue of paragraph (a) above, any person who, under the will or intestacy or, as the case may require, under the terms of the trusts concerned, is beneficially entitled to an interest in the dwelling or the proceeds of sale thereof.

(*Note*: Sale of a dwelling therefore represents a breach of the conditions but not its demise under a will or trust.)

(iii) A person is a member of another's family if that person is:

(a) the other's wife or husband; or

(b) a son or daughter or a son-in-law or daughter-in-law of the other, or of the other's wife or husband ("son" or "daughter" includes any step-son or step-daughter, any illegitimate son or daughter, any adopted son or daughter of that person, and "son-in-law" and "daughter-in-law" are to be construed accordingly); or

(c) a father or mother of the other, or of the other's wife or husband. **[802]**

GRANT CONDITIONS *Form C*

SECTION 74 OF THE HOUSING ACT 1974—OTHER CONDITIONS RELATING TO THE LETTING OF DWELLINGS IMPROVED WITH GRANT

These conditions apply automatically throughout the relevant period when improvement grant, intermediate grant or repairs grant is approved for dwellings situated in housing action areas, general improvement areas or priority neighbourhoods, or may be applied at the discretion of the local authority to dwellings outside those areas when approving improvement or intermediate grant. The relevant period is 5 years beginning on the certified date, except in housing action areas where it is 7 years.

The conditions are:

1. The dwelling will be let or available for letting on a regulated tenancy or a Part VI contract.

2. If the local authority by whom the grant in question was paid serve notice on the owner of the dwelling requiring him to do so, the owner will within the

period of 21 days beginning with the date on which the notice is served furnish to the authority a certificate that the condition set out in paragraph 1 above is being fulfilled.

3. If required to do so by the owner of the dwelling, any tenant of the dwelling will furnish the owner with such information as he may reasonably require for the purpose of enabling him to comply with the condition set out in paragraph 2 above.

4. If on the certified date there is no registered rent for the dwelling and no such application or reference is pending, an application for the registration of a rent for the dwelling will be made to the rent officer before the expiry of the period of 14 days beginning on the relevant day or, as the case may require, the Part VI contract will be referred to the rent tribunal for the district in question before the expiry of that period.

5. Any such application or reference as is referred to in paragraph 4 above which is either pending on the certified date or made as mentioned in that paragraph will be diligently proceeded with and not withdrawn.

6. No premium shall be required as a condition of the grant, renewal or continuance on or after the certified date of any lease, agreement for a lease or Part VI contract of or relating to the dwelling.

Definitions:

(i) "Certified date" means the date certified by the local authority as the date on which the dwelling first becomes fit for occupation after the completion of the relevant works to their satisfaction.

(ii) "Part VI contract" has the same meaning as in Part VI of the Rent Act 1968.

(iii) "Premium" has the same meaning as in Part VII of that Act.

(iv) "Registered rent" means:

(a) in relation to a dwelling which is subject to, or available for letting on, a regulated tenancy, a rent registered under Part IV of that Act; and

(b) in relation to a dwelling which is let, or available for letting, on a Part VI contract, a rent registered in the register kept under section 74 of that Act.

(v) "Regulated tenancy" has the same meaning as in that Act.

(vi) "relevant day", in relation to a dwelling for which there is no registered rent on the certified date, means the first day, not being earlier than the certified date, on which the dwelling is or becomes subject to a regulated tenancy or let on a Part VI contract. **[803]**

GRANT CONDITIONS *Form D*

NOTES ON GRANT CONDITIONS

1. The conditions will be registered by the local authority in the register of local land charges, and so long as the conditions remain in force they are binding on any person, other than a housing authority or registered housing association,

who is for the time being the owner of the dwelling to which the grant relates, and are enforceable against all other persons having an interest in the dwelling as if it were a condition of the terms of every lease, agreement for a lease or statutory tenancy of, or of property including, that dwelling.

2. On breach of a condition of grant, the grant, together with compound interest thereon from the certified date, becomes repayable on demand by the local authority. Where the grant related to two or more dwellings the amount repayable is such part of the relevant grant as appears to the Council to be referable to the dwelling to which the breach relates.

3. The local authority may at their discretion demand a lesser amount than the full amount of grant, or may make no demand for payment at all. This is, however, entirely a matter for the authority concerned to decide in any particular instance.

4. On making payment of the sum demanded for breach of a condition, the condition ceases to be in force with respect to that dwelling.

5. A voluntary repayment of the grant, or such proportion of the grant as the Council may be prepared to accept, may be made at any time, whereupon all the grant conditions cease to be in force with respect to that dwelling. **[804]**

APPENDIX D

Housing Act 1974

Application for Improvement Contribution

.... COUNCIL

Local authority's address ....

....

....

Local authority reference No. ....

ENCLOSURES: Tick as enclosed

(a) Plans of property before and after conversion/improvement.

(b) Specification of proposed works, distinguishing between the various categories of work as listed under question 10 below.

(c) Copy of Council's resolution authorising the application.

(d) Any necessary application for loan consent.

---

1. Address of property to be converted/improved.

---

2. Number and size of dwellings
   (a) Now
   (b) After
   conversion/improvement.

---

3. Approximate age of property.

---

4. Is the building listed or subject to a building preservation notice under the Town and Country Planning Act 1971?

---

5. Date of acquisition if the property has been or is to be purchased for conversion/improvement.

---

6. Has loan consent for acquisition been obtained?

---

7. If not have the terms of acquisition been agreed at the District Valuer's valuation?

---

8. Powers under which the property is held (or will be held after acquisition).

---

9. Do these powers authorise the Council to spend money on improvements?

	£
10. (a) Actual cost of acquisition for conversion/improvement at District Valuer's valuation (including fees).	....
(b) Estimated cost of works of improvement/conversion other than those included in (c) below.	....
	£
(c) Estimated cost of works of repair and replacement needed to enable the dwelling(s) to attain the relevant standard.	....
(d) Estimated cost of professional fees or apportionment of local authority's officers' salaries for conversion/improvement works.	....
(e) Total cost on which approval for contribution and subsidy purposes is sought	__________

....

(f) Costs inadmissible for subsidy purposes (not included above).	
(i) items above Parker Morris standards.	....
(ii) items inadmissible in a new building scheme.	....

(iii) normal repairs and maintenance (i.e. not included in (c) above).	....
(iv) other works (give details).	....
TOTAL COST OF PROPOSAL	
11. Estimated life of property after conversion/improvement.	
12. Will the dwelling reach the other standards required under section 61 (3) after conversion/improvement? If not, which requirements cannot be achieved?	
13. If a contribution under previous legislation has been approved in respect of any dwelling included in this application, give the date of approval and the Department's reference.	

To the Department of the Environment (address to Regional Office where appropriate)

(In Wales address to the Welsh Office, Housing Division, Oxford House, Hills Street, Cardiff CF1 2SY.)

I am directed by the Council to submit this application under section 79 of the Housing Act 1974. The Council are satisfied that the proposals are desirable and economic and that they comply with the statutory requirements.

Date .... (Signed) ....

Chief Executive

Note: This application should not normally be submitted until informal consultations on the proposals have been completed between the Council's appropriate professional officers and the Department's Regional Architect. **[805]**

APPENDIX E

Guidance on Aspects of Compulsory Improvement Powers

1. The purpose of this Appendix is to give guidance on certain of the revised compulsory improvement provisions contained in Part VIII of the Act, and in one instance to issue a directive. It should be noted that the procedure which applies in the case of dwellings outside housing action areas and general improvement areas differs from the procedure applying within those areas.

2. *Reasonable expense* (*Section* 85).—Before serving a provisional notice under section 85—or an improvement notice under section 88—a local authority is required to be satisfied, among other things, that the dwelling concerned is

capable of improvement at reasonable expense. This factor is also relevant in the consideration of an appeal against an improvement notice, one of the grounds of appeal being that it is not practicable to comply with the requirements of the notice at reasonable expense. The interpretation of "reasonable expense" in any particular case is initially for the local authority concerned and ultimately for the courts on appeal. This represents a change from the previous legislation, since Part II of the Housing Act 1964 specifically required that, in determining whether a dwelling was capable of improvement at reasonable expense, regard should be had to the estimated cost of the relevant works and the value of the dwelling after improvement. This restrictive requirement has not been perpetuated in the present Act and a local authority is thus free to have regard to any matters which it considers to be relevant. **[806]**

3. *Housing arrangements* (*Section* 86).—The housing arrangements which are the subject of this section provide a new safeguard for tenants affected by compulsory improvement works. These arrangements consist of a written agreement between the tenant and either his landlord or the local authority, or both, providing for the accommodation of himself and his household during the period when works are taking place in his home, or after that period, or both during and after that.

4. In most cases the tenant concerned will probably be temporarily rehoused, either by the local authority or the landlord, while works are being carried out, and will return to his original home after it has been improved. But the housing arrangements could provide for the tenant to move permanently into another property in the landlord's ownership, or into local authority housing. The situation could also be covered in which, although the tenant returns to his original home, the improvement works have altered the dwelling in such a way that a legal change of identity has occurred and a new tenancy is necessary.

5. Housing arrangements can cover not only the actual housing of an occupying tenant and the rent to be paid, but also matters incidental or ancillary to that housing. This means that the arrangements could provide for such matters as the temporary storage of furniture, and help towards removal costs. Housing arrangements should thus ensure that an occupying tenant's interests are fully protected.

6. The written agreement containing the housing arrangements will give the tenant the power of recourse to an action in the courts for breach of contract if the landlord or local authority fail to fulfil the terms of the housing arrangements; if, for example the landlord does not allow the tenant to return after a temporary absence to allow the improvement works to take place.

7. Before a local authority can take any of the steps in the compulsory improvement procedure which follow the service of a provisional notice the authority must satisfy itself that there are satisfactory housing arrangements where these are required, or that the tenant has been unreasonable in refusing to enter into housing arrangements. And as an additional protection the tenant has the special ground of appeal against an improvement notice as set out in section 91 (3) (b), that the housing arrangements are not satisfactory or that housing arrangements are needed and they have not been made or that he has not been unreasonable in refusing to make them.

8. Local authorities are asked to ensure that both tenants and landlords are made fully aware, at the earliest possible moment in the compulsory improvement procedure, of the existence and scope of the provisions in the Act relating to housing arrangements. This will enable informal discussions about these arrangements to take place at the "time and place" meeting and will allow representations about the arrangements to be fully considered by local authorities before they proceed to take any subsequent action following the service of provisional notices. **[807]**

9. *Acceptance of undertakings* (*Section* 87 (3) (*a*))—The Secretaries of State strongly recommend that a local authority (whether or not it concludes that housing arrangements are required) should make quite certain that a tenant has given his written consent to the carrying out of the works before accepting an undertaking. **[808]**

10. *Terms of loans for compulsory improvement* (*Section* 100). Under section 100 (6) the Secretary of State hereby directs that the rates of interest and periods for repayment of loans to meet the expenses of compulsory improvement shall be those payable in respect of loans made under section 43 of the Housing (Financial Provisions) Act 1958, as amended by section 37 of the Local Government Act 1974. **[809]**

11. *Prescribed forms* (*Section* 104). Under the powers of section 178 of the Housing Act 1957 as applied by section 104 (4) of the Act, it is proposed as soon as possible to prescribe forms for compulsory improvement under Part VIII of the Act. Until this is done local authorities are free to use their own forms and may wish to adapt the earlier forms, as prescribed in the Housing (Prescribed Forms) Regulations 1972, SI 1972 No. 228. **[810]**

12. *Entitlement to Home Loss and Disturbance Payments and to Rehousing* (*Schedule* 13).—Paragraphs 38–41 of Schedule 13 to the Housing Act 1974 widen the scope of sections 29, 37, 39 and 43 of the Land Compensation Act 1973 by including people permanently displaced from a dwelling in consequence of the acceptance of an undertaking under section 87 of 1974 Act, or of the service of an improvement notice within the meaning of Part VIII of the 1974 Act. People thus permanently displaced from their homes may be entitled to home loss payments and or disturbance payments and to rehousing. In addition, where a person thus permanently displaced has no greater interest than that of a tenant for a year or from year to year the displacing authority may pay any reasonable expenses he incurs, other than the purchase price, in connection with the acquisition of an alternative dwelling. A person must make a claim in writing for a home loss payment before the expiration of the period of six months, beginning with the date of displacement, as specified in the 1973 Act. Local authorities are asked to take all necessary steps to ensure that those concerned are made aware of their rights in ample time to make their claims within the six months period specified. (Circulars DOE 130/74 and 139/74, Welsh Office 186/74 and 225/74, refer.) **[811]**

13. *Transitional arrangements.*—Commencement Order No. 3 brings into operation the repeal of the previous legislation on compulsory improvements as listed in Schedule 15 to the Act. The order contains savings which will have the effect of allowing action started under that legislation to continue if a

representation under section 19 of the Housing Act 1964 has been made, or any preliminary notice under section 20 of that Act has been served before 2nd December 1974. Loans can also continue to be offered under section 57 to meet expenses of complying with these notices and purchase notices served under section 59 of that Act. The order also preserves the power of a local authority, under section 26 (4) of the 1964 Act, to withdraw improvement notices served under that Act.

14. A local authority is not obliged to continue with action under the previous legislation in every case in which an immediate or final notice has been served. It could withdraw the notice if it was considered that action could be taken more effectively under the new provisions and that the advantages of doing so would out-weigh any consequential administrative delays. Local authorities are urged to consider taking this course where, in their view, the interests of a tenant would be better protected or where, since the provisions of section 67 (2) of the 1974 Act apply only to improvement notices served under that Act, they are unable to give a person having control an intermediate grant in respect of the works involved. **[812]**

APPENDIX F

Conditions Relating to Payment of Government Contribution for Improvements and Conversions of Housing Accommodation under Part VII of the Housing Act 1974 and Conditions of Grant Approved by the Treasury

1. Section 127 (2) of the Housing Act 1974 provides that any grant, subsidy or contribution payable by the Secretary of State under the Act shall be payable subject to such conditions as to records, certificates, audit or otherwise as the Secretary of State may, with the approval of the Treasury, impose.

2. With the approval of the Treasury, payments on account of Government contributions will be made periodically, and the balances will be paid after the final claims have been duly examined by the District Auditor. Forms of claim will be supplied by the Department.

3. The local authority shall permit the District Auditor, or other officer authorised by the Secretary of State concerned, to have access to and inspect the registers, records and certificates referred to in these conditions and, where necessary, accounts, plans, contracts and other relevant documents and vouchers. The dwellings of the local authorities to which the Government contributions relate shall be open to inspection, if required, by an officer authorised by the Secretary of State.

4. Registers shall be kept of dwellings provided or improved with Government financial assistance as detailed below, and shall be kept separately from the registers which have been kept under superseded legislation relating to improvements and conversions.

5. The register to be maintained in respect of dwellings for which improvement grants have been paid by the local authority under sections 61 to 64 of

the Act shall contain the following particulars of each dwelling or group of dwellings improved or provided by conversion:

(a) Name and address of applicant.
(b) Address of dwelling or dwellings.
(c) Eligible expense of the works.
(d) Rate and amount of improvement grant.
(e) Date of completion of works.
(f) Reference to certificate of completion (see paragraph 9).
(g) Date of payment of grant.

6. The register in respect of dwellings for which intermediate grants under sections 65–68, or houses for which special grants under sections 69 and 70, have been paid by the local authority shall contain the following particulars of each dwelling or group of dwellings, or house in multiple occupation, improved:

(a) Name and address of applicant.
(b) Address of dwelling or dwellings, or house in multiple occupation.
(c) Whether intermediate grant or special grant.
(d) Eligible expense of the works for

(i) provision of standard amenities;
(ii) repairs and replacements for intermediate grant.

(e) Rate and amount of grant.
(f) Date of completion of works.
(g) Reference to certificate of completion (see paragraph 9).
(h) Date of payment of grant.

7. The register in respect of dwellings for which repairs grants have been paid by the local authority under sections 71 and 72 of the Act shall contain the following particulars of each dwelling or group of dwellings repaired:

(a) Name and address of applicant.
(b) Address of dwelling or dwellings.
(c) Eligible expense of the works.
(d) Rate and amount of repairs grant.
(e) Date of completion of works.
(f) Reference to certificate of completion (see paragraph 9).
(g) Date of payment of grant.

8. The register to be kept by housing authorities in respect of dwellings for which improvement contributions are payable under section 79 shall contain the following particulars of each dwelling or group of dwellings improved or provided by conversion:

(a) Address of dwelling or dwellings.
(b) Amount and period of improvement contributions.
(c) Reference to Secretary of State's approval of application.
(d) Date of completion of works.
(e) Reference to certificate of completion (see paragraph 9).

9. The certificates referred to in the foregoing conditions shall be in the following form:

HOUSING ACT 1974

Certificate of Completion of Improvements or Repairs.

This is to certify that in respect of the dwellings described in the Schedule below the work of improvement, conversion or repair was completed to the satisfaction of the Council, and that the dwellings were fit for occupation, before the date set opposite their description in that Schedule. And that, as regards applications approved by the Secretary of State, the work has been carried out in a proper and workmanlike manner in accordance with the application.

SCHEDULE

Address of dwellings	Date	Reference number for register

Date of certificate .... Signed ....
Surveyor or other authorised officer of the .... Council.

[813]

APPENDIX III

STATUTORY INSTRUMENTS

THE HOUSING ACT 1974 (COMMENCEMENT NO. 1) ORDER 1974

S.I. 1974 No. 1406 (C. 25)

Made . . . . 19 *August* 1974

The Secretary of State, in exercise of the powers conferred upon him by section 131 (3) of the Housing Act 1974 and of all other powers enabling him in that behalf, hereby makes the following order:—

1.—(1) This order may be cited as the Housing Act 1974 (Commencement No. 1) Order 1974.

(2) The Interpretation Act 1889 applies for the interpretation of this order as it applies for the interpretation of an Act of Parliament.

(3) In this order "the Act" means the Housing Act 1974.

2. The provisions of the Act specified in the Schedule to this order shall come into operation on 20 August 1974.

3. The provisions of Schedule 9 to the Act shall come into operation on 31 August 1974. [**814**]

SCHEDULE

Section 2, 13, 14, 117, 127, 128 and 129.

Section 130 (1) in so far as it relates to paragraphs 8 and 38 to 45 of Schedule 13.

Section 130 (2).

Section 130 (4) in so far as it relates to the Land Compensation Act 1973 and the Land Compensation (Scotland) Act 1973.

Section 131.

Schedule 2.

Paragraphs 8 and 38 to 45 of Schedule 13.

Schedule 15 in so far as it relates to the Land Compensation Act 1973 and the Land Compensation (Scotland) Act 1973. [**815**]

THE HOUSING ACT 1974 (COMMENCEMENT NO. 2) ORDER 1974

S.I. 1974 No. 1562 (C.28)

Made . . . . 17 *September* 1974

The Secretary of State, in exercise of the powers conferred upon him by section 131 (3) of the Housing Act 1974 and of all other powers enabling him in that behalf, hereby makes the following order:—

1.—(1) This order may be cited as the Housing Act 1974 (Commencement No. 2) Order 1974.

(2) The Interpretation Act 1889 shall apply for the interpretation of this order as it applies for the interpretation of an Act of Parliament.

2. The provisions of the Housing Act 1974 specified in the Schedule to this order shall come into operation on 18 September 1974. **[816]**

SCHEDULE

Section 1.
Section 3 (1), (2) and (6).
Sections 4 to 8.
Section 9 (except in so far as it relates to paragraphs (*a*) and (*b*) of subsection (1) and except subsections (5) and (6)).
Sections 10 to 12.
Sections 29 to 33.
Section 35.
Section 107.
Section 130 (1) in so far as it relates to paragraphs 6, 10 (2), 10 (3), 10 (4), 15, 16, 22, 23 (1) to (4), 30, 31 and 32 of Schedule 13.
Section 130 (4) in so far as it relates to the repeals specified in the Table below.
Schedule 1.
Paragraphs 6, 10 (2), 10 (3), 10 (4), 15, 16, 22, 23 (1) to (4), 30, 31 and 32 of Schedule 13.
Schedule 15 in so far as it relates to the repeals specified in the Table below.

TABLE

REPEALS

Chapter	Short Title	Extent of Repeal
1964 c. 56	The Housing Act 1964	In section 1, in subsection (1) the words from "whose general duty" to the end of the subsection and subsection (1A). Sections 3 and 4. Section 6. In section 8 subsections (6), (7) and (9). Section 9. In section 11 (1) the words "section 3" and "section 6". In section 12, in subsection (1) the definition of "local authority" and subsection (2).
1968 c. 13	The National Loans Act 1968	In Schedule 1 the entries relating to subsections (1), (3) and (5) of section 9 of the Housing Act 1964.
1972 c. 47	The Housing Finance Act 1972	In section 77 subsections (1) and (3).

[817]

THE HOUSING ACT 1974 (COMMENCEMENT NO. 3) ORDER 1974

S.I. 1974 No. 1791 (C. 30)

Made . . . . 30 *October* 1974

The Secretary of State, in exercise of the powers conferred upon him by section 131 (3) and (4) of the Housing Act 1974 and of all other powers enabling him in that behalf, hereby makes the following order:—

1.—(1) This order may be cited as the Housing Act 1974 (Commencement No. 3) Order 1974.

(2) The Interpretation Act 1889 shall apply for the interpretation of this order as it applies for the interpretation of an Act of Parliament.

2. The provisions of the Housing Act 1974 specified in Schedule 1 to this order shall come into operation on 2nd December 1974.

3. The savings contained in Schedule 2 to this order shall have effect. **[818]**

SCHEDULE 1

Section 3 (3), (4) and (5).
Sections 15 to 17.
Section 18 (except in so far as it is already in operation).
Section 19 to 28.
Parts IV, V, VI, VII, and VIII.
Section 106.
Sections 109 to 112.
Sections 114 to 116.
Section 119 (1) in so far as it relates to paragraph 3 (2) of Schedule 11 and so much of paragraph 4 of Schedule 11 as relates to the insertion in section 27 (1) of the Housing Subsidies Act 1967 of the paragraph:—
"(*f*) the Housing Corporation";.
Section 120.
Section 123.
Section 126.
Section 130 (1) in so far as it relates to paragraphs 1, 4, 9, 10 (5), 12, 14, 17, 20, 23 (5), (6) and (7), 24 to 29, 33, 36 and 37 of Schedule 13.
Section 130 (3) (except in so far as it relates to paragraphs 1 and 2 of Schedule 14).
Section 130 (4) in so far as it relates to the repeals specified in the Table below.
Schedule 3 (except in so far as it is already in operation).
Schedule 4 to 7.
Schedule 10.
In Schedule 11, paragraph 3 (2) and so much of paragraph 4 as relates to the insertion in section 27 (1) of the Housing Subsidies Act 1967 of the paragraph:—
"(*f*) the Housing Corporation";.
Paragraphs 1, 4, 9, 10 (5), 12, 14, 17, 20, 23 (5), (6) and (7), 24 to 29, 33, 34, 36 and 37 of Schedule 13.
Schedule 14 (except paragraphs 1 and 2).
Schedule 15 in so far as it relates to the repeals specified in the Table below.

TABLE
REPEALS

Chapter	Short Title	Extent of Repeal
1964 c. 56	The Housing Act 1964	Part II. Sections 57 and 59. In section 72 (1) the words "of twelve months" in each place where they occur.
1969 c. 33	The Housing Act 1969	Part I (including Schedule 1, but except section 21). In section 30, subsections (2) and (3). Section 36. In section 37 (4), paragraph (*b*) and the word "or" immediately preceding it. In section 40 (2) (*a*) the words "Part I of this Act other than sections 17 to 22". Section 41. In section 70 the words "section 20 or". Section 75 (2) (*b*). Sections 76 and 77. In section 88 (1) the words "Part I". In Schedule 8 paragraphs 25 to 28 and 31.
1972 c. 47	The Housing Finance Act 1972	In Schedule 1, in paragraph 1 (1) (*d*), the word "or" at the end of sub-paragraph (iii).
1972 c. 70	The Local Government Act 1972	In section 171 (1) the words "section 6 (4) of the Housing Act 1969".

[**819**]

SCHEDULE 2

SAVINGS

1. The bringing into effect by this order of the repeal of any provision of Part II of the Housing Act 1964 shall not affect the continued exercise by a local authority of their powers under that Part of that Act in pursuance of any representations under section 19 of that Act which have been made, or any preliminary notice under section 20 of that Act which has been served, before 2 December 1974.

2. Sections 57 and 59 of the Housing Act 1964 and sections 70 and 76 of and paragraphs 25, 26 and 27 of Schedule 8 to the Housing Act 1969 shall, notwithstanding the repeal of any of their provisions, have effect for the purpose of the continued exercise by a local authority of their powers under Part II of the Housing Act 1964 in accordance with paragraph 1 of this Schedule. [**820**]

INDEX

All references are to paragraph numbers.

All references are to paragraph numbers.

All references are to paragraph numbers.

All references are to paragraph numbers.

All references are to paragraph numbers.

All references are to paragraph numbers.

All references are to paragraph numbers.

All references are to paragraph numbers.

All references are to paragraph numbers.